Taste of Home

Slow Cooker

THROUGHOUT THE YEAR

Taste of Home
Slow Cooker
THROUGHOUT THE YEAR

EDITORIAL
EDITOR-IN-CHIEF **Catherine Cassidy**
CREATIVE DIRECTOR **Howard Greenberg**
EDITORIAL OPERATIONS DIRECTOR **Kerri Balliet**

MANAGING EDITOR, PRINT & DIGITAL BOOKS **Mark Hagen**
ASSOCIATE CREATIVE DIRECTOR **Edwin Robles Jr.**

EDITOR **Michelle Rozumalski**
ASSOCIATE EDITOR **Molly Jasinski**
ART DIRECTOR **Maggie Conners**
LAYOUT DESIGNER **Nancy Novak**
EDITORIAL PRODUCTION MANAGER **Dena Ahlers**
COPY CHIEF **Deb Warlaumont Mulvey**
COPY EDITOR **Mary C. Hanson**
CONTENT OPERATIONS MANAGER **Colleen King**
CONTENT OPERATIONS ASSISTANT **Shannon Stroud**
EXECUTIVE ASSISTANT **Marie Brannon**

CHIEF FOOD EDITOR **Karen Berner**
FOOD EDITORS **James Schend; Peggy Woodward, RD**
RECIPE EDITORS **Mary King; Annie Rundle; Jenni Sharp, RD; Irene Yeh**

TEST KITCHEN & FOOD STYLING MANAGER **Sarah Thompson**
TEST COOKS **Nicholas Iverson (lead), Matthew Hass, Lauren Knoelke**
FOOD STYLISTS **Kathryn Conrad (senior), Leah Rekau, Shannon Roum**
PREP COOKS **Megumi Garcia, Melissa Hansen, Bethany Van Jacobson, Sara Wirtz**

PHOTOGRAPHY DIRECTOR **Stephanie Marchese**
PHOTOGRAPHERS **Dan Roberts, Jim Wieland**
PHOTOGRAPHER/SET STYLIST **Grace Natoli Sheldon**
SET STYLISTS **Stacey Genaw, Melissa Haberman, Dee Dee Jacq**

EDITORIAL BUSINESS MANAGER **Kristy Martin**

BUSINESS
VICE PRESIDENT, CHIEF SALES OFFICER **Mark S. Josephson**
VICE PRESIDENT, BUSINESS DEVELOPMENT & MARKETING **Alain Begun**

GENERAL MANAGER, TASTE OF HOME COOKING SCHOOL **Erin Puariea**

VICE PRESIDENT, DIGITAL EXPERIENCE & E-COMMERCE **Jennifer Smith**

THE READER'S DIGEST ASSOCIATION, INC.
PRESIDENT AND CHIEF EXECUTIVE OFFICER **Bonnie Kintzer**
VICE PRESIDENT, CHIEF OPERATING OFFICER, NORTH AMERICA **Howard Halligan**
VICE PRESIDENT, ENTHUSIAST BRANDS, BOOKS & RETAIL **Harold Clarke**
VICE PRESIDENT, NORTH AMERICAN OPERATIONS **Philippe Cloutier**
CHIEF MARKETING OFFICER **Leslie Dukker Doty**
VICE PRESIDENT, BRAND MARKETING **Beth Gorry**
VICE PRESIDENT, NORTH AMERICAN HUMAN RESOURCES **Phyllis E. Gebhardt, SPHR**
VICE PRESIDENT, CONSUMER MARKETING PLANNING **Jim Woods**

A TASTE OF HOME/READER'S DIGEST BOOK

FOR OTHER TASTE OF HOME BOOKS AND PRODUCTS,
VISIT US AT TASTEOFHOME.COM.

FOR MORE READER'S DIGEST PRODUCTS AND INFORMATION,
VISIT RD.COM (IN THE UNITED STATES) OR RD.CA (IN CANADA).

INTERNATIONAL STANDARD BOOK NUMBER **978-1-61765-345-2**
LIBRARY OF CONGRESS CONTROL NUMBER **2013944816**

PICTURED ON FRONT COVER **BBQ Chicken Sliders, page 68; Slow-Cooked Lasagna, page 273; Potluck Macaroni and Cheese, page 31; Sweet and Spicy Jerk Ribs, page 114; and Southwestern Pork and Squash Soup, page 214.**

PICTURED ON BACK COVER **Jalapeno Spinach Dip, page 9; Enchilada Pie, page 110; Momma's Turkey Stew with Dumplings, page 216; and Hot Caramel Apples, page 301.**

PICTURED ON TITLE PAGE **Teriyaki Sandwiches, page 140.**

PRINTED IN CHINA
1 3 5 7 9 10 8 6 4 2

Table of Contents

LEMON RED POTATOES (PAGE 20)

MOROCCAN CHICKEN (PAGE 200)

Spring

APPETIZERS & BEVERAGES	8
SIDE DISHES	18
ENTREES	36
SOUPS & SANDWICHES	64
DESSERTS	78

Summer

APPETIZERS & BEVERAGES	88
SIDE DISHES	98
ENTREES	110
SOUPS & SANDWICHES	138
DESSERTS	152

Autumn

APPETIZERS & BEVERAGES	162
SIDE DISHES	172
ENTREES	184
SOUPS, STEWS & SANDWICHES	210
DESSERTS	226

Winter

APPETIZERS & BEVERAGES	236
SIDE DISHES	246
ENTREES	260
SOUPS, STEWS & SANDWICHES	286
DESSERTS	300

INDEXES	308

Slow Cooking 101

The original slow cooker, called a Crock-Pot, was introduced in 1971 by Rival. Today, the term "slow cooker" and the name Crock-Pot are often used interchangeably; however, Crock-Pot is a brand, and a slow cooker is the appliance.

Most slow cookers have two or more settings. Food cooks faster on the high setting, but the low setting is ideal for all-day cooking or for less tender cuts of meat. Use the "warm" setting to keep food hot until it's ready to serve. The slow cooker recipes in this book refer to cooking on either "high" or "low" settings.

Some newer slow cookers seem to heat up faster than older ones. If you have an older model and a recipe directs to cook on low, you may want to set the slow cooker on the highest setting for the first hour of cooking to be sure the food is thoroughly cooked.

When Using Your Slow Cooker...

- Slow cookers come in a range of sizes, from 1½ to 7 quarts. It's important to use the right size for the amount of food you're making. To serve a dip from a buffet, the smallest slow cookers are ideal. For entertaining or potluck dinners, the larger sizes work best. Check the chart below to find a useful size for your household.

- To cook properly and safely, manufacturers and the USDA recommend slow cookers be filled at least half full but no more than two-thirds full.

- With many slow cooker recipes, the ingredients are added at once and are cooked all day. For make-ahead convenience, place the food items in the crock the night before, cover and refrigerate overnight (the removable stoneware insert makes this an easy task). In the morning, place the crock in the slow cooker and select the proper temperature.

- Do not preheat your slow cooker. An insert that has been in the refrigerator overnight should always be put into a cold base unit. Stoneware is sensitive to dramatic temperature changes, and cracking or breakage could occur if the base is preheated.

- After the recipe is finished cooking, if there are any leftovers, allow them to cool, then refrigerate. Slow cookers should not be used to reheat leftovers. Instead, use a microwave, stovetop burner or oven to reheat foods to 165°. This ensures that the food has been thoroughly heated and it is safe to eat.

- Following a power outage of less than two hours, you can finish cooking food from your slow cooker on the stovetop or microwave. If it's been more than two hours or you are unsure how long the power has been out, discard the food for your safety.

Slow Cooker Size

HOUSEHOLD SIZE	SLOW COOKER CAPACITY
1 person	1½ quarts
2 people	2 to 3½ quarts
3 or 4 people	3½ to 4½ quarts
4 or 5 people	4½ to 5 quarts
6 or more people	5 to 7 quarts

Converting Recipes for the Slow Cooker

Almost any recipe that bakes in the oven or simmers on the stovetop can be easily converted for the slow cooker. Here are some guidelines.

- Before converting recipes, check the manufacturer's guidelines for your particular slow cooker. Find a recipe that is similar to the one you want to convert and use it as a guide. Note the amount and size of meat and vegetables, heat setting, cooking time and liquid.

- Since there is no evaporation, adjusting the amount of liquid in your recipe may be necessary. If a recipe calls for 6 to 8 cups of water, try starting with 5 cups. Conversely, recipes should include at least a little liquid. If a recipe does not include liquid, add ½ cup of water or broth.

- In general, 1 hour of simmering on the stovetop or baking at 350° in the oven is equal to 8-10 hours on low or 4-6 hours on high in a slow cooker. Check the chart below.

- Flour and cornstarch are often used to thicken soups, stews and sauces that are cooked in a slow cooker.

BEEF & POTATO SOUP (PAGE 67)

Cook Times

15 to 30 minutes in Conventional Oven
Slow Cooker
Low: 4 to 6 hours • High: 1½ to 2 hours
35 to 45 minutes in Conventional Oven
Slow Cooker
Low: 6 to 8 hours • High: 3 to 4 hours
50 minutes or more in Conventional Oven
Slow Cooker
Low: 8 to 10 hours • High: 4 to 6 hours

When a range in cooking time is provided, this accounts for variables such as thickness of meat, how full the slow cooker is and the temperature of the food going into the cooker. As you become used to how your slow cooker works, you'll be better able to judge which end of the range to use.

Tips for Tasty Outcomes

- No peeking! Refrain from lifting the lid while food cooks in the slow cooker, unless a recipe instructs you to stir or add ingredients. The loss of steam can mean an extra 20-30 minutes of cooking time each time you lift the lid.

- Be sure the lid is well-placed over the ceramic insert, not tilted or askew. The steam during cooking creates a seal.

- When food is finished cooking, remove it from the slow cooker within one hour and promptly refrigerate any leftovers.

- Slow cooking may take longer at higher altitudes.

- Don't forget to bring your slow cooker when you go camping, if electricity is available. When space is limited and you want "set-it-and-forget-it" meals, it's a handy appliance.

- Reheating food in a slow cooker isn't recommended. Cooked food can be heated on the stovetop or in the microwave and then put into a slow cooker to keep hot for serving.

- Use a slow cooker on a buffet table to keep soup, stew, savory dips or mashed potatoes hot.

RACHEL KUNKEL'S
BBQ CHICKEN SLIDERS
page 68

APPETIZERS & BEVERAGES 8

SIDE DISHES 18

ENTREES 36

SOUPS & SANDWICHES 64

DESSERTS 78

Spring

Spring has sprung! Celebrate the season with these slow-cooked dishes. Whether planning a St. Patrick's Day party, hosting Easter dinner, organizing a quaint luncheon or simply thinking about supper, you can't go wrong with these all-time favorites.

Spring

APPETIZERS & BEVERAGES

It's time to shake the winter blues and get together with a group of friends and family! Whip up these easy bites for a surefire celebration that welcomes longer days, warmer weather and Mother Nature's freshest ingredients.

KELLY BYLER'S SOUTHWESTERN NACHOS

Southwestern Nachos

Guests will go crazy when you serve this cheesy nacho casserole featuring tender chunks of pork made easily in the slow cooker! You don't need to worry about filling the chip bowl...the tortilla chips are conveniently baked right in the dish.

—**KELLY BYLER** GOSHEN, IN

PREP: 40 MIN. • **COOK:** 7¼ HOURS
MAKES: 30 SERVINGS

- 2 boneless whole pork loin roasts (3½ pounds each)
- 1 cup unsweetened apple juice
- 6 garlic cloves, minced
- 1 teaspoon salt
- 1 teaspoon liquid smoke, optional
- 2½ cups barbecue sauce, divided
- ⅓ cup packed brown sugar
- 2 tablespoons honey
- 1 package (10 ounces) tortilla chip scoops
- 1½ cups frozen corn
- 1 can (15 ounces) black beans, rinsed and drained
- 1 medium tomato, seeded and chopped
- 1 medium red onion, chopped
- ⅓ cup minced fresh cilantro
- 1 jalapeno pepper, seeded and chopped
- 2 teaspoons lime juice
- 1 package (16 ounces) process cheese (Velveeta), cubed
- 2 tablespoons 2% milk

1. Cut each roast in half; place in two 5-qt. slow cookers. Combine apple juice, garlic, salt and liquid smoke if desired; pour over meat. Cover and cook on low 7-8 hours or until tender.

2. Preheat oven to 375°. Shred pork with two forks; place in a very large bowl. Stir in 2 cups barbecue sauce, brown sugar and honey. Divide tortilla chips between two greased 13x9-in. baking dishes; top with pork mixture. Combine corn, beans, tomato, onion, cilantro, jalapeno and lime juice; spoon over pork mixture. Bake, uncovered, 15-20 minutes or until heated through.

3. Meanwhile, in a small saucepan, melt cheese with milk. Drizzle cheese sauce and remaining barbecue sauce over nachos.

NOTE *Wear disposable gloves when cutting hot peppers; the oils can burn skin. Avoid touching your face.*

DID YOU KNOW?

Light brown sugar and dark brown sugar can be used interchangeably in recipes. The light version has a delicate flavor while the dark kind has a stronger molasses flavor.

JALAPENO SPINACH DIP

Jalapeno Spinach Dip

Everyone loves spinach dip, and this version is as easy as it is delicious. Just mix the ingredients together in the slow cooker for a savory and creamy appetizer.
—**MICHAELA DEBELIUS** WADDELL, AZ

PREP: 10 MIN. • **COOK:** 2 HOURS
MAKES: 16 SERVINGS (¼ CUP EACH)

- 2 **packages (10 ounces each) frozen chopped spinach, thawed and squeezed dry**
- 2 **packages (8 ounces each) cream cheese, softened**
- 1 **cup grated Parmesan cheese**
- 1 **cup half-and-half cream**
- ½ **cup finely chopped onion**
- ¼ **cup chopped seeded jalapeno peppers**
- 2 **teaspoons Worcestershire sauce**
- 2 **teaspoons hot pepper sauce**
- 1 **teaspoon garlic powder**
- 1 **teaspoon dill weed**
  Tortilla chips

In a 1½-qt. slow cooker, combine the first 10 ingredients. Cover and cook on low for 2-3 hours or until heated through. Serve with chips.
NOTE *Wear disposable gloves when cutting hot peppers; the oils can burn skin. Avoid touching your face.*

⑤INGREDIENTS Warm
Strawberry Fondue

You only need a handful of ingredients to fix this spring fondue. Use grapes, bananas, strawberries and angel food cake cubes as dippers.
—**SHARON MENSING** GREENFIELD, IA

START TO FINISH: 15 MIN.
MAKES: 1½ CUPS

- 1 **package (10 ounces) frozen sweetened sliced strawberries, thawed**
- ¼ **cup half-and-half cream**
- 1 **teaspoon cornstarch**
- ½ **teaspoon lemon juice**
  Angel food cake cubes and fresh fruit

1. In a food processor, combine the strawberries, cream, cornstarch and lemon juice; cover and process until smooth.
2. Pour into saucepan. Bring to a boil; cook and stir for 2 minutes or until slightly thickened. Transfer to a 1½-qt. slow cooker; keep warm. Serve with cake cubes and fruit.

WARM STRAWBERRY FONDUE

JAN HABERSTICH'S
SPINACH ARTICHOKE DIP

Spinach Artichoke Dip

Here's a creamy, delicious appetizer that's perfect for special occasions. It is really good served alongside slices of Asiago cheese bread.

—JAN HABERSTICH WATERLOO, IA

PREP: 10 MIN. • **COOK:** 2 HOURS
MAKES: 12 SERVINGS (¼ CUP EACH)

- 1 **can (14 ounces) water-packed artichoke hearts, drained and chopped**
- 1 **cup fresh baby spinach, chopped**
- ½ **cup sour cream**
- ½ **cup mayonnaise**
- ½ **cup shredded part-skim mozzarella cheese**
- ½ **cup shredded Parmesan cheese**
- ⅓ **cup chopped red onion**
- ¼ **teaspoon garlic powder**
  Assorted crackers or sliced breads

1. Place the first eight ingredients in a 1½-qt. slow cooker; stir to combine. Cook, covered, on low 2 to 2½ hours or until heated through.
2. Stir to blend. Serve with crackers.

Mexican Fondue

A handful of items and a few moments of prep work are all you'll need for this festive fondue. Not only does it take advantage of canned goods and other convenience items, but the slow cooker does all the work.

—NELLA PARKER HERSEY, MI

PREP: 15 MIN. • **COOK:** 1½ HOURS
MAKES: 4½ CUPS

- 1 **can (14¾ ounces) cream-style corn**
- 1 **can (14½ ounces) diced tomatoes, drained**
- 3 **tablespoons chopped green chilies**
- 1 **teaspoon chili powder**
- 1 **package (16 ounces) process cheese (Velveeta), cubed**
  French bread cubes

1. In a small bowl, combine the corn, tomatoes, green chilies and chili powder. Stir in cheese. Pour mixture into a 1½-qt. slow cooker coated with cooking spray.
2. Cover and cook on high for 1½ hours, stirring every 30 minutes or until cheese is melted. Serve warm with bread cubes.

Buffalo Wing Dip

If you love spicy wings, you'll adore this dip. It's super cheesy, easy as can be and really has the flavor of Buffalo wings!

—TASTE OF HOME TEST KITCHEN

PREP: 20 MIN. • **COOK:** 2 HOURS
MAKES: 6 CUPS

- 2 **packages (8 ounces each) cream cheese, softened**
- ½ **cup ranch salad dressing**
- ½ **cup sour cream**
- 5 **tablespoons crumbled blue cheese**
- 2 **cups shredded cooked chicken**
- ½ **cup Buffalo wing sauce**
- 2 **cups (8 ounces) shredded cheddar cheese, divided**
- 1 **green onion, sliced**
  Tortilla chips

1. In a small bowl, combine the cream cheese, dressing, sour cream and blue cheese. Transfer to a 3-qt. slow cooker. Layer with chicken, wing sauce and 1 cup cheese. Cover and cook on low for 2-3 hours or until heated through.
2. Sprinkle with remaining cheese and onion. Serve with tortilla chips.

BUFFALO WING DIP

PRETTY ORANGE CIDER

(5) INGREDIENTS
Marmalade Meatballs

I brought this appetizer to a potluck. I started cooking the meatballs in the morning, and by lunch they were ready.

—**JEANNE KISS** GREENSBURG, PA

PREP: 10 MIN. • **COOK:** 4 HOURS
MAKES: ABOUT 5 DOZEN

- 1 **bottle (16 ounces) Catalina salad dressing**
- 1 **cup orange marmalade**
- 3 **tablespoons Worcestershire sauce**
- ½ **teaspoon crushed red pepper flakes**
- 1 **package (32 ounces) frozen fully cooked homestyle meatballs, thawed**

In a 3-qt. slow cooker, combine the salad dressing, marmalade, Worcestershire sauce and pepper flakes. Stir in meatballs. Cover and cook on low for 4-5 hours or until heated through.

Creamy Chipped Beef Fondue

My mother often served fondue at parties, and I've since followed in that tradition. It's nice to offer a hearty appetizer that requires very little work.

—**BETH FOX** LAWRENCE, KS

START TO FINISH: 15 MIN.
MAKES: ABOUT 4 CUPS

- 1⅓ to 1½ **cups milk**
- 2 **packages (8 ounces each) cream cheese, softened**
- 1 **package (2½ ounces) thinly sliced dried beef, chopped**
- ¼ **cup chopped green onions**
- 2 **teaspoons ground mustard**
- 1 **loaf (1 pound) French bread, cubed**

In a large saucepan, heat milk and cream cheese over medium heat; stir until smooth. Stir in beef, onions and mustard; heat through. Transfer to a 1½-qt. slow cooker; keep warm. Serve with bread cubes.

(5) INGREDIENTS
Pretty Orange Cider

As the season warms up, this pretty beverage is sure to be a hit! You just might want to double the recipe, then fill the punch bowl for guests!

—**MARK MORGAN** WATERFORD, WI

START TO FINISH: 20 MIN.
MAKES: 1½ QUARTS

- 4 **cups apple cider or juice**
- 2 **cups orange juice**
- 3 **tablespoons red-hot candies**
- 1½ **teaspoons whole allspice**
- 4½ **teaspoons honey**

1. In a large saucepan, combine the cider, juice and candies. Place the allspice on a double thickness of cheesecloth; bring up corners of cloth and tie with string to form a bag. Add to pan. Bring to a boil. Reduce heat; cover and simmer for 5 minutes or until flavors are blended.
2. Discard spice bag; stir in honey. Transfer to a 3-qt. slow cooker; keep warm over low heat.

MARMALADE MEATBALLS

SWEET 'N' TANGY CHICKEN WINGS

Sweet 'n' Tangy Chicken Wings

Here's a festive recipe that's perfect for parties. Put the wings in before you prepare for the party, and in a few hours, you'll have wonderful appetizers!

—**IDA TUEY** SOUTH LYON, MI

PREP: 20 MIN. • **COOK:** 3¼ HOURS
MAKES: ABOUT 2½ DOZEN

- 3 **pounds chicken wingettes (about 30)**
- ½ **teaspoon salt, divided**
  Dash pepper
- 1½ **cups ketchup**
- ¼ **cup packed brown sugar**
- ¼ **cup red wine vinegar**
- 2 **tablespoons Worcestershire sauce**
- 1 **tablespoon Dijon mustard**
- 1 **teaspoon minced garlic**
- 1 **teaspoon liquid smoke, optional**
  Sesame seeds, optional

1. Sprinkle chicken wings with a dash of salt and pepper. Broil 4-6 in. from the heat for 5-10 minutes on each side or until golden brown. Transfer to a greased 5-qt. slow cooker.
2. Combine the ketchup, brown sugar, vinegar, Worcestershire sauce, mustard, garlic, liquid smoke if desired and remaining salt; pour over wings. Toss to coat.
3. Cover and cook on low for 3¼ to 3¾ hours or until chicken juices run clear. Sprinkle with sesame seeds if desired.

Hot Crab Dip

I have a large family, work full time, and coach soccer and football. So I truly appreciate recipes like this one that are easy to assemble. The rich, creamy dip is a fun recipe for any spring gathering.

—**TERI RASEY** CADILLAC, MI

PREP: 5 MIN. • **COOK:** 3 HOURS
MAKES: ABOUT 5 CUPS

- ½ **cup milk**
- ⅓ **cup salsa**
- 3 **packages (8 ounces each) cream cheese, cubed**
- 2 **packages (8 ounces each) imitation crabmeat, flaked**
- 1 **cup thinly sliced green onions**
- 1 **can (4 ounces) chopped green chilies**
  Assorted crackers

In a small bowl, combine milk and salsa. Transfer to a greased 3-qt. slow cooker. Stir in cream cheese, crab, onions and chilies. Cover and cook on low for 3-4 hours, stirring every 30 minutes. Serve with crackers.

HOT CRAB DIP

SEAFOOD CHEESE DIP

(5)INGREDIENTS
Seafood Cheese Dip

This cheesy recipe has a wonderful combination of seafood flavors and clings nicely to toasted bread.

—**MICHELLE DOMM** ATLANTA, NY

PREP: 15 MIN. • **COOK:** 1½ HOURS
MAKES: 5 CUPS

- 1 **package (32 ounces) process cheese (Velveeta), cubed**
- 2 **cans (6 ounces each) lump crabmeat, drained**
- 1 **can (10 ounces) diced tomatoes and green chilies, undrained**
- 1 **cup frozen cooked salad shrimp, thawed**
  French bread baguettes, sliced and toasted

In a greased 3-qt. slow cooker, combine the cheese, crab, tomatoes and shrimp. Cover and cook on low for 1½ to 2 hours or until cheese is melted, stirring occasionally. Serve with baguettes.

Spicy Apple Tea

Ideal for a chilly spring morning, this comforting beverage is one of my slow-cooker staples.

—**KAREN LARA** KAMLOOPS, BC

PREP: 15 MIN. • **COOK:** 2 HOURS
MAKES: 21 SERVINGS (¾ CUP EACH)

- 2 **quarts water**
- 2 **quarts unsweetened apple juice**
- 1 **cup packed brown sugar**
- 4 **individual black tea bags**
- 4 **cinnamon sticks (3 inches)**
- 1 **tablespoon minced fresh gingerroot**
- 1 **tablespoon whole allspice**
- 1 **tablespoon whole cloves**

1. In a 6-qt. slow cooker, combine the water, apple juice, brown sugar and tea bags. Place the cinnamon sticks, ginger, allspice and cloves on a double thickness of cheesecloth; bring up corners of cloth and tie with string to form a bag. Place in slow cooker.
2. Cover and cook on high for 2-3 hours

or until heated through. Discard tea bags and spice bag. Serve warm in mugs.

Reuben Spread

I love Reuben anything, and this party-starter is a favorite. It's a warm and yummy crowd-pleaser, perfect for rallying a game-day crowd!

—**JUNE HERKE** WATERTOWN, SD

PREP: 10 MIN. • **COOK:** 4 HOURS
MAKES: 30 SERVINGS
(2 TABLESPOONS EACH)

- 2 **packages (8 ounces each) cream cheese, cubed**
- 4 **cups (16 ounces) shredded Swiss cheese**
- 1 **can (14 ounces) sauerkraut, rinsed and well drained**
- 4 **packages (2 ounces each) thinly sliced deli corned beef, chopped**
- ½ **cup Thousand Island salad dressing**
  Snack rye bread or rye crackers

1. Place the first five ingredients in a 1½-qt. slow cooker; stir to combine. Cook, covered, on low 4 to 4½ hours or until heated through.
2. Stir to blend. Serve spread with bread.

REUBEN SPREAD

BARBECUE SAUSAGE BITES

1. In a 3-qt. slow cooker, combine the sausages. In a small bowl, whisk the barbecue sauce, marmalade, mustard and allspice. Pour over sausage mixture; stir to coat.

2. Cover and cook on high for 2½ to 3 hours or until heated through. Stir in pineapple. Serve with toothpicks.

Crispy Snack Mix

This recipe proves that you can make just about anything in the slow cooker—even a delightfully crunchy snack mix!

—JANE PAIR SIMS DE LEON, TX

PREP: 10 MIN. • **COOK:** 2½ HOURS
MAKES: ABOUT 2½ QUARTS

4½ cups crispy chow mein noodles
4 cups Rice Chex

1 can (9¾ ounces) salted cashews
1 cup flaked coconut, toasted
½ cup butter, melted
2 tablespoons reduced-sodium soy sauce
2¼ teaspoons curry powder
¾ teaspoon ground ginger

1. In a 5-qt. slow cooker, combine the noodles, cereal, cashews and coconut. In a small bowl, whisk the butter, soy sauce, curry powder and ginger; drizzle over cereal mixture and mix well.

2. Cover and cook on low 2½ hours, stirring every 30 minutes. Serve warm or at room temperature.

Barbecue Sausage Bites

This sweet-and-tangy appetizer pairs pineapple chunks with barbecue sauce and three kinds of sausage. It'll tide over even the biggest appetites until dinner.

—REBEKAH RANDOLPH GREER, SC

PREP: 10 MIN. • **COOK:** 2½ HOURS
MAKES: 12-14 SERVINGS

1 package (16 ounces) miniature smoked sausages
¾ pound fully cooked bratwurst links, cut into ½-inch slices
¾ pound smoked kielbasa or Polish sausage, cut into ½-inch slices
1 bottle (18 ounces) barbecue sauce
⅔ cup orange marmalade
½ teaspoon ground mustard
⅛ teaspoon ground allspice
1 can (20 ounces) pineapple chunks, drained

CRISPY SNACK MIX

MARINATED CHICKEN WINGS

Marinated Chicken Wings

I've made these slow-cooked chicken wings many times for get-togethers. They're so moist and tender, I always get lots of compliments and many requests for the recipe.

—JANIE BOTTING SULTAN, WA

PREP: 5 MIN. + MARINATING
COOK: 3 HOURS
MAKES: 20 SERVINGS

- 20 **whole chicken wings (about 4 pounds)**
- 1 **cup reduced-sodium soy sauce**
- ¼ **cup white wine or reduced-sodium chicken broth**
- ¼ **cup canola oil**
- 3 **tablespoons sugar**
- 2 **garlic cloves, minced**
- 1 **teaspoon ground ginger**

1. Cut chicken wings into three sections; discard wing tips. Place in a large resealable plastic bag. In a small bowl, whisk remaining ingredients until blended. Add to chicken; seal bag and turn to coat. Refrigerate overnight.

2. Transfer chicken and marinade to a 5-qt. slow cooker. Cook, covered, on low 3-4 hours or until chicken is tender. Using tongs, remove wings to a serving plate.

Fruit Salsa

Serve this fruity salsa anywhere you'd use ordinary salsa. My son and I experimented with different ingredients to find the combination we liked best. Preparing it in a slow cooker not only minimizes prep time but also maximizes flavor.

—FLORENCE BUCHKOWSKY
PRINCE ALBERT, SK

PREP: 10 MIN. • **COOK:** 2 HOURS
MAKES: 4 CUPS

- 3 **tablespoons cornstarch**
- 4 **teaspoons white vinegar**
- 1 **can (11 ounces) mandarin oranges, undrained**
- 1 **can (8½ ounces) sliced peaches, undrained**
- ¾ **cup pineapple tidbits**
- 1 **medium onion, chopped**
- ½ **each medium green, sweet red and yellow peppers, chopped**
- 3 **garlic cloves, minced Tortilla chips**

1. In a 3-qt. slow cooker, combine cornstarch and vinegar until smooth. Stir in the fruits, onion, peppers and garlic.

2. Cover and cook on high for 2-3 hours or until thickened and heated through, stirring occasionally. Serve with tortilla chips.

FRUIT SALSA

Pizza Dip

Everybody loves this pizza-flavored simple dip. If you have any left over, spoon it on a toasted English muffin for a great open-faced sandwich.

—SARA NOWACKI FRANKLIN, WI

PREP: 10 MIN. • **COOK:** 1½ HOURS
MAKES: 5½ CUPS

- 2 **packages (8 ounces each) cream cheese, cubed**
- 1 **can (15 ounces) pizza sauce**
- 1 **package (8 ounces) sliced pepperoni, chopped**
- 1 **can (3.8 ounces) chopped ripe olives, drained**
- 2 **cups (8 ounces) shredded part-skim mozzarella cheese**
  Bagel chips or garlic toast

1. Place cream cheese in a 3-qt. slow cooker. Combine the pizza sauce, pepperoni and olives; pour over cream cheese. Top with mozzarella cheese.
2. Cover and cook on low for 1-2 hours or until cheese is melted. Stir just until combined; serve warm with bagel chips or garlic toast.

Hearty Broccoli Dip

You'll need just five ingredients to stir up my no-fuss spring appetizer. People often ask me to bring this creamy dip to potlucks and parties. Best of all, I never leave with leftovers.

—SUE CALL BEECH GROVE, IN

PREP: 15 MIN. • **COOK:** 2 HOURS
MAKES: 5½ CUPS

- 1 **pound ground beef**
- 1 **pound process cheese (Velveeta), cubed**
- 1 **can (10¾ ounces) condensed cream of mushroom soup, undiluted**
- 3 **cups frozen chopped broccoli, thawed**
- 2 **tablespoons salsa**
  Tortilla chips

1. In a large skillet, cook beef over medium heat until no longer pink; drain. Transfer to a 3-qt. slow cooker. Add cheese, soup, broccoli and salsa; mix well.
2. Cover and cook on low for 2-3 hours or until heated through, stirring after 1 hour. Serve with chips.

Spring

SIDE DISHES

Spring is a great time to round out meals with root vegetables such as carrots and potatoes. Best of all, these savory slow-cooked options free up oven space for entrees. So go ahead and add these sides to your lineup for a fuss-free dinner!

GLORIA SCHUTZ'S
SHOEPEG CORN SIDE DISH

Shoepeg Corn Side Dish

I took this dish to a potluck and everyone asked for the recipe. If shoepeg corn isn't available in your region, then regular canned corn works well, too.
—**GLORIA SCHUTZ** TRENTON, IL

PREP: 20 MIN. • **COOK:** 3 HOURS
MAKES: 8 SERVINGS

- 1 can (14½ ounces) French-style green beans, drained
- 2 cans (7 ounces each) white or shoepeg corn
- 1 can (10¾ ounces) condensed cream of mushroom soup, undiluted
- 1 jar (4½ ounces) sliced mushrooms, drained
- ½ cup slivered almonds
- ½ cup shredded cheddar cheese
- ½ cup sour cream
- ¾ cup French-fried onions

In a 3-qt. slow cooker, combine the first seven ingredients. Cover and cook on low for 3-4 hours or until vegetables are tender, stirring occasionally. Sprinkle with onions during the last 15 minutes of cooking.

Garlic & Herb Mashed Potatoes

Can you keep a secret? Cream cheese is the surprise ingredient in these comforting spuds. Simply mix, mash and let them simmer in the slow cooker.
—**FRIEDA BLIESNER** MCALLEN, TX

PREP: 30 MIN. • **COOK:** 2 HOURS
MAKES: 10 SERVINGS

- 4 pounds Yukon Gold potatoes (about 12 medium), peeled and cubed
- 1 package (8 ounces) cream cheese, softened and cubed
- 1 cup (8 ounces) sour cream
- ½ cup butter, cubed
- ⅓ cup heavy whipping cream
- 3 tablespoons minced chives
- 3 garlic cloves, minced
- 1 tablespoon minced fresh parsley
- 1 teaspoon minced fresh thyme
- ½ teaspoon salt
- ¼ teaspoon pepper

1. Place potatoes in a Dutch oven and cover with water. Bring to a boil. Reduce heat; cover and cook for 10-15 minutes or until tender. Drain. Mash potatoes with cream cheese, sour cream, butter and cream. Stir in the remaining ingredients.
2. Transfer to a greased 3- or 4-qt. slow cooker. Cover and cook on low for 2-3 hours or until heated through.

LOADED MASHED POTATOES

Au Gratin Garlic Potatoes

A can of cheese soup easily helps turn ordinary sliced potatoes into a rich side dish that's a perfect accompaniment to almost any meal.

—**TONYA VOWELS** VINE GROVE, KY

PREP: 10 MIN. • **COOK:** 6 HOURS
MAKES: 6-8 SERVINGS

- ½ cup milk
- 1 can (10¾ ounces) condensed cheddar cheese soup, undiluted
- 1 package (8 ounces) cream cheese, cubed
- 1 garlic clove, minced
- ¼ teaspoon ground nutmeg
- ⅛ teaspoon pepper
- 2 pounds potatoes, peeled and sliced
- 1 small onion, chopped
  Paprika, optional

1. In a large saucepan, heat milk over medium heat until bubbles form around side of saucepan. Remove from the heat. Add the soup, cream cheese, garlic, nutmeg and pepper; stir until smooth.
2. Place the potatoes and onion in a 3-qt. slow cooker. Pour the milk mixture over the potato mixture; mix well. Cover and cook on low for 6-7 hours or until potatoes are tender. Sprinkle with paprika if desired.

AU GRATIN GARLIC POTATOES

Loaded Mashed Potatoes

Every year my mom made incredible potatoes for Thanksgiving. I've tailored her recipe to my family's tastes and carried on the tradition. I also make mine in a slow cooker, which is convenient because I can prepare the potatoes a day ahead, freeing up oven space.

—**ANN NOLTE** RIVERVIEW, FL

PREP: 25 MIN. + CHILLING • **COOK:** 3 HOURS
MAKES: 10 SERVINGS

- 3 pounds potatoes (about 9 medium), peeled and cubed
- 1 package (8 ounces) cream cheese, softened
- 1 cup (8 ounces) sour cream
- ½ cup butter, cubed
- ¼ cup 2% milk
- 1½ cups (6 ounces) shredded cheddar cheese
- 1½ cups (6 ounces) shredded pepper jack cheese
- ½ pound bacon strips, cooked and crumbled
- 4 green onions, chopped
- ½ teaspoon onion powder
- ½ teaspoon garlic powder

1. Place potatoes in a Dutch oven and cover with water. Bring to a boil. Reduce heat; cover and cook for 10-15 minutes or until tender. Drain. Mash potatoes with cream cheese, sour cream, butter and milk. Stir in the cheeses, bacon, onions and seasonings. Transfer to a large bowl; cover and refrigerate overnight.
2. Transfer to a greased 3- or 4-quart slow cooker. Cover and cook on low for 3 to 3½ hours.

LEMON RED POTATOES

Harvard Beets

Fresh beets are delicious when combined with aromatic spices and a hint of orange. These have the perfect balance of sweet and sour flavors.

—*TASTE OF HOME* **TEST KITCHEN**

PREP: 15 MIN. • **COOK:** 7 HOURS
MAKES: 6 SERVINGS

- 2 **pounds small fresh beets, peeled and halved**
- ½ **cup sugar**
- ¼ **cup packed brown sugar**
- 2 **tablespoons cornstarch**
- ½ **teaspoon salt**
- ¼ **cup orange juice**
- ¼ **cup cider vinegar**
- 2 **tablespoons butter**
- 1½ **teaspoons whole cloves**

1. Place beets in a 3-qt. slow cooker. In a small bowl, combine the sugar, brown sugar, cornstarch and salt. Stir in orange juice and vinegar. Pour over beets; dot with butter. Place cloves on a double thickness of cheesecloth; bring up corners of cloth and tie with string to form a bag. Place bag in slow cooker.
2. Cover and cook on low for 7-8 hours or until tender. Discard spice bag.

DID YOU KNOW?

Harvard Beets are simmered in a sugar-vinegar sauce, often flavored with orange juice. The history of this dish isn't clear. Many believe the beets are called this because they resemble the color of a Harvard Crimson football jersey. Others think the beets originated in a tavern in England named "Harwood," which eventually came to be pronounced "Harvard."

Lemon Red Potatoes

Butter, lemon juice, parsley and chives enhance this simple side dish. I usually prepare these potatoes when I'm having company. Since the potatoes cook in the slow cooker, there's plenty of room on the stove for other dishes.

—**TARA BRANHAM** AUSTIN, TX

PREP: 5 MIN. • **COOK:** 2½ HOURS
MAKES: 6 SERVINGS

- 1½ **pounds medium red potatoes**
- ¼ **cup water**
- ¼ **cup butter, melted**
- 3 **tablespoons minced fresh parsley**
- 1 **tablespoon lemon juice**
- 1 **tablespoon minced chives**
  Salt and pepper to taste

1. Cut a strip of peel from around the middle of each potato. Place potatoes and water in a 3-qt. slow cooker. Cover and cook on high for 2½ to 3 hours or until tender (do not overcook); drain.
2. In a small bowl, combine the butter, parsley, lemon juice and chives. Pour over the potatoes and toss to coat. Season with salt and pepper.

HARVARD BEETS

CHEDDAR SPIRALS

[5] INGREDIENTS

Cheddar Spirals

Our kids just love this cheesy pasta and will sample a spoonful right from the slow cooker when they walk by. Sometimes I add cooked cocktail sausages, sliced Polish sausage or cubed ham to make it a hearty dinner.

—HEIDI FERKOVICH PARK FALLS, WI

PREP: 20 MIN. • **COOK:** 2½ HOURS
MAKES: 15 SERVINGS (¾ CUP EACH)

1 **package (16 ounces) spiral pasta**
2 **cups half-and-half cream**
1 **can (10¾ ounces) condensed cheddar cheese soup, undiluted**
½ **cup butter, melted**
4 **cups (16 ounces) shredded cheddar cheese**

Cook pasta according to package directions; drain. In a 5-qt. slow cooker, combine the cream, soup and butter until smooth; stir in the cheese and pasta. Cover and cook on low for 2½ hours or until cheese is melted.

TOP TIP

My entire family loves this recipe. I cut the butter to 1 tablespoon and love to add cooked chicken and different veggies to make it an easy on-the-go dinner.
—IMASK TASTEOFHOME.COM

CREAMY HASH BROWN POTATOES

Creamy Hash Brown Potatoes

I like to fix a batch of these cheesy slow-cooker potatoes for potlucks and other big gatherings. Frozen hash browns, canned soup and flavored cream cheese make it so quick to put together.

—JULIANNE HENSON STREAMWOOD, IL

PREP: 5 MIN. • **COOK:** 3½ HOURS
MAKES: 12-14 SERVINGS

- 1 package (32 ounces) frozen cubed hash brown potatoes
- 1 can (10¾ ounces) condensed cream of potato soup, undiluted
- 2 cups (8 ounces) shredded Colby-Monterey Jack cheese
- 1 cup (8 ounces) sour cream
- ¼ teaspoon pepper
- ⅛ teaspoon salt
- 1 carton (8 ounces) spreadable chive and onion cream cheese

1. Place potatoes in a lightly greased 4-qt. slow cooker. In a large bowl, combine the soup, cheese, sour cream, pepper and salt. Pour over potatoes and mix well.

2. Cover and cook on low for 3½ to 4 hours or until potatoes are tender. Stir in cream cheese.

Black-Eyed Peas & Ham

We have these slow-cooked black-eyed peas regularly at our house. They're supposed to bring good luck!

—DAWN FRIHAUF FORT MORGAN, CO

PREP: 20 MIN. • **COOK:** 6 HOURS
MAKES: 12 SERVINGS

- 1 package (16 ounces) dried black-eyed peas, rinsed and sorted
- ½ pound fully cooked boneless ham, finely chopped
- 1 medium onion, finely chopped
- 1 medium sweet red pepper, finely chopped
- 5 bacon strips, cooked and crumbled
- 1 large jalapeno pepper, seeded and finely chopped
- 2 garlic cloves, minced
- 1½ teaspoons ground cumin
- 1 teaspoon reduced-sodium chicken bouillon granules
- ½ teaspoon salt
- ½ teaspoon cayenne pepper
- ¼ teaspoon pepper
- 6 cups water
  Minced fresh cilantro, optional
  Hot cooked rice

In a 6-qt. slow cooker, combine the first 13 ingredients. Cover and cook on low for 6-8 hours or until peas are tender. Sprinkle with cilantro if desired. Serve with rice.

NOTE *Wear disposable gloves when cutting hot peppers; the oils can burn skin. Avoid touching your face.*

BLACK-EYED PEAS & HAM

PECAN-COCONUT SWEET POTATOES

Here's a recipe that has evolved in all the years we've made it. This version has been a favorite at our Christmas dinners.
—**JUDY BATSON** TAMPA, FL

Pecan-Coconut Sweet Potatoes

It's great to be able to make a tempting sweet potato dish well ahead of time by putting it in the slow cooker. This tasty recipe includes sweet coconut and crunchy pecans. It's yummy!
—**REBECCA CLARK** WARRIOR, AL

PREP: 20 MIN. • **COOK:** 5 HOURS
MAKES: 6 SERVINGS

- ¼ **cup packed brown sugar**
- 2 **tablespoons flaked coconut**
- 2 **tablespoons chopped pecans, toasted**
- 1 **teaspoon vanilla extract**
- ½ **teaspoon salt**
- ¼ **teaspoon ground cinnamon**
- 2 **pounds sweet potatoes, peeled and cut into ¾-inch cubes**
- 1 **tablespoon butter, melted**
- ½ **cup miniature marshmallows**

1. In a small bowl, mix the first six ingredients. Place sweet potatoes in a 3-qt. slow cooker coated with cooking spray; sprinkle with brown sugar mixture. Drizzle with butter.
2. Cook, covered, on low 5-6 hours or until sweet potatoes are tender. Turn off the slow cooker. Sprinkle marshmallows over potatoes; let stand, covered, for 5 minutes before serving.

Banana Applesauce

PREP: 20 MIN. • **COOK:** 3 HOURS
MAKES: 5½ CUPS

- 8 **medium apples, peeled and cubed**
- 1 **medium ripe banana, thinly sliced**
- 1 **cup raisins**
- ¾ **cup orange juice**
- ½ **cup packed brown sugar**
- ¼ **cup honey**
- ¼ **cup butter, melted**
- 2 **teaspoons pumpkin pie spice**
- 1 **small lemon**
- 1 **envelope instant apples and cinnamon oatmeal**
- ½ **cup boiling water**

1. Place the apples, banana and raisins in a 3-qt. slow cooker coated with cooking spray. In a small bowl, combine the orange juice, brown sugar, honey, butter and pie spice; pour over apple mixture. Cut ends off lemon. Cut into six wedges and remove seeds. Transfer to slow cooker. Cover and cook on high for 3-4 hours or until apples are soft.
2. Discard lemon. Mash apple mixture. In a small bowl, combine oatmeal and water. Let stand for 1 minute. Stir into applesauce.

COWBOY CALICO BEANS

Cowboy Calico Beans

This filling dish is a tradition at the table when my girlfriends and I go up North for a girls' weekend. The husbands and kids are left at home, but the slow cooker comes with us!

—**JULIE BUTSCH** HARTLAND, WI

PREP: 30 MIN. • **COOK:** 4 HOURS
MAKES: 8 SERVINGS

- 1 **pound lean ground beef (90% lean)**
- 1 **large sweet onion, chopped**
- ½ **cup packed brown sugar**
- ¼ **cup ketchup**
- 3 **tablespoons cider vinegar**
- 2 **tablespoons yellow mustard**
- 1 **can (16 ounces) butter beans, drained**
- 1 **can (16 ounces) kidney beans, rinsed and drained**
- 1 **can (15 ounces) pork and beans**
- 1 **can (15¼ ounces) lima beans, rinsed and drained**

1. In a large skillet, cook beef and onion over medium heat until meat is no longer pink; drain.

2. Transfer to a 3-qt. slow cooker. Combine the brown sugar, ketchup, vinegar and mustard; add to meat mixture. Stir in the beans. Cover and cook on low for 4-5 hours or until heated through.

Spanish Hominy

I received this recipe from a good friend who is a fabulous cook. The colorful side dish gets its zesty flavor from spicy canned tomatoes with green chilies.

—**DONNA BROCKETT** KINGFISHER, OK

PREP: 15 MIN. • **COOK:** 6 HOURS
MAKES: 12 SERVINGS

- 4 **cans (15½ ounces each) hominy, rinsed and drained**
- 1 **can (14½ ounces) diced tomatoes, undrained**
- 1 **can (10 ounces) diced tomatoes and green chilies, undrained**
- 1 **can (8 ounces) tomato sauce**
- ¾ **pound sliced bacon, diced**
- 1 **large onion, chopped**
- 1 **medium green pepper, chopped**

1. In a 5-qt. slow cooker, combine the hominy, tomatoes and tomato sauce.

2. In a large skillet, cook bacon until crisp; remove with a slotted spoon to paper towels. Drain, reserving 1 tablespoon drippings.

3. In the same skillet, saute onion and green pepper in drippings until tender. Stir onion mixture and bacon into hominy mixture. Cover and cook on low for 6-8 hours or until heated through.

SPANISH HOMINY

CATHY BELL'S
GREEN BEANS WITH BACON AND TOMATOES

Green Beans with Bacon and Tomatoes

If needed, this recipe can be easily doubled or tripled to serve larger crowds. And garlic salt can be substituted for the seasoned salt, if you prefer.

—**CATHY BELL** JOPLIN, MO

PREP: 15 MIN. • **COOK:** 4½ HOURS
MAKES: 12 SERVINGS (¾ CUP)

- 1 **package (14 ounces) thick-sliced bacon strips, chopped**
- 1 **large red onion, chopped**
- 2 **packages (16 ounces each) frozen cut green beans**
- 1 **can (28 ounces) petite diced tomatoes, undrained**
- ¼ **cup packed brown sugar**
- 1 **tablespoon seasoned pepper**
- ½ **teaspoon seasoned salt**
- 1 **can (16 ounces) red beans, rinsed and drained**

1. In a large skillet, cook bacon over medium heat until partially cooked but not crisp, stirring occasionally. Remove with a slotted spoon; drain on paper towels. Discard drippings, reserving 2 tablespoons. Add onion to drippings; cook and stir over medium-high heat until tender.

2. In a 4- or 5-qt. slow cooker, combine green beans, tomatoes, brown sugar, pepper, salt, bacon and onion. Cook, covered, on low 4 hours. Stir in red beans. Cook 30 minutes longer or until heated through.

Black Bean Potato au Gratin

Black beans and vegetables add both protein and fiber to this side dish. For a Southwestern twist, try adding a handful or two of chopped cooked ham or chorizo sausage and replace the peas with one cup of frozen corn, thawed.

—**ERIN CHILCOAT** CENTRAL ISLIP, NY

PREP: 25 MIN. • **COOK:** 8 HOURS
MAKES: 6 SERVINGS

- 2 **cans (15 ounces each) black beans, rinsed and drained**
- 1 **can (10¾ ounces) condensed cream of mushroom soup, undiluted**
- 1 **medium sweet red pepper, chopped**
- 1 **cup frozen peas**
- 1 **cup chopped sweet onion**
- 1 **celery rib, thinly sliced**
- 2 **garlic cloves, minced**
- 1 **teaspoon dried thyme**
- ¼ **teaspoon coarsely ground pepper**
- 1½ **pounds medium red potatoes, cut into ¼-inch slices**
- 1 **teaspoon salt**
- 1 **cup (4 ounces) shredded cheddar cheese**

In a large bowl, combine the beans, soup, red pepper, peas, onion, celery, garlic, thyme and pepper. Spoon half of mixture into a greased 3- or 4-qt. slow cooker. Layer with half of the potatoes, salt and cheese. Repeat layers. Cover and cook on low for 8-10 hours or until potatoes are tender.

BLACK BEAN POTATO AU GRATIN

EASY BEANS & POTATOES WITH BACON

Easy Beans & Potatoes with Bacon

I love the combination of green beans with bacon, so I created this recipe. It's great to serve guests because you can start the side dish in the slow cooker, then continue preparing the rest of your dinner.

—**BARBARA BRITTAIN** SANTEE, CA

PREP: 15 MIN. • **COOK:** 6 HOURS
MAKES: 10 SERVINGS

8 bacon strips, chopped
1½ pounds fresh green beans, trimmed and cut into 2-inch pieces (about 4 cups)
4 medium potatoes, peeled and cubed (½-inch)
1 small onion, halved and sliced
¼ cup reduced-sodium chicken broth
½ teaspoon salt
¼ teaspoon pepper

1. In a large skillet, cook bacon over medium heat until crisp, stirring occasionally. Remove to paper towels with a slotted spoon; drain, reserving 1 tablespoon drippings. Cover and refrigerate bacon until serving.

2. In a 5-qt. slow cooker, combine the remaining ingredients; stir in reserved drippings. Cover and cook on low for 6-8 hours or until potatoes are tender. Stir in bacon; heat through.

SLOW-COOKED VEGETABLES

Scalloped Potatoes & Ham

I adapted this oven favorite to cook on its own while I'm gone. It's ready to serve when I get home, making it a winner!
—**JONI HILTON** ROCKLIN, CA

PREP: 25 MIN. • **COOK:** 8 HOURS
MAKES: 16 SERVINGS (¾ CUP EACH)

- 1 **can (10¾ ounces) condensed cheddar cheese soup, undiluted**
- 1 **can (10¾ ounces) condensed cream of mushroom soup, undiluted**
- 1 **cup 2% milk**
- 10 **medium potatoes, peeled and thinly sliced**
- 3 **cups cubed fully cooked ham**
- 2 **medium onions, chopped**
- 1 **teaspoon paprika**
- 1 **teaspoon pepper**

1. In a small bowl, combine the soups and milk. In a greased 5-qt. slow cooker, layer half of the potatoes, ham, onions and soup mixture. Repeat layers. Sprinkle with paprika and pepper.
2. Cover and cook on low for 8-10 hours or until potatoes are tender.

Slow-Cooked Vegetables

I like to simmer an assortment of garden-fresh vegetables for this satisfying side dish. My sister-in-law shared the recipe with me. It's a favorite at potlucks.
—**KATHY WESTENDORF** WESTGATE, IA

PREP: 10 MIN. • **COOK:** 7 HOURS
MAKES: 8 SERVINGS

- 4 **celery ribs, cut into 1-inch pieces**
- 4 **small carrots, cut into 1-inch pieces**
- 2 **medium tomatoes, cut into chunks**
- 2 **medium onions, thinly sliced**
- 2 **cups cut fresh green beans (1-inch pieces)**
- 1 **medium green pepper, cut into 1-inch pieces**
- ¼ **cup butter, melted**
- 3 **tablespoons quick-cooking tapioca**
- 1 **tablespoon sugar**
- 2 **teaspoons salt, optional**
- ⅛ **teaspoon pepper**

1. Place the vegetables in a 3-qt. slow cooker. In a small bowl, combine the butter, tapioca, sugar, salt if desired and pepper; pour over vegetables and stir well.
2. Cover and cook on low for 7-8 hours or until vegetables are tender. Serve with a slotted spoon.

SCALLOPED POTATOES & HAM

GLAZED SPICED CARROTS

Slow Cooker Goetta

My husband's German grandfather introduced me to goetta. I found a slow cooker recipe, changed some of the ingredients to make it the best goetta around—and now many people request the recipe. It makes a lot, but freezes well.

—SHARON GEERS WILMINGTON, OH

PREP: 45 MIN. • **COOK:** 4 HOURS
MAKES: 2 LOAVES (16 SLICES EACH)

- 6 **cups water**
- 2½ **cups steel-cut oats**
- 6 **bay leaves**
- 3 **tablespoons beef bouillon granules**
- ¾ **teaspoon salt**
- 1 **teaspoon each garlic powder, rubbed sage and pepper**
- ½ **teaspoon ground allspice**
- ½ **teaspoon crushed red pepper flakes**
- 2 **pounds bulk pork sausage**
- 2 **medium onions, chopped**

1. In a 5-qt. slow cooker, combine water, oats and seasonings. Cook, covered, on high for 2 hours. Remove bay leaves.
2. In a large skillet, cook sausage and onions over medium heat 8-10 minutes or until no longer pink, breaking up sausage into crumbles. Drain, reserving 2 tablespoons drippings. Stir sausage mixture and reserved drippings into oats. Cook, covered, on low 2 hours.
3. Transfer mixture to two plastic wrap-lined 9x5-in. loaf pans. Refrigerate, covered, overnight.
4. To serve, slice each loaf into 16 slices. In a large skillet, cook goetta, in batches, over medium heat 3-4 minutes on each side or until lightly browned and heated through.

Glazed Spiced Carrots

Glazed carrots are a classic side dish for special occasions. This recipe is so easy to put together, leaving your oven and stovetop free for other cooking creations.

—TASTE OF HOME TEST KITCHEN

PREP: 10 MIN. • **COOK:** 6 HOURS
MAKES: 6 SERVINGS

- 2 **pounds fresh baby carrots**
- ½ **cup peach preserves**
- ¼ **cup packed brown sugar**
- ½ **cup butter, melted**
- 1 **teaspoon vanilla extract**
- ½ **teaspoon ground cinnamon**
- ¼ **teaspoon salt**
- ⅛ **teaspoon ground nutmeg**
- 2 **tablespoons cornstarch**
- 2 **tablespoons water**
  Toasted chopped pecans, optional

1. Place carrots in a 3-qt. slow cooker. Combine the preserves, brown sugar, butter, vanilla, cinnamon, salt and nutmeg. Combine cornstarch and water until smooth; stir into preserve mixture. Pour over carrots.
2. Cover and cook on low for 6-8 hours or until tender. Stir carrots; sprinkle with pecans if desired.

POTLUCK MACARONI AND CHEESE

Potluck Macaroni and Cheese

Here's a great way to make America's most popular comfort food. The dish turns out cheesy, rich and extra-creamy.
—**JENNIFER BABCOCK** CHICOPEE, MA

PREP: 25 MIN. • **COOK:** 2 HOURS
MAKES: 16 SERVINGS (¾ CUP EACH)

3 cups uncooked elbow macaroni
1 pound process cheese (Velveeta), cubed
2 cups (8 ounces) shredded Mexican cheese blend
2 cups (8 ounces) shredded white cheddar cheese
1¾ cups milk
1 can (12 ounces) evaporated milk
3 eggs, lightly beaten
¾ cup butter, melted

1. Cook macaroni according to package directions; drain. Place in a greased 5-qt. slow cooker. Stir in the remaining ingredients.
2. Cover and cook on low for 2-3 hours or until a thermometer reads 160°, stirring once.

SWEET & SPICY BEANS

Sweet & Spicy Beans

My husband and I love this sweet and savory bean recipe. It's truly a side dish, but we normally eat it as a dip. When you use it to fill a corn chip scoop, the party starts in your mouth! I've shared this slow cooker recipe many times.

—**SONDRA POPE** MOORESVILLE, NC

PREP: 10 MIN. • **COOK:** 5 HOURS
MAKES: 12 SERVINGS (⅔ CUP EACH)

1 can (16 ounces) kidney beans, rinsed and drained
1 can (15¼ ounces) whole kernel corn, drained
1 can (15 ounces) garbanzo beans or chickpeas, rinsed and drained
1 can (15 ounces) black beans, rinsed and drained
1 can (15 ounces) chili with beans
1 cup barbecue sauce
1 cup salsa
⅓ cup packed brown sugar
¼ teaspoon hot pepper sauce
   Chopped green onions, optional

In a 4- or 5-qt. slow cooker, combine the first nine ingredients. Cover and cook on low for 5-6 hours. Top with green onions if desired.

Slow-Cooked Mac 'n' Cheese

Just the name of this recipe is enough to make mouths water. It's truly comfort food at its finest: rich, hearty and extra-cheesy. It serves nine as a side dish, though you might just want to make it your main course!

—**SHELBY MOLINA** WHITEWATER, WI

PREP: 25 MIN. • **COOK:** 2 HOURS
MAKES: 9 SERVINGS

- 2 **cups uncooked elbow macaroni**
- 1 **can (12 ounces) reduced-fat evaporated milk**
- 1½ **cups fat-free milk**
- ⅓ **cup egg substitute**
- 1 **tablespoon butter, melted**
- 8 **ounces reduced-fat process cheese (Velveeta), cubed**
- 2 **cups (8 ounces) shredded sharp cheddar cheese, divided**

1. Cook macaroni according to package directions; drain and rinse in cold water. In a large bowl, combine the evaporated milk, milk, egg substitute and butter. Stir in the process cheese, 1½ cups sharp cheddar cheese and macaroni.

2. Transfer to a 3-qt. slow cooker coated with cooking spray. Cover and cook on low for 2-3 hours or until center is set, stirring once. Sprinkle with remaining sharp cheddar cheese.

Onion-Garlic Hash Browns

Quick to assemble, this is a simple recipe that I've served many times. Stir in hot sauce if you like a bit of heat. I love to top my finished dish with a sprinkling of shredded cheese.

—**CINDI BOGER** ARDMORE, AL

PREP: 20 MIN. • **COOK:** 3 HOURS
MAKES: 12 SERVINGS (½ CUP EACH)

- 1 **large red onion, chopped**
- 1 **small sweet red pepper, chopped**
- 1 **small green pepper, chopped**
- ¼ **cup butter, cubed**
- 1 **tablespoon olive oil**
- 4 **garlic cloves, minced**
- 1 **package (30 ounces) frozen shredded hash brown potatoes**
- ½ **teaspoon salt**
- ½ **teaspoon pepper**
- 3 **drops hot pepper sauce, optional**
- 2 **teaspoons minced fresh parsley**

1. In a large skillet, saute onion and peppers in butter and oil until crisp-tender. Add garlic; cook 1 minute longer. Stir in the hash browns, salt, pepper and pepper sauce if desired.

2. Transfer to a 5-qt. slow cooker coated with cooking spray. Cover and cook on low for 3-4 hours or until heated through. Sprinkle with parsley before serving.

ONION-GARLIC HASH BROWNS

NACHO HASH BROWN CASSEROLE

Nacho Hash Brown Casserole

This tasty slow cooker recipe produces the best hash browns ever! Soft and cheesy, they make a super side dish for meat or poultry.

—**PAT HABIGER** SPEARVILLE, KS

PREP: 15 MIN. • **COOK:** 3¼ HOURS
MAKES: 8 SERVINGS

- 1 package (32 ounces) frozen cubed hash brown potatoes, thawed
- 1 can (10¾ ounces) condensed cream of celery soup, undiluted
- 1 can (10¾ ounces) condensed nacho cheese soup, undiluted
- 1 large onion, finely chopped
- ⅓ cup butter, melted
- 1 cup (8 ounces) reduced-fat sour cream

In a greased 3-qt. slow cooker, combine the first five ingredients. Cover and cook on low for 3-4 hours or until potatoes are tender. Stir in sour cream. Cover and cook 15-30 minutes longer or until heated through.

Italian Mushrooms

Only four ingredients create a rich and flavorful side dish that goes great with beef and mashed potatoes.

—**KIM REICHERT** ST. PAUL, MN

PREP: 10 MIN. • **COOK:** 4 HOURS
MAKES: 6 SERVINGS

- 1 pound medium fresh mushrooms
- 1 large onion, sliced
- ½ cup butter, melted
- 1 envelope Italian salad dressing mix

In a 3-qt. slow cooker, layer mushrooms and onion. Combine butter and salad dressing mix; pour over vegetables. Cover and cook on low for 4-5 hours or until vegetables are tender. Serve with a slotted spoon.

ITALIAN MUSHROOMS

STUFFED SWEET ONIONS

Stuffed Sweet Onions

Here's a unique dish that's perfect to serve alongside steak or pork chops. Even if you're not an onion fan, the low heat and long cooking time of this recipe mellows and sweetens the naturally sharp onion flavors.

—ERIN CHILCOAT CENTRAL ISLIP, NY

PREP: 45 MIN. • **COOK:** 4 HOURS
MAKES: 4 SERVINGS

- 4 **medium sweet onions**
- 2 **small zucchini, shredded**
- 1 **large garlic clove, minced**
- 1 **tablespoon olive oil**
- 1 **teaspoon dried basil**
- 1 **teaspoon dried thyme**
- ¼ **teaspoon salt**
- ¼ **teaspoon pepper**
- ½ **cup dry bread crumbs**
- 4 **thick-sliced bacon strips, cooked and crumbled**
- ¼ **cup grated Parmesan cheese**
- ¼ **cup reduced-sodium chicken broth**

1. Peel onions and cut a ¼-in. slice from the top and bottom. Carefully cut and remove the center of each onion, leaving a ½-in. shell; chop removed onion.

2. In a large skillet, saute the zucchini, garlic and chopped onions in oil until tender and juices are reduced. Stir in the basil, thyme, salt and pepper. Remove from the heat. Stir in the bread crumbs, bacon and Parmesan cheese. Fill onion shells with the zucchini mixture.

3. Place in a greased 3- or 4-qt. slow cooker. Add broth to the slow cooker. Cover and cook on low for 4-5 hours or until onions are tender.

Spring

ENTREES

Spring chicken...glazed ham...St. Patty's Day favorites...these are just a few of the light and lively main courses you'll find here. Whether you're celebrating a special occasion or not, these warm-weather slow-cooked dinners make mealtime a breeze.

DARLENE MORRIS' CHICKEN MOLE

Chicken Mole

If you're not familiar with mole, don't be afraid to try this versatile Mexican sauce. I love sharing the recipe because it's a great one to experiment with.
—**DARLENE MORRIS** FRANKLINTON, LA

PREP: 25 MIN. • **COOK:** 6 HOURS
MAKES: 12 SERVINGS

- 12 **bone-in chicken thighs (about 4½ pounds), skin removed**
- 1 **teaspoon salt**
MOLE SAUCE
- 1 **can (28 ounces) whole tomatoes, drained**
- 1 **medium onion, chopped**
- 2 **dried ancho chilies, stems and seeds removed**
- ½ **cup sliced almonds, toasted**
- ¼ **cup raisins**
- 3 **ounces bittersweet chocolate, chopped**
- 3 **tablespoons olive oil**
- 1 **chipotle pepper in adobo sauce**
- 3 **garlic cloves, peeled and halved**
- ¾ **teaspoon ground cumin**
- ½ **teaspoon ground cinnamon**
  Fresh cilantro leaves, optional

1. Sprinkle chicken with salt; place in a 5- or 6-qt. slow cooker. Place the tomatoes, onion, chilies, almonds, raisins, chocolate, oil, chipotle pepper, garlic, cumin and cinnamon in a food processor; cover and process until blended. Pour over chicken.
2. Cover and cook on low for 6-8 hours or until chicken is tender; skim fat. Serve chicken with sauce and sprinkle with cilantro if desired.

Ratatouille with a Twist

Before this variation, we ate ratatouille as a side dish. My husband's suggestion to incorporate sausage made it an entree.
—**SUSAN TREMBLAY** BERLIN, NH

PREP: 25 MIN. • **COOK:** 6 HOURS
MAKES: 6 SERVINGS

- 4 **hot Italian sausage links (4 ounces each)**
- 4 **cups chopped zucchini**
- 1 **can (14½ ounces) stewed tomatoes, cut-up**
- 1 **can (10¾ ounces) condensed tomato soup, undiluted**
- 1 **medium onion, chopped**
- 1 **garlic clove, minced**
- ½ **teaspoon dried basil**
- ½ **teaspoon dried oregano**
  Hot cooked pasta

In a large skillet, cook sausages until no longer pink. Cut into ½-in. slices; transfer to a 3-qt. slow cooker. Add the zucchini, tomatoes, soup, onion, garlic, basil and oregano. Cover and cook on low for 6-8 hours or until flavors are blended. Serve with pasta.

BEST SHORT RIBS VINDALOO

3. In a large resealable plastic bag, combine the vinegar, bay leaves and onion mixture. Add ribs; seal bag and turn to coat. Refrigerate overnight.

4. Transfer rib mixture to a 4-qt. slow cooker. Cover and cook on low for 8-10 hours or until meat is tender. Stir in peas; cook 8-10 minutes longer or until peas are crisp-tender. Skim fat; discard bay leaves. Serve rib mixture with rice and yogurt.

(5)INGREDIENTS
Glazed Kielbasa

You'll need only three ingredients to prepare this pleasantly sweet sausage. Reduced-fat or turkey kielbasa can also be used.

—**JODY SANDS TAYLOR** RICHMOND, VA

PREP: 5 MIN. • **COOK:** 4 HOURS
MAKES: 12 SERVINGS

- 3 pounds smoked kielbasa or Polish sausage, cut into 1-inch chunks
- ½ cup packed brown sugar
- 1½ cups ginger ale

Place sausage in a 3-qt. slow cooker; sprinkle with brown sugar. Pour ginger ale over the top. Cover and cook on low for 4-5 hours or until heated through. Serve with a slotted spoon.

Best Short Ribs Vindaloo

My sister shared this dish with me, and I've made a few modifications to fit my tastes. I love the aroma as it simmers all day!

—**LORRAINE CARLSTROM** NELSON, BC

PREP: 30 MIN. + MARINATING
COOK: 8¼ HOURS
MAKES: 4 SERVINGS

- 1 tablespoon cumin seeds
- 2 teaspoons coriander seeds
- 1 tablespoon butter
- 1 medium onion, finely chopped
- 8 garlic cloves, minced
- 1 tablespoon minced fresh gingerroot
- 2 teaspoons mustard seed
- ½ teaspoon ground cloves
- ¼ teaspoon kosher salt
- ¼ teaspoon ground cinnamon
- ¼ teaspoon cayenne pepper
- ½ cup red wine vinegar
- 4 bay leaves
- 2 pounds bone-in beef short ribs
- 1 cup fresh sugar snap peas, halved
  Hot cooked rice and plain yogurt

1. In a dry small skillet over medium heat, toast cumin and coriander seeds until aromatic, stirring frequently. Cool. Coarsely crush seeds in a spice grinder or with a mortar and pestle.
2. In a large saucepan, heat butter over medium heat. Add the onion, garlic and ginger; cook and stir for 1 minute. Add the mustard seed, cloves, salt, cinnamon, cayenne pepper and crushed seeds; cook and stir 1 minute longer. Cool completely.

GLAZED KIELBASA

THAI PORK

Tangy Chicken Thighs

I love this dish because it turns affordable chicken thighs into a rich and delicious entree. The creamy and tangy sauce is what makes the meal. Serve with a crisp salad or fresh vegetables.

—**VICKI ROELOFS** WYOMING, MI

PREP: 25 MIN. • **COOK:** 4¾ HOURS
MAKES: 6 SERVINGS

- 1 **envelope Italian salad dressing mix**
- ½ **teaspoon pepper**
- 6 **boneless skinless chicken thighs (about 1½ pounds)**
- 2 **tablespoons butter, melted**
- 1 **large onion, chopped**
- 2 **garlic cloves, minced**
- 1 **can (10¾ ounces) condensed cream of chicken soup, undiluted**
- 1 **package (8 ounces) cream cheese, softened and cubed**
- ¼ **cup chicken broth**
  Hot cooked noodles or rice, optional

1. Combine salad dressing mix and pepper. In a 3-qt. slow cooker, layer half of the chicken, butter, salad dressing mixture, onion and garlic. Repeat layers. Cover and cook on low for 4-5 hours or until chicken is tender. Skim fat.
2. In a small bowl, combine the soup, cream cheese and broth until blended; add to slow cooker. Cover and cook for 45 minutes or until heated through.
3. Remove chicken to a serving platter; stir sauce until smooth. Serve chicken with sauce and noodles or rice if desired.

Thai Pork

My husband and I both work long hours. This slow cooker recipe is large enough for the two of us to eat as much of the pork as we like—and still have leftovers!

—**DAWN SCHMIDT** DURHAM, NC

PREP: 20 MIN. • **COOK:** 8 HOURS
MAKES: 8 SERVINGS

- 2 **medium sweet red peppers, julienned**
- 1 **boneless pork shoulder butt roast (3 pounds)**
- ⅓ **cup reduced-sodium teriyaki sauce**
- 3 **tablespoons rice vinegar**
- 2 **garlic cloves, minced**
- ½ **teaspoon crushed red pepper flakes**
- ¼ **cup creamy peanut butter**
- 4 **cups hot cooked rice**
- ½ **cup chopped unsalted peanuts**
- 4 **green onions, sliced**

1. Place peppers in a 3-qt. slow cooker. Cut roast in half; place on top of peppers. Combine teriyaki sauce, vinegar and garlic; pour over roast. Sprinkle with pepper flakes. Cover and cook on low for 8-9 hours or until meat is tender.
2. Remove meat from slow cooker. When cool enough to handle, shred meat with two forks. Reserve 2 cups cooking juices; skim fat. Stir peanut butter into reserved juices.
3. Return pork and cooking juices to the slow cooker; heat through. Serve with rice; sprinkle with peanuts and green onions.

VICKI ROELOFS'
TANGY CHICKEN THIGHS

After simmering in the slow cooker for hours, this rump roast is fork-tender and has taken on some of the flavors of the sauce. My family looks forward to having it for dinner. I serve it with mashed potatoes and corn.
—**LAURA EHLERS** LAFAYETTE, IN

SPECIAL SAUERBRATEN

Special Sauerbraten

PREP: 25 MIN. • **COOK:** 6 HOURS
MAKES: 6 SERVINGS

- 1 beef rump roast or bottom round roast (3 to 4 pounds), cut in half
- 1 tablespoon olive oil
- 1½ cups cider vinegar
- 1 medium onion, chopped
- ⅔ cup packed brown sugar
- 1 envelope onion soup mix
- ⅓ cup shredded carrot
- 2 tablespoons beef bouillon granules
- 1 tablespoon Worcestershire sauce
- 1 bay leaf
- 1 garlic clove, minced
- 1 teaspoon salt
- 1 teaspoon celery seed
- 1 teaspoon ground ginger
- ½ teaspoon mixed pickling spices
- ¼ teaspoon ground allspice
- ¼ teaspoon pepper
- ¼ cup cornstarch
- ½ cup water

1. In a large skillet, brown meat in oil on all sides. Transfer meat and drippings to a 5-qt. slow cooker. In a large bowl, combine the vinegar, onion, sugar, soup mix, carrot, bouillon, Worcestershire sauce and seasonings; pour over roast. Cover and cook on low for 6-8 hours or until tender.

2. Remove meat to a serving platter; keep warm. Strain cooking juices, discarding vegetables and seasonings.

3. Skim fat from cooking juices; transfer juices to a large saucepan. Bring to a boil. Combine cornstarch and water until smooth; gradually stir into the pan. Bring to a boil; cook and stir for 2 minutes or until thickened. Serve with beef.

Mom's Scalloped Potatoes and Ham

Mom's friend gave her this recipe years ago, and she shared it with me. When we have leftover ham to use up, it's the most-requested recipe at my house.
—**KELLY GRAHAM** ST. THOMAS, ON

PREP: 20 MIN. • **COOK:** 8 HOURS
MAKES: 9 SERVINGS

- 10 medium potatoes (about 3 pounds), peeled and thinly sliced
- 3 cups cubed fully cooked ham
- 2 large onions, thinly sliced
- 2 cups (8 ounces) shredded cheddar cheese
- 1 can (10¾ ounces) condensed cream of mushroom soup, undiluted
- ½ teaspoon paprika
- ¼ teaspoon pepper

1. In a greased 6-qt. slow cooker, layer half of the potatoes, ham, onions and cheese. Repeat layers. Pour soup over top. Sprinkle with paprika and pepper.

2. Cover and cook on low for 8-10 hours or until potatoes are tender.

HEARTY CHEESE TORTELLINI

Hearty Cheese Tortellini

Simple enough for an everyday meal but impressive enough for company, my recipe feeds a group. I serve it with steamed broccoli covered in cheese sauce and fresh bread.

—**CHRISTINE EILERTS** TULSA, OK

PREP: 30 MIN. • **COOK:** 6¼ HOURS
MAKES: 6 SERVINGS

- ½ **pound bulk Italian sausage**
- ½ **pound lean ground beef (90% lean)**
- 1 **jar (24 ounces) marinara sauce**
- 1 **can (14½ ounces) Italian diced tomatoes**
- 1 **cup sliced fresh mushrooms**
- 1 **package (9 ounces) refrigerated cheese tortellini**
- 1 **cup (4 ounces) shredded part-skim mozzarella cheese**

1. In a small skillet, cook sausage and beef over medium heat until no longer pink; drain. Transfer to a 3-qt. slow cooker. Stir in the marinara sauce, tomatoes and mushrooms. Cover and cook on low for 6-7 hours or until heated through.

2. Prepare tortellini according to package directions; stir into meat mixture. Sprinkle with cheese. Cover and cook for 15 minutes or until cheese is melted.

Lemon Chicken Breasts with Veggies

Why bake chicken when this slow-cooked version is so fuss-free? Flecked with herbs, these chicken breasts are nestled among crisp-tender veggies in a subtle lemon sauce. The recipe's everything you need for a satisfying spring meal.

—**AMBER OTIS** MORRIS, OK

PREP: 25 MIN. • **COOK:** 8 HOURS
MAKES: 6 SERVINGS

- 1 **pound fresh baby carrots**
- 3 **cups cubed red potatoes**
- 1 **package (14 ounces) frozen pearl onions, thawed**
- 2 **celery ribs, thinly sliced**
- 6 **bone-in chicken breast halves (10 ounces each), skin removed**
- 1 **can (10¾ ounces) condensed cream of chicken soup, undiluted**
- ½ **cup water**
- ½ **cup lemon juice**
- 1 **teaspoon dried parsley flakes**
- 1 **teaspoon dried thyme**
- ½ **teaspoon pepper**
- ¼ **teaspoon salt**

1. In a 5- or 6-qt. slow cooker, combine the carrots, potatoes, onions and celery. Top with chicken.

2. Combine the soup, water, lemon juice, parsley, thyme, pepper and salt; pour over chicken and vegetables. Cover and cook on low for 8-9 hours or until chicken and vegetables are tender.

LEMON CHICKEN BREASTS WITH VEGGIES

TANGY LAMB TAGINE

Tangy Lamb Tagine

I love lamb stew but wanted to try something a bit different, so I created a recipe that features Moroccan spices. It's a wonderful way to use lamb, and it's easy to make in the slow cooker. The stew tastes even better served a day or two later, when the flavors have really had a chance to blend together.

—BRIDGET KLUSMAN OTSEGO, MI

PREP: 40 MIN. • **COOK:** 8 HOURS
MAKES: 8 SERVINGS

- 3 **pounds lamb stew meat, cut into 1½-inch cubes**
- 1 **teaspoon salt**
- 1 **teaspoon pepper**
- 4 **tablespoons olive oil, divided**
- 6 **medium carrots, sliced**
- 2 **medium onions, chopped**
- 6 **garlic cloves, minced**
- 2 **teaspoons grated lemon peel**
- ¼ **cup lemon juice**
- 1 **tablespoon minced fresh gingerroot**
- 1½ **teaspoons ground cinnamon**
- 1½ **teaspoons ground cumin**
- 1½ **teaspoons paprika**
- 2½ **cups reduced-sodium chicken broth**
- ¼ **cup sweet vermouth**
- ¼ **cup honey**
- ½ **cup pitted dates, chopped**
- ½ **cup sliced almonds, toasted**

1. Sprinkle lamb with salt and pepper. In a Dutch oven, brown meat in 2 tablespoons oil in batches. Using a slotted spoon, transfer to a 4- or 5-qt. slow cooker.

2. In the same pot, saute the carrots, onions, garlic and lemon peel in remaining oil until crisp-tender. Add the lemon juice, ginger, cinnamon, cumin and paprika; cook and stir 2 minutes longer. Add to slow cooker.

3. Stir in the broth, vermouth, honey and dates. Cover and cook on low for 8-10 hours or until lamb is tender. Sprinkle with almonds.

Lucky Corned Beef

It's not luck; it's just an amazing Irish recipe. With this in the slow cooker by sunrise, you can bet to fill seats at the dinner table by sundown.

—HEATHER PARRAZ ROCHESTER, WA

PREP: 20 MIN. • **COOK:** 9 HOURS
MAKES: 5 SERVINGS PLUS LEFTOVERS

- 6 **medium red potatoes, quartered**
- 2 **medium carrots, cut into chunks**
- 1 **large onion, sliced**
- 2 **corned beef briskets with spice packets (3 pounds each)**
- ¼ **cup packed brown sugar**
- 2 **tablespoons sugar**
- 2 **tablespoons coriander seeds**
- 2 **tablespoons whole peppercorns**
- 4 **cups water**

1. In a 6-qt. slow cooker, combine the potatoes, carrots and onion. Add briskets (discard spice packets from corned beef or save for another use). Sprinkle the brown sugar, sugar, coriander and peppercorns over meat. Pour water over top.

2. Cover and cook on low for 9-11 hours or until meat and vegetables are tender.

3. Remove meat and vegetables to a serving platter. Thinly slice one brisket across the grain and serve with vegetables. Save the remaining brisket for Reuben sandwiches, strata or save for another use.

LUCKY CORNED BEEF

SLOW COOKER TWO-MEAT MANICOTTI

Chicken Thighs with Ginger-Peach Sauce

This sweet and sour chicken main dish has become a favorite Sunday recipe. It's easy to prepare and requires very little cleanup. Best of all, the slow cooker leaves me plenty of time to do other things.

—LISA RENSHAW KANSAS CITY, MO

PREP: 15 MIN. • **COOK:** 4 HOURS
MAKES: 10 SERVINGS

- 10 boneless skinless chicken thighs (about 2½ pounds)
- 1 cup sliced peeled fresh or frozen peaches
- 1 cup golden raisins
- 1 cup peach preserves
- ⅓ cup chili sauce
- 2 tablespoons minced crystallized ginger
- 1 tablespoon reduced-sodium soy sauce
- 1 tablespoon minced garlic
  Hot cooked rice, optional

1. Place chicken in a 4-qt. slow cooker coated with cooking spray. Top with peaches and raisins. In a small bowl, combine preserves, chili sauce, ginger, soy sauce and garlic. Spoon over top.
2. Cover and cook on low for 4-5 hours or until chicken is tender. Serve with rice if desired.

CHICKEN THIGHS WITH GINGER-PEACH SAUCE

Slow Cooker Two-Meat Manicotti

I wanted to create my ideal version of stuffed manicotti, with a fantastic filling and a meat sauce to die for. This recipe is the final result, and I don't mind saying it's a huge success!

—SHALIMAR WIECH GLASSPORT, PA

PREP: 45 MIN. • **COOK:** 4 HOURS
MAKES: 7 SERVINGS

- ½ pound medium fresh mushrooms, chopped
- 2 small green peppers, chopped
- 1 medium onion, chopped
- 1½ teaspoons canola oil
- 4 garlic cloves, minced
- ¾ pound ground sirloin
- ¾ pound bulk Italian sausage
- 2 jars (23½ ounces each) Italian sausage and garlic spaghetti sauce
- 1 carton (15 ounces) ricotta cheese
- 1 cup minced fresh parsley
- ½ cup shredded part-skim mozzarella cheese, divided
- ½ cup grated Parmesan cheese, divided
- 2 eggs, lightly beaten
- ½ teaspoon salt
- ¼ teaspoon pepper
- ⅛ teaspoon ground nutmeg
- 1 package (8 ounces) manicotti shells

1. In a large skillet, saute the mushrooms, peppers and onion in oil until tender. Add garlic; cook 1 minute longer. Remove from pan.
2. In the same skillet, cook beef and sausage over medium heat until no longer pink; drain. Stir in mushroom mixture and spaghetti sauce; set aside.
3. In a small bowl, combine the ricotta cheese, parsley, ¼ cup mozzarella cheese, ¼ cup Parmesan cheese, eggs and seasonings. Stuff into uncooked manicotti shells.
4. Spread 2¼ cups sauce onto the bottom of a 6-qt. slow cooker. Arrange five stuffed manicotti shells over sauce; repeat two times, using four shells on the top layer. Top with the remaining sauce. Sprinkle with the remaining cheeses. Cover and cook on low for 4-5 hours or until the pasta is tender.

ROBIN HAAS'
PINEAPPLE CURRY CHICKEN

Pineapple Curry Chicken

Curry has a moderate to strong delivery, so I add it early in the cooking process for good balance with the pineapple, coconut and ginger.

—ROBIN HAAS CRANSTON, RI

PREP: 25 MIN. • **COOK:** 6 HOURS
MAKES: 6 SERVINGS

- 2 cans (8 ounces each) unsweetened pineapple chunks, undrained
- 6 bone-in chicken breast halves, skin removed (12 ounces each)
- 1 can (15 ounces) garbanzo beans or chickpeas, rinsed and drained
- 1 large onion, cut into 1-inch pieces
- 1 cup julienned carrots
- 1 medium sweet red pepper, cut into strips
- ½ cup light coconut milk
- 2 tablespoons cornstarch
- 2 tablespoons sugar
- 3 teaspoons curry powder
- 2 garlic cloves, minced
- 2 teaspoons minced fresh gingerroot
- 1 teaspoon salt
- 1 teaspoon pepper
- 1 teaspoon lime juice
- ½ teaspoon crushed red pepper flakes
  Hot cooked rice
- ⅓ cup minced fresh basil
  Toasted flaked coconut, optional

1. Drain pineapple, reserving ¾ cup juice. Place the chicken, beans, vegetables and pineapple in a 6-qt. slow cooker. In a small bowl, combine coconut milk and cornstarch until smooth. Stir in the sugar, curry powder, garlic, ginger, salt, pepper, lime juice, pepper flakes and reserved pineapple juice; pour over chicken.

2. Cover and cook on low for 6-8 hours or until chicken is tender. Serve with rice; sprinkle with basil and, if desired, coconut.

Potato Pizza Casserole

Here's a fun, full-flavored meal the whole family will go for. It's great on weeknights when everyone comes through the door hungry at the same time.

—TYLER SHERMAN WILLIAMSBURG, VA

PREP: 25 MIN. • **COOK:** 4 HOURS
MAKES: 8 SERVINGS

- 1 pound ground beef
- ½ pound sliced fresh mushrooms
- 1 medium green pepper, chopped
- 1 small onion, chopped
- 2 jars (14 ounces each) pizza sauce
- 1 can (10¾ ounces) condensed cheddar cheese soup, undiluted
- ½ cup 2% milk
- 1 teaspoon Italian seasoning
- ½ teaspoon garlic salt
- ¼ teaspoon crushed red pepper flakes
- 1 package (32 ounces) frozen cubed hash brown potatoes, thawed
- 15 slices pepperoni, chopped
- 2 cups (8 ounces) shredded Italian cheese blend

1. In a large skillet, cook the beef, mushrooms, green pepper and onion until meat is no longer pink; drain.
2. Meanwhile, in a large bowl, combine the pizza sauce, soup, milk, Italian seasoning, garlic salt and pepper flakes. Stir in the potatoes, pepperoni and beef mixture.
3. Transfer half of the meat mixture to a 5-qt. slow cooker. Sprinkle with half of the cheese; repeat layers. Cover and cook on low for 4-5 hours or until potatoes are tender.

POTATO PIZZA CASSEROLE

CANTONESE SWEET AND SOUR PORK

Cantonese Sweet and Sour Pork

Step away from that takeout menu. There'll be no reason to dial up delivery once you get a bite of my take on traditional sweet and sour pork. The tender vegetables, juicy pork and flavorful sauce are delicious over rice.

—**NANCY TEWS** ANTIGO, WI

PREP: 20 MIN. • **COOK:** 7½ HOURS
MAKES: 6 SERVINGS

- 1 **can (15 ounces) tomato sauce**
- 1 **medium onion, halved and sliced**
- 1 **medium green pepper, cut into strips**
- 1 **can (4½ ounces) sliced mushrooms, drained**
- 3 **tablespoons brown sugar**
- 4½ **teaspoons white vinegar**
- 2 **teaspoons steak sauce**
- 1 **teaspoon salt**
- 1½ **pounds pork tenderloin, cut into 1-inch cubes**
- 1 **tablespoon olive oil**
- 1 **can (8 ounces) unsweetened pineapple chunks, drained**
  Hot cooked rice

1. In a large bowl, combine the first eight ingredients; set aside.
2. In a large skillet, brown pork in oil in batches. Transfer to a 3- or 4-qt. slow cooker. Pour tomato sauce mixture over pork. Cover and cook on low for 7-8 hours or until meat is tender.
3. Add pineapple; cover and cook 30 minutes longer or until heated through. Serve with rice.

Easy Citrus Ham

I created this recipe many years ago with items I already had on hand. Since then, it has become a family favorite. The ham is succulent with a mild citrus flavor. I was asked to share the recipe with a church social and there were so many raves, I knew the recipe was a winner!

—**SHEILA CHRISTENSEN** SAN MARCOS, CA

PREP: 15 MIN. • **COOK:** 4 HOURS + STANDING
MAKES: 10-12 SERVINGS

- 1 **boneless fully cooked ham (3 to 4 pounds)**
- ½ **cup packed dark brown sugar**
- 1 **can (12 ounces) lemon-lime soda, divided**
- 1 **medium navel orange, thinly sliced**
- 1 **medium lemon, thinly sliced**
- 1 **medium lime, thinly sliced**
- 1 **tablespoon chopped crystallized ginger**

1. Cut ham in half; place in a 5-qt. slow cooker. In a small bowl, combine brown sugar and ¼ cup soda; rub over ham. Top with orange, lemon and lime slices. Add crystallized ginger and remaining soda to the slow cooker.
2. Cover and cook on low for 4-5 hours or until a meat thermometer reads 140°, basting occasionally with cooking juices. Let stand 10 minutes before slicing.

EASY CITRUS HAM

BBQ CHICKEN BAKED POTATOES

BBQ Chicken Baked Potatoes

These baked potatoes are meals in themselves, with a smoky barbecue flavor that will make your mouth water! You can top them with your favorite cheese and garnish.

—AMBER MASSEY ARGYLE, TX

PREP: 15 MIN. • **COOK:** 6 HOURS
MAKES: 10 SERVINGS

- 4½ **pounds bone-in chicken breast halves, skin removed**
- 2 **tablespoons garlic powder**
- 1 **large red onion, sliced into thick rings**
- 1 **bottle (18 ounces) honey barbecue sauce**
- 1 **cup Italian salad dressing**
- ½ **cup packed brown sugar**
- ½ **cup cider vinegar**
- ¼ **cup Worcestershire sauce**
- 2 **tablespoons liquid smoke, optional**
- 10 **medium potatoes, baked Crumbled blue cheese and chopped green onions, optional**

1. Place chicken in a greased 5- or 6-qt. slow cooker; sprinkle with garlic powder and top with onion. Combine the barbecue sauce, salad dressing, brown sugar, vinegar, Worcestershire sauce and liquid smoke if desired; pour over chicken.
2. Cover and cook on low for 6-8 hours or until chicken is tender. When cool enough to handle, remove chicken from bones; discard bones and onion. Skim fat from cooking juices.
3. Shred meat with two forks and return to slow cooker; heat through. Serve with potatoes, blue cheese and green onions if desired.

Butter & Herb Turkey

My kids love turkey for dinner, and this easy recipe lets me make it whenever I want. No special occasion required! The meat is so tender, it falls right off the bone.

—ROCHELLE POPOVIC SOUTH BEND, IN

PREP: 10 MIN. • **COOK:** 5 HOURS
MAKES: 12 SERVINGS (3 CUPS GRAVY)

- 1 **bone-in turkey breast (6 to 7 pounds)**
- 2 **tablespoons butter, softened**
- ½ **teaspoon dried rosemary, crushed**
- ½ **teaspoon dried thyme**
- ¼ **teaspoon garlic powder**
- ¼ **teaspoon pepper**
- 1 **can (14½ ounces) chicken broth**
- 3 **tablespoons cornstarch**
- 2 **tablespoons cold water**

1. Rub turkey with butter. Combine the rosemary, thyme, garlic powder and pepper; sprinkle over turkey. Place in a 6-qt. slow cooker. Pour broth over top. Cover and cook on low for 5-6 hours or until tender.
2. Remove turkey to a serving platter; keep warm. Skim fat from cooking juices; transfer to a small saucepan. Bring to a boil. Combine cornstarch and water until smooth. Gradually stir into the pan. Bring to a boil; cook and stir for 2 minutes or until thickened. Serve with turkey.

BUTTER & HERB TURKEY

> Nobody steps out of line when yummy pork slow-cooked in chipotle and molasses moves to the table.
> —**JANICE ELDER** CHARLOTTE, NC

CONGA LIME PORK

Conga Lime Pork

PREP: 20 MIN. • **COOK:** 4 HOURS
MAKES: 6 SERVINGS

- 1 **teaspoon salt, divided**
- ½ **teaspoon pepper, divided**
- 1 **boneless pork shoulder butt roast (2 to 3 pounds)**
- 1 **tablespoon canola oil**
- 1 **large onion, chopped**
- 3 **garlic cloves, peeled and thinly sliced**
- ½ **cup water**
- 2 **chipotle peppers in adobo sauce, seeded and chopped**
- 2 **tablespoons molasses**
- 2 **cups broccoli coleslaw mix**
- 1 **medium mango, peeled and chopped**
- 2 **tablespoons lime juice**
- 1½ **teaspoons grated lime peel**
- 6 **prepared corn muffins, halved**

1. Sprinkle ¾ teaspoon salt and ¼ teaspoon pepper over roast. In a large skillet, brown pork in oil on all sides. Transfer meat to a 3- or 4-qt. slow cooker.

2. In the same skillet, saute onion until tender. Add garlic; cook 1 minute longer. Add water, chipotle peppers and molasses, stirring to loosen browned bits from pan. Pour over pork. Cover and cook on high for 4-5 hours or until meat is tender.

3. Remove roast; cool slightly. Skim fat from cooking juices. Shred pork with two forks and return to slow cooker; heat through.

4. In a large bowl, combine the coleslaw mix, mango, lime juice, lime peel and remaining salt and pepper.

5. Place muffin halves cut side down on an ungreased baking sheet. Broil 4 in. from the heat for 2-3 minutes or until lightly toasted. Serve pork with muffins; top with slaw.

HOW TO

DICE A MANGO

❶ Lay washed fruit on the counter, then turn so the top and bottom are now the sides. Using a sharp knife, make a lengthwise cut as close to the long, flat seed as possible to remove each side of the fruit. Trim fruit away from seed.

❷ Score each side of the fruit lengthwise and widthwise, without cutting through the skin.

❸ Using your hand, push the skin up, turning the fruit out. Cut fruit off at the skin with a knife.

HEALTHY SLOW-COOKED MEAT LOAF

Healthy Slow-Cooked Meat Loaf

What could be better than an Italian-inspired meat loaf made in the slow cooker? No fuss, easy cleanup and great taste; it's all right here!

—SHARON DELANEY-CHRONIS
SOUTH MILWAUKEE, WI

PREP: 15 MIN. • **COOK:** 3 HOURS
MAKES: 8 SERVINGS

- 1 cup soft bread crumbs
- 1½ cups spaghetti sauce, divided
- 1 egg, lightly beaten
- 2 tablespoons dried minced onion
- 1 teaspoon salt
- ½ teaspoon garlic powder
- ½ teaspoon Italian seasoning
- ¼ teaspoon pepper
- 2 pounds lean ground beef (90% lean)

1. Cut four 20x3-in. strips of heavy-duty foil; crisscross so they resemble the spokes of a wheel. Place strips on the bottom and up the sides of a 3-qt. slow cooker. Coat the strips with cooking spray.
2. In a large bowl, combine the bread crumbs, 1 cup spaghetti sauce, egg, onion, and seasonings. Crumble beef over mixture and mix well. Shape into a loaf; place in the center of the strips.
3. Spoon remaining spaghetti sauce over meat loaf. Cover and cook on low for 3-4 hours or until a thermometer reads 160°. Using foil strips as handles, remove meat loaf to a platter.

Chicken & Mushroom Alfredo

Everyone in my family loves it when I make this dinner...even my kids! What's special about this recipe is that you can add vegetables you have on hand to make it heartier, such as peas or red bell pepper.
—MARCIA NEIL ONTARIO, CA

PREP: 20 MIN. • **COOK:** 4 HOURS
MAKES: 4 SERVINGS

- 4 bone-in chicken breast halves (12 to 14 ounces each), skin removed
- 2 tablespoons canola oil
- 1 can (10¾ ounces) condensed cream of chicken soup, undiluted
- 1 can (10¾ ounces) condensed cream of mushroom soup, undiluted
- 1 cup chicken broth
- 1 small onion, chopped
- 1 jar (6 ounces) sliced mushrooms, drained
- ¼ teaspoon garlic salt
- ¼ teaspoon pepper
- 8 ounces fettuccine
- 1 package (8 ounces) cream cheese, softened and cubed
  Shredded Parmesan cheese, optional

1. In a large skillet, brown chicken in oil in batches. Transfer to a 4- or 5-qt. slow cooker. In a large bowl, combine the soups, broth, onion, mushrooms, garlic salt and pepper; pour over meat. Cover and cook on low for 4-5 hours or until chicken is tender.
2. Cook fettuccine according to package directions; drain. Remove chicken from slow cooker and keep warm. Turn slow cooker off and stir in cream cheese until melted. Serve with fettucine. Top with Parmesan cheese if desired.

CHICKEN & MUSHROOM ALFREDO

Steak San Marino

I'm a busy pastor's wife and mother of three, and this delicious, inexpensive dish helps my day run smoother. The steak is so tender and flavorful, my kids gobble it up and my husband asks for seconds!

—**LAEL GRIESS** HULL, IA

PREP: 15 MIN. • **COOK:** 7 HOURS
MAKES: 6 SERVINGS

- ¼ **cup all-purpose flour**
- ½ **teaspoon salt**
- ½ **teaspoon pepper**
- 1 **beef top round steak (1½ pounds), cut into six pieces**
- 2 **large carrots, sliced**
- 1 **celery rib, sliced**
- 1 **can (8 ounces) tomato sauce**
- 2 **garlic cloves, minced**
- 1 **bay leaf**
- 1 **teaspoon Italian seasoning**
- ½ **teaspoon Worcestershire sauce**
- 3 **cups hot cooked brown rice**

1. In a large resealable plastic bag, combine the flour, salt and pepper. Add beef, a few pieces at a time, and shake to coat. Transfer to a 4-qt. slow cooker.

2. In a small bowl, combine the carrots, celery, tomato sauce, garlic, bay leaf, Italian seasoning and Worcestershire sauce. Pour over beef. Cover and cook on low for 7-9 hours or until beef is tender. Discard bay leaf. Serve with rice.

Casablanca Chutney Chicken

PREP: 25 MIN. • **COOK:** 7 HOURS
MAKES: 4 SERVINGS

- 1 **pound boneless skinless chicken thighs, cut into ¾-inch pieces**
- 1 **can (14½ ounces) chicken broth**
- ⅓ **cup finely chopped onion**
- ⅓ **cup chopped sweet red pepper**
- ⅓ **cup chopped carrot**
- ⅓ **cup chopped dried apricots**
- ⅓ **cup chopped dried figs**
- ⅓ **cup golden raisins**
- 2 **tablespoons orange marmalade**
- 1 **tablespoon mustard seed**
- 2 **garlic cloves, minced**
- ½ **teaspoon curry powder**
- ¼ **teaspoon crushed red pepper flakes**
- ¼ **teaspoon ground cumin**
- ¼ **teaspoon ground cinnamon**
- ¼ **teaspoon ground cloves**
- 2 **tablespoons minced fresh parsley**
- 2 **tablespoons minced fresh mint**
- 1 **tablespoon lemon juice**
- 4 **tablespoons chopped pistachios**

1. In a 3-qt. slow cooker, combine the first 16 ingredients. Cover and cook on low for 7-8 hours or until chicken is tender.

2. Stir in the parsley, mint and lemon juice; heat through. Sprinkle each serving with pistachios.

If you enjoy Indian food, you'll love this dish. An array of spices and dried fruits cook slowly with boneless chicken thighs to make an aromatic and satisfying meal. To make it complete, serve over jasmine or basmati rice.
—**ROXANNE CHAN** ALBANY, CA

CASABLANCA CHUTNEY CHICKEN

FIESTA BEEF BOWLS

Fiesta Beef Bowls

This easy entree will knock your socks off! Zesty ingredients turn round steak into a complete phenomenal meal in a bowl.

—DEBORAH LINN VALDEZ, AK

PREP: 25 MIN. • **COOK:** 8½ HOURS
MAKES: 6 SERVINGS

- 1½ **pounds boneless beef top round steak**
- 1 **can (10 ounces) diced tomatoes and green chilies**
- 1 **medium onion, chopped**
- 2 **garlic cloves, minced**
- 1 **teaspoon dried oregano**
- 1 **teaspoon chili powder**
- 1 **teaspoon ground cumin**
- ¼ **teaspoon salt**
- ¼ **teaspoon pepper**
- 2 **cans (15 ounces each) pinto beans, rinsed and drained**
- 3 **cups hot cooked rice**
- ½ **cup shredded cheddar cheese**
- 6 **tablespoons sliced ripe olives**
- 6 **tablespoons thinly sliced green onions**
- 6 **tablespoons guacamole**

1. Place round steak in a 3-qt. slow cooker. In a small bowl, combine the tomatoes, onion, garlic and seasonings; pour over steak. Cover and cook on low for 8-9 hours or until meat is tender.
2. Remove meat from slow cooker. Add beans to tomato mixture. Cover and cook on high for 30 minutes or until beans are heated through. When cool enough to handle, slice meat. In individual bowls, layer the rice, meat and bean mixture. Top with cheese, olives, onions and guacamole.

Vegetarian Stuffed Peppers

My favorite appliance is my slow cooker, and I use it more than anyone I know. I love the convenience of walking in the door and having a meal ready to go. For recipes like my slow-cooked stuffed peppers, you don't have to worry about boiling the peppers first and preparing the filling separately.

—MICHELLE GURNSEY LINCOLN, NE

PREP: 15 MIN. • **COOK:** 3 HOURS
MAKES: 4 SERVINGS

- 4 **medium sweet red peppers**
- 1 **can (15 ounces) black beans, rinsed and drained**
- 1 **cup (4 ounces) shredded pepper jack cheese**
- ¾ **cup salsa**
- 1 **small onion, chopped**
- ½ **cup frozen corn**
- ⅓ **cup uncooked converted long grain rice**
- 1¼ **teaspoons chili powder**
- ½ **teaspoon ground cumin**
  Reduced-fat sour cream, optional

1. Cut and discard tops from peppers; remove seeds. In a large bowl, mix beans, cheese, salsa, onion, corn, rice, chili powder and cumin; spoon into peppers. Place in a 5-qt. slow cooker coated with cooking spray.
2. Cook, covered, on low 3-4 hours or until peppers are tender and filling is heated through. If desired, serve with sour cream.

VEGETARIAN STUFFED PEPPERS

INDONESIAN PEANUT CHICKEN

Indonesian Peanut Chicken

Here's a great make-ahead recipe! I cut up fresh chicken, put it in a bag with the remaining slow-cooker ingredients and freeze. To cook, just remove the bag a day ahead to thaw in the fridge, then pour all the contents into the slow cooker.

—**SARAH NEWMAN** MAHTOMEDI, MN

PREP: 15 MIN. • **COOK:** 4 HOURS
MAKES: 6 SERVINGS

- 1½ pounds boneless skinless chicken breasts, cut into 1-inch cubes
- ⅓ cup chopped onion
- ⅓ cup water
- ¼ cup reduced-fat creamy peanut butter
- 3 tablespoons chili sauce
- ¼ teaspoon salt
- ¼ teaspoon cayenne pepper
- ¼ teaspoon pepper
- 3 cups hot cooked brown rice
- 6 tablespoons chopped salted peanuts
- 6 tablespoons chopped sweet red pepper

1. Place chicken in a 4-qt. slow cooker. In a small bowl, combine the onion, water, peanut butter, chili sauce, salt, cayenne and pepper; pour over chicken. Cover and cook on low for 4-6 hours or until chicken is no longer pink.

2. Shred meat with two forks and return to slow cooker; heat through. Serve with rice. Sprinkle with peanuts and red pepper.

Mediterranean Chicken in Eggplant Sauce

Spice-coated chicken thighs simmer in a rich red pepper-eggplant sauce. This savory entree is perfect for an everyday meal or potluck. It's an easy slow-cooker dish to prepare in the morning so that dinner is all ready at the end of the day.

—**JUDY ARMSTRONG** PRAIRIEVILLE, LA

PREP: 45 MIN. • **COOK:** 5 HOURS
MAKES: 8 SERVINGS

- ⅓ cup all-purpose flour
- 2 teaspoons paprika
- 2 teaspoons ground cumin
- 1 teaspoon salt
- 1 teaspoon freshly ground pepper
- 3 pounds boneless skinless chicken thighs, cut into 2-inch pieces
- 2 tablespoons olive oil
- 1¼ cups white wine or chicken broth
- 1 small eggplant (1 pound), peeled and cubed
- 1 jar (12 ounces) roasted sweet red peppers, drained
- 1 medium onion, chopped
- 1 jalapeno pepper, seeded and chopped
- 2 tablespoons tomato paste
- 1 tablespoon brown sugar
- 3 garlic cloves, minced
- 1 cup pitted ripe olives, halved
- ¼ cup minced fresh Italian parsley
- 1 cup (4 ounces) crumbled feta cheese
- 8 naan flatbreads, quartered

1. In a large bowl, combine the first five ingredients. Add chicken; toss to coat. In a large skillet, brown chicken in oil in batches. Transfer to a 4-qt. slow cooker.

2. Add wine to the skillet, stirring to loosen browned bits from pan. Stir in the eggplant, red peppers, onion, jalapeno, tomato paste, brown sugar and garlic. Bring to a boil. Reduce heat; simmer, uncovered, for 5 minutes. Cool slightly. Transfer to a blender; cover and process until pureed. Pour over chicken.

3. Cover and cook on low for 5-6 hours or until chicken is tender, adding olives and parsley during the last 30 minutes. Just before serving, sprinkle with feta cheese. Serve with naan.

NOTE *Wear disposable gloves when cutting hot peppers; the oils can burn skin. Avoid touching your face.*

JUDY ARMSTRONG'S
MEDITERRANEAN CHICKEN IN EGGPLANT SAUCE

LOUISIANA ROUND STEAK

Greek Shrimp Orzo

One of our favorite dishes, this delicious recipe is satisfying and reheats well. My husband would rather have this meal than go out to eat. Serve it with crusty bread and a green salad.

—**MOLLY SEIDEL** EDGEWOOD, NM

PREP: 45 MIN. • **COOK:** 2 HOURS
MAKES: 6 SERVINGS

- 2 **cups uncooked orzo pasta**
- 2 **tablespoons minced fresh basil or 2 teaspoons dried basil**
- 3 **tablespoons olive oil, divided**
- 1½ **tablespoons chopped shallot**
- 2 **tablespoons butter**
- 1 **can (14½ ounces) diced tomatoes, drained**
- 2 **tablespoons minced fresh oregano or 2 teaspoons dried oregano**
- 3 **garlic cloves, minced**
- 1 **pound uncooked large shrimp, peeled and deveined**
- 1 **cup oil-packed sun-dried tomatoes, chopped**
- 2½ **cups (10 ounces) crumbled feta cheese**
- 1½ **cups pitted Greek olives**

1. Cook orzo according to package directions; rinse in cold water and drain. Transfer to a large bowl. Add basil and 1 tablespoon oil; toss to coat and set aside.
2. In a large skillet, saute shallot in butter and remaining oil until tender. Add the diced tomatoes, oregano and garlic; cook and stir for 1-2 minutes. Add shrimp and sun-dried tomatoes; cook and stir for 2-3 minutes or until shrimp turn pink.
3. Transfer to a greased 5-qt. slow cooker. Stir in the orzo mixture, cheese and olives. Cover and cook on low for 2-3 hours or until heated through.

Louisiana Round Steak

This beefy main dish is always a big hit with the men in my family. After simmering in a slow cooker, the steak takes on a robust flavor, and the filling portions are just perfect if you ask me!

—**MEGAN ROHLCK** VERMILLION, SD

PREP: 20 MIN. • **COOK:** 7 HOURS
MAKES: 6 SERVINGS

- 2 **pounds sweet potatoes, peeled and cut into 1-inch pieces**
- 1 **large onion, chopped**
- 1 **medium green pepper, sliced**
- 2 **beef top round steaks (¾ inch thick and 1 pound each)**
- 1 **teaspoon salt, divided**
- 2 **tablespoons olive oil**
- 1 **garlic clove, minced**
- 3 **tablespoons all-purpose flour**
- 1 **can (28 ounces) diced tomatoes, undrained**
- ½ **cup beef broth**
- 1 **teaspoon sugar**
- ½ **teaspoon dried thyme**
- ½ **teaspoon pepper**
- ¼ **teaspoon hot pepper sauce**

1. Place the sweet potatoes, onion and green pepper in a 6-qt. slow cooker. Cut each steak into three serving-size pieces; sprinkle with ½ teaspoon salt. In a large skillet over medium heat, brown steaks in oil in batches on both sides. Place steaks over vegetables, reserving drippings in pan.
2. Add garlic to drippings; cook and stir for 1 minute. Stir in flour until blended. Stir in the remaining ingredients and remaining salt. Bring to a boil, stirring constantly. Cook and stir for 4-5 minutes or until thickened. Pour over the meat. Cover and cook on low for 7-9 hours or until the beef is tender.

ASIAN RIBS

Asian Ribs

My husband adores this dish, and I love its wonderful aroma filling our house! The tangy, salty-sweet sauce with fresh ginger and garlic is delicious with rice or noodles.

—JULIE KO ROGERS, AR

PREP: 15 MIN. • **COOK:** 6 HOURS
MAKES: 6 SERVINGS (ABOUT 4 CUPS SAUCE)

- 6 pounds pork baby back ribs, cut into serving-size pieces
- 1⅓ cups packed brown sugar
- 1 cup reduced-sodium soy sauce
- ¼ cup rice vinegar
- ¼ cup sesame oil
- ¼ cup minced fresh gingerroot
- 6 garlic cloves, minced
- 1 teaspoon crushed red pepper flakes
- ¼ cup cornstarch
- ¼ cup cold water
  Thinly sliced green onions and sesame seeds, optional

1. Place ribs in a 6-qt. slow cooker. In a small bowl, combine the brown sugar, soy sauce, vinegar, oil, ginger, garlic and pepper flakes; pour over ribs. Cover and cook on low for 6-7 hours or until meat is tender.

2. Remove meat to a serving platter; keep warm. Skim fat from cooking juices; transfer to a small saucepan. Bring to a boil.

3. Combine cornstarch and water until smooth. Gradually stir into the pan. Bring to a boil; cook and stir for 2 minutes or until thickened. Serve with ribs. Garnish with onions and sesame seeds if desired.

German Potato Salad with Sausage

Hearty and saucy, this potato salad is an old family recipe that was updated using canned soup for easy preparation. The sausage and sauerkraut give it a special zip, and the slow cooker makes it a snap!

—TERESA MCGILL TROTWOOD, OH

PREP: 30 MIN. • **COOK:** 6 HOURS
MAKES: 5 SERVINGS

- 8 bacon strips, finely chopped
- 1 large onion, chopped
- 1 pound smoked kielbasa or Polish sausage, halved and cut into ½-inch slices
- 2 pounds medium red potatoes, cut into chunks
- 1 can (10¾ ounces) condensed cream of potato soup, undiluted
- 1 cup sauerkraut, rinsed and well drained
- ½ cup water
- ¼ cup cider vinegar
- 1 tablespoon sugar
- ½ teaspoon salt
- ½ teaspoon coarsely ground pepper

1. In a large skillet, cook bacon over medium heat until crisp. Remove to paper towels with a slotted spoon to drain. Saute onion in drippings for 1 minute. Add sausage; cook until lightly browned. Add potatoes; cook 2 minutes longer. Drain.

2. Transfer sausage mixture to a 3-qt. slow cooker. In a small bowl, combine the soup, sauerkraut, water, vinegar, sugar, salt and pepper. Pour over the sausage mixture. Sprinkle with bacon. Cover and cook on low for 6-7 hours or until potatoes are tender.

GERMAN POTATO SALAD WITH SAUSAGE

SPRING-THYME CHICKEN STEW

Spring-Thyme Chicken Stew

During one long spring, my husband and I were in need of something warm, comforting and bright. This hearty stew proved the perfect answer. It fills the house with the aroma of Mom's chicken soup...coupled with a little something extra all my own.

—**AMY CHASE** VANDERHOOF, BC

PREP: 15 MIN. • **COOK:** 7 HOURS
MAKES: 4 SERVINGS

- 1 **pound small red potatoes, halved**
- 1 **large onion, finely chopped**
- ¾ **cup shredded carrots**
- 3 **tablespoons all-purpose flour**
- 6 **garlic cloves, minced**
- 2 **teaspoons grated lemon peel**
- 2 **teaspoons dried thyme**
- ½ **teaspoon salt**
- ¼ **teaspoon pepper**
- 1½ **pounds boneless skinless chicken thighs, halved**
- 2 **cups reduced-sodium chicken broth**
- 2 **bay leaves**
- 2 **tablespoons minced fresh parsley**

1. Place potatoes, onion and carrots in a 3-qt. slow cooker. Sprinkle with flour, garlic, lemon peel, thyme, salt and pepper; toss to coat. Place chicken on top. Add broth and bay leaves.
2. Cook, covered, on low 7-9 hours or until chicken and vegetables are tender. Remove bay leaves. Sprinkle with parsley.

Island Pork Roast

This fork-tender roast is a nice mixture of sweet and tangy, and it's especially tasty when served over rice. Leftovers make wonderful sandwiches the next day.

—**HEATHER CAMPBELL** LAWRENCE, KS

PREP: 25 MIN. • **COOK:** 5 HOURS
MAKES: 10 SERVINGS

- 1 **boneless pork loin roast (about 4 pounds)**
- 1 **large onion, sliced**
- 2 **cans (8 ounces each) unsweetened pineapple chunks, undrained**
- ½ **cup sugar**
- ½ **cup lime juice**
- ½ **cup soy sauce**
- ¼ **cup packed brown sugar**
- 2 **tablespoons teriyaki sauce**
- 2 **garlic cloves, minced**
- 1 **teaspoon ground ginger**
- 1 **teaspoon curry powder**
- ¼ **teaspoon salt**
- ¼ **teaspoon pepper**
- 1 **bay leaf**
- ¼ **cup cornstarch**
- ½ **cup cold water**

1. Cut roast in half. Place onion in a 4- or 5-qt. slow cooker. Add pork. Drain pineapple, reserving juice; set pineapple aside. In a small bowl, combine the sugar, lime juice, soy sauce, brown sugar, teriyaki sauce, garlic, ginger, curry, salt, pepper, bay leaf and reserved juice. Pour over roast.
2. Cover and cook on low for 5-6 hours or until a thermometer reads 160°. Add pineapple during the last hour of cooking.
3. Remove the meat, onion and pineapple to a serving platter; keep warm. Discard bay leaf. Skim the fat from cooking juices; transfer to a small saucepan. Bring liquid to a boil. Combine cornstarch and water until smooth; gradually stir into the pan. Bring to a boil; cook and stir for 2 minutes or until thickened. Serve with the pork.

ISLAND PORK ROAST

HAM WITH CRANBERRY-PINEAPPLE SAUCE

Ham with Cranberry-Pineapple Sauce

Flag this dish for the times you want that mouthwatering flavor combo of cranberries, pineapple and stone-ground mustard served with smoky ham slices.
—**CAROLE RESNICK** CLEVELAND, OH

PREP: 15 MIN. • **COOK:** 5 HOURS
MAKES: 20 SERVINGS (4½ CUPS SAUCE)

- 1 **fully cooked boneless ham (5 to 6 pounds)**
- 12 **whole cloves**
- 1 **can (20 ounces) crushed pineapple, undrained**
- 1 **can (14 ounces) whole-berry cranberry sauce**
- 2 **garlic cloves, minced**
- 2 **tablespoons stone-ground mustard**
- ½ **teaspoon coarsely ground pepper**
- 2 **tablespoons cornstarch**
- 2 **tablespoons cold water**

1. Score the ham, making ½-in.-deep diamond shapes; insert a clove in each diamond. Place ham in a 5-qt. slow cooker. In a large bowl, combine the pineapple, cranberry sauce, garlic, mustard and pepper; pour over ham.
2. Cover and cook on low for 5-6 hours or until a thermometer reads 140°. Remove meat to a cutting board and keep warm; remove and discard cloves.
3. Transfer sauce to a small saucepan. Bring to a boil. Combine cornstarch and water until smooth; gradually stir into pan. Bring to a boil; cook and stir for 2 minutes or until thickened. Slice ham and serve with sauce.

Caramelized Onion Chuck Roast

Wonderfully fork-tender, this tasty roast with sweet onions makes the perfect comfort food at the end of a long day.
—**JEANNIE KLUGH** LANCASTER, PA

PREP: 25 MIN. • **COOK:** 8 HOURS
MAKES: 4 SERVINGS PLUS LEFTOVERS

- 1 **cup water**
- 1 **cup beer or beef broth**
- ½ **cup beef broth**
- ¼ **cup packed brown sugar**
- 3 **tablespoons Dijon mustard**
- 2 **tablespoons cider vinegar**
- 1 **boneless beef chuck roast (4 pounds), trimmed**
- 1 **teaspoon onion salt**
- 1 **teaspoon coarsely ground pepper**
- 1 **tablespoon olive oil**
- 3 **large sweet onions, halved and sliced**
- 2 **tablespoons cornstarch**
- 2 **tablespoons cold water**

1. In a large bowl, combine the first six ingredients; set aside. Sprinkle roast with onion salt and pepper. In a large skillet, brown meat in oil on all sides. Place onions and roast in a 5-qt. slow cooker; pour beer mixture over top. Cover and cook on low for 8-10 hours or until meat is tender.
2. Remove roast and onions and keep warm. Skim fat from cooking juices; transfer 2 cups to a small saucepan. Bring liquid to a boil. Combine cornstarch and water until smooth; gradually stir into the pan. Bring to a boil; cook and stir for 2 minutes or until thickened. Serve the gravy with the roast and onions.

ENTREES

Spring

AMAZING SLOW COOKER ORANGE CHICKEN

1. In a small bowl, combine the first 11 ingredients; stir in molasses if desired. In a 4-qt. slow cooker, combine chicken, cornstarch, salt and pepper; toss to coat. Top with red pepper. Pour stock mixture over top. Cover and cook on low for 4 hours or until chicken is tender.
2. Stir in broccoli. Cover and cook on high 30-40 minutes longer or until broccoli is crisp-tender. Serve with rice. Sprinkle with toppings of your choice.

Light Ham Tetrazzini

This creamy pasta is an easy way to serve a hungry crowd. If you're bringing this tetrazzini to a potluck, cook and add the spaghetti to the slow cooker just before heading to the gathering.
—**SUSAN BLAIR** STERLING, MI

PREP: 15 MIN. • **COOK:** 4 HOURS
MAKES: 10 SERVINGS

- 2 cans (10¾ ounces each) reduced-fat reduced-sodium condensed cream of mushroom soup, undiluted
- 2 cups sliced fresh mushrooms
- 2 cups cubed fully cooked ham
- 1 cup fat-free evaporated milk
- ¼ cup white wine or water
- 2 teaspoons prepared horseradish
- 1 package (14½ ounces) uncooked multigrain spaghetti
- 1 cup shredded Parmesan cheese

1. In a 5-qt. slow cooker, combine the soup, mushrooms, ham, milk, wine and horseradish. Cover and cook on low for 4 hours.
2. Cook spaghetti according to package directions; drain. Add spaghetti and cheese to slow cooker; toss to coat.

Amazing Slow Cooker Orange Chicken

Orange chicken is my favorite Chinese takeout food, but I know that it's very high in sodium and fat. So I got to work at home and created this healthier version. Now I have peace of mind knowing what ingredients are in it and that it's better for my family.
—**BARB MILLER** OAKDALE, MN

PREP: 25 MIN. • **COOK:** 4 HOURS
MAKES: 8 SERVINGS

- 1 cup chicken stock
- 1 cup orange juice
- 1 cup orange marmalade
- ½ cup ketchup
- ¼ cup Dijon mustard
- 2 tablespoons brown sugar
- 2 tablespoons rice vinegar
- 2 tablespoons reduced-sodium soy sauce
- 1 tablespoon minced fresh gingerroot
- 1 teaspoon garlic powder
- ¾ teaspoon crushed red pepper flakes
- 2 tablespoons molasses, optional
- 2 pounds boneless skinless chicken breasts, cut into ¾-inch pieces
- ½ cup cornstarch
- ¾ teaspoon salt
- ½ teaspoon pepper
- 1 large sweet red pepper, cut into 1-inch pieces
- 2 cups fresh broccoli florets
  Hot cooked rice
  Optional toppings: chopped green onions, peanuts and fresh cilantro

ZIPPY SPAGHETTI SAUCE

Zippy Spaghetti Sauce

This spaghetti sauce is perfect for putting together a flavorful meal. Serve it with any kind of noodles for a fabulous yet no-fuss dinner option.
—**ELAINE PRIEST** DOVER, PA

PREP: 20 MIN. • **COOK:** 6 HOURS
MAKES: ABOUT 3 QUARTS

- 2 pounds lean ground beef (90% lean)
- 1 cup chopped onion
- ½ cup chopped green pepper
- 2 cans (15 ounces each) tomato sauce
- 1 can (28 ounces) diced tomatoes, undrained
- 1 can (12 ounces) tomato paste
- ½ pound sliced fresh mushrooms
- 1 cup grated Parmesan cheese
- ½ to ¾ cup dry red wine or beef broth
- ½ cup sliced pimiento-stuffed olives
- ¼ cup dried parsley flakes
- 1 to 2 tablespoons dried oregano
- 2 teaspoons Italian seasoning
- 2 teaspoons minced garlic
- ½ teaspoon salt
- 1 teaspoon pepper
  Hot cooked spaghetti

1. In a large skillet, cook the beef, onion and green pepper over medium heat until meat is no longer pink; drain. Transfer to a 5-qt. slow cooker.
2. Stir in the tomato sauce, tomatoes, tomato paste, mushrooms, cheese, wine, olives, parsley, oregano, Italian seasoning, garlic, salt and pepper.
3. Cover and cook on low for 6-8 hours. Serve with spaghetti.

Mango-Pineapple Chicken Tacos

I lived in the Caribbean as a child, and the fresh tropical fruits in this slow cooker chicken recipe always bring me back to those childhood days.
—**LISSA NELSON** PROVO, UT

PREP: 25 MIN. • **COOK:** 5 HOURS
MAKES: 16 SERVINGS

- 2 medium mangoes, peeled and chopped
- 1½ cups cubed fresh pineapple or canned pineapple chunks, drained
- 2 medium tomatoes, chopped
- 1 medium red onion, finely chopped
- 2 small Anaheim peppers, seeded and chopped
- 2 green onions, finely chopped
- 1 tablespoon lime juice
- 1 teaspoon sugar
- 4 pounds bone-in chicken breast halves, skin removed
- 3 teaspoons salt
- ¼ cup packed brown sugar
- 32 taco shells, warmed
- ¼ cup minced fresh cilantro

1. In a large bowl, combine the first eight ingredients. Place chicken in a 6-qt. slow cooker; sprinkle with salt and brown sugar. Top with mango mixture. Cover and cook on low for 5-6 hours or until chicken is tender.
2. Remove chicken; cool slightly. Strain cooking juices, reserving mango mixture and ½ cup juices. Discard remaining juices. When cool enough to handle, remove chicken from bones; discard bones.
3. Shred chicken with two forks. Return chicken and reserved mango mixture and cooking juices to slow cooker; heat through. Serve in taco shells; sprinkle with cilantro.

MANGO-PINEAPPLE CHICKEN TACOS

KAEL HARVEY'S
SOY-GINGER CHICKEN

Soy-Ginger Chicken

Bone-in chicken turns tender when cooked with sliced carrots and green onions in a rich ginger-soy sauce. Flavored with brown sugar, balsamic vinegar and coriander, here's a sauce you have to try!

—**KAEL HARVEY** BROOKLYN, NY

PREP: 25 MIN. • **COOK:** 5 HOURS
MAKES: 4 SERVINGS

- 4 **bone-in chicken thighs (about 1½ pounds), skin removed**
- 4 **chicken drumsticks (about 1 pound), skin removed**
- 2 **medium carrots, sliced**
- 4 **green onions, thinly sliced**
- ⅓ **cup soy sauce**
- 2 **tablespoons brown sugar**
- 1 **piece fresh gingerroot (about 2 inches), peeled and thinly sliced**
- 5 **garlic cloves, minced**
- 1 **tablespoon balsamic vinegar**
- 1 **teaspoon ground coriander**
- ½ **teaspoon pepper**
- 1 **tablespoon cornstarch**
- 1 **tablespoon cold water**
  Hot cooked rice and minced fresh cilantro

1. Place chicken, carrots and green onions in a 3-qt. slow cooker. Combine the soy sauce, brown sugar, ginger, garlic, vinegar, coriander and pepper in a small bowl. Pour over top. Cover and cook on low for 5-6 hours or until chicken is tender.

2. Remove chicken to a serving platter; keep warm. Pour juices into a small saucepan. Bring to a boil. Combine cornstarch and water until smooth; gradually stir into pan. Bring to a boil; cook and stir for 1-2 minutes or until thickened. Serve with the chicken and rice; sprinkle servings with cilantro.

Beef Braciole

My great aunt used to make the most amazing braciole, but it was a laborious and time-consuming effort. I took her basic recipe and transformed it into a slow cooker version, making it easier for today's hurried world. My great aunt always served the flank steak sliced over orzo that had been tossed with olive oil and Romano cheese. Delicioso!

—**LISA RENSHAW** KANSAS CITY, MO

PREP: 30 MIN. • **COOK:** 6 HOURS
MAKES: 6 SERVINGS

- 2 **jars (24 ounces each) tomato basil pasta sauce**
- 1 **teaspoon crushed red pepper flakes**
- 1 **beef flank steak (1½ pounds)**
- ½ **teaspoon salt**
- ½ **teaspoon pepper**
- 2 **eggs, beaten**
- ½ **cup seasoned bread crumbs**
- 8 **thin slices prosciutto or deli ham**
- 1 **cup (4 ounces) shredded Italian cheese blend**
- 2 **tablespoons olive oil**

1. In a 5- or 6-qt. oval slow cooker, combine pasta sauce and pepper flakes. Pound steak with a meat mallet to ½-in. thickness; sprinkle with salt and pepper.

2. In a small bowl, combine eggs and bread crumbs. Spoon over beef to within 1 in. of edges; press onto meat. Layer with prosciutto and cheese. Roll up jelly-roll style, starting with a long side; tie at 2-in. intervals with kitchen string.

3. In a Dutch oven, brown meat in oil on all sides. Transfer to slow cooker; spoon sauce over meat. Cover and cook on low for 6-8 hours or until the beef is tender.

4. Remove meat from sauce and discard string. Cut into slices; serve with sauce.

BEEF BRACIOLE

Slow-Cooked Caribbean Pot Roast

This dish may feature spring's root vegetables, but it comes together so easily, you will want to simmer it up all year long!

—**JENN TIDWELL** FAIR OAKS, CA

PREP: 30 MIN. • **COOK:** 6 HOURS
MAKES: 10 SERVINGS

- 2 **medium sweet potatoes, cubed**
- 2 **large carrots, sliced**
- ¼ **cup chopped celery**
- 1 **boneless beef chuck roast (2½ pounds)**
- 1 **tablespoon canola oil**
- 1 **large onion, chopped**
- 2 **garlic cloves, minced**
- 1 **tablespoon all-purpose flour**
- 1 **tablespoon sugar**
- 1 **tablespoon brown sugar**
- 1 **teaspoon ground cumin**
- ¾ **teaspoon salt**
- ¾ **teaspoon ground coriander**
- ¾ **teaspoon chili powder**
- ½ **teaspoon dried oregano**
- ⅛ **teaspoon ground cinnamon**
- ¾ **teaspoon grated orange peel**
- ¾ **teaspoon baking cocoa**
- 1 **can (15 ounces) tomato sauce**

1. Place potatoes, carrots and celery in a 5-qt. slow cooker. In a large skillet, brown meat in oil on all sides. Transfer meat to slow cooker.
2. In the same skillet, saute onion in drippings until tender. Add garlic; cook 1 minute longer. Combine the flour, sugar, brown sugar, seasonings, orange peel and cocoa. Stir in tomato sauce; add to skillet and heat through. Pour over beef.
3. Cover and cook on low for 6-8 hours or until beef and vegetables are tender.

Creamy Chicken & Broccoli Stew

This recipe is so simple, but you'd never know it. My husband, who normally doesn't like chicken, asks for it regularly.

—**MARY WATKINS** LITTLE ELM, TX

PREP: 15 MIN. • **COOK:** 6 HOURS
MAKES: 8 SERVINGS

- 8 **bone-in chicken thighs, skin removed (about 3 pounds)**
- 1 **cup Italian salad dressing**
- ½ **cup white wine or chicken broth**
- 6 **tablespoons butter, melted, divided**
- 1 **tablespoon dried minced onion**
- 1 **tablespoon garlic powder**
- 1 **tablespoon Italian seasoning**
- ¾ **teaspoon salt, divided**
- ¾ **teaspoon pepper, divided**
- 1 **can (10¾ ounces) condensed cream of mushroom soup, undiluted**
- 1 **package (8 ounces) cream cheese, softened**
- 2 **cups frozen broccoli florets, thawed**
- 2 **pounds red potatoes, quartered**

1. Place chicken in a 4-qt. slow cooker. Combine salad dressing, wine, 4 tablespoons butter, onion, garlic powder, Italian seasoning, ½ teaspoon salt and ½ teaspoon pepper in a small bowl; pour over chicken.
2. Cover and cook on low for 5 hours. Skim fat. Combine the soup, cream cheese and 2 cups of liquid from slow cooker in a small bowl until blended; add to slow cooker.
3. Cover and cook 45 minutes longer or until chicken is tender, adding the broccoli during the last 30 minutes of cooking.
4. Meanwhile, place potatoes in a large saucepan and cover with water. Bring to a boil. Reduce heat; cover and simmer for 15-20 minutes or until tender. Drain and return to pan. Mash potatoes with the remaining butter, salt and pepper. Serve with chicken and broccoli mixture.

CREAMY CHICKEN & BROCCOLI STEW

Spiced Lamb Stew with Apricots

My family loves lamb, especially my son. After his first year of college, he claimed to be a vegetarian. When he came home, I had a pot of this slow-cooked lamb stew simmering on the counter. When my husband and I wanted to eat dinner, there were only a few shreds of meat left floating in the gravy—and my son confessed that he was the culprit!

—**ARLENE ERLBACH** MORTON GROVE, IL

PREP: 30 MIN. • **COOK:** 5 HOURS
MAKES: 5 SERVINGS

- 2 **pounds lamb stew meat, cut into ¾-inch cubes**
- 3 **tablespoons butter**
- 1½ **cups chopped sweet onion**
- ¾ **cup dried apricots**
- ½ **cup orange juice**
- ½ **cup chicken broth**
- 2 **teaspoons paprika**
- 2 **teaspoons ground allspice**
- 2 **teaspoons ground cinnamon**
- 1½ **teaspoons salt**
- 1 **teaspoon ground cardamom**

Hot cooked couscous
Chopped dried apricots, optional

1. In a large skillet, brown lamb in butter in batches. With a slotted spoon, transfer to a 3-qt. slow cooker. In the same skillet, saute onion in drippings until tender. Stir in the apricots, orange juice, broth and seasonings; pour over lamb.
2. Cover and cook on high for 5-6 hours or until meat is tender. Serve with couscous. Sprinkle with more chopped apricots if desired.

Spinach and Sausage Lasagna

Dig into the rich layers of this hearty lasagna that features plenty of Italian sausage and gooey cheese. No-cook noodles, frozen spinach and jarred spaghetti sauce simplify the prep. But it tastes far from ordinary!

—**KATHY MORROW** HUBBARD, OH

PREP: 25 MIN. • **COOK:** 3 HOURS
MAKES: 8 SERVINGS

- 1 **pound bulk Italian sausage**
- 1 **jar (24 ounces) garden-style spaghetti sauce**
- ½ **cup water**
- 1 **teaspoon Italian seasoning**
- ½ **teaspoon salt**
- 1 **carton (15 ounces) ricotta cheese**
- 1 **package (10 ounces) frozen chopped spinach, thawed and squeezed dry**
- 2 **cups (8 ounces) shredded part-skim mozzarella cheese, divided**
- 9 **no-cook lasagna noodles**
  Grated Parmesan cheese

1. Cook sausage in a large skillet over medium heat until no longer pink; drain. Stir in the spaghetti sauce, water, Italian seasoning and salt. Combine ricotta, spinach and 1 cup mozzarella cheese in a small bowl.
2. Spread 1 cup sauce mixture in a greased oval 5-qt. slow cooker. Layer with three noodles (breaking noodles if necessary to fit), 1¼ cups sauce mixture and half of the cheese mixture. Repeat layers. Layer with remaining noodles and sauce mixture; sprinkle with remaining mozzarella cheese.
3. Cover and cook on low for 3-4 hours or until noodles are tender. Sprinkle servings with Parmesan cheese.

Spring

SOUPS & SANDWICHES

Nothing tops the popular combination of soup and a sandwich, so why not use your slow cooker to create the tasty duo? Loaded with convenience, the recipes found here deliver spring's freshest flavors.

NICHOLE JONES'
TURKEY SLOPPY JOES

Turkey Sloppy Joes

The chili sauce and ground turkey that are used to make these sloppy joes create a deliciously unique flavor. And the avocado adds a special spring-summer touch to the sandwiches.

—**NICHOLE JONES** IDAHO FALLS, ID

PREP: 35 MIN. • **COOK:** 4 HOURS
MAKES: 8 SERVINGS

- 1½ pounds lean ground turkey
- 2 medium onions, finely chopped
- 4 garlic cloves, minced
- 1 jar (12 ounces) chili sauce
- 1 jalapeno pepper, seeded and chopped
- 1 tablespoon Worcestershire sauce
- 2 teaspoons dried oregano
- 1 teaspoon ground cumin
- 1 teaspoon paprika
- ½ teaspoon salt
- ½ teaspoon pepper
- 2 cups (8 ounces) shredded Monterey Jack cheese
- 8 onion rolls, split
- 2 medium ripe avocados, peeled and thinly sliced

1. In a large skillet coated with cooking spray, cook the turkey, onions and garlic over medium heat until meat is no longer pink; drain.

2. Transfer to a 1½-qt. slow cooker. Stir in the chili sauce, jalapeno, Worcestershire sauce, oregano, cumin, paprika, salt and pepper. Cover and cook on low for 4-5 hours or until heated through. Just before serving, stir in cheese. Serve on rolls topped with avocado.

NOTE *Wear disposable gloves when cutting hot peppers; the oils can burn skin. Avoid touching your face.*

Slow-Cooked Cannellini Turkey Soup

All you have to do is add these ingredients to the slow cooker and let everything simmer to a delicious goodness!

—**GARY FENSKI** HURON, SD

PREP: 20 MIN. • **COOK:** 5 HOURS
MAKES: 4 SERVINGS

- 2 cans (15 ounces each) white kidney or cannellini beans, rinsed and drained
- 2 cups cubed cooked turkey
- 1 can (14½ ounces) chicken broth
- 1 can (10 ounces) diced tomatoes and green chilies, undrained
- 1 cup salsa
- ½ teaspoon ground cumin
- ¼ teaspoon curry powder
- ¼ teaspoon ground ginger
- ¼ teaspoon paprika

In a 3-qt. slow cooker, combine all ingredients. Cover and cook on low for 5-6 hours or until heated through.

SATAY-STYLE PORK STEW

Satay-Style Pork Stew

Thai cuisine features flavors that are hot and sour, salty and sweet. This one-dish pork satay balances all of them using ginger and red pepper flakes, rice vinegar, garlic, lime juice and creamy peanut butter.

—**NICOLE WERNER** ANN ARBOR, MI

PREP: 25 MIN. • **COOK:** 8 HOURS
MAKES: 6 SERVINGS

- 1 **boneless pork shoulder butt roast (3 to 4 pounds), cut into 1½ inch cubes**
- 2 **medium parsnips, peeled and sliced**
- 1 **small sweet red pepper, thinly sliced**
- 1 **cup chicken broth**
- ¼ **cup reduced-sodium teriyaki sauce**
- 2 **tablespoons rice vinegar**
- 1 **tablespoon minced fresh gingerroot**
- 1 **tablespoon honey**
- 2 **garlic cloves, minced**
- ½ **teaspoon crushed red pepper flakes**
- ¼ **cup creamy peanut butter**
  Hot cooked rice, optional
- 2 **green onions, chopped**
- 2 **tablespoons chopped dry roasted peanuts**

In a 3-qt. slow cooker, combine the first 10 ingredients. Cover and cook on low for 8-10 hours or until pork is tender. Skim fat; stir in peanut butter. Serve with rice if desired; top with onions and peanuts.

(5) INGREDIENTS

Tex-Mex Shredded Beef Sandwiches

Slow cooker meals, like this shredded beef sandwich, are my favorite kind because after I combine a few ingredients and let them cook, there is time for me to do my own thing. Plus, I have a hearty, satisfying and enticing meal when I come home!

—**KATHERINE WHITE** CLEMMONS, NC

PREP: 5 MIN. • **COOK:** 8 HOURS
MAKES: 8 SERVINGS

- 1 **boneless beef chuck roast (3 pounds)**
- 1 **envelope chili seasoning**
- ½ **cup barbecue sauce**
- 8 **onion rolls, split**
- 8 **slices cheddar cheese**

1. Cut roast in half; place in a 3-qt. slow cooker. Sprinkle with chili seasoning. Pour barbecue sauce over top. Cover and cook on low for 8-10 hours or until meat is tender.

2. Remove roast; cool slightly. Shred meat with two forks. Skim fat from cooking juices. Return meat to slow cooker; heat through. Using a slotted spoon, place ½ cup meat mixture on each roll bottom; top with cheese. Replace tops.

TEX-MEX SHREDDED BEEF SANDWICHES

KAROL CHANDLER-EZELL'S
MACHACA BEEF DIP SANDWICHES

Machaca Beef Dip Sandwiches

The winning combination of beef, cumin, chili powder and the spicy heat of chipotle peppers makes these sandwiches game-day food at its finest!

—KAROL CHANDLER-EZELL

NACOGDOCHES, TX

PREP: 20 MIN. • **COOK:** 8 HOURS
MAKES: 6 SERVINGS

- 1 **boneless beef chuck roast (2 to 3 pounds)**
- 1 **large sweet onion, thinly sliced**
- 1 **can (14½ ounces) reduced-sodium beef broth**
- ½ **cup water**
- 3 **chipotle peppers in adobo sauce, chopped**
- 1 **tablespoon adobo sauce**
- 1 **envelope au jus gravy mix**
- 1 **tablespoon Creole seasoning**
- 1 **tablespoon chili powder**
- 2 **teaspoons ground cumin**
- 6 **French rolls, split**
  Guacamole and salsa, optional

1. Place roast in a 3- to 4-qt. slow cooker; top with onion. Combine the broth, water, chipotle peppers, adobo sauce, gravy mix, Creole seasoning, chili powder and cumin; pour over meat. Cover and cook on low for 8-10 hours or until meat is tender.

2. Remove roast; cool slightly. Skim fat from cooking juices. Shred beef with two forks and return to slow cooker; heat through. Using a slotted spoon, place meat on rolls. Serve with cooking juices and guacamole or salsa if desired.

NOTE *Wear disposable gloves when cutting hot peppers; the oils can burn skin. Avoid touching your face.*

BEEF & POTATO SOUP

Beef & Potato Soup

Slow-cooker easy, this lightened-up soup is a bit of a tradition after church services at our house.

—SHEILA HOLDERMAN BERTHOLD, ND

PREP: 30 MIN. • **COOK:** 6½ HOURS
MAKES: 10 SERVINGS (3 QUARTS)

- 1½ **pounds lean ground beef (90% lean)**
- ¾ **cup chopped onion**
- ½ **cup all-purpose flour**
- 2 **cans (14½ ounces each) reduced-sodium chicken broth, divided**
- 5 **medium potatoes, peeled and cubed**
- 5 **medium carrots, chopped**
- 3 **celery ribs, chopped**
- 3 **teaspoons dried basil**
- 2 **teaspoons dried parsley flakes**
- 1 **teaspoon garlic powder**
- ½ **teaspoon pepper**
- 12 **ounces reduced-fat process cheese (Velveeta), cubed**
- 1½ **cups 2% milk**
- ½ **cup reduced-fat sour cream**

1. In a large skillet, cook beef and onion over medium heat until meat is no longer pink; drain. Combine flour and 1 can broth until smooth. Add to beef mixture. Bring to a boil; cook and stir for 2 minutes or until thickened.

2. Transfer to a 5-qt. slow cooker. Stir in the potatoes, carrots, celery, seasonings and remaining broth. Cover and cook on low for 6-8 hours or until vegetables are tender.

3. Stir in cheese and milk. Cover and cook 30 minutes longer or until cheese is melted. Just before serving, stir in sour cream.

BBQ CHICKEN SLIDERS

BBQ Chicken Sliders

Brining the chicken overnight helps it taste exceptionally good, making it so tender it literally melts in your mouth.

—RACHEL KUNKEL SCHELL CITY, MO

PREP: 25 MIN. + BRINING • **COOK:** 4 HOURS
MAKES: 8 SERVINGS (2 SLIDERS EACH)

BRINE
- 1½ quarts water
- ¼ cup packed brown sugar
- 2 tablespoons salt
- 1 tablespoon liquid smoke
- 2 garlic cloves, minced
- ½ teaspoon dried thyme

CHICKEN
- 2 pounds boneless skinless chicken breast halves
- ⅓ cup liquid smoke
- 1½ cups hickory smoke-flavored barbecue sauce
- 16 slider buns or dinner rolls, split and warmed

1. In a large bowl, mix the brine ingredients, stirring to dissolve brown sugar. Reserve 1 cup brine for cooking chicken; cover and refrigerate.

2. Place chicken in a large resealable bag; add remaining brine. Seal bag, pressing out as much air as possible; turn to coat chicken. Place in a large bowl; refrigerate 18-24 hours, turning occasionally.

3. Remove chicken from brine and transfer to a 3-qt. slow cooker; discard brine in bag. Add reserved 1 cup brine and ⅓ cup liquid smoke to chicken. Cook, covered, on low 4-5 hours or until chicken is tender.

4. Remove chicken; cool slightly. Discard cooking juices. Shred chicken with two forks and return to slow cooker. Stir in barbecue sauce; heat through. Serve on buns.

HEARTY SPLIT PEA SOUP

cook on low for 7-8 hours or until peas are tender.

3. Cool slightly. In a blender, process half of the soup until smooth. Return all to the slow cooker. Add bacon and pepper; heat through.

Mulligatawny Soup

I learned to cook and bake from my mom and grandmother, and always try to use fresh fruits, vegetables and herbs. This is a delicious, satisfying and versatile soup that I make with leftover chicken, turkey, beef, pork or lamb.

—**MARY ANN MARINO** WEST PITTSBURGH, PA

PREP: 20 MIN. • **COOK:** 6 HOURS
MAKES: 8 SERVINGS (2 QUARTS)

- 1 carton (32 ounces) chicken broth
- 1 can (14½ ounces) diced tomatoes
- 2 cups cubed cooked chicken
- 1 large tart apple, peeled and chopped
- ¼ cup finely chopped onion
- ¼ cup chopped carrot
- ¼ cup chopped green pepper
- 1 tablespoon minced fresh parsley
- 2 teaspoons lemon juice
- 1 teaspoon salt
- 1 teaspoon curry powder
- ½ teaspoon sugar
- ¼ teaspoon pepper
- 2 whole cloves

In a 3- or 4-qt. slow cooker, combine all ingredients. Cover and cook on low for 6-8 hours or until vegetables are tender. Discard cloves.

Hearty Split Pea Soup

We started a 39-day soup challenge to eat healthfully, figuring if *Survivor* contestants could last for 39 days on little food, surely we could survive on soup! This was one of our family favorites.

—**DEBRA KEIL** OWASSO, OK

PREP: 30 MIN. • **COOK:** 7 HOURS
MAKES: 6 SERVINGS (2¼ QUARTS)

- 1 large onion, chopped
- 1 cup chopped celery
- 1 cup chopped fresh carrots
- 2 tablespoons olive oil
- 1 teaspoon dried thyme
- 1 package (16 ounces) dried green split peas, rinsed
- 4 cups vegetable broth
- 2 cups water
- 6 ounces Canadian bacon, chopped
- ¼ teaspoon pepper

1. In a large skillet, saute the onion, celery and carrots in oil until tender. Add thyme; cook 1 minute longer.
2. Transfer to a 5-qt. slow cooker. Add the peas, broth and water. Cover and

MULLIGATAWNY SOUP

SWEET & SAVORY SLOW-COOKED BEEF

Herbed Chicken & Spinach Soup

I love this slow cooker dish because it combines some of my favorite ingredients, such as savory spices, kidney beans and fresh spinach. To create a hearty meal, I eat the chicken soup with a side of crusty bread slathered in butter.

—TANYA MACDONALD
ANTIGONISH COUNTY, NS

PREP: 20 MIN. • **COOK:** 4½ HOURS
MAKES: 4 SERVINGS

- 1 pound boneless skinless chicken thighs, cut into ½-inch pieces
- 1 can (16 ounces) kidney beans, rinsed and drained
- 1 can (14½ ounces) chicken broth
- 1 medium onion, chopped
- 1 medium sweet red pepper, chopped
- 1 celery rib, chopped
- 2 tablespoons tomato paste
- 3 garlic cloves, minced
- ½ teaspoon minced fresh rosemary or ¼ teaspoon dried rosemary, crushed
- ½ teaspoon minced fresh thyme or ¼ teaspoon dried thyme
- ½ teaspoon dried oregano
- ¼ teaspoon salt
- ¼ teaspoon pepper
- 3 cups fresh baby spinach
- ¼ cup shredded Parmesan cheese

In a 3-qt. slow cooker, combine the first 13 ingredients. Cover and cook on low for 4-5 hours or until chicken is tender. Stir in spinach; cook 30 minutes longer or until spinach is wilted. Top with cheese.

Sweet & Savory Slow-Cooked Beef

There's plenty of sweet and a little heat from the chipotle pepper in this family-friendly shredded beef. Add your favorite barbecue sauce or stir things up each time you make it by varying the flavor to see which way you like it best.

—DAVID KLEIMAN NEW BEDFORD, MA

PREP: 20 MIN. • **COOK:** 8 HOURS
MAKES: 16 SERVINGS

- 1 beef top round roast (4 pounds)
- 1 bottle (18 ounces) barbecue sauce
- ½ cup water
- ¼ cup packed brown sugar
- 1 chipotle pepper in adobo sauce, chopped
- 2 tablespoons Worcestershire sauce
- 2 tablespoons steak sauce
- 1½ teaspoons reduced-sodium soy sauce
- 1 teaspoon celery salt
- 1 teaspoon garlic salt
- 1 teaspoon seasoned salt
- 1 teaspoon pepper
- 16 onion rolls, split

1. Cut roast in half; place in a 6-qt. slow cooker. Combine the barbecue sauce, water, brown sugar, chipotle pepper, Worcestershire sauce, steak sauce, soy sauce and seasonings. Pour over meat.

2. Cover and cook on low for 8-10 hours or until meat is tender. Remove roast and cool slightly. Skim fat from cooking juices. Shred meat with two forks and return to slow cooker; heat through. Serve on rolls.

NOTE *Wear disposable gloves when cutting hot peppers; the oils can burn skin. Avoid touching your face.*

TANYA MACDONALD'S
HERBED CHICKEN & SPINACH SOUP

Vegetable Pork Soup

Packed with tender pork, veggies and savory flavor, this nutritious soup fills the house with a wonderful aroma as it cooks.

—**DEB HALL** HUNTINGTON, IN

PREP: 20 MIN. • **COOK:** 7 HOURS
MAKES: 6 SERVINGS (2 QUARTS)

- 1 **pork tenderloin (1 pound), cut into 1-inch pieces**
- 1 **teaspoon garlic powder**
- 2 **teaspoons canola oil**
- 1 **can (28 ounces) diced tomatoes**
- 4 **medium carrots, cut into ½-inch pieces**
- 2 **medium potatoes, cubed**
- 1 **can (12 ounces) light or nonalcoholic beer**
- ¼ **cup quick-cooking tapioca**
- 2 **bay leaves**
- 1 **tablespoon Worcestershire sauce**
- 1 **tablespoon honey**
- 1 **teaspoon dried thyme**
- ¼ **teaspoon salt**
- ¼ **teaspoon pepper**
- ⅛ **teaspoon ground nutmeg**

1. Sprinkle pork with garlic powder. In a large skillet, brown pork in oil; drain.

2. Transfer to a 4-qt. slow cooker. Add the remaining ingredients. Cover and cook on low for 7-8 hours or until meat is tender. Discard bay leaves.

TOP TIP

Store honey, tightly sealed, in a cool dry place for up to one year. Honey shouldn't be kept in the refrigerator because that only accelerates the crystallization process.

Navy Bean Dinner

This is one of my favorite recipes because the chili simmers all day in a slow cooker. When your hungry family calls for dinner, you can ladle out bowlfuls in a hurry.

—**LANA RUTLEDGE** SHEPHERDSVILLE, KY

PREP: 5 MIN. • **COOK:** 8 HOURS
MAKES: 12 SERVINGS (3 QUARTS)

- 2 **medium onions, chopped**
- 4 **garlic cloves, minced**
- 2 **quarts water**
- 3 **pounds chicken breasts or thighs, skin removed**
- 1 **pound dried navy beans**
- 2 **cans (4 ounces each) chopped green chilies**
- 1 **tablespoon ground cumin**
- 2 **teaspoons dried oregano**
- 1 **teaspoon salt, optional**
- ½ **to 1 teaspoon cayenne pepper**
- ½ **teaspoon ground cloves**
- 2 **chicken bouillon cubes**
  Shredded Monterey Jack cheese, optional
  Sour cream, optional
  Minced chives and crushed red pepper flakes

1. Place the onions and garlic in a 5-qt. slow cooker. Add the next 10 ingredients; do not stir. Cook on high for 8-10 hours.

2. Uncover and stir (the meat should fall off the bones). Remove bones. Stir to break up the meat. Spoon into bowls; top with cheese and sour cream if desired. Sprinkle with chives and red pepper flakes.

NAVY BEAN DINNER

ITALIAN PULLED PORK SANDWICHES

Italian Pulled Pork Sandwiches

Enjoy all the flavors of classic Italian sausage sandwiches with a healthier alternative that uses spicy and tender pulled pork instead.

—**DELLARIO LIA** MIDDLEPORT, NY

PREP: 20 MIN. • **COOK:** 8 HOURS
MAKES: 12 SERVINGS

- 1 tablespoon fennel seed, crushed
- 1 tablespoon steak seasoning
- 1 teaspoon cayenne pepper, optional
- 1 boneless pork shoulder butt roast (3 pounds)
- 1 tablespoon olive oil
- 2 medium green or sweet red peppers, thinly sliced
- 2 medium onions, thinly sliced
- 1 can (14½ ounces) diced tomatoes, undrained
- 12 whole wheat hamburger buns, split

1. In a small bowl, combine the fennel seed, steak seasoning and cayenne if desired. Cut roast in half. Rub seasoning mixture over pork. In a large skillet, brown roast in oil on all sides. Place in a 4- or 5-qt. slow cooker. Add the peppers, onions and tomatoes; cover and cook on low for 7-9 hours or until meat is tender.

2. Remove roast; cool slightly. Skim fat from cooking juices. Shred pork with two forks and return to slow cooker; heat through. Using a slotted spoon, place ½ cup meat mixture on each bun.

NOTE *This recipe was tested with McCormick's Montreal Steak Seasoning. Look for it in the spice aisle.*

Lentil Stew

This vegetarian stew is perfect when you want to take a break from meat. Adding the cream at the end gives it a smoother texture.

—**MICHELLE COLLINS** SUFFOLK, VA

PREP: 45 MIN. • **COOK:** 6 HOURS
MAKES: 8 SERVINGS (2¾ QUARTS)

- 2 large onions, thinly sliced, divided
- 2 tablespoons canola oil
- 2 tablespoons minced fresh gingerroot
- 3 garlic cloves, minced
- 8 plum tomatoes, chopped
- 2 teaspoons ground coriander
- 1½ teaspoons ground cumin
- ¼ teaspoon cayenne pepper
- 3 cups vegetable broth
- 2 cups water
- 2 cups dried lentils, rinsed
- 1 can (4 ounces) chopped green chilies
- ¾ cup heavy whipping cream
- 2 tablespoons butter
- 1 teaspoon cumin seeds
- 6 cups hot cooked basmati or jasmine rice
   Sliced green onions or minced fresh cilantro, optional

1. In a large skillet, saute half of the onions in oil until tender. Add ginger and garlic; saute for 1 minute. Add the tomatoes, coriander, cumin and cayenne; cook and stir 5 minutes longer.

2. In a 4- or 5-qt. slow cooker, combine the vegetable broth, water, lentils, green chilies, tomato mixture and remaining onion. Cover and cook on low for 6-8 hours or until lentils are tender.

3. Just before serving, stir cream into slow cooker. In a small skillet, heat butter over medium heat. Add cumin seeds; cook and stir for 1-2 minutes or until golden brown. Add to lentil mixture.

4. To serve, spoon over rice. Sprinkle with green onions or cilantro if desired.

Vegetarian Chili Ole!

I combine ingredients for this hearty chili the night before, start my trusty slow cooker in the morning and come home to a rich, spicy meal at night.

—MARJORIE AU HONOLULU, HI

PREP: 35 MIN. • **COOK:** 6 HOURS
MAKES: 7 SERVINGS

- 1 can (16 ounces) kidney beans, rinsed and drained
- 1 can (15 ounces) black beans, rinsed and drained
- 1 can (14½ ounces) diced tomatoes, undrained
- 1½ cups frozen corn
- 1 large onion, chopped
- 1 medium zucchini, chopped
- 1 medium sweet red pepper, chopped
- 1 can (4 ounces) chopped green chilies
- 1 ounce Mexican chocolate, chopped
- 1 cup water
- 1 can (6 ounces) tomato paste
- 1 tablespoon cornmeal
- 1 tablespoon chili powder
- ½ teaspoon salt
- ½ teaspoon dried oregano
- ½ teaspoon ground cumin
- ¼ teaspoon hot pepper sauce, optional
  Optional toppings: diced tomatoes, chopped green onions and crumbled queso fresco

1. In a 4-qt. slow cooker, combine first nine ingredients. Combine the water, tomato paste, cornmeal, chili powder, salt, oregano, cumin and pepper sauce if desired until smooth; stir into slow cooker. Cover and cook on low for 6-8 hours or until vegetables are tender.

2. Serve with toppings of your choice.

Gyro Soup

If you're a fan of lamb, don't pass up this Greek-style soup. Seasoned with classic flavors of rosemary, marjoram and mint, it will transport you straight to the Mediterranean!

—BRIDGET KLUSMAN OTSEGO, MI

PREP: 25 MIN. • **COOK:** 6 HOURS
MAKES: 6 SERVINGS

- 2 pounds ground lamb
- 5 cups water
- 1 can (14½ ounces) diced tomatoes, undrained
- 1 medium onion, chopped
- ¼ cup red wine
- 3 tablespoons minced fresh mint or 1 tablespoon dried mint
- 6 garlic cloves, minced
- 1 tablespoon dried marjoram
- 1 tablespoon dried rosemary, crushed
- 2 teaspoons salt
- ½ teaspoon pepper
  Optional toppings: plain Greek yogurt and crumbled feta cheese

1. In a large skillet, cook lamb until no longer pink; drain. Transfer to a 4- or 5-qt. slow cooker. Add the water, tomatoes, onion, wine, mint, garlic, marjoram, rosemary, salt and pepper. Cover and cook on low for 6-8 hours or until flavors are blended.

2. Serve with yogurt and feta cheese if desired.

VEGETARIAN CHILI OLE!

Mint Lamb Stew

The lamb here isn't just tender, it melts in your mouth! This recipe is an adaptation of a stew my mother used to make while I was growing up in England. Now I round it out with local root vegetables.

—**MAUREEN EVANS** RANCHO CUCAMONGA, CA

PREP: 40 MIN. • **COOK:** 7 HOURS
MAKES: 6 SERVINGS

- ½ cup all-purpose flour
- ½ teaspoon salt
- ¼ teaspoon pepper
- 1½ pounds lamb stew meat, cubed
- 2 shallots, sliced
- 2 tablespoons olive oil
- ½ cup red wine
- 2 cans (14½ ounces each) beef broth
- 2 medium potatoes, cubed
- 1 large sweet potato, peeled and cubed
- 2 large carrots, cut into 1-inch pieces
- 2 medium parsnips, peeled and cubed
- 1 garlic clove, minced
- 1 tablespoon mint jelly
- 4 bacon strips, cooked and crumbled

1. In a large resealable plastic bag, combine the flour, salt and pepper. Add the meat, a few pieces at a time, and shake to coat. In a large skillet, brown meat and shallots in oil in batches.

2. Transfer to a 5- or 6-qt. slow cooker. Add wine to the skillet, stirring to loosen browned bits from pan. Bring to a boil. Reduce heat; simmer, uncovered, for 1-2 minutes. Add to slow cooker.

3. Stir in the broth, potatoes, sweet potato, carrots, parsnips and garlic. Cover and cook on low for 7-9 hours or until meat is tender. Stir in jelly; sprinkle with bacon.

MOJITO PULLED PORK

Mojito Pulled Pork

This fork-tender pulled pork tastes fabulous in a bun, lettuce wrap or tortilla. My kids like to eat it spooned over rice in its citrus-flavored juices.

—**MINDY OSWALT** WINNETKA, CA

PREP: 20 MIN. • **COOK:** 7 HOURS
MAKES: 16 SERVINGS

- 1 boneless pork shoulder roast (4 to 5 pounds)
- 2 teaspoons salt
- 2 teaspoons dried oregano
- 2 teaspoons each ground cumin, paprika and pepper
- 1 bunch fresh cilantro, divided
- 2 medium onions, halved and sliced
- ¼ cup canned chopped green chilies
- 4 garlic cloves, minced
- 2 cans (14½ ounces each) reduced-sodium chicken broth
- ⅔ cup orange juice
- ½ cup lime juice
- 16 sandwich buns, split
  Barbecue sauce

1. Cut roast in half. Combine the salt, oregano, cumin, paprika and pepper; rub over pork. Place in a 4- or 5-qt. slow cooker.

2. Mince cilantro to measure ¼ cup; set aside. Trim remaining cilantro, discarding stems. Add the whole cilantro leaves, onions, chilies and garlic to the slow cooker. Combine the broth, orange juice and lime juice; pour over roast. Cover and cook on low for 7-9 hours or until meat is tender.

3. Remove roast; cool slightly. Skim fat from cooking juices; set aside 3 cups juices. Discard remaining juices. Shred pork with two forks and return to slow cooker. Stir in minced cilantro and reserved cooking juices; heat through. Spoon ½ cup meat onto each bun. Serve with barbecue sauce.

LISA MORIARTY'S CIOPPINO

Cioppino

If you're looking for a great seafood recipe to create in your slow cooker, this classic fish stew is just the ticket. It's full to the brim with clams, crab, fish and shrimp, and is fancy enough to be an elegant meal.
—**LISA MORIARTY** WILTON, NH

PREP: 20 MIN. • **COOK:** 4½ HOURS
MAKES: 8 SERVINGS (2½ QUARTS)

- 1 **can (28 ounces) diced tomatoes, undrained**
- 2 **medium onions, chopped**
- 3 **celery ribs, chopped**
- 1 **bottle (8 ounces) clam juice**
- 1 **can (6 ounces) tomato paste**
- ½ **cup white wine or vegetable broth**
- 5 **garlic cloves, minced**
- 1 **tablespoon red wine vinegar**
- 1 **tablespoon olive oil**
- 1 **to 2 teaspoons Italian seasoning**
- ½ **teaspoon sugar**
- 1 **bay leaf**
- 1 **pound haddock fillets, cut into 1-inch pieces**
- 1 **pound uncooked small shrimp, peeled and deveined**
- 1 **can (6 ounces) lump crabmeat, drained**
- 1 **can (6 ounces) chopped clams**
- 2 **tablespoons minced fresh parsley or 2 teaspoons dried parsley flakes**

In a 4- or 5-qt. slow cooker, combine the first 12 ingredients. Cover and cook on low for 4-5 hours. Stir in the haddock, shrimp, crabmeat and clams. Cover and cook 30 minutes longer or until fish flakes easily with a fork and shrimp turn pink. Stir in parsley. Discard bay leaf.

Coffee-Braised Pulled Pork Sandwiches

I love coffee with meat—it adds such a deep flavor, and leftovers make a great sandwich with pepper jack cheese and mayo. I also love that I can just assemble this before work, and by the time I get home, dinner is all ready!
—**JACQUELYNN SANDERS** BURNSVILLE, MN

PREP: 30 MIN. • **COOK:** 8 HOURS
MAKES: 10 SERVINGS

- 1 **boneless pork shoulder butt roast (3 to 3½ pounds)**
- ⅓ **cup ground coffee beans**
- ½ **teaspoon salt**
- ½ **teaspoon pepper**
- 2 **tablespoons canola oil**
- 2 **celery ribs, chopped**
- 1 **large carrot, chopped**
- 1 **medium onion, chopped**
- 2 **cups chicken stock**
- 1½ **cups strong brewed coffee**
- 2 **tablespoons minced fresh parsley**
- 1 **teaspoon coriander seeds**
- 1 **teaspoon ground cumin**
- 1 **teaspoon whole peppercorns, crushed**
- 1 **cinnamon stick (3 inches)**
- 1 **bay leaf**
- 10 **hoagie or kaiser buns, split**
- 10 **slices pepper jack cheese**

1. Cut roast into thirds. Combine the ground coffee, salt and pepper; rub over roast. In a large skillet, brown meat in oil on all sides; drain.

2. Transfer meat to a 5-qt. slow cooker. Add the celery, carrot, onion, chicken stock, brewed coffee, parsley, coriander seeds, cumin, peppercorns, cinnamon stick and bay leaf; pour over roast.

3. Cover and cook on low for 8-10 hours or until meat is tender. When cool enough to handle, shred meat. Skim fat from cooking juices. Strain cooking juices, discarding the vegetables, cinnamon stick and the bay leaf.

4. Spoon about ½ cup pork onto each bun; top with cheese. Serve with cooking juices.

COFFEE-BRAISED PULLED PORK SANDWICHES

Spring

DESSERTS

Who has time to make dessert? You do! After all, slow cookers aren't just for savory dishes anymore. Check out this colorful selection of sweet treats featuring the season's freshest berries, fruits and more!

SHERRY NIESE'S
RAISIN BREAD PUDDING

Raisin Bread Pudding

My sister gave me the recipe for this delicious bread pudding that's dotted with raisins. A homemade vanilla sauce goes together quickly on the stovetop and is yummy drizzled over warm servings of this old-fashioned-tasting treat.

—**SHERRY NIESE** MCCOMB, OH

PREP: 20 MIN. • **COOK:** 4 HOURS
MAKES: 6 SERVINGS

- 8 slices bread, cubed
- 4 eggs
- 2 cups milk
- ¼ cup sugar
- ¼ cup butter, melted
- ¼ cup raisins
- ½ teaspoon ground cinnamon

SAUCE
- 2 tablespoons butter
- 2 tablespoons all-purpose flour
- 1 cup water
- ¾ cup sugar
- 1 teaspoon vanilla extract

1. Place bread cubes in a greased 3-qt. slow cooker. In a large bowl, beat eggs and milk; stir in the sugar, butter, raisins and cinnamon. Pour over bread; stir.

2. Cover and cook on high for 1 hour. Reduce heat to low; cook for 3-4 hours or until a thermometer reads 160°.

3. For sauce, melt butter in a small saucepan. Stir in flour until smooth. Gradually add water, sugar and vanilla. Bring to a boil; cook and stir for 2 minutes or until thickened. Serve with warm bread pudding.

Butterscotch Apple Crisp

I give this classic dessert a rich twist with butterscotch pudding. The warm apple filling bubbles to perfection in a mini slow cooker.

—**JOLANTHE ERB** HARRISONBURG, VA

PREP: 10 MIN. • **COOK:** 2½ HOURS
MAKES: 3 SERVINGS

- 3 cups thinly sliced peeled tart apples (about 3 medium)
- ⅓ cup packed brown sugar
- ¼ cup all-purpose flour
- ¼ cup quick-cooking oats
- ⅓ cup cook-and-serve butterscotch pudding mix
- ½ teaspoon ground cinnamon
- ¼ cup cold butter, cubed
  Vanilla ice cream, optional

1. Place apples in a 1½-qt. slow cooker. In a small bowl, combine the brown sugar, flour, oats, pudding mix and cinnamon. Cut in butter until mixture resembles coarse crumbs. Sprinkle over apples.

2. Cover and cook on low for 2½ to 3½ hours or until apples are tender. Serve with ice cream if desired.

BANANAS FOSTER

Chocolate-Raspberry Fondue

You don't need a fancy fondue pot to make this melt-in-your-mouth concoction. I serve the dip in my small slow cooker. Folks of all ages love the chocolate-raspberry combination.
—**HEATHER MAXWELL** FORT RILEY, KS

START TO FINISH: 15 MIN.
MAKES: 5 CUPS

- 1 **package (14 ounces) caramels**
- 2 **cups (12 ounces) semisweet chocolate chips**
- 1 **can (12 ounces) evaporated milk**
- ½ **cup butter**
- ½ **cup seedless raspberry jam**
  Frozen pound cake, thawed
  Assorted fresh fruit

1. In a large saucepan, combine the first five ingredients. Cook over low heat until caramels, chips and butter are melted, about 15 minutes. Stir until smooth.
2. Transfer to a 1½-qt. slow cooker or fondue pot. Serve warm with pound cake or fruit.

Bananas Foster

The flavors of caramel, rum and walnut naturally complement fresh bananas in this classic dessert made easy!
—**CRYSTAL JO BRUNS** ILIFF, CO

PREP: 10 MIN. • **COOK:** 2 HOURS
MAKES: 5 SERVINGS

- 5 **medium firm bananas**
- 1 **cup packed brown sugar**
- ¼ **cup butter, melted**
- ¼ **cup rum**
- 1 **teaspoon vanilla extract**
- ½ **teaspoon ground cinnamon**
- ⅓ **cup chopped walnuts**
- ⅓ **cup flaked coconut**
  Vanilla ice cream or sliced pound cake

1. Cut bananas in half lengthwise, then widthwise; layer in the bottom of a 1½-qt. slow cooker. Combine the brown sugar, butter, rum, vanilla and cinnamon; pour over bananas. Cover and cook on low for 1½ hours or until heated through.
2. Sprinkle with walnuts and coconut; cook 30 minutes longer. Serve with ice cream or pound cake.

CHOCOLATE-RASPBERRY FONDUE

ELVIS' PUDDING CAKE

Chocolate Malt Pudding Cake

When I make this warm, comforting cake, I chop the malted milk balls by putting them in a plastic bag and pounding it with a rubber mallet. It completely eliminates the mess.

—**SARAH SKUBINNA** CASCADE, MT

PREP: 25 MIN. • **COOK:** 2 HOURS + STANDING
MAKES: 8 SERVINGS

- ½ **cup 2% milk**
- 2 **tablespoons canola oil**
- ½ **teaspoon almond extract**
- 1 **cup all-purpose flour**
- ½ **cup packed brown sugar**
- 2 **tablespoons baking cocoa**
- 1½ **teaspoons baking powder**
- ½ **cup coarsely chopped malted milk balls**
- ½ **cup semisweet chocolate chips**
- ¾ **cup sugar**
- ¼ **cup malted milk powder**
- 1¼ **cups boiling water**
- 4 **ounces cream cheese, softened and cubed**
  Vanilla ice cream and sliced almonds

1. In a large bowl, combine milk, oil and extract. Combine flour, brown sugar, cocoa and baking powder; gradually beat into milk mixture until blended. Stir in malted milk balls and chocolate chips.
2. Spoon into a greased 3-qt. slow cooker. In a small bowl, combine sugar and milk powder; stir in water and cream cheese. Pour over batter (do not stir).
3. Cover and cook on high for 2-3 hours or until a toothpick inserted in center of cake comes out clean. Turn off heat. Let stand 15 minutes. Serve warm with ice cream; sprinkle with almonds.

I love the flavors of peanut butter and banana together, and this slow cooker pudding cake is just like eating an Elvis sandwich...only sweeter! Banana chips add a surprisingly crunchy texture—find them near the dried fruit in your grocery store.

—**LISA RENSHAW** KANSAS CITY, MO

Elvis' Pudding Cake

PREP: 10 MIN.
COOK: 3 HOURS + STANDING
MAKES: 12 SERVINGS

- 3 **cups cold 2% milk**
- 1 **package (3.4 ounces) instant banana cream pudding mix**
- 1 **package banana cake mix (regular size)**
- ½ **cup creamy peanut butter**
- 2 **cups peanut butter chips**
- 1 **cup chopped dried banana chips**

1. In a small bowl, whisk milk and pudding mix for 2 minutes. Let stand for 2 minutes or until soft-set. Transfer to a greased 5-qt. slow cooker.
2. Prepare cake mix batter according to package directions, adding peanut butter before mixing. Pour over pudding. Cover and cook on low for 3 to 3½ hours or until a toothpick inserted near the center comes out with moist crumbs.
3. Sprinkle with peanut butter chips; cover and let stand for 15-20 minutes or until partially melted. Top with banana chips.

##

⑤ INGREDIENTS

Chunky Applesauce

My mother gave me the recipe for this cinnamony apple delight that fills the house with a wonderful aroma.

—**LISA ROESSNER** FORT RECOVERY, OH

PREP: 5 MIN. • **COOK:** 6 HOURS
MAKES: 5 CUPS

- 8 to 10 large tart apples, peeled and cut into chunks
  Sugar substitute equivalent to ½ to 1 cup sugar
- ½ cup water
- 1 teaspoon ground cinnamon

Combine apples, sugar, water and cinnamon in a 3-qt. slow cooker; stir gently. Cover and cook on low for 6-8 hours or until apples are tender.

BUTTERSCOTCH DIP

Rice Pudding

For an old-fashioned sweet treat just like Grandma used to make, try my rich and delicious pudding dessert.

—**JENNIFER BENNETT** SALEM, IN

PREP: 15 MIN. • **COOK:** 3 HOURS + CHILLING
MAKES: 4 SERVINGS

RICE PUDDING

- 1¼ cups 2% milk
- ½ cup sugar
- ½ cup uncooked converted rice
- ½ cup raisins
- 2 eggs, lightly beaten
- 1 teaspoon ground cinnamon
- 1 teaspoon butter, melted
- 1 teaspoon vanilla extract
- ¾ teaspoon lemon extract
- 1 cup heavy whipping cream, whipped
  Additional whipped cream and ground cinnamon, optional

1. In a 1½-qt. slow cooker, combine the first nine ingredients. Cover and cook on low for 2 hours; stir. Cover and cook 1-2 hours longer or until rice is tender. Transfer to a small bowl; cool. Refrigerate until chilled.
2. Just before serving, fold in whipped cream. If desired, garnish with additional whipped cream and cinnamon.

⑤ INGREDIENTS

Butterscotch Dip

If you like butterscotch, you'll enjoy this warm rum-flavored fruit dip.

—**JEAUNE HADL VAN METER** LEXINGTON, KY

PREP: 5 MIN. • **COOK:** 45 MIN.
MAKES: ABOUT 3 CUPS

- 2 packages (10 to 11 ounces each) butterscotch chips
- ⅔ cup evaporated milk
- ⅔ cup chopped pecans
- 1 tablespoon rum extract
  Apple and pear wedges

In a 1½-qt. slow cooker, combine butterscotch chips and milk. Cover and cook on low for 45-50 minutes or until chips are softened; stir until smooth. Stir in pecans and extract. Serve warm with fruit.

GRANOLA APPLE CRISP

Chocolate Bread Pudding

I love chocolate and I love berries, so I was thrilled to come across a slow-cooker recipe that combines the two. I like to use egg bread when making this rich dessert.

—**BECKY FOSTER** UNION, OR

PREP: 10 MIN. • **COOK:** 2¼ HOURS
MAKES: 6-8 SERVINGS

- 6 cups cubed day-old bread (¾-inch cubes)
- 1½ cups semisweet chocolate chips
- 1 cup fresh raspberries
- 4 eggs
- ½ cup heavy whipping cream
- ½ cup milk
- ¼ cup sugar
- 1 teaspoon vanilla extract
  Whipped cream and additional raspberries, optional

1. In a greased 3-qt. slow cooker, layer half of the bread cubes, chocolate chips and raspberries. Repeat layers. In a bowl, whisk the eggs, cream, milk, sugar and vanilla. Pour over bread mixture.

2. Cover and cook on high for 2¼ to 2½ hours or until a thermometer reads 160°. Let stand for 5-10 minutes. Serve with whipped cream and additional raspberries if desired.

Granola Apple Crisp

Tender apple slices are tucked beneath a sweet crunchy topping in my comforting dessert. For variety, replace the apples with your favorite fruit.

—**BARBARA SCHINDLER** NAPOLEON, OH

PREP: 20 MIN. • **COOK:** 5 HOURS
MAKES: 6-8 SERVINGS

- 8 medium tart apples, peeled and sliced
- ¼ cup lemon juice
- 1½ teaspoons grated lemon peel
- 2½ cups granola with fruit and nuts
- 1 cup sugar
- 1 teaspoon ground cinnamon
- ½ cup butter, melted

1. In a large bowl, toss the apples, lemon juice and peel. Transfer to a greased 3-qt. slow cooker. Combine the granola, sugar and cinnamon; sprinkle over apples. Drizzle with the butter.

2. Cover and cook on low for 5-6 hours or until the apples are tender. Serve warm.

CHOCOLATE BREAD PUDDING

PINK GRAPEFRUIT CHEESECAKE

Pink Grapefruit Cheesecake

Cheesecake from a slow cooker? It's true! I experimented a few times to turn this iconic dessert into a slow-cooker classic! Give it a try. You'll be amazed at the delightful results!

—**KRISTA LANPHIER** MILWAUKEE, WI

PREP: 20 MIN. • **COOK:** 2 HOURS + CHILLING
MAKES: 6 SERVINGS

- ¾ cup graham cracker crumbs
- 1 tablespoon plus ⅔ cup sugar, divided
- 1 teaspoon grated grapefruit peel
- ¼ teaspoon ground ginger
- 2½ tablespoons butter, melted
- 2 packages (8 ounces each) cream cheese, softened
- ½ cup sour cream
- 2 tablespoons pink grapefruit juice
- 2 eggs, lightly beaten

1. Place a greased 6-in. springform pan on a double thickness of heavy-duty foil (about 12 in. square). Wrap foil securely around pan. Pour 1 in. of water in a 6-qt. slow cooker. Layer two 24-in. pieces of aluminum foil. Starting with a long side, fold up foil to create a 1-in.-wide strip; roll into a coil. Place in slow cooker to form a rack for the cheesecake.

2. In a small bowl, mix cracker crumbs, 1 tablespoon sugar, peel and ginger; stir in butter. Press onto bottom and about 1 in. up sides of prepared pan.

3. In a large bowl, beat cream cheese and remaining sugar until smooth. Beat in sour cream and grapefruit juice. Add eggs and beat on low speed just until combined.

4. Pour into crust. Place springform pan on top of coil. Cover slow cooker with a double layer of paper towels; place lid securely over towels. Cook, covered, on high 2 hours. Do not remove lid; turn off slow cooker and let cheesecake stand, covered, in slow cooker 1 hour. Center of cheesecake will be just set and top will appear dull.

5. Remove springform pan from slow cooker; remove foil from pan. Cool cheesecake on a wire rack 1 hour. Loosen sides from pan with a knife. Refrigerate overnight, covering when completely cooled. Remove rim from the pan.

Pear-Blueberry Granola

Oatmeal fans will love this dish! It is a delicious dessert when served with vanilla ice cream, but the pears, blueberries and granola make it a beautiful breakfast or brunch item as well.

—**LISA WORKMAN** BOONES MILL, VA

PREP: 15 MIN. • **COOK:** 3 HOURS
MAKES: 10 SERVINGS

- 5 medium pears, peeled and thinly sliced
- 2 cups fresh or frozen unsweetened blueberries
- ½ cup packed brown sugar
- ⅓ cup apple cider or unsweetend apple juice
- 1 tablespoon all-purpose flour
- 1 tablespoon lemon juice
- 2 teaspoons ground cinnamon
- 2 tablespoons butter
- 3 cups granola without raisins

In a 4-qt. slow cooker, combine the first seven ingredients. Dot with butter. Sprinkle granola over top. Cover and cook on low for 3-4 hours or until fruit is tender.

CHERRY COLA CHOCOLATE CAKE

Cherry Cola Chocolate Cake

For a truly different chocolate cake, think outside the box...and inside the slow cooker! This easy dessert comes out warm, moist, fudgy and wonderful. And it won't heat up your kitchen.
—ELAINE SWEET DALLAS, TX

PREP: 30 MIN. + STANDING
COOK: 2 HOURS + STANDING
MAKES: 8 SERVINGS

- ½ cup cola
- ½ cup dried tart cherries
- 1½ cups all-purpose flour
- ½ cup sugar
- 2 ounces semisweet chocolate, chopped
- 2½ teaspoons baking powder
- ½ teaspoon salt
- 1 cup chocolate milk
- ½ cup butter, melted
- 2 teaspoons vanilla extract
TOPPING
- 1¼ cups cola

- ½ cup sugar
- ½ cup packed brown sugar
- 2 ounces semisweet chocolate, chopped
- ¼ cup dark rum
  Vanilla ice cream and maraschino cherries, optional

1. In a small saucepan, bring cola and dried cherries to a boil. Remove from the heat; let stand for 30 minutes.
2. In a large bowl, combine the flour, sugar, chocolate, baking powder and salt. Combine the chocolate milk, butter and vanilla; stir into dry ingredients just until moistened. Fold in cherry mixture. Pour into a 3-qt. slow cooker coated with cooking spray.
3. For topping, in a small saucepan, combine the cola, sugar and brown sugar. Cook and stir until sugar is dissolved. Remove from the heat; stir in chocolate and rum until smooth. Pour over batter; do not stir.

4. Cover and cook on high for 2 to 2½ hours or until set. Turn off heat; let stand, covered, for 30 minutes. Serve warm with ice cream and maraschino cherries if desired.
NOTE *This recipe does not use eggs.*

Tropical Compote Dessert

To make a more adult version of this recipe, use brandy instead of the extra tropical fruit juice.
—TASTE OF HOME TEST KITCHEN

PREP: 15 MIN. • **COOK:** 2¼ HOURS
MAKES: 6 SERVINGS

- 1 jar (23½ ounces) mixed tropical fruit
- 1 jalapeno pepper, seeded and chopped
- ¼ cup sugar
- 1 tablespoon chopped crystallized ginger
- ¼ teaspoon ground cinnamon
- 1 can (15 ounces) mandarin oranges, drained
- 1 jar (6 ounces) maraschino cherries, drained
- 1 medium firm banana, sliced
- 6 individual round sponge cakes
- 6 tablespoons flaked coconut, toasted

1. Drain tropical fruit, reserving ¼ cup liquid. Combine tropical fruit and jalapeno in a 1½-qt. slow cooker. Combine the sugar, ginger, cinnamon and reserved juice; pour over fruit. Cover and cook on low for 2 hours. Stir in the mandarin oranges, cherries and banana; cook 15 minutes longer.
2. Place sponge cakes on dessert plates; top with compote. Sprinkle with coconut.
NOTE *Wear disposable gloves when cutting hot peppers; the oils can burn skin. Avoid touching your face.*

TROPICAL COMPOTE DESSERT

ESTELLA PETERSON'S
PEPPERONI PIZZA SOUP
page 141

APPETIZERS & BEVERAGES 88
SIDE DISHES 98
ENTREES 110
SOUPS & SANDWICHES 138
DESSERTS 152

Summer

Keep the kitchen cool and family meals hot with this warm-weather selection of slow-cooked favorites. Whether you're going to a block party, entertaining in the backyard or just whipping up a weeknight dinner, these summertime recipes promise to spice up every menu!

Summer

APPETIZERS & BEVERAGES

Summer brings with it friendly barbecues, tailgates, church picnics and neighborhood parties. Thanks to these slow-cooked snacks, you can enjoy these get-togethers without much effort!

1. In a 3-qt. slow cooker, combine the cheeses, mayonnaise, mushrooms, olives, pepperoni and onion.
2. Cover and cook on low 1½ hours; stir. Cover and cook 1 hour longer or until heated through. Serve with assorted crackers.

Mocha Mint Coffee

This dressed-up coffee benefits from subtle hints of mint, cocoa and cinnamon. The marshmallows on top are a playful addition and bring out the youngster in everyone!

—**MINDIE HILTON** SUSANVILLE, CA

PREP: 10 MIN. • **COOK:** 2 HOURS
MAKES: 8 SERVINGS

- 6 **cups hot brewed coffee**
- 2 **packets instant hot cocoa mix**
- ½ **cup dulce de leche**
- ¼ **cup peppermint crunch baking chips or mint chocolate chips**
- 4 **teaspoons sugar**
- 1 **cup miniature marshmallows**
- ½ **teaspoon ground cinnamon**

1. In a 3-qt. slow cooker, combine the coffee, hot cocoa mix, dulce de leche, baking chips and sugar. Cover and cook on low for 2-3 hours or until hot.
2. Ladle into mugs. Top with the marshmallows; sprinkle with cinnamon.
NOTE *This recipe was tested with Nestle La Lechera dulce de leche; look for it in the international foods section. If using Eagle Brand dulce de leche (caramel flavored sauce), thicken according to package directions before using.*

LISA FRANCIS'
PEPPERONI PIZZA DIP

Pepperoni Pizza Dip

This dip is so easy to make and transport. You won't have to keep it warm long, because it'll be gone in a flash. It's a great appetizer for a backyard barbecue or any party.

—**LISA FRANCIS** ELBA, AL

PREP: 20 MIN. • **COOK:** 2½ HOURS
MAKES: 5 CUPS

- 4 **cups (16 ounces) shredded cheddar cheese**
- 4 **cups (16 ounces) shredded part-skim mozzarella cheese**
- 1 **cup mayonnaise**
- 1 **jar (6 ounces) sliced mushrooms, drained**
- 2 **cans (2¼ ounces each) sliced ripe olives, drained**
- 1 **package (3½ ounces) pepperoni slices, quartered**
- 1 **tablespoon dried minced onion**
  Assorted crackers

SUNNY AMBROSIA PUNCH

Green Olive Dip

Olive fans will love this dip. It's cheesy and full of beef and beans. I like to use it as a festive filling for taco shells, too.

—**BETH DUNAHAY** LIMA, OH

PREP: 30 MIN. • **COOK:** 3 HOURS
MAKES: 8 CUPS

- 1 **pound ground beef**
- 1 **medium sweet red pepper, chopped**
- 1 **small onion, chopped**
- 1 **can (16 ounces) refried beans**
- 1 **jar (16 ounces) mild salsa**
- 2 **cups (8 ounces) shredded part-skim mozzarella cheese**
- 2 **cups (8 ounces) shredded cheddar cheese**
- 1 **jar (5¾ ounces) sliced green olives with pimientos, drained Tortilla chips**

1. In a large skillet, cook the beef, pepper and onion over medium heat until meat is no longer pink; drain.
2. Transfer to a greased 3-qt. slow cooker. Add the beans, salsa, cheeses and olives. Cover and cook on low for 3-4 hours or until cheese is melted, stirring occasionally. Serve with chips.

GREEN OLIVE DIP

Sunny Ambrosia Punch

I love this unique twist on cider punch because it was inspired by the spices in chai. It's so easy to make, and everyone seems wonderfully surprised by the summery apricot and peach twist.

—**AYSHA SCHURMAN** AMMON, ID

PREP: 15 MIN. • **COOK:** 3 HOURS
MAKES: 10 SERVINGS (¾ CUP EACH)

- 3½ **cups apple cider or juice**
- 3 **cups apricot nectar**
- 1 **cup peach nectar or additional apricot nectar**
- ¼ **cup water**
- 3 **tablespoons lemon juice**
- ½ **teaspoon ground cardamom**
- ½ **teaspoon ground nutmeg**
- 2 **cinnamon sticks (3 inches)**
- 1 **teaspoon finely chopped fresh gingerroot**
- 1 **teaspoon grated orange peel**
- 8 **whole cloves**
  Lemon or orange slices, optional

1. In a 3- or 4-qt. slow cooker, combine the first seven ingredients. Place cinnamon sticks, ginger, orange peel and cloves on a double thickness of cheesecloth. Gather corners of cloth to enclose seasonings; tie securely with string. Place bag in slow cooker.
2. Cook, covered, on low 3-4 hours or until heated through. Remove and discard spice bag. Serve warm, with lemon slices, if desired.

HOT CHILI DIP

(5) INGREDIENTS Hot Chili Dip

I first made this dip for my husband's birthday party. So many of our guests asked for the yummy recipe that I actually photocopied it to share with them all.

—NIKKI ROSATI FRANKSVILLE, WI

PREP: 5 MIN. • **COOK:** 1 HOUR
MAKES: ABOUT 2 CUPS

- 1 jar (24 ounces) salsa
- 1 can (15 ounces) chili with beans
- 2 cans (2¼ ounces each) sliced ripe olives, drained
- 12 ounces process cheese (Velveeta), cubed
  Tortilla chips

In a 1½-qt. slow cooker, combine the salsa, chili and olives. Stir in cheese. Cover and cook on low for 1-2 hours or until cheese is melted, stirring halfway through. Serve with chips.

Loaded Veggie Dip

Packed with veggies and bursting with flavor, this chunky appetizer will be a hit at your next get-together. Serve it with a thick cracker that can be used as a scoop.

—PATRICE SLAUGHTER PALM BAY, FL

PREP: 1 HOUR • **COOK:** 1 HOUR
MAKES: 5 CUPS

- ¾ cup finely chopped fresh broccoli
- ½ cup finely chopped cauliflower
- ½ cup finely chopped fresh carrot
- ½ cup finely chopped red onion
- ½ cup finely chopped celery
- 2 garlic cloves, minced
- 4 tablespoons olive oil, divided
- 1 can (14 ounces) water-packed artichoke hearts, rinsed, drained and chopped
- 1 package (6½ ounces) spreadable garlic and herb cream cheese
- 1 package (1.4 ounces) vegetable recipe mix (Knorr)
- 1 teaspoon garlic powder
- ½ teaspoon white pepper
- ⅛ to ¼ teaspoon cayenne pepper
- ¼ cup vegetable broth
- ¼ cup half-and-half cream
- 3 cups (12 ounces) shredded Italian cheese blend
- ½ cup minced fresh basil
- 1 package (9 ounces) fresh spinach, finely chopped
  Assorted crackers or baked pita chips

1. In a large skillet, saute the broccoli, cauliflower, carrot, onion, celery and garlic in 2 tablespoons oil until tender. Stir in the artichokes, cream cheese, vegetable recipe mix, garlic powder, white pepper and cayenne; set aside.
2. In a 3-qt. slow cooker, combine the broth, cream and remaining oil. Stir in the broccoli mixture, Italian cheese blend and basil. Fold in spinach. Cover and cook on low for 1-2 hours or until cheese is melted and spinach is tender. Serve with crackers.

TOP TIP

When purchasing fresh cauliflower, look for a head with compact florets that are free of yellow or brown spots. The leaves should be crisp and green, not withered or discolored. Tightly wrap an unwashed head of cauliflower and refrigerate for up to 5 days. Before using, wash and remove the leaves at the base and trim the stem.

Makeover Creamy Artichoke Dip

Folks are sure to gather around this ooey-gooey treat whenever it's placed on the buffet table. It's a lightened-up take on a treasured family favorite.

—MARY SPENCER GREENDALE, WI

PREP: 20 MIN. • **COOK:** 1 HOUR
MAKES: 5 CUPS

- 2 cans (14 ounces each) water-packed artichoke hearts, rinsed, drained and coarsely chopped
- 1 package (8 ounces) reduced-fat cream cheese, cubed
- ¾ cup (6 ounces) plain yogurt
- 1 cup (4 ounces) shredded part-skim mozzarella cheese
- 1 cup reduced-fat ricotta cheese
- ¾ cup shredded Parmesan cheese, divided
- ½ cup shredded reduced-fat Swiss cheese
- ¼ cup reduced-fat mayonnaise
- 2 tablespoons lemon juice
- 1 tablespoon chopped seeded jalapeno pepper
- 1 teaspoon garlic powder
- 1 teaspoon seasoned salt
  Tortilla chips

1. In a 3-qt. slow cooker, combine the artichokes, cream cheese, yogurt, mozzarella cheese, ricotta cheese, ½ cup Parmesan cheese, Swiss cheese, mayonnaise, lemon juice, jalapeno, garlic powder and seasoned salt. Cover and cook on low for 1 hour or until heated through.

2. Sprinkle with remaining Parmesan cheese. Serve with tortilla chips.

NOTE *Wear disposable gloves when cutting hot peppers; the oils can burn skin. Avoid touching your face.*

Moist & Tender Wings

These no-fuss wings are fall-off-the-bone tender. Chili sauce offers a bit of spice, while molasses lends a hint of sweetness. Serve them with a side of rice or a green salad, and you've got a meal!

—SHARON MORCILIO JOSHUA TREE, CA

PREP: 15 MIN. • **COOK:** 8 HOURS
MAKES: ABOUT 4 DOZEN

MOIST & TENDER WINGS

- 5 pounds chicken wings (about 25 wings)
- 1 bottle (12 ounces) chili sauce
- ¼ cup lemon juice
- ¼ cup molasses
- 2 tablespoons Worcestershire sauce
- 6 garlic cloves, minced
- 1 tablespoon chili powder
- 1 tablespoon salsa
- 1 teaspoon garlic salt
- 3 drops hot pepper sauce

1. Cut chicken wings into three sections; discard wing tips. Place the wings in a 5-qt. slow cooker.

2. In a small bowl, combine the remaining ingredients; pour over chicken. Stir to coat. Cover and cook on low for 6-8 hours or until chicken is tender.

NOTE *Uncooked chicken wing sections (wingettes) may be substituted for whole chicken wings.*

MAKEOVER CREAMY ARTICHOKE DIP

SUSAN D'AMORE'S
SLOW-COOKED CRAB DIP

Slow-Cooked Crab Dip

Slow-cooked appetizers are ideal for entertaining because they free up your oven. Leftover dips are also great served over baked potatoes the next day.

—**SUSAN D'AMORE** WEST CHESTER, PA

PREP: 20 MIN. • **COOK:** 2 HOURS
MAKES: 2⅓ CUPS

- 1 **package (8 ounces) cream cheese, softened**
- 2 **green onions, chopped**
- ¼ **cup chopped sweet red pepper**
- 2 **tablespoons minced fresh parsley**
- 2 **tablespoons mayonnaise**
- 1 **tablespoon Dijon mustard**
- 1 **teaspoon Worcestershire sauce**
- ¼ **teaspoon salt**
- ¼ **teaspoon pepper**
- 2 **cans (6 ounces each) lump crabmeat, drained**
- 2 **tablespoons capers, drained**
    Dash hot pepper sauce
    Assorted crackers

1. In a 1½-qt. slow cooker, combine the first nine ingredients; stir in crab.
2. Cover and cook on low for 1-2 hours. Stir in capers and pepper sauce; cook 30 minutes longer to allow the flavors to blend. Serve with crackers.

Sweet & Spicy Peanuts

With a caramel-like coating, these crunchy peanuts have a touch of heat from the hot sauce. They make a tasty snack any time of day.

—*TASTE OF HOME* TEST KITCHEN

PREP: 10 MIN. • **COOK:** 1½ HOURS + COOLING
MAKES: 4 CUPS

- 3 **cups salted peanuts**
- ½ **cup sugar**
- ⅓ **cup packed brown sugar**
- 2 **tablespoons hot water**

SWEET & SPICY PEANUTS

- 2 **tablespoons butter, melted**
- 1 **tablespoon Sriracha Asian hot chili sauce or hot pepper sauce**
- 1 **teaspoon chili powder**

1. Place peanuts in a greased 1½-qt. slow cooker. In a small bowl, combine the sugars, water, butter, hot sauce and chili powder. Pour over peanuts. Cover and cook on high for 1½ hours, stirring once.
2. Spread on waxed paper to cool. Store in an airtight container.

Sweet Kahlua Coffee

Here's a fun way to dress up your morning coffee! Or simmer up a batch for an after-dinner treat when friends visit.

—**RUTH GRUCHOW** YORBA LINDA, CA

PREP: 10 MIN. • **COOK:** 3 HOURS
MAKES: 8 SERVINGS (2¼ QUARTS)

- 2 **quarts hot water**
- ½ **cup Kahlua (coffee liqueur)**
- ¼ **cup creme de cacao**
- 3 **tablespoons instant coffee granules**
- 2 **cups heavy whipping cream**
- ¼ **cup sugar**
- 1 **teaspoon vanilla extract**
- 2 **tablespoons grated semisweet chocolate**

1. In a 4-qt. slow cooker, mix water, Kahlua, creme de cacao and coffee granules. Cook, covered, on low 3-4 hours or until heated through.
2. In a large bowl, beat cream until it begins to thicken. Add sugar and vanilla; beat until soft peaks form. Serve warm coffee with whipped cream and chocolate.

CHAI TEA

water to a 5- or 6-qt. slow cooker. Cover and cook on low for 8 hours.

2. Add tea bags; cover and steep for 3-5 minutes. Discard tea bags and spice bag. Stir in milk; heat through. Serve warm.

(5) INGREDIENTS

Slow Cooker Cheese Dip

I brought this slightly spicy cheese dip to a gathering with friends, and it was a huge hit! The pork sausage provides the zip.

—**MARION BARTONE** CONNEAUT, OH

PREP: 15 MIN. • **COOK:** 4 HOURS
MAKES: 2 QUARTS

- 1 **pound ground beef**
- ½ **pound bulk spicy pork sausage**
- 2 **pounds process cheese (Velveeta), cubed**
- 2 **cans (10 ounces each) diced tomatoes and green chilies Tortilla chips**

1. In a large skillet, cook beef and sausage over medium heat until no longer pink; drain. Transfer to a 3- or 4-qt. slow cooker. Stir in cheese and tomatoes.

2. Cover and cook on low for 4-5 hours or until cheese is melted, stirring occasionally. Serve with tortilla chips.

NOTE *If you're planning on serving Slow Cooker Cheese Dip at a party or family get-together, make it ahead and freeze it. Than all you need to do is thaw and reheat it.*

Chai Tea

A wonderfully sweet and spicy aroma wafts from the slow cooker as this pleasantly flavored chai tea simmers.

—**CRYSTAL JO BRUNS** ILIFF, CO

PREP: 20 MIN. • **COOK:** 8 HOURS
MAKES: 12 SERVINGS (3 QUARTS)

- 3½ **ounces fresh gingerroot, peeled and thinly sliced**
- 25 **whole cloves**
- 15 **cardamom pods, crushed**
- 3 **cinnamon sticks (3 inches)**
- 3 **whole peppercorns**
- 3½ **quarts water**
- 8 **individual black tea bags**
- 1 **can (14 ounces) sweetened condensed milk**

1. Place the ginger, cloves, cardamom, cinnamon sticks and peppercorns on a double thickness of cheesecloth; bring up corners of cloth and tie with string to form a bag. Add spice bag and

SLOW COOKER CHEESE DIP

CHEESE-TRIO ARTICHOKE & SPINACH DIP

Slow Cooker Party Mix

A nicely seasoned snack mix is always a party standard. For variety, try substituting cashews for the peanuts in this recipe. It's great any time of year!

—**DANA HUGHES** GRESHAM, OR

PREP: 5 MIN. • **COOK:** 1 HOUR
MAKES: ABOUT 3 QUARTS

- 4 cups Wheat Chex
- 4 cups Cheerios
- 3 cups pretzel sticks
- 1 can (12 ounces) salted peanuts
- ¼ cup butter, melted
- 2 to 3 tablespoons grated Parmesan cheese
- 1 teaspoon celery salt
- ½ to ¾ teaspoon seasoned salt

In a 5-qt. slow cooker, combine cereals, pretzels and peanuts. Combine the butter, cheese, celery salt and seasoned salt; drizzle over cereal mixture and mix well. Cover and cook on low for 1 to 1½ hours, stirring every 20 minutes. Serve warm or at room temperature.

Cheese-Trio Artichoke & Spinach Dip

No spread of appetizers is complete without at least one amazing dip, and this slow-cooked specialty is it! Creamy, cheesy and chock-full of veggies, it will quickly become your new go-to favorite.

—**DIANE SPEARE** KISSIMMEE, FL

PREP: 20 MIN. • **COOK:** 2 HOURS
MAKES: 4 CUPS

- 1 cup chopped fresh mushrooms
- 1 tablespoon butter
- 2 garlic cloves, minced
- 1½ cups mayonnaise
- 1 package (8 ounces) cream cheese, softened
- 1 cup plus 2 tablespoons grated Parmesan cheese, divided
- 1 cup (4 ounces) shredded part-skim mozzarella cheese, divided
- 1 can (14 ounces) water-packed artichoke hearts, rinsed, drained and chopped
- 1 package (10 ounces) frozen chopped spinach, thawed and squeezed dry
- ¼ cup chopped sweet red pepper
  Toasted French bread baguette slices

1. In a large skillet, saute mushrooms in butter until tender. Add garlic; cook 1 minute longer.

2. In a large bowl, combine the mayonnaise, cream cheese, 1 cup of Parmesan cheese and ¾ cup mozzarella cheese. Add the mushroom mixture, artichokes, spinach and red pepper.

3. Transfer to a 3-qt slow cooker. Sprinkle with remaining cheeses. Cover and cook on low for 2-3 hours or until heated through. Serve with baguette slices.

SLOW COOKER PARTY MIX

SLOW-COOKED SALSA

cover and process until blended. Refrigerate leftovers.

NOTE *Wear disposable gloves when cutting hot peppers; the oils can burn skin. Avoid touching your face.*

Hawaiian Kielbasa

Savory sausage teams up with juicy, tangy pineapple for a winning combination that you can prep in a flash. The sweet barbecue-style sauce makes a tasty way to tie the two together.

—LOUISE KLINE CARROLLTOWN, PA

PREP: 15 MIN. • **COOK:** 3 HOURS
MAKES: 12 SERVINGS

- 2 **pounds smoked kielbasa or Polish sausage, cut into 1-inch pieces**
- 1 **can (20 ounces) unsweetened pineapple chunks, undrained**
- ½ **cup ketchup**
- 2 **tablespoons brown sugar**
- 2 **tablespoons yellow mustard**
- 1 **tablespoon cider vinegar**
- ¾ **cup lemon-lime soda**
- 2 **tablespoons cornstarch**
- 2 **tablespoons cold water**

1. Place sausage in a 3- or 4-qt. slow cooker. Drain pineapple, reserving ¾ cup juice; set pineapple aside. In a small bowl, whisk the ketchup, brown sugar, mustard and vinegar. Stir in soda and reserved pineapple juice. Pour over sausage; stir to coat. Cover and cook on low for 2-3 hours or until heated through.

2. Stir in pineapple. In a small bowl, combine cornstarch and water until smooth. Stir into slow cooker. Cover and cook 30 minutes longer or until sauce is thickened. Serve with toothpicks.

(5) INGREDIENTS

Slow-Cooked Salsa

I love the fresh taste of homemade salsa, but as a working mother, I don't have much time to make it. So I came up with this slow-cooked version that practically makes itself!

—TONI MENARD LOMPOC, CA

PREP: 15 MIN. • **COOK:** 2½ HOURS + COOLING
MAKES: ABOUT 2 CUPS

- 10 **plum tomatoes**
- 2 **garlic cloves**
- 1 **small onion, cut into wedges**
- 2 **jalapeno peppers**
- ¼ **cup cilantro leaves**
- ½ **teaspoon salt, optional**

1. Core tomatoes. Cut a small slit in two tomatoes; insert a garlic clove into each slit. Place tomatoes and onion in a 3-qt. slow cooker.

2. Cut stems off jalapenos; remove seeds if a milder salsa is desired. Place jalapenos in the slow cooker.

3. Cover and cook on high for 2½ to 3 hours or until vegetables are softened (some may brown slightly); cool.

4. In a blender, combine the tomato mixture, cilantro and salt if desired;

Tomato Fondue

Both the young and young at heart will gobble up this cheesy tomato fondue when served alongside hot dogs and bread cubes.

—**MARLENE MUCKENHIRN** DELANO, MN

START TO FINISH: 20 MIN.
MAKES: ABOUT 1 CUP

- 1 **garlic clove, halved**
- ½ **cup condensed tomato soup, undiluted**
- 1½ **teaspoons ground mustard**
- 1½ **teaspoons Worcestershire sauce**
- 10 **slices process American cheese (Velveeta), cubed**
- ¼ **to ⅓ cup milk**
- 1 **package (16 ounces) miniature hot dogs or smoked sausage, warmed**
  Cubed French bread

1. Rub garlic clove over the bottom and sides of a 1½-qt. slow cooker; discard garlic and set the slow cooker aside.

2. In a small saucepan, combine the tomato soup, mustard and Worcestershire sauce; heat through. Stir in cheese until melted. Stir in milk; heat through.

3. Transfer to prepared slow cooker and keep warm. Serve with hot dogs and bread cubes.

> **TOP TIP**
>
> Slow-cooked appetizers are perfect for sharing at get-togethers. If you plan on bringing your party contribution in a slow cooker, be sure to pack an extension cord, too, so you don't have to bother the hostess.

Bacon Cheese Dip

I've tried several appetizer recipes, but this one is a surefire people-pleaser. The thick dip has lots of bacon flavor and keeps friends happily munching.

—**SUZANNE WHITAKER** KNOXVILLE, TN

PREP: 15 MIN. • **COOK:** 2 HOURS
MAKES: 4 CUPS

- 2 **packages (8 ounces each) cream cheese, cubed**
- 4 **cups (16 ounces) shredded cheddar cheese**
- 1 **cup half-and-half cream**
- 2 **teaspoons Worcestershire sauce**
- 1 **teaspoon dried minced onion**
- 1 **teaspoon prepared mustard**
- 16 **bacon strips, cooked and crumbled**
  Tortilla chips or French bread slices

1. In a 1½-qt. slow cooker, combine the first six ingredients. Cover and cook on low for 2-3 hours or until cheeses are melted, stirring occasionally.

2. Just before serving, stir in bacon. Serve warm with tortilla chips or bread.

BACON CHEESE DIP

Summer

SIDE DISHES

Looking for something to serve alongside your grilled specialty? Need a quick contribution to the family reunion or church picnic? Your slow cooker has you covered! Consider these easy alternatives when you want to round out summer meals.

MELISSA MARZOLF'S
CHEESY POTATOES

Cheesy Potatoes

For a side dish that feeds a crowd, try these saucy slow-cooked potatoes. A simple topping of buttered croutons enhances the creamy combination.
—**MELISSA MARZOLF** MARYSVILLE, MI

PREP: 10 MIN. • **COOK:** 8 HOURS
MAKES: 10-12 SERVINGS

- 6 **medium potatoes, peeled and cut into ¼-inch strips**
- 2 **cups (8 ounces) shredded cheddar cheese**
- 1 **can (10¾ ounces) condensed cream of chicken soup, undiluted**
- 1 **small onion, chopped or 1 tablespoon dried minced onion**
- 7 **tablespoons butter, melted, divided**
- 1 **teaspoon salt**
- 1 **teaspoon pepper**
- 1 **cup (8 ounces) sour cream**
- 2 **cups seasoned stuffing cubes**

1. Toss the potatoes and cheese; place in a 5-qt. slow cooker. Combine soup, onion, 4 tablespoons butter, salt and pepper; pour over potato mixture.
2. Cover and cook on low for 8-10 hours or until potatoes are tender. Stir in sour cream. Toss stuffing cubes and remaining butter; sprinkle over potatoes.

Marmalade-Glazed Carrots

This side dish is ideal when you'd like to do something different with your vegetables for a special dinner. Cinnamon and nutmeg season baby carrots that are simmered with orange marmalade and a little brown sugar.
—**BARB RUDYK** VERMILION, AB

PREP: 10 MIN. • **COOK:** 5½ HOURS
MAKES: 6 SERVINGS

- 2 **pounds fresh baby carrots**
- ½ **cup orange marmalade**
- 3 **tablespoons cold water, divided**
- 2 **tablespoons brown sugar**
- 1 **tablespoon butter, melted**
- ½ **teaspoon ground cinnamon**
- ¼ **teaspoon salt**
- ¼ **teaspoon ground nutmeg**
- ⅛ **teaspoon pepper**
- 1 **tablespoon cornstarch**

1. In a 3-qt. slow cooker, combine the carrots, marmalade, 1 tablespoon water, brown sugar, butter and seasonings. Cover and cook on low for 5-6 hours or until carrots are tender.
2. Combine cornstarch and remaining water until smooth; stir into carrot mixture. Cover and cook on high for 30 minutes or until thickened. Serve with a slotted spoon.

MAPLE BAKED BEANS

1 cup chopped carrots
1 small onion, chopped
1 tablespoon olive oil
1½ teaspoons brown sugar
1½ teaspoons curry powder
1 garlic clove, minced
½ teaspoon ground cinnamon
¼ teaspoon ground ginger
⅛ teaspoon salt
1 medium butternut squash (about 2½ pounds), cut into 1-inch cubes
2½ cups vegetable broth
¾ cup coconut milk
½ cup uncooked basmati or jasmine rice

1. In a large skillet, saute carrots and onion in oil until onion is tender. Add the brown sugar, curry, garlic, cinnamon, ginger and salt. Cook and stir 2 minutes longer.
2. In a 3- or 4-qt. slow cooker, combine the butternut squash, broth, coconut milk, rice and carrot mixture. Cover and cook on low for 4-5 hours or until rice is tender.

BUTTERNUT COCONUT CURRY

Maple Baked Beans

This recipe came from my mother and was always a hit. Chopped jalapeno pepper spices it up a bit. The recipe is easy to remember—it's a half-cup of this and a half-cup of that!
—**NADINE BRISSEY** JENKS, OK

PREP: 15 MIN. • **COOK:** 6 HOURS
MAKES: 8 SERVINGS

3 cans (15 ounces each) pork and beans
½ cup finely chopped onion
½ cup chopped green pepper
½ cup ketchup
½ cup maple syrup
2 tablespoons finely chopped seeded jalapeno pepper
½ cup crumbled cooked bacon

In a 3-qt. slow cooker, combine the first six ingredients. Cover and cook on low for 6-8 hours or until vegetables are tender. Just before serving, stir in bacon.
NOTE *Wear disposable gloves when cutting hot peppers; the oils can burn skin. Avoid touching your face.*

Butternut Coconut Curry

I love my slow cooker because it makes dinner so easy! I first created this flavorful curry for a potluck supper, and since then, I've been asked many times for the recipe.
—**JESSIE APFE** BERKELEY, CA

PREP: 35 MIN. • **COOK:** 4 HOURS
MAKES: 9 SERVINGS

(5) INGREDIENTS
Jalapeno Creamed Corn

My version of creamed corn gets its spicy kick from jalapeno peppers. Try a chopped poblano or a small red bell pepper for a milder side dish.

—**JUDY CARTY** WICHITA, KS

PREP: 15 MIN. • **COOK:** 4 HOURS
MAKES: 8 SERVINGS

- 2 packages (16 ounces each) frozen corn
- 1 package (8 ounces) cream cheese, softened and cubed
- 4 jalapeno peppers, seeded and finely chopped
- ¼ cup butter, cubed
- 2 tablespoons water
- ½ teaspoon salt
- ¼ teaspoon pepper

In a 3-qt. slow cooker, combine all ingredients. Cover and cook on low for 4-5 hours or until corn is tender, stirring occasionally.

NOTE *Wear disposable gloves when cutting hot peppers; the oils can burn skin. Avoid touching your face.*

Slow-Cooked Ranch Potatoes

Even after 7 years, my family still asks for this tasty potato and bacon dish. Try it one time, and I'll bet your family will be hooked, too.

—**LYNN IRELAND** LEBANON, WI

PREP: 15 MIN. • **COOK:** 7 HOURS
MAKES: 10 SERVINGS

- 6 bacon strips, chopped
- 2½ pounds small red potatoes, cubed
- 1 package (8 ounces) cream cheese, softened

SLOW-COOKED RANCH POTATOES

- 1 can (10¾ ounces) condensed cream of potato soup, undiluted
- ¼ cup 2% milk
- 1 envelope buttermilk ranch salad dressing mix
- 3 tablespoons thinly sliced green onions

1. In a large skillet, cook bacon over medium heat until crisp, stirring occasionally. Remove with a slotted spoon; drain on paper towels, reserving 1 tablespoon drippings.
2. Place potatoes in a 3-qt. slow cooker. In a bowl, beat cream cheese, soup, milk, dressing mix and reserved drippings until blended; stir into potatoes. Sprinkle with bacon.
3. Cook, covered, on low 7-8 hours or until potatoes are tender. Top with green onions.

DID YOU KNOW?

Have you ever wondered why red potatoes are so popular in slow-cooker recipes? There are a few reasons why this sensational spud finds itself simmering to perfection in slow cookers across the country.

One is that the skin of these potatoes is very thin, allowing busy cooks to prepare dishes without having to peel them. What a time-saver!

In addition, red potatoes have a firm flesh that helps them hold their shape during slow cooking (as well as boiling).

It's benefits like these that make red potatoes a natural fit for salads, soups and casseroles—regardless of how the recipe is prepared.

Summer Side Dish

I use my slow cooker to make these tasty potatoes in a rich and creamy sauce. Be sure to stir them well before serving to help the cheese mixture thicken.

—**ELAINE RYAN** HOLLEY, NY

PREP: 15 MIN. • **COOK:** 5 HOURS
MAKES: 8 SERVINGS

- 7 cups cubed uncooked red potatoes
- 1 cup (8 ounces) 4% cottage cheese
- ½ cup sour cream
- ½ cup cubed process cheese (Velveeta)
- 1 tablespoon dried minced onion
- 2 garlic cloves, minced
- ½ teaspoon salt
  Paprika and minced chives, optional

1. Place the potatoes in a 3-qt. slow cooker. In a blender, puree cottage cheese and sour cream until smooth. Transfer to a large bowl; stir in the process cheese, onion, garlic and salt. Pour over potatoes and mix well.
2. Cover and cook on low for 5-6 hours or until potatoes are tender. Stir well before serving. Garnish with paprika and chives if desired.

Stewed Zucchini and Tomatoes

A fresh take on traditional vegetable sides, zucchini, tomatoes and green peppers star in this make-ahead dish. Bubbly cheddar cheese adds a down-home feel.

—**BARBARA SMITH** SALEM, OR

PREP: 20 MIN. • **COOK:** 3½ HOURS
MAKES: 6 SERVINGS

- 3 medium zucchini, cut into ¼-inch slices
- 1 teaspoon salt, divided
- ½ teaspoon pepper, divided
- 1 medium onion, thinly sliced
- 1 medium green pepper, thinly sliced
- 3 medium tomatoes, sliced
- ⅔ cup condensed tomato soup, undiluted
- 1 teaspoon dried basil
- 1 cup (4 ounces) shredded cheddar cheese

1. Place zucchini in greased 3-qt. slow cooker. Sprinkle with ½ teaspoon salt and ¼ teaspoon pepper. Layer with onion, green pepper and tomatoes. In a small bowl, combine the soup, basil and remaining salt and pepper; spread over tomatoes.
2. Cover and cook on low for 3-4 hours or until vegetables are tender. Sprinkle with cheese. Cover and cook 30 minutes longer or until cheese is melted.

(5)INGREDIENTS Hawaiian Barbecue Beans

The ingredient list is short, but it's creative! Guests rave and wonder about the unique flavor of these beans (it's the fresh ginger)—and they're always a hit.

—**HELEN REYNOLDS** QUINCY, CA

PREP: 10 MIN. • **COOK:** 5 HOURS
MAKES: 9 SERVINGS

- 4 cans (15 ounces each) black beans, rinsed and drained
- 1 can (20 ounces) crushed pineapple, drained
- 1 bottle (18 ounces) barbecue sauce
- 1½ teaspoons minced fresh gingerroot
- ½ pound bacon strips, cooked and crumbled

In a 4-qt. slow cooker, combine the beans, pineapple, barbecue sauce and ginger. Cover and cook on low for 5-6 hours. Stir in bacon before serving.

HAWAIIAN BARBECUE BEANS

SLOW COOKER MUSHROOM RICE PILAF

Slow Cooker Mushroom Rice Pilaf

A few modifications to our Great Aunt Bernice's mushroom rice pilaf recipe made this dish an always-requested favorite. Perfect for potlucks, barbecues and family get-togethers, it is sure to become a slow cooker favorite in your home as well.

—AMY WILLIAMS RIALTO, CA

PREP: 20 MIN. • **COOK:** 3 HOURS
MAKES: 6 SERVINGS

- 1 cup medium grain rice
- ¼ cup butter, cubed
- 6 green onions, chopped
- 2 garlic cloves, minced
- ½ pound sliced baby portobello mushrooms
- 2 cups warm water
- 4 teaspoons beef base

1. In a large skillet, saute rice in butter until lightly browned. Add green onions and garlic; cook and stir until tender. Stir in mushrooms.

2. Transfer to a 1½-qt. slow cooker. In a small bowl, whisk water and beef base; pour over rice mixture. Cover and cook on low for 3 to 3½ hours or until rice is tender and liquid is absorbed. Fluff with a fork.

NOTE *Look for beef base near the broth and bouillon in your grocery.*

Slow Cooker Ratatouille

Try this ratatouille in the summer with your garden-fresh vegetables. Feel free to toss a handful of frozen peas or corn kernels into the slow cooker, too, if you'd like. They add color and nutrition.

—JOLENE WALTERS NORTH MIAMI, FL

PREP: 20 MIN. + STANDING • **COOK:** 3 HOURS
MAKES: 10 SERVINGS

- 1 large eggplant, peeled and cut into 1-inch cubes
- 2 teaspoons salt, divided
- 3 medium tomatoes, chopped
- 3 medium zucchini, halved lengthwise and sliced
- 2 medium onions, chopped
- 1 large green pepper, chopped
- 1 large sweet yellow pepper, chopped
- 1 can (6 ounces) pitted ripe olives, drained and chopped
- 1 can (6 ounces) tomato paste
- ½ cup minced fresh basil
- 2 garlic cloves, minced
- ½ teaspoon pepper
- 2 tablespoons olive oil

1. Place eggplant in a colander over a plate; sprinkle with 1 teaspoon salt and toss. Let stand for 30 minutes. Rinse and drain well. Transfer to a 5-qt. slow cooker coated with cooking spray.

2. Stir in the tomatoes, zucchini, onions, green and yellow peppers, olives, tomato paste, basil, garlic, pepper and remaining salt. Drizzle with oil. Cover and cook on high for 3-4 hours or until vegetables are tender.

TOP TIP

Not only does ratatouille make a phenomenal side dish, but you can also serve it with sliced French bread for a warm (and easy) appetizer!
—JOLENE W. NORTH MIAMI, FL

JOLENE WALTERS'
SLOW COOKER RATATOUILLE

Hash Browns with Ham

Convenient grocery store items like frozen hash browns and a can of chicken soup make this an easy-to-prepare dish. Both kids and adults love it because it's super-tasty and chock-full of cheese.

—LIGHTNINGBUG

TASTEOFHOME.COM

PREP: 15 MIN. • **COOK:** 3¼ HOURS
MAKES: 8 SERVINGS

1 package (32 ounces) frozen cubed hash brown potatoes, thawed
1 cup cubed fully cooked ham
1 small onion, chopped
2 cups (8 ounces) shredded cheddar cheese, divided
1 can (14¾ ounces) condensed cream of chicken soup, undiluted
½ cup butter, melted
1 cup (8 ounces) sour cream

1. In a 3-qt. slow cooker, combine the potatoes, ham, onion and 1 cup cheese. Combine soup and butter; pour over potato mixture. Cover and cook on low for 3-4 hours or until potatoes are tender.

2. Stir in sour cream. Sprinkle with remaining cheese. Cover and cook for 15 minutes or until cheese is melted.

HASH BROWNS WITH HAM

GREEN BEANS AND NEW POTATOES

Vegetable Medley

Here's a wonderful side dish to make when summer's vegetables are plentiful. It's a great complement to any entree.

—**TERRY MALY** OLATHE, KS

PREP: 15 MIN. • **COOK:** 5 HOURS
MAKES: 8 SERVINGS

> 4 **cups diced peeled potatoes**
> 1½ **cups frozen whole kernel corn or 1 can (15¼ ounces) whole kernel corn, drained**
> 4 **medium tomatoes, seeded and diced**
> 1 **cup sliced carrots**
> ½ **cup chopped onion**
> ¾ **teaspoon salt**
> ½ **teaspoon sugar**
> ½ **teaspoon dill weed**
> ⅛ **teaspoon pepper**

In a 3-qt. slow cooker, combine all ingredients. Cover and cook on low for 5-6 hours or until vegetables are tender.

HOW TO

SEED A TOMATO

❶ To seed a tomato, cut in half horizontally and remove the stem.
❷ Holding a tomato half over a bowl or sink, scrape out seeds with a small spoon or squeeze the tomato to force out the seeds. Then slice or dice as directed in the recipe.

Green Beans and New Potatoes

The beans and potatoes are so tender in this side dish, and the broth so flavorful!

—**ANN BAKER** TEXARKANA, TX

PREP: 15 MIN. • **COOK:** 6 HOURS
MAKES: 10 SERVINGS

> 1 **pound fresh green beans, trimmed**
> 1 **pound small red potatoes, quartered**
> ½ **pound medium fresh mushrooms, halved**
> ½ **cup thinly sliced sweet onion**
> 2 **cans (14½ ounces each) beef broth**
> 2 **tablespoons beefy onion soup mix**
> 2 **teaspoons Worcestershire sauce**
> 1 **teaspoon grated lemon peel**
> ½ **teaspoon salt**
> ½ **teaspoon pepper**
> ¼ **teaspoon garlic powder**

In a 5-qt. slow cooker, layer the green beans, potatoes, mushrooms and onion. In a small bowl, combine the remaining ingredients; pour over vegetables. Cover and cook on low for 6-8 hours or until vegetables are tender. Serve with a slotted spoon.

JOYCE JOHNSON'S
CORN AND BROCCOLI IN CHEESE SAUCE

Corn and Broccoli in Cheese Sauce

This popular dish is a standby at our house. My daughter likes to add leftover ham to it. No one will guess it's on the lighter side!

—JOYCE JOHNSON UNIONTOWN, OH

PREP: 10 MIN. • **COOK:** 3 HOURS
MAKES: 8 SERVINGS

- 1 package (16 ounces) frozen corn, thawed
- 1 package (16 ounces) frozen broccoli florets, thawed
- 4 ounces reduced-fat process cheese (Velveeta), cubed
- ½ cup shredded cheddar cheese
- 1 can (10¼ ounces) reduced-fat reduced-sodium condensed cream of chicken soup, undiluted
- ¼ cup fat-free milk

1. In a 4-qt. slow cooker, combine the corn, broccoli and cheeses. In a small bowl, combine soup and milk; pour over vegetable mixture.

2. Cover and cook on low for 3-4 hours or until heated through. Stir before serving.

Brown Rice and Vegetables

Here's a nutritious rice dish, full of big chunks of butternut squash and sweet potatoes, that's a tasty combination of sweet and savory flavors.

—TASTE OF HOME TEST KITCHEN

PREP: 20 MIN. • **COOK:** 5 HOURS
MAKES: 12 SERVINGS

- 1 cup uncooked brown rice
- 1 medium butternut squash (about 3 pounds), cubed
- 2 medium apples, coarsely chopped
- 1 medium sweet potato, peeled and cubed
- 1 medium onion, chopped
- 1 teaspoon salt
- ½ teaspoon pepper
- 1 can (14½ ounces) reduced-sodium chicken broth
- ½ cup raisins
- 1 tablespoon minced fresh tarragon or 1 teaspoon dried tarragon

1. Place rice in a greased 4- or 5-qt. slow cooker. In a large bowl, combine the squash, apples, sweet potato, onion, salt and pepper; add to slow cooker. Pour broth over vegetables.

2. Cover and cook on low for 5-6 hours or until vegetables are tender. Stir in raisins and tarragon.

BROWN RICE AND VEGETABLES

SMOKY BAKED BEANS

Smoky Baked Beans

They'll be standing in line for this saucy bean recipe, full of campfire flavor. A variation on colorful calico beans, it makes a nice side dish with all your cookout favorites.

—**LYNNE GERMAN** WOODLAND HILLS, CA

PREP: 25 MIN. • **COOK:** 7 HOURS
MAKES: 16 SERVINGS

- 1 **pound bulk spicy pork sausage**
- 1 **medium onion, chopped**
- 1 **can (31 ounces) pork and beans**
- 1 **can (16 ounces) kidney beans, rinsed and drained**
- 1 **can (16 ounces) butter beans, rinsed and drained**
- 1 **can (15½ ounces) navy beans, rinsed and drained**
- 1 **can (15 ounces) black beans, rinsed and drained**
- 1 **can (10 ounces) diced tomatoes and green chilies, drained**
- ½ **cup hickory smoke-flavored barbecue sauce**
- ½ **cup ketchup**
- ½ **cup packed brown sugar**
- 1 **teaspoon ground mustard**
- 1 **teaspoon steak seasoning**
- 1 **teaspoon liquid smoke, optional**

1. In a large skillet, cook sausage and onion over medium heat until meat is no longer pink; drain.

2. In a 5-qt. slow cooker, combine the beans, tomatoes and sausage mixture. In a small bowl, combine the barbecue sauce, ketchup, brown sugar, mustard, steak seasoning and liquid smoke if desired. Stir into bean mixture.

3. Cover and cook on low for 7-8 hours or until heated through.
NOTE *This recipe was tested with McCormick's Montreal Steak Seasoning. Look for it in the spice aisle of your grocery store.*

Scalloped Taters

This creamy side dish goes well with almost any entree and is a snap to assemble with frozen hash browns. It's a handy way to make potatoes when your oven is full of other foods.

—**LUCINDA WOLKER** SOMERSET, PA

PREP: 10 MIN. • **COOK:** 4½ HOURS
MAKES: 12 SERVINGS

- 1 **package (2 pounds) frozen cubed hash brown potatoes**
- 1 **can (10¾ ounces) condensed cream of chicken soup, undiluted**
- 1½ **cups whole milk**
- 1 **cup (4 ounces) shredded cheddar cheese**
- ½ **cup plus 1 tablespoon butter, melted, divided**
- ¼ **cup dried minced onion**
- ½ **teaspoon salt**
- ⅛ **teaspoon pepper**
- ¾ **cup crushed cornflakes**

1. In a large bowl, combine the hash browns, soup, milk, cheese, ½ cup butter, onion, salt and pepper. Pour into a greased 5-qt. slow cooker. Cover and cook on low for 4-5 hours or until potatoes are tender.

2. Just before serving, combine the cornflake crumbs and remaining butter in a pie plate. Bake at 350° for 4-6 minutes or until golden brown. Stir the potatoes; sprinkle with crumb topping.

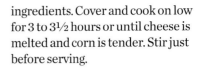

(5) INGREDIENTS
Creamed Corn

Five ingredients are all you'll need for my popular dinner accompaniment. It's wonderful no matter what the occasion is. Try it with a barbecue buffet.

—BARBARA BRIZENDINE HARRISONVILLE, MO

PREP: 10 MIN. • **COOK:** 3 HOURS
MAKES: 5 SERVINGS

- 2 packages (one 16 ounces, one 10 ounces) frozen corn
- 1 package (8 ounces) cream cheese, softened and cubed
- ¼ cup butter, cubed
- 1 tablespoon sugar
- ½ teaspoon salt

In a 3-qt. slow cooker coated with cooking spray, combine all the ingredients. Cover and cook on low for 3 to 3½ hours or until cheese is melted and corn is tender. Stir just before serving.

Fiesta Corn and Beans

Bursting with Southwestern flavors, this zesty veggie medley can be served either as a side dish or a meatless meal. A dollop of yogurt adds a cool and creamy finishing touch.

—GERALD HETRICK ERIE, PA

PREP: 25 MIN. • **COOK:** 3 HOURS
MAKES: 10 SERVINGS

- 1 large onion, chopped
- 1 medium green pepper, cut into 1-inch pieces
- 1 to 2 jalapeno peppers, seeded and sliced
- 1 tablespoon olive oil
- 1 garlic clove, minced
- 2 cans (16 ounces each) kidney beans, rinsed and drained
- 1 package (16 ounces) frozen corn
- 1 can (14½ ounces) diced tomatoes, undrained
- 1 teaspoon chili powder
- ¾ teaspoon salt
- ½ teaspoon ground cumin
- ½ teaspoon pepper
  Optional toppings: plain yogurt and sliced ripe olives

1. In a large skillet, saute onion and peppers in oil until tender. Add garlic; cook 1 minute longer. Transfer to a 4-qt. slow cooker. Stir in the beans, corn, tomatoes and seasonings.
2. Cover and cook on low for 3-4 hours or until heated through. Serve with yogurt and olives if desired.
NOTE *Wear disposable gloves when cutting hot peppers; the oils can burn skin. Avoid touching your face.*

CREAMED CORN

Summer

ENTREES

Don't feel like standing over a hot grill all summer? Want to keep the oven off and the kitchen cool? You've come to the right spot! Turn here for slow-cooked main dishes just perfect for steamy summer nights.

JACQUELINE CORREA'S
ENCHILADA PIE

Enchilada Pie

Stacked with layers of beans, vegetables and cheese, this mile-high pie makes for a fun fiesta night with the family. Who would ever guess that it all comes together in the slow cooker?

—**JACQUELINE CORREA** LANDING, NJ

PREP: 40 MIN. • **COOK:** 4 HOURS
MAKES: 8 SERVINGS

- 1 package (12 ounces) frozen vegetarian meat crumbles
- 1 cup chopped onion
- ½ cup chopped green pepper
- 2 teaspoons canola oil
- 1 can (16 ounces) kidney beans, rinsed and drained
- 1 can (15 ounces) black beans, rinsed and drained
- 1 can (10 ounces) diced tomatoes and green chilies, undrained
- ½ cup water
- 1½ teaspoons chili powder
- ½ teaspoon ground cumin
- ¼ teaspoon pepper
- 6 whole wheat tortillas (8 inches)
- 2 cups (8 ounces) shredded reduced-fat cheddar cheese

1. Cut three 25x3-in. strips of heavy-duty foil; crisscross so they resemble spokes of a wheel. Place strips on the bottom and up the sides of a 5-qt. slow cooker. Coat strips with cooking spray.

2. In a large saucepan, cook the meat crumbles, onion and green pepper in oil until vegetables are tender. Stir in both cans of beans, tomatoes, water, chili powder, cumin and pepper. Bring to a boil. Reduce heat; simmer, uncovered, for 10 minutes.

3. In the prepared slow cooker, layer about a cup of bean mixture, one tortilla and ⅓ cup cheese. Repeat layers five times. Cover and cook on low for 4-5 hours or until heated through and cheese is melted.

4. Using foil strips as handles, remove the pie to a platter.

NOTE *Vegetarian meat crumbles are a nutritious protein source made from soy. Look for them in the natural foods freezer section.*

TOP TIP

Feel free to change up any of the ingredients for the Enchilada Pie with others your family might enjoy more.
- Swap out the vegetarian meat crumbles for ground beef, turkey or chicken if that suits them better.
- Use a can of plain tomatoes if green chilies aren't your thing.
- Try the recipe with full-fat cheese or flour tortillas if you like.

JAMAICAN-ME-CRAZY CHICKEN TROPICALE

Jamaican-Me-Crazy Chicken Tropicale

I sample the sauce about 30 minutes before this chicken is done and adjust the seasonings to taste. You can thicken it with a tablespoon of cornstarch if you wish.
—**MARY LOUISE LEVER** ROME, GA

PREP: 25 MIN. • **COOK:** 5 HOURS
MAKES: 4 SERVINGS

- 3 **medium sweet potatoes, peeled and cut into 2-inch pieces**
- 1 **can (8 ounces) sliced water chestnuts, drained**
- 1 **cup dried cranberries**
- 1 **can (20 ounces) unsweetened pineapple tidbits**
- 2 **pounds bone-in chicken breast halves, skin removed**
- 2 **tablespoons Caribbean jerk seasoning**
- ¼ **cup dried minced onion**
- 3 **tablespoons minced fresh gingerroot**
- 2 **tablespoons Worcestershire sauce**
- 1 **tablespoon grated lime peel**
- 1 **teaspoon cumin seeds, crushed**
- 3 **fresh thyme sprigs**
  Hot cooked rice

1. Place potatoes in a 4- or 5-qt. slow cooker. Add water chestnuts and cranberries. Drain pineapple, reserving juice; add pineapple to slow cooker. Top with chicken. Sprinkle jerk seasoning over chicken.
2. Combine the onion, ginger, Worcestershire sauce, lime peel, cumin seeds and reserved juice. Pour over the chicken. Top with thyme sprigs.
3. Cover and cook on low for 5-6 hours or until chicken and vegetables are tender. Serve with rice.

Chili Coney Dogs

Everyone in our family, from kids to adults, simply loves these dogs. They're so easy to throw together and they heat up nicely in the slow cooker.
—**MICHELE HARRIS** VICKSBURG, MI

PREP: 20 MIN. • **COOK:** 4 HOURS
MAKES: 8 SERVINGS

- 1 **pound lean ground beef (90% lean)**
- 1 **can (15 ounces) tomato sauce**
- ½ **cup water**
- 2 **tablespoons Worcestershire sauce**
- 1 **tablespoon dried minced onion**
- ½ **teaspoon garlic powder**
- ½ **teaspoon ground mustard**
- ½ **teaspoon chili powder**
- ½ **teaspoon pepper**
  Dash cayenne pepper
- 8 **hot dogs**
- 8 **hot dog buns, split**
  Shredded cheddar cheese, relish and chopped onion, optional

1. In a large skillet, cook beef over medium heat until no longer pink; drain. Stir in the tomato sauce, water, Worcestershire sauce, onion and spices.
2. Place hot dogs in a 3-qt. slow cooker; top with beef mixture. Cover and cook on low for 4-5 hours or until heated through. Serve on buns with cheese, relish and onion if desired.

CHILI CONEY DOGS

CHICKEN THIGHS WITH SAUSAGE

Chicken Thighs with Sausage

Whether you're serving your family or special guests, this delicious entree is one that always hits the spot.

—JOANNE IOVINO KINGS PARK, NY

PREP: 25 MIN. • **COOK:** 6 HOURS
MAKES: 8 SERVINGS

- 2 **medium carrots, chopped**
- 2 **celery ribs, chopped**
- 1 **large onion, finely chopped**
- 8 **bone-in chicken thighs (about 3 pounds), skin removed**
- 1 **package (14 ounces) smoked turkey sausage, cut into ½-inch slices**
- ¼ **cup ketchup**
- 6 **garlic cloves, minced**
- 1 **tablespoon Louisiana-style hot sauce**
- 1 **teaspoon dried basil**
- 1 **teaspoon paprika**
- 1 **teaspoon dried thyme**
- ½ **teaspoon dried oregano**
- ½ **teaspoon pepper**
- ¼ **teaspoon ground allspice**
- 1 **teaspoon browning sauce, optional**

1. In a 4- or 5-qt. slow cooker, combine the carrots, celery and onion. Top with chicken and sausage.

2. In a small bowl, combine the ketchup, garlic, hot sauce, seasonings and, if desired, browning sauce. Spoon over meats. Cover and cook on low for 6-8 hours or until chicken is tender.

Pork and Green Chili Stew

An easily adaptable stew, this makes a delicious change of pace from beef stews and hearty staples like chili. Serve it with crispy tortilla chips.

—PAUL SEDILLO PLAINFIELD, IL

PREP: 40 MIN. • **COOK:** 7 HOURS
MAKES: 8 SERVINGS (2 QUARTS)

- 2 **pounds boneless pork shoulder butt roast, cut into ¾-inch cubes**
- 1 **large onion, cut into ½-in. pieces**
- 2 **tablespoons canola oil**
- 1 **teaspoon salt**
- 1 **teaspoon coarsely ground pepper**
- 4 **large potatoes, peeled and cut into ¾-inch cubes**
- 3 **cups water**
- 1 **can (16 ounces) hominy, rinsed and drained**
- 2 **cans (4 ounces each) chopped green chilies**
- 2 **tablespoons quick-cooking tapioca**
- 2 **garlic cloves, minced**
- ½ **teaspoon dried oregano**
- ½ **teaspoon ground cumin**
- 1 **cup minced fresh cilantro**
  Sour cream, optional

1. In a large skillet, brown pork and onion in oil in batches. Sprinkle with salt and pepper. Transfer to a 4-qt. slow cooker.

2. Stir in the potatoes, water, hominy, chilies, tapioca, garlic, oregano and cumin. Cover and cook on low for 7-9 hours or until meat is tender, stirring in cilantro during the last 30 minutes of cooking. Serve with sour cream if desired.

PORK AND GREEN CHILI STEW

SLOW-COOKED PORK AND BEANS

Slow-Cooked Pork and Beans

I like to get this dish started before leaving for work in the morning. When I come home, my supper's ready! It's a hearty slow cooker meal that is also good for an outdoor potluck. A generous helping of tender pork and beans is perfect alongside corn bread or grilled items.

—PATRICIA HAGER NICHOLASVILLE, KY

PREP: 15 MIN. • **COOK:** 6 HOURS
MAKES: 12 SERVINGS

- 1 **boneless pork loin roast (3 pounds)**
- 1 **medium onion, sliced**
- 3 **cans (15 ounces each) pork and beans**
- 1½ **cups barbecue sauce**
- ¼ **cup packed brown sugar**
- 1 **teaspoon garlic powder**

1. Cut roast in half; place in a 5-qt. slow cooker. Top with onion. In a large bowl, combine the beans, barbecue sauce, brown sugar and garlic powder; pour over meat. Cover and cook on low for 6-8 hours or until meat is tender.

2. Remove roast; shred with two forks. Return meat to slow cooker; heat through.

Beer-Braised Stew

Friends and family will never guess that the secret ingredient in this wonderful stew is beer! What a nice meal to come home to. Just cook the noodles and dinner is done.

—GERI FAUSTICH APPLETON, WI

PREP: 20 MIN. • **COOK:** 6 HOURS
MAKES: 8 SERVINGS

- 3 **bacon strips, diced**
- 2 **pounds beef stew meat, cut into 1-inch cubes**
- ½ **teaspoon pepper**
- ¼ **teaspoon salt**
- 2 **tablespoons canola oil**
- 2 **cups fresh baby carrots**
- 1 **medium onion, cut into wedges**
- 1 **teaspoon minced garlic**
- 1 **bay leaf**
- 1 **can (12 ounces) beer or nonalcoholic beer**
- 1 **tablespoon soy sauce**
- 1 **tablespoon Worcestershire sauce**
- 1 **teaspoon dried thyme**
- 2 **tablespoons all-purpose flour**
- ¼ **cup water**
  Hot cooked noodles

1. In a large skillet, cook bacon over medium heat until crisp. Remove to paper towels; drain, discarding drippings. Sprinkle beef with pepper and salt. In the same skillet, brown beef in oil in batches; drain.

2. Transfer to a 5-qt. slow cooker. Add the carrots, bacon, onion, garlic and bay leaf. In a small bowl, combine the beer, soy sauce, Worcestershire sauce and thyme. Pour over beef mixture.

3. Cover and cook on low for 5½ to 6 hours or until meat and vegetables are tender.

4. In a small bowl, combine flour and water until smooth. Gradually stir into slow cooker. Cover and cook on high for 30 minutes or until thickened. Discard bay leaf. Serve beef with noodles.

BEER-BRAISED STEW

SOUTHWEST CHICKEN

Southwest Chicken

Chicken simmers until it's tender before being combined with corn, beans, cheese, and salsa for a delicious meal with Southwestern flair.

—**MADDYMOO** TASTEOFHOME.COM

PREP: 15 MIN. • **COOK:** 4 HOURS
MAKES: 6 SERVINGS

- 1 can (15¼ ounces) whole kernel corn, drained
- 1 can (15 ounces) black beans, rinsed and drained
- 1 jar (16 ounces) mild salsa
- 4 boneless skinless chicken breast halves (5 ounces each)
  Sweet red and yellow pepper strips, sour cream, shredded cheddar cheese and sliced green onions, optional

1. In a 3-qt. slow cooker, layer three-fourths each of the corn and beans and half of the salsa. Arrange chicken over salsa; top with remaining corn, beans and salsa. Cover and cook on low for 4-5 hours or until chicken is tender.
2. Shred chicken with two forks and return to the slow cooker; heat through. Top with the peppers, sour cream, cheese and onions if desired.

Java Roast Beef

Coffee adds richness to this gravy, which is perfect to sop up with crusty bread or drape over mashed potatoes.

—**CHARLA SACKMANN** ORANGE CITY, IA

PREP: 10 MIN. • **COOK:** 8 HOURS
MAKES: 12 SERVINGS

- 5 garlic cloves, minced
- 1½ teaspoons salt
- ¾ teaspoon pepper
- 1 boneless beef chuck roast (3 to 3½ pounds)
- 1½ cups strong brewed coffee
- 2 tablespoons cornstarch
- ¼ cup cold water

1. Combine the garlic, salt and pepper; rub over beef. Transfer to a 4-qt. slow cooker. Pour coffee around meat. Cover and cook on low for 8-10 hours or until meat is tender. Remove meat to a serving platter; keep warm.
2. Skim fat from cooking juices; transfer to a small saucepan. Bring to a boil. Combine cornstarch and water until smooth; gradually stir into the pan. Bring to a boil; cook and stir for 2 minutes or until thickened. Serve with meat.

(5)INGREDIENTS Sweet and Spicy Jerk Ribs

Here's a no-fuss ribs recipe that the whole family will love. The spicy rub and sweet sauce make it an instant favorite. Best of all, it cooks on its own in the slow cooker!

—**GERI LESCH** NEW PORT RICHEY, FL

PREP: 10 MIN. • **COOK:** 6 HOURS
MAKES: 5 SERVINGS

- 4½ pounds pork baby back ribs
- 3 tablespoons olive oil
- ⅓ cup Caribbean jerk seasoning
- 3 cups honey barbecue sauce
- 3 tablespoons apricot preserves
- 2 tablespoons honey

1. Cut ribs into serving-size pieces; brush with oil and rub with jerk seasoning. Place in a 5- or 6-qt. slow cooker. Combine the remaining ingredients; pour over ribs.
2. Cover and cook on low for 6-8 hours or until meat is tender. Skim fat from sauce before serving.

GERI LESCH'S
SWEET AND SPICY JERK RIBS

Fiesta-Twisted Brunswick Stew

Traditionally made with game meat, this updated Brunswick stew, using spicy sausage, is a modern mom's best friend.

—**DONNA MARIE RYAN** TOPSFIELD, MA

PREP: 20 MIN. • **COOK:** 5 HOURS
MAKES: 9 SERVINGS (3½ QUARTS)

- ½ **pound uncooked chorizo or bulk spicy pork sausage**
- 1 **large potato, cubed**
- 1 **large onion, chopped**
- 1 **large green pepper, chopped**
- 3 **jalapeno peppers, seeded and chopped**
- 1 **can (28 ounces) crushed tomatoes**
- 1 **jar (26 ounces) marinara sauce**
- 1 **can (14¾ ounces) cream-style corn**
- 1 **tablespoon Cajun seasoning**
- 1 **garlic clove, minced**
- ½ **teaspoon sugar**
- ½ **teaspoon pepper**
- ¼ **teaspoon salt**
- ⅓ **cup all-purpose flour**
- 1 **can (14½ ounces) chicken broth**
- 2 **pounds bone-in chicken breast halves, skin removed**
- 1 **cup cut fresh green beans**
- 2 **tablespoons minced fresh cilantro Shredded Asiago cheese**

1. Crumble chorizo into a small skillet; cook over medium heat for 6-8 minutes or until fully cooked. Drain. Transfer to a 6-qt. slow cooker. Add the potato, onion, green pepper, jalapenos, tomatoes, marinara sauce, corn, Cajun seasoning, garlic, sugar, pepper and salt.
2. In a small bowl, combine flour and broth until smooth; stir into slow cooker. Add the chicken. Cover and cook on low for 5-6 hours or until chicken and vegetables are tender, adding green beans and cilantro during the last 2 hours of cooking.
3. Remove chicken from slow cooker. When cool enough to handle, remove meat from bones; discard bones. Cut meat into bite-size pieces and return to slow cooker; heat through. Sprinkle servings with cheese.
NOTE *Wear disposable gloves when cutting hot peppers; the oils can burn skin. Avoid touching your face.*

Greek Orzo Chicken

Take your first bite of this change-of-pace dish and you'll be on a tour of the sunny Greek Isles. Sprinkle lemon zest on top to give it a little extra flair.

—**ANGELA BUCHANAN** LONGMONT, CO

PREP: 15 MIN. • **COOK:** 5½ HOURS
MAKES: 6 SERVINGS

- 6 **bone-in chicken thighs, (about 2¼ pounds), skin removed**
- 1 **cup sliced fresh carrots**
- 1 **cup chicken broth**
- ¼ **cup lemon juice**
- 1 **garlic clove, minced**
- 1 **teaspoon dried oregano**
- ½ **teaspoon salt**
- 1 **cup uncooked orzo pasta**
- ½ **cup sliced pitted green olives**
- ¼ **cup golden raisins**
- ½ **cup minced fresh parsley**
- ½ **cup crumbled feta cheese**

1. In a 3-qt. slow cooker, combine the chicken, carrots, broth, lemon juice, garlic, oregano and salt. Cover and cook on low for 5-6 hours or until chicken is tender.
2. Stir in the orzo, olives and raisins. Cover and cook 30 minutes longer or until pasta is tender. Sprinkle with parsley and feta cheese.

FIESTA-TWISTED BRUNSWICK STEW

LOUISIANA RED BEANS AND RICE

Lime Chicken Tacos

Lime juice adds a burst of flavor to my easy taco filling that's surprisingly healthy. The fun recipe is great for casual dinners with friends and family.

—TRACY GUNTER BOISE, ID

PREP: 10 MIN. • **COOK:** 5½ HOURS
MAKES: 12 TACOS

- 1½ **pounds boneless skinless chicken breasts**
- 3 **tablespoons lime juice**
- 1 **tablespoon chili powder**
- 1 **cup frozen corn**
- 1 **cup chunky salsa**
- 12 **fat-free flour tortillas (6 inches), warmed**
  Sour cream, shredded cheddar cheese and shredded lettuce, optional

1. Place the chicken in a 3-qt. slow cooker. Combine lime juice and chili powder; pour over chicken. Cover and cook on low for 5-6 hours or until chicken is tender.
2. Remove chicken; cool slightly. Shred meat with two forks and return to the slow cooker. Stir in corn and salsa.
3. Cover and cook on low 30 minutes or until heated through. Serve in tortillas with sour cream, cheese and lettuce if desired.

LIME CHICKEN TACOS

Louisiana Red Beans and Rice

Smoked turkey sausage and red pepper flakes add zip to this saucy, slow-cooked version of the New Orleans classic. For extra heat, add red pepper sauce at the table.

—JULIA BUSHREE COMMERCE CITY, CO

PREP: 20 MIN. • **COOK:** 8 HOURS
MAKES: 8 SERVINGS

- 4 **cans (16 ounces each) kidney beans, rinsed and drained**
- 1 **can (14½ ounces) diced tomatoes, undrained**
- 1 **package (14 ounces) smoked turkey sausage, sliced**
- 3 **celery ribs, chopped**
- 1 **large onion, chopped**
- 1 **cup chicken broth**
- 1 **medium green pepper, chopped**
- 1 **small sweet red pepper, chopped**
- 6 **garlic cloves, minced**
- 1 **bay leaf**
- ½ **teaspoon crushed red pepper flakes**
- 2 **green onions, chopped**
  Hot cooked rice

1. In a 4- or 5-qt. slow cooker, combine the first 11 ingredients. Cook, covered, on low 8-10 hours or until vegetables are tender.
2. Stir before serving. Remove bay leaf. Serve with green onions and rice.

LEMON CILANTRO CHICKEN

Bayou Gulf Shrimp Gumbo

This recipe skips the traditional hard-to-find spices and still delivers the true seafood flavor that's beloved in the Louisiana Bayou and beyond.

—WOLFGANG HANAU WEST PALM BEACH, FL

PREP: 35 MIN. • **COOK:** 5 HOURS
MAKES: 6 SERVINGS

- ½ **pound bacon strips, chopped**
- 3 **celery ribs, chopped**
- 1 **medium onion, chopped**
- 1 **medium green pepper, chopped**
- 2 **garlic cloves, minced**
- 2 **bottles (8 ounces each) clam juice**
- 1 **can (14½ ounces) diced tomatoes, undrained**
- 2 **tablespoons Worcestershire sauce**
- 1 **teaspoon kosher salt**
- 1 **teaspoon dried marjoram**
- 2 **pounds uncooked large shrimp, peeled and deveined**
- 2½ **cups frozen sliced okra, thawed**
    Hot cooked rice

1. In a large skillet, cook bacon over medium heat until crisp. Remove to paper towels with a slotted spoon; drain, reserving 2 tablespoons drippings. Saute the celery, onion, green pepper and garlic in drippings until tender.

2. Transfer to a 4-qt. slow cooker. Stir in the bacon, clam juice, tomatoes, Worcestershire sauce, salt and marjoram. Cover and cook on low for 4 hours.

3. Stir in shrimp and okra. Cover and cook 1 hour longer or until shrimp turn pink and okra is heated through. Serve with rice.

Lemon Cilantro Chicken

Here's a wonderful way to cook a whole chicken. The fall-off-the-bone meat with lemony gravy is so easy to prepare, making it ideal for busy weekdays.

—TASTE OF HOME TEST KITCHEN

PREP: 25 MIN. • **COOK:** 4 HOURS + STANDING
MAKES: 6 SERVINGS

- ½ **cup chopped fresh cilantro**
- 3 **tablespoons canola oil, divided**
- 2 **tablespoons lemon juice**
- 2 **garlic cloves, minced**
- 2 **teaspoons salt**
- 1 **teaspoon grated lemon peel**
- 1 **broiler/fryer chicken (3 to 4 pounds)**
- ½ **teaspoon paprika**
- ½ **teaspoon pepper**
- ½ **cup white wine or chicken broth**

1. In a small bowl, combine the cilantro, 2 tablespoons oil, lemon juice, garlic, salt and lemon peel. Loosen skin around the chicken breast, leg and thigh. Rub the cilantro mixture under and over the skin. Rub any remaining mixture into the cavity. Drizzle with remaining oil. Sprinkle with paprika and pepper.

2. Place in a 6- or 7-qt. slow cooker. Add wine to slow cooker. Cover and cook on low for 4-5 hours or until a meat thermometer reads 180°. Remove chicken to a serving platter; cover and let stand 15 minutes before carving. Skim fat and thicken juices if desired. Serve with chicken.

Mexican Pork Roast

Friends who live in Mexico shared this dinner years ago. They cooked the roast in a clay pot in a slow oven, but I found it works well in a slow cooker. The leftovers make great burritos and tacos.

—**CHUCK ALLEN** DANA POINT, CA

PREP: 15 MIN. • **COOK:** 8 HOURS
MAKES: 8 SERVINGS

- 2 medium onions, sliced
- 2 medium carrots, sliced
- 2 jalapeno peppers, seeded and chopped
- 2 tablespoons olive oil
- 3 garlic cloves, minced
- ½ cup water
- ½ cup chicken broth
- 1 teaspoon ground coriander
- ½ teaspoon salt
- ½ teaspoon ground cumin
- ½ teaspoon dried oregano
- ¼ teaspoon pepper
- 1 boneless pork shoulder butt roast (3 pounds)

1. In a large skillet, saute the onions, carrots and jalapenos in oil 3 minutes. Add garlic; cook 1 minute longer. Transfer to a 5-qt. slow cooker; add water and broth.

2. In a small bowl, combine the coriander, salt, cumin, oregano and pepper; rub over roast. Cut roast in half; place in the slow cooker. Cover and cook on low for 8-9 hours or until meat is tender.

3. Transfer roast and vegetables to a serving platter; keep warm. Strain cooking juices and skim fat. Pour into a small saucepan. Bring to a boil; cook until liquid is reduced to about 1 cup.

MEXICAN PORK ROAST

Serve with roast and vegetables.
NOTE *Wear disposable gloves when cutting hot peppers; the oils can burn skin. Avoid touching your face.*

Cajun Chicken Lasagna

Destined to be a new favorite with all around the table, this zesty take on traditional Italian lasagna nods to the Gulf Coast. Increase the amount of Cajun seasoning if you like spicier fare.

—**MARY LOU COOK** WELCHES, OR

PREP: 20 MIN. • **COOK:** 3 HOURS
MAKES: 8 SERVINGS

- 2 pounds ground chicken
- 2 celery ribs with leaves, chopped
- 1 medium green pepper, chopped
- 1 medium onion, chopped
- 1 can (28 ounces) crushed tomatoes, undrained
- 1 cup water
- 1 can (6 ounces) tomato paste
- 3 teaspoons Cajun seasoning
- 1 teaspoon sugar
- 2 cups (8 ounces) shredded part-skim mozzarella cheese
- 1 carton (15 ounces) ricotta cheese
- 9 uncooked lasagna noodles

1. In a large skillet, cook chicken over medium heat until no longer pink. Add the celery, green pepper and onion; cook and stir 5 minutes longer or until tender. Stir in the tomatoes, water, tomato paste, Cajun seasoning and sugar. In a small bowl, combine cheeses.

2. Spread 1 cup meat sauce in a greased oval 5- or 6-qt. slow cooker. Layer with 3 noodles (breaking noodles if necessary to fit), a third of the remaining meat sauce and a third of the cheese mixture. Repeat layers twice. Cover and cook on low for 3-4 hours or until noodles are tender.

ANITA BELL'S
SLOW-ROASTED CHICKEN WITH VEGETABLES

> The aroma of rosemary and garlic is mouth-watering, and this recipe could not be easier. Just a few minutes of prep and you'll come home to a delicious dinner. Even a beginner cook could make this and have it turn out perfectly.
>
> —**ANITA BELL** HERMITAGE, TN

Slow-Roasted Chicken with Vegetables

PREP: 15 MIN. • **COOK:** 6 HOURS + STANDING
MAKES: 6 SERVINGS

- 2 **medium carrots, halved lengthwise and cut into 3-inch pieces**
- 2 **celery ribs, halved lengthwise and cut into 3-inch pieces**
- 8 **small red potatoes, quartered**
- ¾ **teaspoon salt, divided**
- ⅛ **teaspoon pepper**
- 1 **medium lemon, halved**
- 2 **garlic cloves, crushed**
- 1 **broiler/fryer chicken (3 to 4 pounds)**
- 1 **tablespoon dried rosemary, crushed**
- 1 **tablespoon lemon juice**
- 1 **tablespoon olive oil**
- 2 **teaspoons paprika**

1. Place carrots, celery and potatoes in a 6-qt. slow cooker; toss with ¼ teaspoon salt and pepper. Place lemon halves and garlic in chicken cavity. Tuck wings under chicken; tie drumsticks together. Place chicken over vegetables in slow cooker, breast side up. Mix rosemary, lemon juice, oil, paprika and remaining salt; rub over chicken.

2. Cook, covered, on low 6-8 hours or until a thermometer reads 165° when inserted in center of stuffing and thigh reaches at least 170° and vegetables are tender.

3. Remove chicken to a serving platter; tent with foil. Let stand 15 minutes before carving. Serve with vegetables.

Pork with Peach Sauce

When fresh peaches are in season, I cook these pork ribs for family and friends. I just love the recipe because it calls for only six ingredients, the slow cooker does the work for me and the ribs turn out tender and tasty!

—**CONNIE JENISTA** VALRICO, FL

PREP: 20 MIN. + CHILLING • **COOK:** 5½ HOURS
MAKES: 6 SERVINGS

- 2 **pounds boneless country-style pork ribs**
- 2 **tablespoons taco seasoning**
- ½ **cup mild salsa**
- ¼ **cup peach preserves**
- ¼ **cup barbecue sauce**
- 2 **cups chopped fresh peeled peaches or frozen unsweetened sliced peaches, thawed and chopped**

1. In a large bowl, toss ribs with taco seasoning. Cover and refrigerate overnight.

2. Place pork in a 3-qt. slow cooker. In a small bowl, combine the salsa, preserves and barbecue sauce. Pour over ribs. Cover and cook on low for 5-6 hours or until meat is tender.

3. Add peaches; cover and cook 30 minutes longer or until peaches are tender.

PORK WITH PEACH SAUCE

BEEF OSSO BUCCO

Beef Osso Bucco

Our beef entree boasts a thick, savory sauce complemented by the addition of gremolata, a chopped herb condiment made of lemon zest, garlic and parsley.

—*TASTE OF HOME* TEST KITCHEN

PREP: 30 MIN. • **COOK:** 7 HOURS
MAKES: 6 SERVINGS

- ½ cup all-purpose flour
- ½ teaspoon pepper
- ¾ teaspoon salt, divided
- 6 beef shanks (14 ounces each)
- 2 tablespoons butter
- 1 tablespoon olive oil
- ½ cup white wine or beef broth
- 1 can (14½ ounces) diced tomatoes, undrained
- 1½ cups beef broth
- 2 medium carrots, chopped
- 1 medium onion, chopped
- 1 celery rib, sliced
- 1 tablespoon dried thyme
- 1 tablespoon dried oregano
- 2 bay leaves
- 3 tablespoons cornstarch
- ¼ cup cold water

GREMOLATA

- ⅓ cup minced fresh parsley
- 1 tablespoon grated lemon peel
- 1 tablespoon grated orange peel
- 2 garlic cloves, minced

1. In a large resealable plastic bag, combine the flour, pepper and ½ teaspoon salt. Add beef, a few pieces at a time, and shake to coat.
2. In a large skillet, brown beef in butter and oil. Transfer meat and drippings to a 6-qt. slow cooker. Add wine to skillet, stirring to loosen browned bits from pan; pour over meat. Add the tomatoes, broth, carrots, onion, celery, thyme, oregano, bay leaves and remaining salt.
3. Cover and cook on low for 7-9 hours or until meat is tender. Discard bay leaves.
4. Skim fat from cooking juices; transfer juices to a large saucepan. Bring to a boil. Combine cornstarch and water until smooth; gradually stir into the pan. Bring to a boil; cook and stir for 2 minutes or until thickened.
5. In a small bowl, combine the gremolata ingredients. Serve beef with gremolata and sauce.

Cola Barbecue Ribs

No matter what the weather is like, you can enjoy the smoky goodness of a summer barbecue by preparing these moist and tender ribs in your slow cooker!

—**KAREN SHUCK** EDGAR, NE

PREP: 10 MIN. • **COOK:** 9 HOURS
MAKES: 4 SERVINGS

- ¼ cup packed brown sugar
- 2 garlic cloves, minced
- 1 teaspoon salt
- ½ teaspoon pepper
- 3 tablespoons liquid smoke, optional
- 4 pounds pork spareribs, cut into serving-size pieces
- 1 medium onion, sliced
- ½ cup cola
- 1½ cups barbecue sauce

1. In a small bowl, combine the brown sugar, garlic, salt, pepper and liquid smoke if desired; rub over ribs.
2. Layer ribs and onion in a greased 5- or 6-qt. slow cooker; pour cola over ribs. Cover and cook on low for 8-10 hours or until ribs are tender. Drain liquid. Pour sauce over ribs and cook 1 hour longer.

COLA BARBECUE RIBS

CHILI-LIME CHICKEN TOSTADAS

Chili-Lime Chicken Tostadas

The flavor of this tender chicken with a hint of lime is delicious. It has just the right amount of heat to spice up the week while keeping dinner family-friendly.

—**LAURA POWELL** SOUTH JORDAN, UT

PREP: 10 MIN. • **COOK:** 5 HOURS
MAKES: 5 SERVINGS

- **4 pounds bone-in chicken breast halves, skin removed**
- **1 medium onion, chopped**
- **1 can (4 ounces) chopped green chilies**
- **3 tablespoons lime juice**
- **4½ teaspoons chili powder**
- **4 garlic cloves, minced**
- **10 tostada shells**
- **1 can (16 ounces) fat-free refried beans**
- **Optional ingredients: Shredded cabbage, shredded cheddar cheese, salsa, sour cream, sliced ripe olives and guacamole**

1. In a 4-qt. slow cooker, combine chicken and onion. In a small bowl, combine the green chilies, lime juice, chili powder and garlic; pour over chicken. Cover and cook on low for 5-6 hours or until meat is tender.
2. Remove chicken; cool slightly. Set aside ⅔ cup cooking juices. Discard remaining juices. Shred chicken with two forks and return to slow cooker. Stir in reserved cooking juices.
3. Spread tostadas with refried beans; top with chicken. Layer with cabbage, cheese, salsa, sour cream, olives and guacamole if desired.

Glazed Lamb Shanks

Ideal for small households, these slow-cooked shanks are packed with complex flavors. The Guinness and honey nicely balance the lamb, while garlic lends zing.

—**ELIZABETH MITCHELL** COCHRANVILLE, PA

PREP: 30 MIN. + MARINATING • **COOK:** 6 HOURS
MAKES: 4 SERVINGS

- **4 lamb shanks (about 20 ounces each)**
- **4 garlic cloves, thinly sliced**
- **1 cup lemon juice**
- **4 tablespoons olive oil, divided**
- **1 tablespoon each minced fresh thyme, rosemary and parsley**
- **1 teaspoon salt**
- **½ teaspoon pepper**
  SAUCE
- **1 cup Guinness (dark beer)**
- **¼ cup honey**
- **3 fresh thyme sprigs**
- **2 bay leaves**
- **1 tablespoon Dijon mustard**
- **2 garlic cloves, minced**
- **½ teaspoon salt**
- **¼ teaspoon pepper**
- **⅛ teaspoon crushed red pepper flakes**
- **2 pounds Yukon Gold potatoes, peeled and cut into chunks**

1. Cut slits into each lamb shank; insert garlic slices. In a large resealable plastic bag, combine the lemon juice, 2 tablespoons oil, thyme, rosemary, parsley, salt and pepper. Add the lamb; seal bag and turn to coat. Refrigerate overnight.
2. Drain and discard marinade. In large skillet, brown shanks in remaining oil on all sides in batches. Place shanks in a 5- or 6-qt. slow cooker.
3. In the same skillet, combine the beer, honey, thyme, bay leaves, Dijon, garlic, salt, pepper and pepper flakes. Bring to a boil, stirring constantly. Pour over meat. Cover and cook on low for 6-8 hours or until meat and potatoes are tender, adding the potatoes during the last 2 hours of cooking.
4. Remove lamb and potatoes from slow cooker. Strain sauce and discard bay leaves. If desired, thicken sauce. Serve with lamb and potatoes.

MOROCCAN VEGETABLE CHICKEN TAGINE

Moroccan Vegetable Chicken Tagine

Take a trip to Morocco with this exotic dish. Tagine is a rich North African slow-cooked stew that is named after the pot in which it is traditionally cooked.
—*TASTE OF HOME* **TEST KITCHEN**

PREP: 45 MIN. • **COOK:** 7½ HOURS
MAKES: 6 SERVINGS

- 1 **medium butternut squash (about 3 pounds), peeled and cut into 1-inch cubes**
- 2 **medium red potatoes, cut into 1-inch cubes**
- 1 **medium sweet potato, peeled and cut into 1-inch cubes**
- 1 **large onion, halved and sliced**
- 2 **garlic cloves, minced**
- 6 **chicken leg quarters, skin removed**
- ½ **teaspoon salt**
- ¼ **teaspoon pepper**
- ½ **cup dried apricots, chopped**
- ½ **cup dried cranberries, chopped**
- 2 **tablespoons all-purpose flour**
- 1 **can (14¾ ounces) reduced-sodium chicken broth**
- ¼ **cup chili sauce**
- 1 **tablespoon minced fresh gingerroot**
- 1 **teaspoon curry powder**
- ½ **teaspoon ground cinnamon**
- ½ **teaspoon ground cumin**
- 1 **can (15 ounces) garbanzo beans or chickpeas, rinsed and drained
  Hot cooked couscous, optional**

1. In a 6-qt. slow cooker, combine the squash, potatoes, onion and garlic. Sprinkle chicken with salt and pepper; place over vegetables. Top with apricots and cranberries.

2. In a small bowl, combine flour and broth until smooth. Stir in the chili sauce, ginger, curry, cinnamon and cumin. Pour over chicken. Cover and cook on low for 7-8 hours or until chicken and vegetables are tender.

3. Stir in garbanzo beans; cover and cook for 30 minutes or until heated through. Serve with couscous if desired.

Tasty Chicken Marsala

A friend shared this company-worthy recipe with me. There's enough of the smooth, creamy sauce to dress both the meat and the noodles, should you choose to serve them, too.
—**PATRICIA CAMPBELL** VALENCIA, PA

PREP: 20 MIN. • **COOK:** 5 HOURS
MAKES: 6 SERVINGS

- ¾ **cup water**
- ¼ **cup butter, melted**
- 1 **teaspoon garlic salt**
- 1 **teaspoon dried basil**
- 1 **teaspoon dried oregano**
- 6 **boneless skinless chicken breast halves (5 ounces each)**
- 2 **cups sliced fresh mushrooms**
- 2 **cans (10¾ ounces each) condensed golden mushroom soup, undiluted**
- 1 **package (8 ounces) reduced-fat cream cheese, cubed**
- ¾ **cup Marsala wine
  Hot cooked noodles, optional**

In a greased 4- or 5-qt. slow cooker, combine the water, butter, garlic salt, basil and oregano. Add chicken and mushrooms. In a large bowl, combine the soup, cream cheese and wine; pour over chicken. Cover and cook on low for 5-6 hours or until chicken is tender. Serve with noodles if desired.

Slow Cooker Salmon Loaf

I'm always looking for quick, easy recipes that can be prepared ahead of time. I also don't like to heat up my oven during our hot Georgia summers. I adapted this recipe from one I found in an old slow-cooker book of my grandma's. I serve it with macaroni and cheese and pinto beans.

—KELLY RITTER DOUGLASVILLE, GA

PREP: 10 MIN. • **COOK:** 4 HOURS
MAKES: 6 SERVINGS

- 2 **eggs, lightly beaten**
- 2 **cups seasoned stuffing croutons**
- 1 **cup chicken broth**
- 1 **cup grated Parmesan cheese**
- ¼ **teaspoon ground mustard**
- 1 **can (14¾ ounces) salmon, drained, bones and skin removed**

1. Cut three 20x3-in. strips of heavy duty foil; crisscross so they resemble spokes of a wheel. Place strips on the bottom and up the sides of a 3-qt. slow cooker coated with cooking spray.
2. In a large bowl, combine the first five ingredients. Add salmon and mix well. Gently shape mixture into a round loaf. Place in the center of the strips.
3. Cover and cook on low for 4-6 hours or until a thermometer reads 160°. Using foil strips as handles, remove the loaf to a platter.

Slow-Cooked Pulled Pork with Mojito Sauce

This Cuban twist on a pulled pork classic will knock your socks off! Wrap the pork in tortillas and serve with rice if you'd like.

—KRISTINA WILEY JUPITER, FL

PREP: 15 MIN. + MARINATING • **COOK:** 9 HOURS
MAKES: 12 SERVINGS (1½ CUPS SAUCE)

- 2 **large onions, quartered**
- 12 **garlic cloves**
- 1 **bottle (18 ounces) Cuban-style mojo sauce and marinade**
- ½ **cup lime juice**
- ½ **teaspoon salt**
- ¼ **teaspoon pepper**
- 1 **bone-in pork shoulder butt roast (5 to 5¼ pounds)**

MOJITO SAUCE
- ¾ **cup canola oil**
- 1 **medium onion, finely chopped**
- 6 **garlic cloves, finely chopped**
- ⅓ **cup lime juice**
- ½ **teaspoon salt**
- ¼ **teaspoon pepper**
    Additional chopped onion and lime wedges, optional

1. Place onions and garlic in a food processor; process until finely chopped. Add mojo marinade, lime juice, salt and pepper; process until blended. Pour half of the marinade into a large resealable plastic bag. Cut roast into quarters; add to bag. Seal bag and turn to coat. Refrigerate 8 hours or overnight. Transfer remaining marinade to a small bowl; refrigerate, covered, while marinating meat.
2. Drain pork, discarding marinade in bag. Place pork in a 5-qt. slow cooker coated with cooking spray. Top with reserved marinade. Cook, covered, on low 8-10 hours or until meat is tender.
3. For sauce, in a small saucepan, heat oil over medium heat 2½ to 3 minutes or until a thermometer reads 200°. Carefully add onion; cook 2 minutes, stirring occasionally. Stir in garlic; remove from heat. Stir in lime juice, salt and pepper.
4. Remove pork from slow cooker; cool slightly. Skim fat from cooking juices. Remove meat from bone; discard bone. Shred pork with two forks. Return cooking juices and pork to slow cooker; heat through.
5. Using tongs, remove pork to a platter. Serve with chopped onion, lime wedges and mojito sauce, stirring just before serving.

SLOW-COOKED PULLED PORK WITH MOJITO SAUCE

SLOW COOKER BUFFALO CHICKEN LASAGNA

Simple Chicken Tagine

Flavored with cinnamon and a touch of sweetness from the apricots, this stew tastes like it took a chef hours to make. I like to garnish it with toasted almonds or cashews and serve it with hot couscous.

—ANGELA BUCHANAN LONGMONT, CO

PREP: 15 MIN. • **COOK:** 6 HOURS
MAKES: 6 SERVINGS

- 2¼ **pounds bone-in chicken thighs, skin removed**
- 1 **large onion, chopped**
- 2 **medium carrots, sliced**
- ¾ **cup unsweetened apple juice**
- 1 **garlic clove, minced**
- 1 **teaspoon salt**
- ½ **teaspoon ground cinnamon**
- ½ **teaspoon pepper**
- 1 **cup chopped dried apricots**
  Hot cooked couscous

1. Place the chicken, onion and carrots in a 3- or 4-qt. slow cooker coated with cooking spray. In a small bowl, combine the apple juice, garlic, salt, cinnamon and pepper; pour over vegetables.
2. Cover and cook on low for 6-8 hours or until chicken is tender.
3. Remove chicken from slow cooker; shred meat with two forks. Skim fat from cooking juices; stir in apricots. Return shredded chicken to slow cooker; heat through. Serve with couscous.

DID YOU KNOW?

Minced garlic that you purchase, garlic that's been finely chopped by hand and garlic that's been put through a press can all be used interchangeably in recipes. Choose whichever is easiest and most convenient for you.

Slow Cooker Buffalo Chicken Lasagna

When I make this tasty chicken lasagna at home, I use a whole bottle of Buffalo wing sauce because my family likes food nice and spicy. Use less if you prefer, and simply increase the pasta sauce.

—HEIDI PEPIN SYKESVILLE, MD

PREP: 25 MIN. • **COOK:** 4 HOURS + STANDING
MAKES: 8 SERVINGS

- 1½ **pounds ground chicken**
- 1 **tablespoon olive oil**
- 1 **bottle (12 ounces) Buffalo wing sauce**
- 1½ **cups meatless spaghetti sauce**
- 1 **carton (15 ounces) ricotta cheese**
- 2 **cups (8 ounces) shredded part-skim mozzarella cheese**
- 9 **no-cook lasagna noodles**
- 2 **medium sweet red peppers, chopped**
- ½ **cup crumbled blue cheese or feta cheese**
  Chopped celery and additional crumbled blue cheese, optional

1. In a Dutch oven, cook chicken in oil over medium heat until no longer pink; drain. Stir in wing sauce and spaghetti sauce. In a small bowl, mix ricotta and mozzarella cheeses.
2. Spread 1 cup sauce onto the bottom of an oval 6-qt. slow cooker. Layer with three noodles (breaking noodles to fit), 1 cup sauce, a third of the peppers and a third of the cheese mixture. Repeat layers twice. Top with remaining sauce; sprinkle with blue cheese.
3. Cover and cook on low for 4-5 hours or until noodles are tender. Let stand 15 minutes before serving. Top with celery and additional blue cheese if desired.

ANGELA BUCHANAN'S
SIMPLE CHICKEN TAGINE

LIP SMACKIN' RIBS

Lip Smackin' Ribs

No matter what time of year you eat them, these ribs taste like summer. They're feel-good food at its best!

—RON BYNAKER LEBANON, PA

PREP: 20 MIN. • **COOK:** 6 HOURS
MAKES: 8 SERVINGS

- 3 tablespoons butter
- 3 pounds boneless country-style pork ribs
- 1 can (15 ounces) tomato sauce
- 1 cup packed brown sugar
- 1 cup ketchup
- ¼ cup prepared mustard
- 2 tablespoons honey
- 3 teaspoons pepper
- 2 teaspoons dried savory
- 1 teaspoon salt

In a large skillet, heat butter over medium heat. Brown ribs in batches; transfer to a 5-qt. slow cooker. Add remaining ingredients. Cook, covered, on low 6-8 hours or until meat is tender.

Moist Turkey Breast with White Wine Gravy

I modified a favorite dish for slow-cooker ease. It's moist and tender each time and perfectly complemented by the white wine gravy. I prefer to make it with regular wine, not cooking wine.

—TINA MACKISSOCK MANCHESTER, NH

PREP: 20 MIN. • **COOK:** 6 HOURS
MAKES: 8 SERVINGS

- 1 cup white wine
- 1 medium apple, chopped
- ½ cup sliced fennel bulb
- ⅓ cup chopped celery
- ⅓ cup chopped carrot
- 3 garlic cloves, minced
- 1 teaspoon ground mustard
- 1 bay leaf
- ½ teaspoon dried rosemary, crushed
- ½ teaspoon dried thyme
- ½ teaspoon rubbed sage
- ¼ teaspoon pepper
- 1 package (3 pounds) frozen boneless turkey roast with gravy, thawed
- 2 tablespoons plus 1½ teaspoons cornstarch
- ½ cup half-and-half cream

1. In a 6-qt. slow cooker, combine the wine, apple, fennel, celery, carrot, garlic, mustard and bay leaf. In a small bowl, combine the rosemary, thyme, sage and pepper; rub over turkey. (Discard gravy packet or save for another use.) Add turkey to slow cooker. Cover and cook on low for 6-8 hours or until meat is tender.

2. Remove meat to a serving platter and keep warm. Strain drippings into a measuring cup to measure 1 cup. Skim fat. In a small saucepan, combine cornstarch and cream; stir until smooth. Gradually add drippings. Bring to a boil; cook and stir for 2 minutes or until thickened. Serve with turkey.

MOIST TURKEY BREAST WITH WHITE WINE GRAVY

SPICY CHICKEN AND RICE

Italian Sausages with Provolone

Here's a simple recipe everyone will rave about. These sausages, with their pepper and onion topping, disappear quickly. Better make a double batch!

—**SHELLY BEVINGTON** HERMISTON, OR

PREP: 15 MIN. • **COOK:** 4 HOURS
MAKES: 10 SERVINGS

- 10 **Italian sausage links (4 ounces each)**
- 1 **tablespoon canola oil**
- 1 **each small sweet red, yellow and orange peppers, cut into strips**
- 2 **medium onions, halved and sliced**
- 2 **cups Italian salad dressing**
- 10 **slices provolone cheese**
- 10 **brat buns**

1. In a large skillet, brown sausages in batches in oil. Drain. Transfer to a 5-qt. slow cooker. Add the peppers, onions and salad dressing. Cover and cook on low for 4-5 hours or until a thermometer reads 160° and vegetables are tender.

2. Place the sausages and cheese in buns; using a slotted spoon, top with pepper mixture.

ITALIAN SAUSAGES WITH PROVOLONE

Spicy Chicken and Rice

As a working mom, I have little time to prepare something hearty for dinner during the week. This recipe is easily tossed together in the morning, and it's fabulous to come home to at night. Even my picky eaters love it!

—**JESSICA COSTELLO** FITCHBURG, MA

PREP: 20 MIN. • **COOK:** 5½ HOURS
MAKES: 8 SERVINGS

- 1½ **pounds boneless skinless chicken breast halves**
- 2 **cans (14½ ounces each) diced tomatoes with mild green chilies, undrained**
- 2 **medium green peppers, chopped**
- 1 **medium onion, chopped**
- 1 **garlic clove, minced**
- 1 **teaspoon smoked paprika**
- ¾ **teaspoon salt**
- ½ **teaspoon ground cumin**
- ½ **teaspoon ground chipotle pepper**
- 6 **cups cooked brown rice**
- 1 **can (15 ounces) black beans, rinsed and drained**
- ½ **cup shredded cheddar cheese**
- ½ **cup reduced-fat sour cream**

1. Place chicken in a 4- or 5-qt. slow cooker. In a large bowl, combine the tomatoes, green peppers, onion, garlic, paprika, salt, cumin and chipotle pepper; pour over chicken. Cover and cook on low for 5-6 hours or until chicken is tender.

2. Remove chicken; cool slightly. Shred with two forks and return to the slow cooker. Stir in rice and beans; heat through. Garnish with cheese and sour cream.

SUNDAY DINNER BRISKET

Sunday Dinner Brisket

We love the tenderness of this brisket done in the slow cooker. The sauce has a robust, beefy flavor with a slight tang from the balsamic vinegar, and the rich caramelized onions complete the entree.

—*TASTE OF HOME* TEST KITCHEN

PREP: 45 MIN. • **COOK:** 8 HOURS
MAKES: 10 SERVINGS

- 4 **cups sliced onions (about 4 medium)**
- 3 **tablespoons olive oil, divided**
- 4 **garlic cloves, minced**
- 1 **tablespoon brown sugar**
- ⅓ **cup all-purpose flour**
- 1 **fresh beef brisket (4 to 5 pounds)**
- 1 **teaspoon salt**
- 1 **teaspoon coarsely ground pepper**
- ¼ **cup balsamic vinegar**
- 1 **can (14 ounces) reduced-sodium beef broth**
- 2 **tablespoons tomato paste**
- 2 **teaspoons Italian seasoning**
- 1 **teaspoon Worcestershire sauce**
- ½ **teaspoon paprika**
- 1 **tablespoon cornstarch**
- 2 **tablespoons cold water**

1. In a large skillet, saute onions in 1 tablespoon of oil until softened. Sprinkle with garlic and brown sugar. Reduce heat to medium-low; cook 10 minutes or until onions are golden brown, stirring occasionally. Transfer to a 4- or 5-qt. slow cooker.

2. Sprinkle flour over both sides of brisket; shake off excess. In the same skillet, brown beef in remaining oil on all sides. Remove from heat; sprinkle with salt and pepper. Place beef on top of onions. Add balsamic vinegar to skillet; increase heat to medium-high. Cook, stirring to loosen browned bits from pan. Pour over beef.

3. In a small bowl, combine the broth, tomato paste, Italian seasoning, Worcestershire sauce and paprika; pour over beef. Cover and cook on low for 8-10 hours or until meat is tender.

4. Remove roast to a serving platter; keep warm. Pour cooking juices into a small saucepan; skim fat and bring to a boil. In a small bowl, combine cornstarch and water until smooth; stir into cooking juices. Return to a boil; cook and stir for 1-2 minutes or until thickened. Thinly slice beef across the grain; serve with sauce. **NOTE** *This is a fresh beef brisket, not corned beef.*

Tender Salsa Beef

This is my Mexican twist on comfort food. To keep the dinner kid-friendly, consider using a mild salsa.

—**STACIE STAMPER** NORTH WILKESBORO, NC

PREP: 15 MIN. • **COOK:** 8 HOURS
MAKES: 8 SERVINGS

- 1½ **pounds beef stew meat, cut into ¾-inch cubes**
- 2 **cups salsa**
- 1 **tablespoon brown sugar**
- 1 **tablespoon reduced-sodium soy sauce**
- 1 **garlic clove, minced**
- 4 **cups hot cooked brown rice**

In a 3-qt. slow cooker, combine the beef, salsa, brown sugar, soy sauce and garlic. Cover and cook on low for 8-10 hours or until meat is tender. Using a slotted spoon, serve beef with rice.

TENDER SALSA BEEF

**RED, WHITE AND BREW
SLOW-COOKED CHICKEN**

1. Place the first eight ingredients in a food processor; cover and process until pureed. Stir in beer; set aside.
2. Rub chicken pieces with chili seasoning. Place in a 5-qt. slow cooker. Pour tomato mixture over chicken. Cover and cook on low for 6-7 hours or until chicken is tender.
3. Thicken cooking liquid if desired. Serve the chicken with pasta.
NOTE *Wear disposable gloves when cutting hot peppers; the oils can burn skin. Avoid touching your face.*

Sweet 'n' Tangy Chicken

My slow cooker comes in really handy during the haying and harvest seasons. We're so busy that if supper isn't prepared before I serve lunch, it doesn't seem to get done on time.
—**JOAN AIREY** RIVERS, MB

PREP: 15 MIN. • **COOK:** 4 HOURS
MAKES: 4 SERVINGS

- 1 **medium onion, chopped**
- 1½ **teaspoons minced garlic**
- 1 **broiler/fryer chicken (3 pounds), cut up, skin removed**

⅔ **cup ketchup**
⅓ **cup packed brown sugar**
1 **tablespoon chili powder**
1 **tablespoon lemon juice**
1 **teaspoon dried basil**
½ **teaspoon salt**
¼ **teaspoon pepper**
⅛ **teaspoon hot pepper sauce**
2 **tablespoons cornstarch**
3 **tablespoons cold water**

1. In a 3-qt. slow cooker, combine onion and garlic; top with chicken. In a small bowl, combine the ketchup, brown sugar, chili powder, lemon juice, basil, salt, pepper and pepper sauce; pour over chicken. Cover and cook on low for 4-5 hours or until meat is tender. Remove chicken to a serving platter; keep warm.
2. Skim fat from cooking juices; transfer to a small saucepan. Bring liquid to a boil. Combine cornstarch and water until smooth. Gradually stir into the pan. Bring to a boil; cook and stir for 2 minutes or until thickened. Serve with chicken.

Red, White and Brew Slow-Cooked Chicken

Cut up economical whole chicken and simmer it in a spicy tomato sauce. Then serve it with crusty slices of bread so you can mop up every last drop of sauce!
—**GILDA LESTER** MILLSBORO, DE

PREP: 25 MIN. • **COOK:** 6 HOURS
MAKES: 6 SERVINGS

- 1 **can (14½ ounces) fire-roasted diced tomatoes, undrained**
- 1 **medium onion, chopped**
- 1 **jalapeno pepper, seeded and chopped**
- 3 **tablespoons brown sugar**
- 3 **tablespoons balsamic vinegar**
- 1 **tablespoon ground mustard**
- 1 **teaspoon dried basil**
- ¼ **teaspoon crushed red pepper flakes**
- 1 **cup beer or nonalcoholic beer**
- 1 **broiler/fryer chicken (3 to 4 pounds), cut up and skin removed**
- 1 **envelope (1¼ ounces) chili seasoning**
  Hot cooked pasta

SWEET 'N' TANGY CHICKEN

TEX-MEX CHICKEN & RICE

Tex-Mex Chicken & Rice

I came up with this recipe for my sister after she received her first slow cooker. She cooks mostly by throwing canned goods into a pot, so this is a delicious go-to recipe for her on busy days.
—**ELIZABETH DUMONT** BOULDER, CO

PREP: 15 MIN. • **COOK:** 7 HOURS
MAKES: 6 SERVINGS

- 6 **chicken leg quarters, skin removed**
- 1 **envelope taco seasoning, divided**
- 1 **can (14½ ounces) Mexican diced tomatoes, undrained**
- 1 **can (10¾ ounces) condensed cream of chicken soup, undiluted**
- 1 **large onion, chopped**
- 1 **can (4 ounces) chopped green chilies**
- 1 **cup uncooked instant rice**
- 1 **cup canned black beans, rinsed and drained**
- 1 **container (8 ounces) sour cream**
- 1 **cup (4 ounces) shredded cheddar cheese**
- 1½ **cups crushed tortilla chips**
  Minced fresh cilantro

1. Sprinkle chicken with 1 tablespoon taco seasoning; transfer to a 5- or 6-qt. slow cooker. In a large bowl, combine the tomatoes, soup, onion, chilies and remaining taco seasoning; pour over chicken. Cover and cook on low for 7-9 hours or until chicken is tender.
2. Prepare rice according to package directions. Stir in beans; heat through.
3. Remove chicken from cooking juices; stir sour cream into cooking juices. Serve chicken with rice mixture and sauce. Sprinkle servings with cheese, tortilla chips and cilantro.

Brat Sauerkraut Supper

My stick-to-your-ribs German dish is sure to satisfy even the biggest appetites at your house. Sliced apple and apple juice lend mellowing sweetness to the tangy sauerkraut, flavorful bratwurst, red potatoes and bacon.
—**ANN CHRISTENSEN** MESA, AZ

PREP: 15 MIN. • **COOK:** 4 HOURS
MAKES: 6 SERVINGS

- 1 **jar (32 ounces) sauerkraut, rinsed and well drained**
- 2 **medium red potatoes, peeled, halved and cut into thin slices**
- 1 **medium tart apple, peeled and cut into thick slices**
- 1 **small onion, chopped**
- ½ **cup apple juice**
- ¼ **cup water**
- 2 **tablespoons brown sugar**
- 1 **teaspoon chicken bouillon granules**
- 1 **teaspoon caraway seeds**
- 1 **garlic clove, minced**
- 1 **bay leaf**
- 1 **pound fully cooked bratwurst links**
- 6 **bacon strips, cooked and crumbled**

In a 5-qt. slow cooker, combine the first 11 ingredients. Top with the bratwurst. Cover and cook on high for 4-5 hours or until the potatoes are tender. Discard bay leaf. Sprinkle with the bacon.

BRAT SAUERKRAUT SUPPER

> With a busy day ahead, I threw this jambalaya-style main dish together using items I had on hand—it was so easy! When I served it at dinner, it earned rave reviews from my guests.
> —**DEE GUELCHER** ACWORTH, GA

Tropical Triple Pork

PREP: 25 MIN. • **COOK:** 5 HOURS
MAKES: 8 SERVINGS

- 1½ pounds boneless pork loin roast
- ¾ pound fully cooked andouille sausage links, sliced
- 1½ cups cubed fully cooked ham
- 1 can (28 ounces) diced tomatoes, undrained
- 2 medium mangoes, peeled and chopped
- 1 medium onion, chopped
- 1 cup roasted sweet red peppers, cut into strips
- 1 bay leaf
- 1 teaspoon salt
- ½ teaspoon pepper
  Hot cooked rice

1. Place roast in a 5-qt. slow cooker. Add sausage and ham. Stir in the tomatoes, mangoes, onion, red peppers, bay leaf, salt and pepper. Cover and cook on low for 5-6 hours or until meat is tender.
2. Remove roast to a plate. Discard bay leaf. Shred meat with two forks and return to slow cooker; heat through. Serve with rice.

Tempting Teriyaki Chicken Stew

I created this dish that combines two of my favorite tastes—salty and sweet. I'm always looking for new ideas for my slow cooker, and this one's a keeper!
—**AMY SIEGEL** CLIFTON, NJ

PREP: 20 MIN. • **COOK:** 7 HOURS
MAKES: 6 SERVINGS

- 1 tablespoon olive oil
- 6 bone-in chicken thighs (about 2 pounds)
- 2 medium sweet potatoes, cut into 1-inch pieces
- 3 medium carrots, cut into 1-inch pieces
- 1 medium parsnip, peeled and cut into 1-inch pieces
- 1 medium onion, sliced
- 1 cup apricot preserves
- ½ cup maple syrup
- ½ cup teriyaki sauce
- ½ teaspoon ground ginger
- ⅛ teaspoon cayenne pepper
- 2 tablespoons cornstarch
- 2 tablespoons cold water

1. In a large skillet, heat oil over medium-high heat; brown chicken on both sides. Place vegetables in a 4-qt. slow cooker; add chicken. In a small bowl, mix the preserves, maple syrup, teriyaki sauce, ginger and cayenne; pour over chicken.
2. Cover and cook on low for 6-8 hours or until the chicken is tender. Remove chicken and vegetables to a platter; keep warm.
3. Transfer cooking liquid to a small saucepan. Skim the fat. Bring cooking liquid to a boil. In a small bowl, combine cornstarch and water until smooth; gradually stir into the pan. Return to a boil, stirring constantly; cook and stir for 2 minutes or until thickened. Serve with chicken and vegetables.

TEMPTING TERIYAKI CHICKEN STEW

SLOW COOKER
ROTISSERIE-STYLE CHICKEN

Slow Cooker Rotisserie-Style Chicken

No one will believe this golden brown chicken was made in the slow cooker! Packed with flavor, the meat is moist, the carrots are tender and the juices would make a nice gravy.

—TASTE OF HOME TEST KITCHEN

PREP: 30 MIN.
COOK: 6 HOURS + STANDING
MAKES: 6 SERVINGS

- 4 teaspoons seasoned salt
- 4 teaspoons poultry seasoning
- 1 tablespoon paprika
- 1½ teaspoons onion powder
- 1½ teaspoons brown sugar
- 1½ teaspoons salt-free lemon-pepper seasoning
- ¾ teaspoon garlic powder
- 1 broiler/fryer chicken (4 pounds)
- 1 pound carrots, halved lengthwise and cut into 1½-inch lengths
- 2 large onions, chopped
- 2 tablespoons cornstarch

1. In a small bowl, combine the first seven ingredients. Carefully loosen skin from the chicken breast; rub 1 tablespoon spice mixture under the skin. Rub remaining spice mixture over chicken. In another bowl, toss carrots and onions with cornstarch; transfer to a 6-qt. slow cooker. Place chicken on vegetables.

2. Cover and cook on low for 6-7 hours or until a thermometer inserted in thigh reads 180°. Remove chicken and vegetables to a serving platter; cover and let stand for 15 minutes before carving. Skim fat from cooking juices. Serve with chicken and vegetables.

No-Fuss Pork Roast Dinner

This delicious recipe will give you the most delightful pork you've ever tasted! You can cut it with a fork, and it's just as juicy and tender the next day...if there are any leftovers, that is!

—JANE MONTGOMERY PIQUA, OH

PREP: 25 MIN. • **COOK:** 6 HOURS
MAKES: 8 SERVINGS

- 1 large onion, halved and sliced
- 1 boneless pork loin roast (2½ pounds)
- 4 medium potatoes, peeled and cubed
- 1 package (16 ounces) frozen sliced carrots
- 1 cup hot water
- ¼ cup sugar
- 3 tablespoons cider vinegar
- 2 tablespoons reduced-sodium soy sauce
- 1 tablespoon ketchup
- ½ teaspoon salt
- ½ teaspoon pepper
- ¼ teaspoon garlic powder
- ¼ teaspoon chili powder
- 2 tablespoons cornstarch
- 2 tablespoons cold water

1. Place onion in a 5-qt. slow cooker. Add the pork, potatoes and carrots. Whisk the hot water, sugar, vinegar, soy sauce, ketchup, salt, pepper, garlic powder and chili powder; pour over pork and vegetables. Cover and cook on low for 6-8 hours or until the meat is tender.

2. Remove pork and vegetables to a serving platter; keep warm. Skim fat from cooking juices; transfer to a small saucepan. Bring liquid to a boil. Combine cornstarch and cold water until smooth. Gradually stir into the pan. Bring to a boil; cook and stir for 2 minutes or until thickened. Serve with meat and vegetables.

NO-FUSS PORK ROAST DINNER

SAVORY LEMONADE CHICKEN

Savory Lemonade Chicken

I don't know where this recipe originally came from, but my mother used to prepare it for our family when I was little. Now I love to make it! A sweet and tangy sauce nicely coats poultry that's ready to serve in just a few hours.

—**JENNY COOK** EAU CLAIRE, WI

PREP: 10 MIN. • **COOK:** 3 HOURS
MAKES: 6 SERVINGS

- 6 boneless skinless chicken breast halves (4 ounces each)
- ¾ cup thawed lemonade concentrate
- 3 tablespoons ketchup
- 2 tablespoons brown sugar
- 1 tablespoon cider vinegar
- 2 tablespoons cornstarch
- 2 tablespoons cold water

1. Place chicken in a 5-qt. slow cooker. In a small bowl, combine the lemonade concentrate, ketchup, brown sugar and vinegar; pour over chicken. Cover and cook on low for 2½ hours or until chicken is tender.

2. Remove chicken and keep warm. Combine cornstarch and water until smooth; gradually stir into cooking juices. Cover and cook on high for 30 minutes or until thickened. Return chicken to slow cooker; heat through.

Polynesian Roast Beef

This easy and delicious recipe from my sister has been a family favorite for years. Pineapple and peppers perfectly complement the rich and savory beef.

—**ANNETTE MOSBARGER** PEYTON, CO

PREP: 15 MIN. • **COOK:** 7 HOURS
MAKES: 10-11 SERVINGS

- 1 beef top round roast (3¼ pounds)
- 2 tablespoons browning sauce, optional
- ¼ cup all-purpose flour
- 1 teaspoon salt
- ¼ teaspoon pepper
- 1 medium onion, sliced
- 1 can (8 ounces) unsweetened sliced pineapple
- ¼ cup packed brown sugar
- 2 tablespoons cornstarch
- ¼ teaspoon ground ginger
- ½ cup beef broth
- ¼ cup reduced-sodium soy sauce
- ½ teaspoon minced garlic
- 1 medium green pepper, sliced

1. Cut roast in half; brush with browning sauce if desired. Combine the flour, salt and pepper; rub over meat. Place onion in a 3-qt. slow cooker; top with roast.

2. Drain pineapple, reserving juice; refrigerate the pineapple. In a small bowl, combine the brown sugar, cornstarch and ginger; whisk in the broth, soy sauce, garlic and reserved pineapple juice until smooth. Pour over meat. Cover and cook on low for 6-8 hours.

3. Add pineapple and green pepper. Cook 1 hour longer or until the meat is tender.

POLYNESIAN ROAST BEEF

PORK ROAST CUBANO

Pork Roast Cubano

It takes me just minutes to assemble this recipe, and the slow cooker does the rest of the work! It's a one-dish meal that's real comfort food for my family.

—ROXANNE CHAN ALBANY, CA

PREP: 30 MIN. • **COOK:** 7 HOURS
MAKES: 8 SERVINGS

- 3 **pounds boneless pork shoulder butt roast**
- 2 **tablespoons olive oil**
- 1 **can (15 ounces) black beans, rinsed and drained**
- 1 **medium sweet potato, cut into ½-inch cubes**
- 1 **small sweet red pepper, cubed**
- 1 **can (13.66 ounces) light coconut milk**
- ½ **cup salsa verde**
- 1 **teaspoon minced fresh gingerroot**
- 2 **green onions, thinly sliced**
   Sliced papaya

1. In a large skillet, brown roast in oil on all sides. Transfer to a 5-qt. slow cooker. Add black beans, sweet potato and red pepper. In a small bowl, mix coconut milk, salsa and ginger; pour over top.

2. Cook, covered, on low 7-9 hours or until pork is tender. Sprinkle with green onions; serve with papaya.

Italian Sausage and Vegetables

This easy and complete meal-in-a-pot is both healthy and delicious. It's wonderful served with a slice of hot garlic bread. I found the recipe in a magazine and made just a few adjustments to suit myself. Enjoy!

—GINNY STUBY ALTOONA, PA

PREP: 20 MIN. • **COOK:** 5½ HOURS
MAKES: 6 SERVINGS

- 1¼ **pounds sweet or hot Italian turkey sausage links**
- 1 **can (28 ounces) diced tomatoes, undrained**
- 2 **medium potatoes, cut into 1-inch pieces**
- 4 **small zucchini, cut into 1-inch slices**
- 1 **medium onion, cut into wedges**
- ½ **teaspoon garlic powder**
- ¼ **teaspoon crushed red pepper flakes**
- ¼ **teaspoon dried oregano**
- ¼ **teaspoon dried basil**
- 1 **tablespoon dry bread crumbs**
- ¾ **cup shredded pepper jack cheese**

1. In a nonstick skillet, brown sausages over medium heat. Place in a 5-qt. slow cooker. Add the vegetables and seasonings. Cover and cook on low for 5½ to 6½ hours or until a thermometer reads 165°.

2. Remove sausages and cut into 1-in. pieces; return to slow cooker. Stir in bread crumbs. Serve in bowls; sprinkle with cheese.

ITALIAN SAUSAGE AND VEGETABLES

Summer

SOUPS & SANDWICHES

The classic pairing of a soup and sandwich is a hit any time of year! Here, you'll find soups featuring the season's freshest ingredients and hearty sandwiches ideal for all of the appetites at your table.

JUDY DAMES'
HAWAIIAN SAUSAGE SUBS

(5) INGREDIENTS

Hawaiian Sausage Subs

If you are looking for a different way to use kielbasa, the sweet and mildly spicy flavor of these sandwiches is a nice change of pace.

—JUDY DAMES BRIDGEVILLE, PA

PREP: 15 MIN. • **COOK:** 3 HOURS
MAKES: 12 SERVINGS

- 3 **pounds smoked kielbasa or Polish sausage, cut into 3-inch pieces**
- 2 **bottles (12 ounces each) chili sauce**
- 1 **can (20 ounces) pineapple tidbits, undrained**
- ¼ **cup packed brown sugar**
- 12 **hoagie buns, split**

Place kielbasa in a 3-qt. slow cooker. Combine the chili sauce, pineapple and brown sugar; pour over kielbasa. Cover and cook on low for 3-4 hours or until heated through. Serve on buns.

Southwestern Chicken & Lima Bean Soup

I love to cook for my family and to see them fill their plates up again and comment on how tasty something is. This simple supper is so colorful, delicious and healthy that you're sure to love it.

—PAM CORDER MONROE, LA

PREP: 20 MIN. • **COOK:** 6 HOURS
MAKES: 6 SERVINGS

- 4 **bone-in chicken thighs (1½ pounds), skin removed**
- 2 **cups frozen lima beans**
- 2 **cups frozen corn**
- 1 **large green pepper, chopped**
- 1 **large onion, chopped**
- 2 **cans (14 ounces each) fire-roasted diced tomatoes, undrained**
- ¼ **cup tomato paste**
- 3 **tablespoons Worcestershire sauce**
- 3 **garlic cloves, minced**
- 1½ **teaspoons ground cumin**
- 1½ **teaspoons dried oregano**
- ¼ **teaspoon salt**
- ¼ **teaspoon pepper**
  Chopped fresh cilantro or parsley

1. Place the first five ingredients in a 5-qt. slow cooker. In a large bowl, combine tomatoes, tomato paste, Worcestershire sauce, garlic and dry seasonings; pour over top.

2. Cook, covered, on low 6-8 hours or until chicken is tender. Remove chicken from slow cooker. When cool enough to handle, remove meat from bones; discard bones. Shred meat with two forks; return to slow cooker and heat through. If desired, sprinkle with cilantro.

These saucy sandwiches are great for a hungry crowd. Best of all, they're easy to prepare. Once the meat is cooked, simply transfer it to a slow cooker to keep it nice and warm.

—**KIMBERLY WALLACE** DENNISON, OH

Slow Cooked Barbecued Pork Sandwiches

PREP: 20 MIN. • **COOK:** 9 HOURS
MAKES: 10 SERVINGS

- 1 medium onion, chopped
- 1 tablespoon butter
- 1 can (15 ounces) tomato puree
- ½ cup packed brown sugar
- ¼ cup steak sauce
- 2 tablespoons lemon juice
- ½ teaspoon salt
- 1 boneless pork shoulder butt roast (3 pounds)
- 10 hard rolls, split

1. In a large skillet, saute onion in butter until tender. Stir in the tomato puree, brown sugar, steak sauce, lemon juice and salt. Cook over medium heat until sugar is dissolved and heated through.
2. Place roast in a 5-qt. slow cooker; pour sauce over the top. Cover and cook on low for 7-9 hours or until meat is tender. Remove roast; cool slightly. Skim fat from cooking juices. Shred meat with two forks and return to the slow cooker. Heat through. Serve on rolls.

ZIPPY SPANISH RICE SOUP

Zippy Spanish Rice Soup

I created this recipe after ruining a dinner of Spanish rice. I tried to salvage the dish by adding green chilies, cilantro and more water. It was a hit with the family! Add a salad and corn bread, and it's a meal.

—**MARILYN SCHETZ** CUYAHOGA FALLS, OH

PREP: 20 MIN. • **COOK:** 4 HOURS
MAKES: 8 SERVINGS (2 QUARTS)

- 1 pound lean ground beef (90% lean)
- 1 medium onion, chopped
- 3 cups water
- 1 jar (16 ounces) salsa
- 1 can (14½ ounces) diced tomatoes, undrained
- 1 jar (7 ounces) roasted sweet red peppers, drained and chopped
- 1 can (4 ounces) chopped green chilies
- 1 envelope taco seasoning
- 1 tablespoon dried cilantro flakes
- ½ cup uncooked converted rice

1. In a large skillet, cook beef and onion over medium heat until meat is no longer pink; drain.
2. Transfer to a 4- or 5-qt. slow cooker. Add the water, salsa, tomatoes, red peppers, chilies, taco seasoning and cilantro. Stir in rice. Cover and cook on low for 4-5 hours or until rice is tender.

SLOW COOKED BARBECUED PORK SANDWICHES

SOUTHWEST PULLED PORK

Southwest Pulled Pork

I made this on a whim one Sunday morning when friends called and said they planned to drop by in the afternoon. It makes a lot, and I was able to serve our friends and the neighbors a casual supper. The seasonings and green chilies give the meat a spicy kick. I top servings with sour cream and fresh salsa.

—**DEB LEBLANC** PHILLIPSBURG, KS

PREP: 20 MIN. • **COOK:** 8 HOURS
MAKES: 14 SERVINGS

- 1 **boneless pork shoulder butt roast (4 pounds)**
- 2 **tablespoons chili powder**
- 1 **tablespoon brown sugar**
- 1½ **teaspoons ground cumin**
- 1 **teaspoon salt**
- ½ **teaspoon pepper**
- ½ **teaspoon cayenne pepper**
- 1 **large sweet onion, coarsely chopped**
- 2 **cans (4 ounces each) chopped green chilies**
- 1 **cup chicken broth**
- 14 **kaiser rolls, split**

1. Cut roast in half. In a small bowl, combine the chili powder, brown sugar, cumin, salt, pepper and cayenne; rub over meat. Transfer to a 5-qt. slow cooker. Top with onion and chilies. Pour broth around meat.

2. Cover and cook on low for 8-10 hours or until tender. Remove roast; cool slightly. Skim fat from cooking juices. Shred pork with two forks and return to slow cooker; heat through. Serve on rolls.

Teriyaki Sandwiches

The meat for these sandwiches comes out of the slow cooker tender and flavorful. Living as we do in the foothills of the Cascades, we frequently have deer and elk in the freezer. I sometimes substitute that in this recipe, and it never tastes like game.

—**BERNICE MUILENBURG** MOLALLA, OR

PREP: 30 MIN. • **COOK:** 7 HOURS
MAKES: 8 SERVINGS

- 2 **pounds beef boneless chuck steak**
- ¼ **cup soy sauce**
- 1 **tablespoon brown sugar**
- 1 **teaspoon ground ginger**
- 1 **garlic clove, minced**
- 4 **teaspoons cornstarch**
- 2 **tablespoons water**
- 8 **French rolls, split**
- ¼ **cup butter, melted**
  Pineapple rings
  Chopped green onions

1. Cut steak into thin bite-size slices. In a 3-qt. slow cooker, combine the soy sauce, sugar, ginger and garlic. Add steak. Cover and cook on low for 7-9 hours or until meat is tender.

2. Remove meat with a slotted spoon; set aside. Carefully pour liquid into a 2-cup measuring cup; skim fat. Add water to liquid to measure 1½ cups.

3. Pour into a large saucepan. Combine cornstarch and water until smooth; add to pan. Cook and stir until thick and bubbly, about 2 minutes. Add meat and heat through.

4. Brush rolls with butter; broil 4-5 in. from the heat for 2-3 minutes or until lightly toasted. Fill with meat, pineapple and green onions.

TERIYAKI SANDWICHES

1. In a 4-qt. slow cooker, combine the first eight ingredients. Cook, covered, on low 8-9 hours.

2. Stir in ravioli; cook, covered, on low 15-30 minutes or until pasta is tender. Top servings with cheese and olives.

Mango & Coconut Chicken Soup

I love preparing dinner in a slow cooker because it's such carefree cooking. This hearty chicken soup uses ingredients that I love, like coconut milk, edamame and fresh ginger. It's a perfect party dish.

—ROXANNE CHAN ALBANY, CA

PREP: 25 MIN. • **COOK:** 6 HOURS
MAKES: 6 SERVINGS

- 1 **broiler/fryer chicken (3 to 4 pounds), skin removed and cut up**
- 2 **tablespoons canola oil**
- 1 **can (15 ounces) whole baby corn, drained**
- 1 **package (10 ounces) frozen chopped spinach, thawed**
- 1 **cup frozen shelled edamame, thawed**
- 1 **small sweet red pepper, chopped**
- 1 **can (13.66 ounces) light coconut milk**
- ½ **cup mango salsa**
- 1 **teaspoon minced fresh gingerroot**
- 1 **medium mango, peeled and chopped**
- 2 **tablespoons lime juice**
- 2 **green onions, chopped**

1. In a large skillet, brown chicken in oil in batches. Transfer chicken and drippings to a 5-qt. slow cooker. Add the corn, spinach, edamame and pepper. In a small bowl, combine the coconut milk, salsa and ginger; pour over vegetables.

2. Cover and cook on low for 6-8 hours or until chicken is tender. Remove chicken; cool slightly. When cool enough to handle, remove meat from bones; cut or shred meat into bite-size pieces. Return meat to slow cooker.

3. Just before serving, stir in mango and lime juice. Sprinkle servings with green onions.

Pepperoni Pizza Soup

Once upon a time, my husband and I owned a pizzeria—and this dish was always popular. We've since sold the restaurant, but I still make the soup for all kinds of potlucks and gatherings. It's always a big hit and everyone asks for the recipe.

—ESTELLA PETERSON MADRAS, OR

PREP: 20 MIN. • **COOK:** 8¼ HOURS
MAKES: 6 SERVINGS (2¼ QUARTS)

- 2 **cans (14½ ounces each) Italian stewed tomatoes, undrained**
- 2 **cans (14½ ounces each) reduced-sodium beef broth**
- 1 **small onion, chopped**
- 1 **small green pepper, chopped**
- ½ **cup sliced fresh mushrooms**
- ½ **cup sliced pepperoni, halved**
- 1½ **teaspoons dried oregano**
- ⅛ **teaspoon pepper**
- 1 **package (9 ounces) refrigerated cheese ravioli**
  Shredded part-skim mozzarella cheese and sliced ripe olives

MANGO & COCONUT CHICKEN SOUP

SLOW-COOKED SPICY PORTUGUESE CACOILA

Slow-Cooked Spicy Portuguese Cacoila

You're probably used to pulled pork coated with barbecue sauce and made into sandwiches. Portuguese pulled pork is a spicy dish often served at our large family functions. Each cook generally adds his or her own touches that reflect their taste and Portuguese heritage. A mixture of beef roast and pork can also be used.

—**MICHELE MERLINO** EXETER, RI

PREP: 20 MIN. • **COOK:** 6 HOURS
MAKES: 12 SERVINGS

- 4 **pounds boneless pork shoulder butt roast, cut into 2-in. pieces**
- 1½ **cups dry red wine or reduced-sodium chicken broth**
- 4 **garlic cloves, minced**
- 4 **bay leaves**
- 1 **tablespoon salt**
- 1 **tablespoon paprika**
- 2 **to 3 teaspoons crushed red pepper flakes**
- 1 **teaspoon ground cinnamon**
- 1 **large onion, chopped**
- ½ **cup water**
- 12 **bolillos or hoagie buns, split, optional**

1. Place pork in a large resealable bag; add wine, garlic and seasonings. Seal bag and turn to coat. Refrigerate overnight.
2. Transfer pork mixture to a 5- or 6-qt. slow cooker; add onion and water. Cook, covered, on low 6-8 hours or until meat is tender.
3. Skim fat. Remove bay leaves. Shred meat with two forks. If desired, serve with a slotted spoon on bolillos.

Lime Chicken Chili

Lime juice gives this chili a zesty twist, while canned tomatoes and beans make preparation a snap. Try topping bowls with toasted tortilla strips.

—**DIANE RANDAZZO** SINKING SPRING, PA

PREP: 25 MIN. • **COOK:** 40 MIN.
MAKES: 6 SERVINGS

- 1 **medium onion, chopped**
- 1 **each medium sweet yellow, red and green pepper, chopped**
- 2 **tablespoons olive oil**
- 3 **garlic cloves, minced**
- 1 **pound ground chicken**
- 2 **cans (14½ ounces each) diced tomatoes, undrained**
- 1 **can (15 ounces) white kidney or cannellini beans, rinsed and drained**
- ¼ **cup lime juice**
- 1 **tablespoon all-purpose flour**
- 1 **tablespoon baking cocoa**
- 1 **tablespoon ground cumin**
- 1 **tablespoon chili powder**
- 2 **teaspoons ground coriander**
- 1 **teaspoon grated lime peel**
- ½ **teaspoon salt**
- ½ **teaspoon garlic pepper blend**
- ¼ **teaspoon pepper**
- 2 **flour tortillas (8 inches), cut into ¼-inch strips**
- 6 **tablespoons reduced-fat sour cream**

1. In a large skillet, saute onion and peppers in oil for 7-8 minutes or until crisp-tender. Add the garlic; cook for 1 minute longer. Add chicken; cook and stir over medium heat for 8-9 minutes or until the meat is no longer pink.
2. Transfer to a 3-qt. slow cooker. Stir in the tomatoes, beans, lime juice, flour, cocoa, cumin, chili powder, coriander, lime peel, salt, garlic pepper and pepper.
3. Cover and cook on low for 4-5 hours or until heated through.
4. Place tortilla strips on a baking sheet coated with cooking spray. Bake at 400° for 8-10 minutes or until crisp. Serve chili with sour cream and tortilla strips.

DIANE RANDAZZO'S
LIME CHICKEN CHILI

Easy Philly Cheesesteaks

Since we live in a rural area where there aren't any restaurants to speak of, I thought it would be fun to come up with a take on this classic sandwich for home. The resulting cheesesteaks are delicious! Grab a bottle of steak sauce to top them off and give them an extra bolt of flavor.

—LENETTE BENNETT COMO, CO

PREP: 20 MIN. • **COOK:** 6 HOURS
MAKES: 6 SERVINGS

- **2 medium onions, halved and sliced**
- **2 medium sweet red or green peppers, halved and sliced**
- **1 beef top sirloin steak (1½ pounds), cut into thin strips**
- **1 envelope onion soup mix**
- **1 can (14½ ounces) reduced-sodium beef broth**
- **6 hoagie buns, split**
- **12 slices provolone cheese, halved Pickled hot cherry peppers, optional**

1. Place onions and red peppers in a 4- or 5-qt. slow cooker. Add beef, soup mix and broth. Cook, covered, on low 6-8 hours or until meat is tender.
2. Arrange buns on a baking sheet, cut side up. Using tongs, place the meat mixture on bun bottoms; top with cheese.
3. Broil 2-3 in. from heat for 30-60 seconds or until cheese is melted and bun tops are toasted. If desired, serve with cherry peppers.

Zesty Italian Soup

While visiting my sister-in-law, we had a delicious Italian soup at a local restaurant. We decided to duplicate it at home and created this dish. You can vary the seasonings and types of canned tomatoes to suit your own family's tastes.

—MYRNA SIPPEL THOMPSON, IL

PREP: 15 MIN. • **COOK:** 7 HOURS
MAKES: 10 SERVINGS (3½ QUARTS)

ZESTY ITALIAN SOUP

- **1 pound bulk Italian sausage**
- **3 cans (14½ ounces each) reduced-sodium chicken broth**
- **1 can (15 ounces) black beans, rinsed and drained**
- **1 can (15 ounces) pinto beans, rinsed and drained**
- **1 can (14½ ounces) diced tomatoes and green chilies, undrained**
- **1 can (14½ ounces) Italian diced tomatoes**
- **1 large carrot, chopped**
- **1 jalapeno pepper, seeded and chopped**
- **1½ teaspoons Italian seasoning**
- **1 teaspoon dried minced garlic**
- **1½ cups cooked elbow macaroni**

1. In a large skillet, cook sausage over medium heat until no longer pink; drain.
2. Transfer to a 5-qt. slow cooker. Stir in the broth, beans, tomatoes, carrot, jalapeno, Italian seasoning and garlic.
3. Cover and cook on low for 7-8 hours or until heated through. Just before serving, stir in macaroni.
NOTE *Wear disposable gloves when cutting hot peppers; the oils can burn skin. Avoid touching your face.*

EASY PHILLY CHEESESTEAKS

SOUTHWESTERN CHICKEN SOUP

Southwestern Chicken Soup

Here's the perfect recipe for a busy week. It serves a crowd, reheats well, and the slow cooker does most of the work!

—**HAROLD TARTAR** WEST PALM BEACH, FL

PREP: 10 MIN. • **COOK:** 7 HOURS
MAKES: 10 SERVINGS (2½ QUARTS)

- 1¼ **pounds boneless skinless chicken breasts, cut into thin strips**
- 1 **tablespoon canola oil**
- 2 **cans (14½ ounces each) reduced-sodium chicken broth**
- 1 **package (16 ounces) frozen corn, thawed**
- 1 **can (14½ ounces) diced tomatoes, undrained**
- 1 **medium onion, chopped**
- 1 **medium green pepper, chopped**
- 1 **medium sweet red pepper, chopped**
- 1 **can (4 ounces) chopped green chilies**
- 1½ **teaspoons seasoned salt, optional**
- 1 **teaspoon ground cumin**
- ½ **teaspoon garlic powder**

1. In a large skillet, saute chicken in oil until lightly browned. Transfer to a 5-qt. slow cooker. Stir in all the remaining ingredients.

2. Cover and cook on low for 7-8 hours or until chicken and vegetables are tender. Stir before serving.

Very Best Barbecue Beef Sandwiches

Simple and so good, this recipe is sure to be popular with your friends. The sweet and tangy barbecue beef sandwiches definitely live up to their name.

—*TASTE OF HOME* **TEST KITCHEN**

PREP: 20 MIN. • **COOK:** 8 HOURS
MAKES: 12 SERVINGS

- 1 **boneless beef chuck roast (3 to 4 pounds)**
- 1½ **cups ketchup**
- 1 **small onion, finely chopped**
- ¼ **cup packed brown sugar**
- ¼ **cup red wine vinegar**
- 1 **tablespoon Dijon mustard**
- 1 **tablespoon Worcestershire sauce**
- 2 **garlic cloves, minced**
- ½ **teaspoon salt**
- ¼ **teaspoon celery seed**
- ¼ **teaspoon paprika**
- ¼ **teaspoon pepper**
- 2 **tablespoons cornstarch**
- 2 **tablespoons cold water**
- 12 **kaiser rolls, split**
   Dill pickle slices, optional

1. Cut roast in half. Place in a 5-qt. slow cooker. In a small bowl, combine the ketchup, onion, brown sugar, vinegar, mustard, Worcestershire sauce, garlic, salt, celery seed, paprika and pepper; pour over roast. Cover and cook on low for 8-10 hours or until meat is tender.

2. Remove meat. Skim fat from cooking juices; transfer to a large saucepan. Bring to a boil. Combine cornstarch and water until smooth; gradually stir into juices. Return to a boil; cook and stir for 2 minutes or until thickened.

3. When meat is cool enough to handle, shred with two forks. Return to slow cooker and stir in sauce mixture; heat through. Serve on rolls with pickle slices if desired.

VERY BEST BARBECUE BEEF SANDWICHES

TEX-MEX BEEF SANDWICHES

Tex-Mex Beef Sandwiches

Everyone loves these when I serve them. The cocoa is a surprise ingredient that adds a depth of flavor and can be hard to identify, so I'm often asked, "What's that great taste?"

—BRENDA THEISEN ADDISON, MI

PREP: 25 MIN. • **COOK:** 8 HOURS
MAKES: 8 SERVINGS

- 1 **boneless beef chuck roast (3 pounds)**
- 1 **envelope burrito seasoning**
- 2 **tablespoons baking cocoa**
- 1 **large green pepper, coarsely chopped**
- 1 **large sweet red pepper, coarsely chopped**
- 1 **large onion, chopped**
- 1 **cup beef broth**
- ½ **cup ketchup**
- 8 **hoagie buns, split**

1. Cut roast in half. Combine burrito seasoning and cocoa; rub over meat. Place peppers and onion in a 3- or 4-qt. slow cooker; top with meat. Combine broth and ketchup; pour over meat.

2. Cover and cook on low for 8-10 hours or until meat is tender.

3. Skim fat. When cool enough to handle, shred meat with two forks and return to slow cooker; heat through. Using a slotted spoon, spoon ½ cup onto each bun.

Posole Verde

With fresh tomatillos, green chilies and hominy, this hearty, healthy soup nods to authentic Mexican fare. Family and friends frequently request it when they're invited for dinner.

—GAYLE EHRENMAN WHITE PLAINS, NY

PREP: 30 MIN. • **COOK:** 7 HOURS
MAKES: 8 SERVINGS (3 QUARTS)

- 1 **pork tenderloin (1 pound), cubed**
- 1 **package (12 ounces) fully cooked spicy chicken sausage links, sliced**
- 8 **tomatillos, husks removed and cut into 1-inch pieces**
- 2 **cans (14 ounces each) hominy, rinsed and drained**
- 1 **can (16 ounces) kidney beans, rinsed and drained**
- 1 **can (14½ ounces) chicken broth**
- 3 **cans (4 ounces each) chopped green chilies**
- 1 **large red onion, quartered and sliced**
- 2 **tablespoons brown sugar**
- 3 **garlic cloves, minced**
- 1 **tablespoon ground cumin**
- 1 **tablespoon chili powder**
- 1 **teaspoon dried oregano**
  Minced fresh cilantro, optional

In a 6-qt. slow cooker, combine the first 13 ingredients. Cover and cook on low for 8-10 hours or until pork is tender. Sprinkle with cilantro if desired.

DID YOU KNOW?

Tomatillos resemble small green tomatoes in size and shape and have brown papery husks. Once the husks are removed, tomatillos can be added to dishes, offering hints of lemon and apple flavors.

Spinach Bean Soup

This meatless soup is great for a busy weeknight supper after I get home from my job as a college nursing professor. It offers plenty of nutrients to keep me both healthy and satisfied.

—**BRENDA JEFFERS** OTTUMWA, IA

PREP: 20 MIN. • **COOK:** 6¼ HOURS
MAKES: 8 SERVINGS (2 QUARTS)

- 3 cans (14½ ounces each) vegetable broth
- 1 can (15½ ounces) great northern beans, rinsed and drained
- 1 can (15 ounces) tomato puree
- ½ cup finely chopped onion
- ½ cup uncooked converted long grain rice
- 2 garlic cloves, minced
- 1 teaspoon dried basil
- ½ teaspoon salt
- ¼ teaspoon pepper
- 1 package (6 ounces) fresh baby spinach, coarsely chopped
- ¼ cup shredded Parmesan cheese

In a 4-qt. slow cooker, combine the first nine ingredients. Cover and cook on low for 6-7 hours or until heated through. Stir in spinach. Cover and cook for 15 minutes or until spinach is wilted. Sprinkle with cheese.

COUNTRY RIB SANDWICHES

Country Rib Sandwiches

Perfect for a weekday dinner, these slow-cooked sandwiches are packed with down-home flavor.

—**MARGARET LUCHSINGER** JUPITER, FL

PREP: 30 MIN. • **COOK:** 6 HOURS
MAKES: 8 SERVINGS

- 1 large onion, chopped
- 2 pounds boneless country-style pork ribs
- ½ cup ketchup
- ¼ cup plum sauce
- ¼ cup chili sauce
- 2 tablespoons brown sugar
- 1 teaspoon celery seed
- 1 teaspoon garlic powder
- 1 teaspoon liquid smoke, optional
- ½ teaspoon ground allspice
- 8 kaiser rolls, split

1. Place onion in a 3-qt. slow cooker; top with ribs. Combine the ketchup, plum sauce, chili sauce, brown sugar, celery seed, garlic powder, liquid smoke if desired and allspice; pour over ribs.

2. Cover and cook on low for 6-7 hours or until meat is tender. Shred meat with two forks. Serve on rolls.

SPINACH BEAN SOUP

ALICE PEACOCK'S
VEGETABLE MINESTRONE

Vegetable Minestrone

My husband and I created this recipe to replicate the minestrone soup at our favorite Italian hot spot. It's nice to have this ready to eat for our evening meal on days when we have a real busy schedule. To make the soup vegetarian, use vegetable broth instead of beef.

—ALICE PEACOCK GRANDVIEW, MO

PREP: 15 MIN. • **COOK:** 6½ HOURS
MAKES: 8 SERVINGS (2½ QUARTS)

- 2 cans (14½ ounces each) beef broth
- 1 can (16 ounces) kidney beans, rinsed and drained
- 1 can (15 ounces) great northern beans, rinsed and drained
- 1 can (14½ ounces) Italian-style stewed tomatoes
- 1 large onion, chopped
- 1 medium zucchini, thinly sliced
- 1 medium carrot, shredded
- ¾ cup tomato juice
- 1 teaspoon dried basil
- ¾ teaspoon dried oregano
- ¼ teaspoon garlic powder
- 1 cup frozen cut green beans, thawed
- ½ cup frozen chopped spinach, thawed
- ½ cup small shell pasta
- ½ cup shredded Parmesan cheese

1. In a 4- or 5-qt. slow cooker, combine the first 11 ingredients. Cover and cook on low for 6-7 hours or until vegetables are tender.
2. Stir in the green beans, spinach and pasta. Cover and cook for 30 minutes or until heated through. Sprinkle with cheese.

Slow-Cooked Reuben Brats

Sauerkraut gives these beer-simmered brats big flavor, but it's the special chili sauce and melted cheese that makes them a home run! Top your favorite burger with some of the chili sauce; you won't be sorry!

—ALANA SIMMONS JOHNSTOWN, PA

PREP: 30 MIN. • **COOK:** 7¼ HOURS
MAKES: 10 SERVINGS

- 10 uncooked bratwurst links
- 3 cans (12 ounces each) light beer or nonalcoholic beer
- 1 large sweet onion, sliced
- 1 can (14 ounces) sauerkraut, rinsed and well drained
- ¾ cup mayonnaise
- ¼ cup chili sauce
- 2 tablespoons ketchup
- 1 tablespoon finely chopped onion
- 2 teaspoons sweet pickle relish
- 1 garlic clove, minced
- ⅛ teaspoon pepper
- 10 hoagie buns, split
- 10 slices Swiss cheese

1. In a large skillet, brown bratwurst in batches; drain. In a 5-qt. slow cooker, combine beer, sliced onion and sauerkraut; top with bratwurst. Cook, covered, on low 7-9 hours or until sausages are cooked through.
2. Preheat oven to 350°. In a small bowl, mix mayonnaise, chili sauce, ketchup, chopped onion, relish, garlic and pepper until blended. Spread over cut sides of buns; top with cheese, bratwurst and sauerkraut mixture. Place on an ungreased baking sheet. Bake for 8-10 minutes or until the cheese is melted.

SLOW-COOKED REUBEN BRATS

VEGETABLE BEEF BARLEY SOUP

Vegetable Beef Barley Soup

Seasoned beef and a host of fresh vegetables give this slow cooker soup a real down-home flavor. Serve with a loaf of bread and dinner is done!

—**TARA MCDONALD** KANSAS CITY, MO

PREP: 45 MIN. • **COOK:** 7 HOURS
MAKES: 8 SERVINGS (2¾ QUARTS)

- 1 teaspoon seasoned salt
- 1 teaspoon onion powder
- 1 teaspoon garlic powder
- 1½ pounds beef stew meat, cut into 1-inch cubes
- 2 tablespoons canola oil
- 3 cups water
- 3 medium potatoes, peeled and diced
- 1 cup sliced fresh carrots
- 1 cup chopped celery
- ½ cup chopped onion
- 1 teaspoon beef bouillon granules
- 1 can (15¼ ounces) whole kernel corn, drained
- 1 can (14½ ounces) diced tomatoes, undrained
- 1 can (8½ ounces) peas, drained
- 1 cup tomato juice
- ¾ cup medium pearl barley
- ½ teaspoon salt
- ¼ teaspoon pepper

1. In a large resealable plastic bag, combine seasoned salt, onion powder and garlic powder. Add beef and toss to coat. In a large skillet, brown beef in oil until meat is no longer pink; drain.

2. Transfer to a 5- or 6-qt. slow cooker. Add the water, potatoes, carrots, celery, onion and bouillon. Cover and cook on low for 5-6 hours or until meat and vegetables are almost tender.

3. Add the corn, tomatoes, peas, tomato juice, barley, salt and pepper; cover and cook 2 hours longer or until barley is tender.

Chicago-Style Beef Rolls

I have fond memories of eating these big, messy sandwiches at a neighbor's house when I was growing up. This makes enough to freeze some leftovers and save for another meal.

—**TRISHA KRUSE** EAGLE, ID

PREP: 20 MIN. • **COOK:** 8 HOURS
MAKES: 16 SERVINGS

- 1 boneless beef chuck roast (4 to 5 pounds)
- 1 tablespoon olive oil
- 3 cups beef broth
- 1 medium onion, chopped
- 1 package Italian salad dressing mix
- 3 garlic cloves, minced
- 1 tablespoon Italian seasoning
- ½ teaspoon crushed red pepper flakes
- 16 sourdough rolls, split
  Sliced pepperoncini and pickled red pepper rings, optional

1. Brown roast in oil on all sides in a large skillet; drain. Transfer beef to a 5-qt. slow cooker. Combine the broth, onion, dressing mix, garlic, Italian seasoning and pepper flakes in a large bowl; pour over roast.

2. Cover and cook on low for 8-10 hours or until tender. Remove meat; cool slightly. Skim fat from cooking juices. Shred beef with two forks and return to slow cooker; heat through. Place ½ cup on each roll, using a slotted spoon. Serve with pickled pepper rings and pepperoncini if desired.

CHICAGO-STYLE BEEF ROLLS

Cuban-Style Pork Sandwiches

Loaded with tangy flavor, this is a lighter version of a favorite restaurant-style sandwich. If you don't have a panini maker, tuck the sandwiches under the broiler until the bread is browned and the cheese melted.

—**ROBIN HAAS** CRANSTON, RI

PREP: 20 MIN.
COOK: 6 HOURS + STANDING
MAKES: 10 SERVINGS

- 1 **large onion, cut into wedges**
- ¾ **cup reduced-sodium chicken broth**
- 1 **cup minced fresh parsley**
- 7 **garlic cloves, minced and divided**
- 2 **tablespoons cider vinegar**
- 1 **tablespoon plus 1½ teaspoons lemon juice, divided**
- 2 **teaspoons ground cumin**
- 1 **teaspoon ground mustard**
- 1 **teaspoon dried oregano**
- ½ **teaspoon salt**
- ½ **teaspoon pepper**
- 1 **boneless pork shoulder butt roast (3 to 4 pounds)**
- 1¼ **cups fat-free mayonnaise**
- 2 **tablespoons Dijon mustard**
- 10 **whole wheat hamburger buns, split**
- 1¼ **cups (5 ounces) shredded reduced-fat Swiss cheese**
- 1 **medium onion, thinly sliced and separated into rings**
- 2 **whole dill pickles, sliced**

1. Place onion wedges and broth in a 5-qt. slow cooker. In a small bowl, combine the parsley, 5 garlic cloves, vinegar, 1 tablespoon lemon juice, cumin, mustard, oregano, salt and pepper; rub over pork. Add to slow cooker. Cover and cook on low for 6-8 hours or until meat is tender.

2. Remove meat; let stand for 10 minutes before slicing. In another small bowl, combine the mayonnaise, mustard and remaining garlic and lemon juice; spread over buns. Layer bun bottoms with pork, cheese, sliced onion and pickles; replace tops.

3. Cook on a panini maker or indoor grill for 2-3 minutes or until buns are browned and cheese is melted.

Summer

DESSERTS

You don't need a special occasion to enjoy a scrumptious dessert. Make summer even sweeter with these slow-cooked treats filled with berries, bananas, coconut and more. What a terrific way to top off a meal!

KAREN JAROCKI'S
SLOW-COOKER
BERRY COBBLER

Slow-Cooker Berry Cobbler

During warm weather, you can enjoy the comforting taste of homemade cobbler without heating up the kitchen.
—**KAREN JAROCKI** YUMA, AZ

PREP: 15 MIN. • **COOK:** 2 HOURS
MAKES: 8 SERVINGS

- 1¼ cups all-purpose flour, divided
- 2 tablespoons plus 1 cup sugar, divided
- 1 teaspoon baking powder
- ¼ teaspoon ground cinnamon
- 1 egg, lightly beaten
- ¼ cup fat-free milk
- 2 tablespoons canola oil
- ⅛ teaspoon salt
- 2 cups fresh or frozen raspberries, thawed
- 2 cups fresh or frozen blueberries, thawed
  Low-fat vanilla frozen yogurt, optional

1. In a large bowl, combine 1 cup flour, 2 tablespoons sugar, baking powder and cinnamon. Combine the egg, milk and oil; stir into dry ingredients just until moistened (batter will be thick). Spread batter evenly into a 5-qt. slow cooker coated with cooking spray.
2. In a large bowl, combine the salt and remaining flour and sugar; add the berries and toss to coat. Spread over the batter.
3. Cover and cook on high for 2-2½ hours or until a toothpick inserted into cobbler comes out clean. Serve with frozen yogurt if desired.

Apple Granola Dessert

I would be lost without my slow cooker! Besides using it to fix our evening meal, I often pull it out to make sweet treats, including these tender apples.
—**JANIS LAWRENCE** CHILDRESS, TX

PREP: 10 MIN. • **COOK:** 6 HOURS
MAKES: 4-6 SERVINGS

- 4 medium tart apples, peeled and sliced
- 2 cups granola cereal with fruit and nuts
- ¼ cup honey
- 2 tablespoons butter, melted
- 1 teaspoon ground cinnamon
- ½ teaspoon ground nutmeg
  Whipped topping, optional

In a 1½-qt. slow cooker, combine the apples and cereal. In a small bowl, combine the honey, butter, cinnamon and nutmeg; pour over apple mixture and mix well. Cover and cook on low for 6-8 hours. Serve with whipped topping if desired.

Minty Hot Fudge Sundae Cake

The best part about a slow-cooked dessert is that when we're done eating dinner, a hot treat is ready to serve. In this case, it's a chocolaty, gooey, minty delight that everyone finds irresistible!

—TERRI MCKITRICK DELAFIELD, WI

PREP: 15 MIN. • **COOK:** 4 HOURS
MAKES: 12 SERVINGS

- 1¾ cups packed brown sugar, divided
- 1 cup all-purpose flour
- 5 tablespoons baking cocoa, divided
- 2 teaspoons baking powder
- ½ teaspoon salt
- ½ cup evaporated milk
- 2 tablespoons butter, melted
- ½ teaspoon vanilla extract
- ⅛ teaspoon almond extract
- 1 package (4.67 ounces) mint Andes candies
- 1¾ cups boiling water
- 4 teaspoons instant coffee granules
  Vanilla ice cream, whipped cream and maraschino cherries

1. In a large bowl, combine 1 cup brown sugar, flour, 3 tablespoons cocoa, baking powder and salt. In another bowl, combine the milk, butter and extracts. Stir into dry ingredients just until moistened. Transfer to a 3-qt. slow cooker coated with cooking spray. Sprinkle with candies.

2. Combine the water, instant coffee granules and remaining brown sugar and cocoa; pour over batter (do not stir). Cover and cook on high 4 to 4½ hours or until a toothpick inserted near the center of the cake comes out clean. Serve with ice cream, whipped cream and cherries.

CHERRY & SPICE RICE PUDDING

Cherry & Spice Rice Pudding

I live in Traverse City, Michigan, which is known as the Cherry Capital of the World. What better way is there to celebrate our bountiful orchards than by cooking with cherries? A bowlful of my creamy rice pudding always goes over well.

—DEB PERRY TRAVERSE CITY, MI

PREP: 10 MIN. • **COOK:** 2 HOURS
MAKES: 12 SERVINGS

- 4 cups cooked long grain rice
- 1 can (12 ounces) evaporated milk
- 1 cup 2% milk
- ⅓ cup sugar
- ¼ cup water
- ¾ cup dried cherries
- 3 tablespoons butter, softened
- 2 teaspoons vanilla extract
- ½ teaspoon ground cinnamon
- ¼ teaspoon ground nutmeg

1. In a large bowl, combine the rice, evaporated milk, milk, sugar and water. Stir in remaining ingredients. Transfer to a 3-qt. slow cooker coated with cooking spray.

2. Cover and cook on low for 2-3 hours or until mixture is thickened. Stir lightly before serving. Serve warm or cold. Refrigerate leftovers.

MINTY HOT FUDGE SUNDAE CAKE

FRUIT COMPOTE DESSERT

Caribbean Bread Pudding

Indulge in the ultimate comfort-food dessert: bread pudding. It gets a tropical twist when you add cream of coconut, pineapple and pina colada mix.

—ELIZABETH DOSS CALIFORNIA CITY, CA

PREP: 30 MIN. • **COOK:** 4 HOURS
MAKES: 16 SERVINGS

- 1 cup raisins
- 1 can (8 ounces) crushed pineapple, undrained
- 2 large firm bananas, halved
- 1 can (12 ounces) evaporated milk
- 1 can (10 ounces) frozen non-alcoholic pina colada mix
- 1 can (6 ounces) unsweetened pineapple juice
- 3 eggs
- ½ cup cream of coconut
- ¼ cup light rum, optional
- 1 loaf (1 pound) French bread, cut into 1-inch cubes
  Whipped cream and maraschino cherries, optional

1. In a small bowl, combine raisins and pineapple; set aside. In a blender, combine bananas, milk, pina colada mix, pineapple juice, eggs, cream of coconut and rum if desired. Cover and process until smooth.

2. Place two-thirds of the bread in a greased 5- or 6-qt. slow cooker. Top with 1 cup raisin mixture. Layer with remaining bread and raisin mixture. Pour the banana mixture into the slow cooker. Cover and cook on low for 4-5 hours or until a knife inserted near the center comes out clean. Serve warm with whipped cream if desired.

Fruit Compote Dessert

This is one of the first slow-cooked treats I learned to make, and it's still the one my guests enjoy the most. They say it tastes like it came from a fancy restaurant.

—LAURA BRYANT GERMAN

WEST WARREN, MA

PREP: 15 MIN. • **COOK:** 3 HOURS
MAKES: 8 SERVINGS

- 2 medium tart apples, peeled
- 2 medium peaches, peeled and cubed
- 2 cups unsweetened pineapple chunks
- 1¼ cups unsweetened pineapple juice
- ¼ cup honey
- 2 lemon slices (⅛ inch)
- 1 cinnamon stick (3½ inches)
- 1 medium firm banana, thinly sliced
  Whipped cream, sliced almonds and maraschino cherries, optional

1. Cut the apples into ¼-in. slices and then in half; place in a 3-qt. slow cooker. Add the peaches, pineapple, pineapple juice, honey, lemon and cinnamon. Cover and cook on low for 3-4 hours.

2. Just before serving, stir in banana slices. Serve with a slotted spoon if desired. Garnish with whipped cream, almonds and cherries if desired.

STRAWBERRY RHUBARB SAUCE

Strawberry Rhubarb Sauce

A neighbor shared this tangy fruit topping with me. It's a wonderful way to use up a bumper crop of homegrown rhubarb. We like it over ice cream, pancakes and even fresh-from-the-oven biscuits.

—NANCY COWLISHAW BOISE, ID

PREP: 15 MIN. • **COOK:** 4¼ HOURS
MAKES: 4½ CUPS

- 6 **cups sliced fresh or frozen rhubarb, thawed**
- 1 **cup sugar**
- ½ **cup unsweetened apple juice**
- 3 **cinnamon sticks (3 inches)**
- ½ **teaspoon grated orange peel**
- ¼ **teaspoon ground ginger**
- 1 **pint fresh strawberries, halved**
  Vanilla ice cream

1. Place the rhubarb, sugar, juice, cinnamon sticks, orange peel and ginger in a 3-qt. slow cooker. Cover and cook on low for 4-5 hours or until rhubarb is tender.
2. Stir in the strawberries; cover and cook 15 minutes longer or until heated through. Discard the cinnamon sticks. Serve with ice cream.

Black and Blue Cobbler

It never occurred to me that a cobbler could be made in the slow cooker. Then I discovered some recipes and decided to give my favorite version a try. It took a little bit of experimenting, but the yummy results were well worth it.

—MARTHA CREVELING ORLANDO, FL

PREP: 15 MIN. • **COOK:** 2 HOURS + STANDING
MAKES: 6 SERVINGS

- 1 **cup all-purpose flour**
- 1½ **cups sugar, divided**
- 1 **teaspoon baking powder**
- ¼ **teaspoon salt**
- ¼ **teaspoon ground cinnamon**
- ¼ **teaspoon ground nutmeg**
- 2 **eggs, lightly beaten**
- 2 **tablespoons milk**
- 2 **tablespoons canola oil**
- 2 **cups fresh or frozen blackberries**
- 2 **cups fresh or frozen blueberries**
- ¾ **cup water**
- 1 **teaspoon grated orange peel**
  Whipped cream or vanilla ice cream, optional

1. In a large bowl, combine flour, ¾ cup sugar, baking powder, salt, cinnamon and nutmeg. Combine the eggs, milk and oil; stir into dry ingredients just until moistened. Spread the batter evenly onto the bottom of a greased 5-qt. slow cooker.
2. In a large saucepan, combine the berries, water, orange peel and remaining sugar; bring to a boil. Remove from the heat; immediately pour over the batter. Cover and cook on high for 2 to 2½ hours or until a toothpick inserted into the batter comes out clean.
3. Turn cooker off. Uncover and let stand for 30 minutes before serving. Serve with whipped cream or ice cream if desired.

BLACK AND BLUE COBBLER

MAPLE CREME BRULEE

until caramelized. Serve immediately.

4. If broiling the custards, place the ramekins on a baking sheet; let stand at room temperature for 15 minutes. Sprinkle with sugar mixture. Broil 8 in. from the heat for 3-5 minutes or until sugar is caramelized. Refrigerate for 1-2 hours or until firm.

Blueberry Grunt

If you love blueberries, you can't go wrong with this home-style treat. Serve it warm with a scoop of vanilla ice cream.

—CLEO GONSKE REDDING, CA

PREP: 20 MIN. • **COOK:** 2½ HOURS
MAKES: 6 SERVINGS

- 4 **cups fresh or frozen blueberries**
- ¾ **cup sugar**
- ½ **cup water**
- 1 **teaspoon almond extract**

DUMPLINGS
- 2 **cups all-purpose flour**
- 4 **teaspoons baking powder**
- 1 **teaspoon sugar**
- ½ **teaspoon salt**
- 1 **tablespoon cold butter**
- 1 **tablespoon shortening**
- ¾ **cup 2% milk**
  Vanilla ice cream, optional

1. In a 3-qt. slow cooker, combine the blueberries, sugar, water and extract. Cover and cook on high for 2-3 hours or until bubbly.

2. For the dumplings, in a small bowl, combine flour, baking powder, sugar and salt. Cut in butter and shortening until crumbly. Add the milk; stir just until moistened.

3. Drop by tablespoonfuls onto hot blueberry mixture. Cover and cook 30 minutes longer or until a toothpick inserted in a dumpling comes out clean. Serve warm with ice cream if desired.

Maple Creme Brulee

The slow cooker is a great way to prepare classic creme brulee. Your guests are sure to enjoy the smooth and creamy custard, crunchy sugar topping and unexpected but yummy maple flavor.

—TASTE OF HOME TEST KITCHEN

PREP: 20 MIN. • **COOK:** 2 HOURS + CHILLING
MAKES: 3 SERVINGS

- 1⅓ **cups heavy whipping cream**
- 3 **egg yolks**
- ½ **cup packed brown sugar**
- ¼ **teaspoon ground cinnamon**
- ½ **teaspoon maple flavoring**

TOPPING
- 1½ **teaspoons sugar**
- 1½ **teaspoons brown sugar**

1. In a small saucepan, heat cream until bubbles form around sides of pan. In a small bowl, whisk the egg yolks, brown sugar and cinnamon. Remove cream from the heat; stir a small amount of hot cream into egg mixture. Return all to the pan, stirring constantly. Stir in maple flavoring.

2. Transfer to three 6-oz. ramekins or custard cups. Place in a 6-qt. slow cooker; add 1 in. of boiling water to slow cooker. Cover and cook on high for 2 to 2½ hours or until centers are just set (mixture will jiggle). Carefully remove cups from slow cooker; cool for 10 minutes. Cover and refrigerate for at least 4 hours.

3. For topping, combine sugar and brown sugar. If using a creme brulee torch, sprinkle custards with sugar mixture. Heat sugar with the torch

CLEO GONSKE'S
BLUEBERRY GRUNT

CHOCOLATE PECAN FONDUE

Chocolate Pecan Fondue

When our kids have friends sleep over, I like to surprise them with my chocolate fondue. Our favorite dippers include fruit, marshmallows, cookies and pound cake.

—**SUZANNE MCKINLEY** LYONS, GA

START TO FINISH: 15 MIN.
MAKES: 1⅓ CUPS

- ½ **cup half-and-half cream**
- 2 **tablespoons honey**
- 9 **ounces semisweet chocolate, broken into small pieces**
- ¼ **cup finely chopped pecans**
- 1 **teaspoon vanilla extract**
  Fresh fruit and shortbread cookies

1. In a heavy saucepan over low heat, combine the cream and honey; heat until warm. Add chocolate; stir until melted. Stir in pecans and vanilla.
2. Transfer to a warmed fondue pot or a 1½-qt. slow cooker and keep warm. Serve with fruit and cookies.

Amaretto Cherries with Dumplings

It's hard to beat the flavor combination of cherries and almond. They come together wonderfully in this dessert.

—*TASTE OF HOME* TEST KITCHEN

PREP: 15 MIN. • **COOK:** 7¾ HOURS
MAKES: 6 SERVINGS

- 2 **cans (14½ ounces each) pitted tart cherries**
- ¾ **cup sugar**
- ¼ **cup cornstarch**
- ⅛ **teaspoon salt**
- ¼ **cup amaretto or ½ teaspoon almond extract**

DUMPLINGS

- 1 **cup all-purpose flour**
- ¼ **cup sugar**
- 1 **teaspoon baking powder**
- ½ **teaspoon grated lemon peel**
- ⅛ **teaspoon salt**
- ⅓ **cup 2% milk**
- 3 **tablespoons butter, melted**
  Vanilla ice cream, optional

1. Drain the cherries, reserving ¼ cup juice. Place the cherries in a 3-qt. slow cooker.
2. In a small bowl, mix the sugar, cornstarch and salt; stir in reserved juice until smooth. Stir into cherries. Cook, covered, on high 7 hours. Drizzle amaretto over cherry mixture.
3. For dumplings, in a small bowl, whisk flour, sugar, baking powder, lemon peel and salt. In another bowl, whisk milk and melted butter. Add to flour mixture; stir just until moistened.
4. Drop by tablespoonfuls on top of the hot cherry mixture. Cook, covered, 45 minutes or until a toothpick inserted in center of dumplings comes out clean. If desired, serve warm with ice cream.

AMARETTO CHERRIES WITH DUMPLINGS

SLOW-COOKER BREAD PUDDING

Slow-Cooker Bread Pudding

Have leftovers from yesterday's breakfast? Let your slow cooker transform day-old cinnamon rolls into an old-fashioned treat everyone will love. This yummy pudding is especially good with a dollop of whipped cream or a drizzle of vanilla sauce.

—**EDNA HOFFMAN** HEBRON, IN

PREP: 15 MIN. • **COOK:** 3 HOURS
MAKES: 6 SERVINGS

- 8 **cups cubed day-old unfrosted cinnamon rolls**
- 4 **eggs**
- 2 **cups milk**
- ¼ **cup sugar**
- ¼ **cup butter, melted**
- ½ **teaspoon vanilla extract**
- ¼ **teaspoon ground nutmeg**
- 1 **cup raisins**

Place the cubed rolls in a 3-qt. slow cooker. In a small bowl, whisk the eggs, milk, sugar, butter, vanilla and nutmeg. Stir in raisins. Pour over rolls; stir gently. Cover and cook on low for 3 hours or until a knife inserted near the center comes out clean.

NOTE *8 slices of cinnamon or white bread, cut into 1-inch cubes, may be substituted for the cinnamon rolls.*

⑤ INGREDIENTS

Blueberry Cobbler

If you like, replace the blueberry filling to make an apple or cherry cobbler instead.

—**NELDA CRONBAUGH** BELLE PLAINE, IA

PREP: 10 MIN. • **COOK:** 3 HOURS
MAKES: 6 SERVINGS

- 1 **can (21 ounces) blueberry pie filling**
- 1 **package (9 ounces) yellow cake mix**
- ¼ **cup chopped pecans**
- ¼ **cup butter, melted**
   Vanilla ice cream, optional

Place the blueberry pie filling in a greased 1½-qt. slow cooker. Sprinkle with the yellow cake mix and pecans. Drizzle with butter. Cover and cook on high for 3 hours or until the topping is golden brown. Serve warm with ice cream if desired.

DID YOU KNOW?

A fruit cobbler gets its name from the biscuit (or biscuit-like) topping that covers the fruit. While the topping can be in a single layer, the dough is often dropped in sections over the fruit, creating a cobblestone effect.

TONYA SWAIN'S
OKTOBERFEST PORK ROAST
page 208

APPETIZERS & BEVERAGES 162

SIDE DISHES 172

ENTREES 184

SOUPS, STEWS & SANDWICHES 210

DESSERTS 226

Autumn

For many, comfort food is at its very best when the weather turns crisp, the nights become longer and harvest-fresh delights abound. Enjoy all of the colors, aromas and flavors of the fall season with the satisfying slow-cooked dishes featured here.

Autumn

APPETIZERS & BEVERAGES

Harvest festivals...Halloween...Thanksgiving... these are just a few of the wonderful reasons to host an open house this fall. Brimming with heartwarming goodness, the slow-cooked dishes here promise to help you build happy memories for years to come.

NOEL LICKENFELT'S HOT SPICED WINE

Hot Spiced Wine

My friends, family and I enjoy this during cold-weather gatherings. It's especially popular with fans of dry red wines.
—**NOEL LICKENFELT** BOLIVAR, PA

PREP: 15 MIN. • **COOK:** 4 HOURS
MAKES: 8 SERVINGS

- 2 **cinnamon sticks (3 inches)**
- 3 **whole cloves**
- 2 **bottles (750 milliliters each) dry red wine**
- 3 **medium tart apples, peeled and sliced**
- ½ **cup sugar**
- 1 **teaspoon lemon juice**

1. Place cinnamon sticks and cloves on a double thickness of cheesecloth. Gather the corners of the cheesecloth to enclose the seasonings; tie securely with string.
2. In a 3-qt. slow cooker, combine the remaining ingredients. Add the spice bag. Cook, covered, on low 4-5 hours or until heated through. Discard spice bag. Serve warm.

Creamy Onion Dip

Here's a rich, indulgent appetizer fit for a classic cocktail party. Caramelized onions are paired with flavorful Gruyere cheese.
—**BECKY WALCH** MANTECA, CA

PREP: 20 MIN. • **COOK:** 5 HOURS
MAKES: 5 CUPS

- 4 **cups finely chopped sweet onions**
- ¼ **cup butter, cubed**
- ¼ **cup white wine or chicken broth**
- 6 **garlic cloves, minced**
- 1 **bay leaf**
- 2 **cups (8 ounces) shredded Gruyere or Swiss cheese**
- 1 **package (8 ounces) cream cheese, softened**
- ¼ **cup sour cream**
  Assorted crackers or breadsticks

1. In a 3-qt. slow cooker, combine the sweet onions, butter, wine, garlic and bay leaf. Cover and cook on low for 4-5 hours or until onions are tender and golden brown.
2. Discard bay leaf. Stir in the Gruyere cheese, cream cheese and sour cream. Cover and cook 1 hour longer or until the cheese is melted. Serve warm with crackers.

TOP TIP

An appetizer buffet is a fun twist on entertaining and creates a less formal atmosphere than a traditional sit-down dinner. For a buffet that will serve as your meal, offer five or six different appetizers (including some substantial selections) and plan on roughly 8-9 pieces per guest.

CHILI CHEESE DIP

Buffet Meatballs

I need only five simple ingredients to make these easy little bites. Grape juice and apple jelly are the secrets behind the sweet yet tangy sauce, which coats convenient packaged meatballs.

—**JANET ANDERSON** CARSON CITY, NV

PREP: 10 MIN. • **COOK:** 4 HOURS
MAKES: ABOUT 10½ DOZEN

- 1 **cup grape juice**
- 1 **cup apple jelly**
- 1 **cup ketchup**
- 1 **can (8 ounces) tomato sauce**
- 1 **package (64 ounces) frozen fully cooked Italian meatballs**

1. In a small saucepan, combine the juice, jelly, ketchup and tomato sauce. Cook and stir over medium heat until jelly is melted.
2. Place the meatballs in a 5-qt. slow cooker. Pour the sauce over the top and gently stir to coat. Cover and cook on low for 4-5 hours or until heated through.

BUFFET MEATBALLS

Chili Cheese Dip

While trying to create a recipe for Mexican soup, I came up with a cheesy, beefy dip that eats like a meal. My husband and two children love digging in with corn chips when they watch football games.

—**SANDRA FICK** LINCOLN, NE

PREP: 20 MIN. • **COOK:** 4½ HOURS
MAKES: 8 CUPS

- 1 **pound lean ground beef (90% lean)**
- 1 **medium onion, chopped**
- 1 **can (16 ounces) kidney beans, rinsed and drained**
- 1 **can (15 ounces) black beans, rinsed and drained**
- 1 **can (14½ ounces) diced tomatoes in sauce, undrained**
- 1 **cup frozen corn, thawed**
- ¾ **cup water**
- 1 **can (2¼ ounces) sliced ripe olives, drained**
- 3 **teaspoons chili powder**
- ½ **teaspoon dried oregano**
- ½ **teaspoon chipotle hot pepper sauce**
- ¼ **teaspoon garlic powder**
- ¼ **teaspoon ground cumin**
- 1 **package (16 ounces) reduced-fat process cheese (Velveeta), cubed Corn chips or tortilla chips**

1. In a large skillet, cook the beef and onion over medium heat 6-8 minutes or until the beef is no longer pink and the onion is tender, breaking up beef into crumbles; drain. Transfer to a 4-qt. slow cooker.
2. Stir in beans, tomatoes, corn, water, olives, chili powder, oregano, pepper sauce, garlic powder and cumin. Cook, covered, on low 4-5 hours or until heated through.
3. Stir in cheese. Cook, covered, on low 30 minutes longer or until cheese is melted. Serve with corn chips.

AMY WARREN'S CREAMY CRANBERRY MEATBALLS
SUE BAYLESS' SWEET & SPICY CHICKEN WINGS

(5)INGREDIENTS Creamy Cranberry Meatballs

For a terrific entree the next day, serve leftover meatballs over hot pasta or rice.
—**AMY WARREN** MAINEVILLE, OH

PREP: 10 MIN. • **COOK:** 3 HOURS
MAKES: ABOUT 5 DOZEN

- 2 **envelopes brown gravy mix**
- 1 **package (32 ounces) frozen fully cooked Swedish meatballs**
- ⅔ **cup jellied cranberry sauce**
- 2 **teaspoons Dijon mustard**
- ¼ **cup heavy whipping cream**

Prepare the gravy mix according to the package directions. In a 4-qt. slow cooker, combine the meatballs, cranberry sauce, mustard and gravy. Cover and cook on low for 3-4 hours or until heated through, adding cream during the last 30 minutes of cooking.

Sweet & Spicy Chicken Wings

The spice lovers in your life are sure to get a kick out of these zippy wings.
—**SUE BAYLESS** PRIOR LAKE, MN

PREP: 25 MIN. • **COOK:** 5 HOURS
MAKES: ABOUT 2½ DOZEN

- 3 **pounds chicken wings**
- 1½ **cups ketchup**
- 1 **cup packed brown sugar**
- 1 **small onion, finely chopped**
- ¼ **cup finely chopped sweet red pepper**
- 2 **tablespoons chili powder**
- 2 **tablespoons Worcestershire sauce**
- 1½ **teaspoons crushed red pepper flakes**
- 1 **teaspoon ground mustard**
- 1 **teaspoon dried basil**
- 1 **teaspoon dried thyme**
- 1 **teaspoon pepper**

Cut wings into three sections; discard wing tip sections. Place the chicken in a 4-qt. slow cooker. In a small bowl, combine the remaining ingredients. Pour over chicken; stir until coated. Cover and cook on low for 5-6 hours or until chicken juices run clear.

NOTE *Uncooked chicken wing sections (wingettes) may be substituted for whole chicken wings.*

Easy Hot Spiced Cider

Sipping from a mug of slow-cooked apple cider is such a cozy treat after a day of raking fall leaves or picking pumpkins.
—**TRINDA HEINRICH** LAKEMOOR, IL

PREP: 5 MIN. • **COOK:** 2 HOURS
MAKES: 3 SERVINGS

- 2½ **cups apple cider or unsweetened apple juice**
- ⅔ **cup orange juice**
- ⅓ **cup sugar**
- 2 **tablespoons lemon juice**
- ¼ **teaspoon ground nutmeg**
- 1 **cinnamon stick (3 inches)**
- 12 **whole cloves**

1. In a 1½-qt. slow cooker, combine the first five ingredients. Place the cinnamon stick and cloves on a double thickness of cheesecloth; bring up the corners of the cheesecloth and tie with string to form a bag. Place the bag in the slow cooker.

2. Cover and cook on low for 1 hour. Discard spice bag; continue to cook 1-2 hours or until heated through.

EASY HOT SPICED CIDER

SLOW-COOKED APPLE CRANBERRY CIDER

(5) INGREDIENTS Slow-Cooked Apple Cranberry Cider

Buffets are my favorite way to feed a crowd. This cranberry-flavored cider can be made ahead, then kept warm in a slow cooker so guests can serve themselves.

—**KATHY WELLS** BRODHEAD, WI

PREP: 5 MIN. • **COOK:** 2 HOURS
MAKES: 11 CUPS

- 3 cinnamon sticks (3 inches), broken
- 1 teaspoon whole cloves
- 2 quarts apple cider or juice
- 3 cups cranberry juice
- 2 tablespoons brown sugar

1. Place cinnamon sticks and cloves on a double thickness of cheesecloth; bring up corners of cloth and tie with string to form a bag.
2. In a 5-qt. slow cooker, combine the apple cider, cranberry juice and brown sugar; add spice bag. Cover and cook on high for 2 hours or until the cider reaches desired temperature. Discard the spice bag.

Hot Wing Dip

I usually have the ingredients for my wing dip on hand. It's a great go-to recipe when unexpected visitors drop by.

—**COLEEN CORNER** GROVE CITY, PA

PREP: 10 MIN. • **COOK:** 1 HOUR
MAKES: 18 SERVINGS (¼ CUP EACH)

- 2 cups shredded cooked chicken
- 1 package (8 ounces) cream cheese, cubed
- 2 cups (8 ounces) shredded cheddar cheese
- 1 cup ranch salad dressing
- ½ cup Louisiana-style hot sauce
  Tortilla chips and celery sticks
  Minced fresh parsley, optional

In a 3-qt. slow cooker, mix the first five ingredients. Cook, covered, on low for 1-2 hours or until the cheese is melted. Serve with chips and celery. If desired, sprinkle with parsley.

(5) INGREDIENTS Slow-Cooked Smokies

Just about every time I put together a party or picnic menu, I include miniature smoked sausages smothered in a zesty barbecue sauce. They're popular with both children and adults.

—**SUNDRA HAUCK** BOGALUSA, LA

PREP: 5 MIN. • **COOK:** 6 HOURS
MAKES: 8 SERVINGS

- 1 package (1 pound) miniature smoked sausages
- 1 bottle (28 ounces) barbecue sauce
- 1¼ cups water
- 3 tablespoons Worcestershire sauce
- 3 tablespoons steak sauce
- ½ teaspoon pepper

In a 3-qt. slow cooker, combine all ingredients. Cover and cook on low for 5-6 hours or until heated through. Serve with a slotted spoon.

HOT WING DIP

TANGY BARBECUE WINGS

Spiced Coffee

Even people who normally don't drink coffee find this special spiced blend appealing. Stirring in a little chocolate syrup adds a touch of decadence.

—**JOANNE HOLT** BOWLING GREEN, OH

PREP: 10 MIN. • **COOK:** 2 HOURS
MAKES: 8 SERVINGS

- 8 **cups brewed coffee**
- ⅓ **cup sugar**
- ¼ **cup chocolate syrup**
- ½ **teaspoon anise extract**
- 4 **cinnamon sticks (3 inches)**
- 1½ **teaspoons whole cloves**
  Additional cinnamon sticks, optional

1. In a 3-qt. slow cooker, combine brewed coffee, sugar, chocolate syrup and extract. Place the cinnamon sticks and cloves on a double thickness of cheesecloth. Gather the corners of the cloth to enclose the spices; tie securely with string. Add to slow cooker. Cook, covered, on low 2-3 hours.
2. Discard spice bag. If desired, serve coffee with cinnamon sticks.

SPICED COFFEE

Tangy Barbecue Wings

When I took these sensational chicken wings to work, my co-workers snatched them up before I could get a single bite!
—**SHERRY PITZER** TROY, MO

PREP: 1½ HOURS • **COOK:** 3 HOURS
MAKES: ABOUT 4 DOZEN

- 5 **pounds chicken wings**
- 2½ **cups hot and spicy ketchup**
- ⅔ **cup white vinegar**
- ½ **cup plus 2 tablespoons honey**
- ½ **cup molasses**
- 1 **teaspoon salt**
- 1 **teaspoon Worcestershire sauce**
- ½ **teaspoon onion powder**
- ½ **teaspoon chili powder**
- ½ **to 1 teaspoon liquid smoke, optional**

1. Cut the chicken wings into three sections; discard wing tip sections. Place wings in two greased 15x10x1-in. baking pans. Bake, uncovered, at 375° for 30 minutes; drain. Turn wings; bake 20-25 minutes longer or until juices run clear.
2. Meanwhile, in a large saucepan, combine the ketchup, vinegar, honey, molasses, salt, Worcestershire sauce, onion powder and chili powder. Add liquid smoke if desired. Bring to a boil. Reduce heat; simmer, uncovered, for 25-30 minutes.
3. Drain the wings; place a third of them in a 5-qt. slow cooker. Top with about 1 cup sauce. Repeat layers twice. Cover and cook on low for 3-4 hours. Stir before serving.
NOTE *Uncooked chicken wing sections (wingettes) may be substituted for whole chicken wings.*

(5) INGREDIENTS Hot Spiced Cherry Sipper

Come in from the cool autumn weather to a glass of comforting cherry-apple cider. It'll warm you from head to toe!
—**MARLENE WICZEK** LITTLE FALLS, MN

PREP: 5 MIN. • **COOK:** 4 HOURS
MAKES: 4 QUARTS

- 1 gallon apple cider or juice
- 2 cinnamon sticks (3 inches)
- 2 packages (3 ounces each) cherry gelatin

Place cider in a 6-qt. slow cooker; add cinnamon sticks. Cover and cook on high for 3 hours. Stir in gelatin; cook 1 hour longer. Discard cinnamon sticks before serving.

Five-Cheese Spinach & Artichoke Dip

I'm always asked to bring my artichoke dip to events. It's rich, cheesy and just plain yummy! Need to use your slow cooker for another recipe? Bake this in the oven at 400° for 30 minutes or until it's hot and bubbly.
—**NOELLE MYERS** GRAND FORKS, ND

PREP: 20 MIN. • **COOK:** 2½ HOURS
MAKES: 16 SERVINGS (¼ CUP EACH)

- 1 jar (12 ounces) roasted sweet red peppers
- 1 jar (6½ ounces) marinated quartered artichoke hearts
- 1 package (10 ounces) frozen chopped spinach, thawed and squeezed dry
- 8 ounces fresh mozzarella cheese, cubed
- 1½ cups (6 ounces) shredded Asiago cheese
- 2 packages (3 ounces each) cream cheese, softened and cubed
- 1 cup (4 ounces) crumbled feta cheese
- ⅓ cup shredded provolone cheese
- ⅓ cup minced fresh basil
- ¼ cup finely chopped red onion
- 2 tablespoons mayonnaise
- 2 garlic cloves, minced
  Assorted crackers

1. Drain the red peppers, reserving 1 tablespoon liquid; chop the peppers. Drain the artichokes, reserving 2 tablespoons liquid; coarsely chop the artichokes.

2. In a 3-qt. slow cooker coated with cooking spray, combine the spinach, cheeses, basil, onion, mayonnaise, garlic, artichoke hearts and peppers. Stir in reserved pepper and artichoke liquids. Cook, covered, on high 2 hours. Stir dip; cook, covered, 30-60 minutes longer. Stir dip before serving; serve with crackers.

TOP TIP

Feel free to change the flavor of Hot Spiced Cherry Sipper. For example, replace the apple cider and cherry gelatin with orange juice and orange gelatin...or use a combination of lemonade and lemon gelatin.

HOT SPICED CHERRY SIPPER

NOELLE MYERS'
FIVE-CHEESE SPINACH & ARTICHOKE DIP

MULLED DR PEPPER

Sweet & Sour Turkey Meatballs

Thanks to the blend of sweet and sour flavors, these special appetizer meatballs are guaranteed to tingle taste buds.

—**CHRISTINE WENDLAND** BROWNS MILLS, NJ

PREP: 30 MIN. • **COOK:** 2 HOURS
MAKES: ABOUT 5½ DOZEN

- 4 **thick-sliced peppered bacon strips**
- 1 **egg, beaten**
- ½ **cup seasoned bread crumbs**
- 3 **tablespoons minced fresh cilantro**
- 1 **teaspoon salt**
- 1 **teaspoon white pepper**
- 2 **pounds ground turkey**
- 1 **jar (18 ounces) apricot preserves**
- 1 **can (14½ ounces) diced tomatoes, undrained**
- 1 **bottle (8 ounces) taco sauce**
- ½ **cup pomegranate juice**

1. Place the peppered bacon in a food processor; cover and process until finely chopped. In a large bowl, combine egg, seasoned bread crumbs, cilantro, salt and pepper. Crumble the turkey and bacon over mixture; mix well. Shape into 1-in. balls.
2. Place in two ungreased 15x10x1-in. baking pans. Bake at 400° for 8-10 minutes or until no longer pink.
3. In a 4-qt. slow cooker, combine the apricot preserves, tomatoes, taco sauce and juice. Stir in the meatballs. Cover and cook on high for 2-3 hours or until heated through.

Mulled Dr Pepper

I like to serve this with ham sandwiches and deviled eggs when we have guests.
—**BERNICE MORRIS** MARSHFIELD, MO

PREP: 10 MIN. • **COOK:** 2 HOURS
MAKES: 8-10 SERVINGS

- 8 **cups Dr Pepper**
- ¼ **cup packed brown sugar**
- ¼ **cup lemon juice**
- ½ **teaspoon ground allspice**
- ½ **teaspoon whole cloves**
- ¼ **teaspoon salt**
- ¼ **teaspoon ground nutmeg**
- 3 **cinnamon sticks (3 inches)**

In a 3-qt. slow cooker, combine all ingredients. Cover and cook on low for 2 hours or until heated through. Discard cloves and cinnamon sticks.

⑤INGREDIENTS Butterscotch Mulled Cider

Here's the perfect treat for chilly nights. Five minutes and three ingredients are all you need to mix it together. Let your slow cooker do the rest of the work, then enjoy a warm butterscotch delight.
—**KAREN MACK** WEBSTER, NY

PREP: 5 MIN. • **COOK:** 3 HOURS
MAKES: 18 SERVINGS (1 CUP EACH)

- 1 **gallon apple cider or juice**
- 2 **cups butterscotch schnapps liqueur**
- 8 **cinnamon sticks (3 inches)**

In a 6-qt. slow cooker, combine all ingredients. Cover and cook on low for 3-4 hours or until heated through.

TACO JOE DIP

In a 5-qt. slow cooker, combine the first eight ingredients. Cover and cook on low for 5-6 hours. Serve with tortilla chips.

NOTE *To make Taco Joe Soup, add a 29-ounce can of tomato sauce to the slow cooker. It will serve 6-8.*

Apricot-Apple Cider

Dried apricots give this heartwarming apple cider a refreshing twist. With ginger ale, ruby-red cranberries and plenty of spices, it's a wonderful drink for holiday gatherings or any time at all.

—GINNIE BUSAM PEWEE VALLEY, KY

PREP: 20 MIN. • **COOK:** 3 HOURS
MAKES: 13 SERVINGS (2½ QUARTS)

- 8 **cups unsweetened apple juice**
- 1 **can (12 ounces) ginger ale**
- ½ **cup dried apricots, halved**
- ½ **cup dried cranberries**
- 2 **cinnamon sticks (3 inches)**
- 1 **tablespoon whole allspice**
- 1 **tablespoon whole cloves**

1. In a 5-qt. slow cooker, combine the apple juice and ginger ale. Place the apricots, cranberries, cinnamon sticks, allspice and cloves on a double thickness of cheesecloth; bring up corners of cloth and tie with string to form a bag. Place in slow cooker.
2. Cover and cook on high for 3-4 hours or until heated through. Discard the spice bag.

Taco Joe Dip

The chunky Southwestern dip recipe my daughter tried became an instant favorite with my husband and me. We think it's one of the best ever! Fill a big basket with tortilla chips, then invite family and friends to start scooping.

—LANG SECREST SIERRA VISTA, AZ

PREP: 5 MIN. • **COOK:** 5 HOURS
MAKES: ABOUT 7 CUPS

- 1 **can (16 ounces) kidney beans, rinsed and drained**
- 1 **can (15¼ ounces) whole kernel corn, drained**
- 1 **can (15 ounces) black beans, rinsed and drained**
- 1 **can (14½ ounces) stewed tomatoes, undrained**
- 1 **can (8 ounces) tomato sauce**
- 1 **can (4 ounces) chopped green chilies, drained**
- 1 **envelope taco seasoning**
- ½ **cup chopped onion**
  Tortilla chips

APRICOT-APPLE CIDER

Autumn

SIDE DISHES

When it's time to round out menus, nothing satisfies like Coconut-Pecan Sweet Potatoes, Slow-Cooked Sausage Dressing, Mushroom Wild Rice and other fall favorites. Turn here for all of those comforting dishes that are ideal for cozy meals.

MARY ANN JONNS'
WARM FRUIT SALAD

⑤ INGREDIENTS

Warm Fruit Salad

I use canned goods and my slow cooker to whip up this old-fashioned side dish that's loaded with sweet fruits. It makes a heartwarming accompaniment to holiday menus as well as everyday meals.

—MARY ANN JONNS MIDLOTHIAN, IL

PREP: 10 MIN. • **COOK:** 2 HOURS
MAKES: 14-18 SERVINGS

- 2 **cans (29 ounces each) sliced peaches, drained**
- 2 **cans (29 ounces each) pear halves, drained and sliced**
- 1 **can (20 ounces) pineapple chunks, drained**
- 1 **can (15¼ ounces) apricot halves, drained and sliced**
- 1 **can (21 ounces) cherry pie filling**

In a 5-qt. slow cooker, combine the peaches, pears, pineapple and apricots. Top with pie filling. Cover and cook on high for 2 hours or until heated through. Serve with a slotted spoon.

Cheesy Sausage Gravy

You'll appreciate the make-ahead convenience of this breakfast dish shared by a friend many years ago. I've served it often to overnight guests, and they never fail to ask for the recipe.

—P.J. PRUSIA RAYMORE, MO

PREP: 15 MIN. • **COOK:** 7 HOURS
MAKES: 8 SERVINGS

- 1 **pound bulk pork sausage**
- ¼ **cup butter, cubed**
- ¼ **cup all-purpose flour**
- ¼ **teaspoon pepper**
- 2½ **cups milk**
- 2 **cans (10¾ ounces each) condensed cheddar cheese soup, undiluted**
- 6 **hard-cooked eggs, chopped**
- 1 **jar (4½ ounces) sliced mushrooms, drained**
  Warm biscuits

1. In a large skillet, cook sausage over medium heat until no longer pink; drain and remove sausage. In the same skillet, melt butter. Stir in flour and pepper until smooth. Gradually whisk in milk. Bring to a boil; cook and stir for 2 minutes or until thickened and bubbly.

2. Stir in soup until blended. Stir in eggs, mushrooms and sausage. Transfer to a 3-qt. slow cooker. Cover and cook on low for 7-8 hours. Stir; serve over biscuits.

Spiced Acorn Squash

Working full-time, I found I didn't always have time to cook the meals my family loved. So I re-created many of our favorites in the slow cooker. This treatment for squash is one of them.

—**CAROL GRECO** CENTEREACH, NY

PREP: 15 MIN. • **COOK:** 3½ HOURS
MAKES: 4 SERVINGS

- ¾ **cup packed brown sugar**
- 1 **teaspoon ground cinnamon**
- 1 **teaspoon ground nutmeg**
- 2 **small acorn squash, halved and seeded**
- ¾ **cup raisins**
- 4 **tablespoons butter**
- ½ **cup water**

1. In a small bowl, mix brown sugar, cinnamon and nutmeg; spoon into squash halves. Sprinkle with raisins.

Top each with 1 tablespoon butter. Wrap each half individually in heavy-duty foil, sealing tightly.
2. Pour water into a 5-qt. slow cooker. Place squash in slow cooker, cut side up (packets may be stacked). Cook, covered, on high 3½ to 4 hours or until squash is tender. Open foil carefully to allow steam to escape.

Corn Spoon Bread

My spoon bread is moister then corn pudding made in the oven, plus the cream cheese is a nice addition. It goes great with Thanksgiving turkey or Christmas ham.

—**TAMARA ELLEFSON** FREDERIC, WI

PREP: 15 MIN. • **COOK:** 3 HOURS
MAKES: 8 SERVINGS

- 1 **package (8 ounces) cream cheese, softened**
- ⅓ **cup sugar**

CORN SPOON BREAD

- 1 **cup 2% milk**
- 2 **eggs**
- 2 **tablespoons butter, melted**
- 1 **teaspoon salt**
- ¼ **teaspoon ground nutmeg**
  Dash pepper
- 2⅓ **cups frozen corn, thawed**
- 1 **can (14¾ ounces) cream-style corn**
- 1 **package (8½ ounces) corn bread/muffin mix**

1. In a large bowl, beat cream cheese and sugar until smooth. Gradually beat in milk. Beat in the eggs, butter, salt, nutmeg and pepper until blended. Stir in corn and cream-style corn. Stir in corn bread mix just until moistened.
2. Pour into a greased 3-qt. slow cooker. Cover and cook on high for 3-4 hours or until center is almost set.

SPICED ACORN SQUASH

APPLESAUCE SWEET POTATOES

(5)INGREDIENTS Applesauce Sweet Potatoes

Using your slow cooker not only frees up oven space, but time, too! Popular sweet potatoes are a must on many of our family menus, and this no-fuss version will fool everyone into thinking that you spent hours in the kitchen.

—**PAMELA ALLEN** MARYSVILLE, OH

PREP: 15 MIN. • **COOK:** 4 HOURS
MAKES: 8 SERVINGS

- 2 **pounds sweet potatoes, peeled and sliced**
- 1½ **cups unsweetened applesauce**
- ⅔ **cup packed brown sugar**
- 3 **tablespoons butter, melted**
- 1 **teaspoon ground cinnamon**
- ½ **cup chopped glazed pecans, optional**

Place sweet potatoes in a 4-qt. slow cooker. Combine the applesauce, brown sugar, butter and cinnamon; pour over sweet potatoes. Cover and cook on low for 4-5 hours or until potatoes are tender. Sprinkle with the pecans. Serve with a slotted spoon.

Easy Squash Stuffing

My friends rave about this creamy side dish. It really jazzes up a packaged stuffing mix with nothing more than fresh summer squash, carrots and onion.

—**PAMELA THORSON** HOT SPRINGS, AR

PREP: 15 MIN. • **COOK:** 4 HOURS
MAKES: 8 SERVINGS

- ¼ **cup all-purpose flour**
- 1 **can (10¾ ounces) condensed cream of chicken soup, undiluted**
- 1 **cup (8 ounces) sour cream**
- 2 **medium yellow summer squash, cut into ½-inch slices**
- 1 **small onion, chopped**
- 1 **cup shredded carrots**
- 1 **package (8 ounces) stuffing mix**
- ½ **cup butter, melted**

1. In a large bowl, combine the flour, soup and sour cream. Add the vegetables and gently stir to coat.
2. Combine stuffing mix and butter; sprinkle half into a 3-qt. slow cooker. Top with vegetable mixture and remaining stuffing mixture. Cover and cook on low for 4-5 hours or until vegetables are tender.

EASY SQUASH STUFFING

COCONUT-PECAN SWEET POTATOES

Coconut-Pecan Sweet Potatoes

These delicious sweet potatoes cook effortlessly in the slow cooker, so you can tend to other things. Coconut gives the classic dish a new twist.

—**RAQUEL HAGGARD** EDMOND, OK

PREP: 15 MIN. • **COOK:** 4 HOURS
MAKES: 12 SERVINGS (¾ CUP EACH)

- 4 **pounds sweet potatoes (about 6 medium), peeled and cubed**
- ½ **cup chopped pecans**
- ½ **cup flaked coconut**
- ⅓ **cup sugar**
- ⅓ **cup packed brown sugar**
- ¼ **cup reduced-fat butter, melted**
- ½ **teaspoon ground cinnamon**
- ¼ **teaspoon salt**
- ½ **teaspoon coconut extract**
- ½ **teaspoon vanilla extract**

1. Place sweet potatoes in a 5-qt. slow cooker coated with cooking spray. In a small bowl, combine pecans, coconut, sugars, butter, cinnamon and salt; sprinkle over potatoes.
2. Cook, covered, on low 4-4½ hours or until potatoes are tender. Stir in the extracts.
NOTE *This recipe was tested with Land O'Lakes light stick butter.*

Fall Garden Medley

I like to make this recipe in the fall and winter for special occasions because it's so colorful, tasty and hearty. It's a nourishing side dish that complements many different entrees.

—**KRYSTINE KERCHER** LINCOLN, NE

PREP: 20 MIN. • **COOK:** 5 HOURS
MAKES: 8 SERVINGS

- 4 **large carrots, cut into 1½-inch pieces**
- 3 **fresh beets, peeled and cut into 1½-inch pieces**
- 2 **medium sweet potatoes, peeled and cut into 1½-inch pieces**
- 2 **medium onions, peeled and quartered**
- ½ **cup water**
- 2 **teaspoons salt**
- ½ **teaspoon pepper**
- ¼ **teaspoon dried thyme**
- 1 **tablespoon olive oil**
  Fresh parsley or dried parsley flakes, optional

1. Place the carrots, beets, sweet potatoes, onions and water in a greased 3-qt. slow cooker. Sprinkle with salt, pepper and thyme. Drizzle with olive oil. Cover and cook on low for 5-6 hours or until tender.
2. Stir vegetables and sprinkle with parsley if desired.

⑤INGREDIENTS

Ginger Applesauce

This is my favorite way to prepare applesauce. It's simple and makes the whole house smell like fall!

—**RENEE PAJESTKA** BRUNSWICK, OH

PREP: 25 MIN. • **COOK:** 4 HOURS
MAKES: ABOUT 5 CUPS

- 4 **pounds apples (about 12 medium), peeled and cubed**
- ¼ **cup water**
- 2 **tablespoons brown sugar**
- 2 **teaspoons ground cinnamon**
- 2 **teaspoons minced fresh gingerroot**
- 2 **teaspoons vanilla extract**

1. Place all ingredients in a 4-qt. slow cooker; stir until combined.
2. Cover and cook on low for 4-5 hours or until apples are tender. Mash if desired. Refrigerate leftovers.

NANCY MOORE'S
CHUCK WAGON BEANS

Chuck Wagon Beans

Following in the footsteps of cooks on the Old Western cattle ranges, I came up with these savory beans. Sweet and smoky, they're made extra hearty by adding smoked sausage.

—**NANCY MOORE** BUCKLIN, KS

PREP: 15 MIN. • **COOK:** 8 HOURS
MAKES: 24 SERVINGS (⅔ CUP EACH)

- 2 **cans (28 ounces each) baked beans**
- 3 **cans (16 ounces each) kidney beans, rinsed and drained**
- 2 **cans (15 ounces each) pinto beans, rinsed and drained**
- 1 **pound smoked kielbasa or Polish sausage, sliced**
- 1 **jar (12 ounces) pickled jalapeno slices, drained**
- 1 **medium onion, chopped**
- 1 **cup barbecue sauce**
- ½ **cup spicy brown mustard**
- ¼ **cup steak seasoning**

In a greased 6-qt. slow cooker, combine all ingredients. Cover and cook on low for 8-10 hours or until heated through.

NOTE *This recipe was tested with McCormick's Montreal Steak Seasoning. Look for it in the spice aisle of your grocery store.*

Slow-Cooked Sausage Dressing

This dressing is so delicious, no one will know it's lower in fat. Best of all, it cooks effortlessly in the slow cooker, so I don't have to think about it. It couldn't be easier, particularly when hosting a large dinner!

—**RAQUEL HAGGARD** EDMOND, OK

PREP: 20 MIN. • **COOK:** 3 HOURS
MAKES: 8 CUPS

- ½ **pound reduced-fat bulk pork sausage**
- 2 **celery ribs, chopped**
- 1 **large onion, chopped**
- 7 **cups seasoned stuffing cubes**
- 1 **can (14½ ounces) reduced-sodium chicken broth**
- 1 **medium tart apple, chopped**
- ⅓ **cup chopped pecans**
- 2 **tablespoons reduced-fat butter, melted**
- 1½ **teaspoons rubbed sage**
- ½ **teaspoon pepper**

1. In a large nonstick skillet, cook the sausage, celery and onion over medium heat until meat is no longer pink; drain. Transfer to a large bowl; stir in the remaining ingredients.

2. Place in a 5-qt. slow cooker coated with cooking spray. Cover and cook on low for 3-4 hours or until heated through and the apple is tender, stirring once.

NOTE *This recipe was tested with Land O'Lakes light stick butter.*

SLOW-COOKED SAUSAGE DRESSING

RICH & CREAMY MASHED POTATOES

Stir in the potato flakes, garlic salt and pepper. Cover and cook on low for 2-3 hours or until heated through. Sprinkle with parsley if desired.

Cranberry Apple Topping

A generous spoonful of this sweet-tart sauce makes a tasty addition to cooked chicken, turkey or pork. The ruby-red color lends a festive look to any meal.
—LISE ODE DELRAY BEACH, FL

PREP: 15 MIN.
COOK: 3½ HOURS + COOLING
MAKES: 3¾ CUPS

> 4 cups fresh or frozen cranberries, thawed
> 2 medium tart apples, peeled and chopped
> 1¼ cups sugar
> ¼ cup orange juice
> 2 teaspoons grated orange peel
> ½ teaspoon ground cinnamon
> 2 tablespoons cornstarch
> 2 tablespoons cold water

1. In a 3-qt. slow cooker, combine the first six ingredients. Cover and cook on low for 3-4 hours or until bubbly.
2. In a small bowl, combine cornstarch and water until smooth; stir into cranberry mixture. Cover and cook 30 minutes longer or until thickened. Transfer to a serving bowl; cool. Serve with cooked turkey, chicken or pork.

DID YOU KNOW?

It's easy to mince parsley without dirtying a cutting board. Just place sprigs of parsley in a small glass container and snip them with kitchen shears until minced.

Rich & Creamy Mashed Potatoes

It's a cinch to jazz up instant mashed potatoes with sour cream and cream cheese, then cook and serve the versatile side dish in a slow cooker. For a special touch, sprinkle the potatoes with chopped fresh chives, canned French-fried onions or grated Parmesan cheese.
—DONNA BARDOCZ HOWELL, MI

PREP: 15 MIN. • **COOK:** 2 HOURS
MAKES: 10 SERVINGS

> 3¾ cups boiling water
> 1½ cups 2% milk
> 1 package (8 ounces) cream cheese, softened
> ½ cup butter, cubed
> ½ cup sour cream
> 4 cups mashed potato flakes
> 1 teaspoon garlic salt
> ¼ teaspoon pepper
>   Minced fresh parsley, optional

In a greased 4-qt. slow cooker, whisk the boiling water, milk, cream cheese, butter and sour cream until smooth.

Sweet Potato Stuffing

Mom likes to make sure there will be enough stuffing to satisfy our large family. So for our holiday gatherings, she slow-cooks this tasty sweet potato dressing in addition to the traditional stuffing cooked inside the turkey.

—KELLY POLLOCK LONDON, ON

PREP: 15 MIN. • **COOK:** 4 HOURS
MAKES: 10 SERVINGS

- ¼ cup butter, cubed
- ½ cup chopped celery
- ½ cup chopped onion
- ½ cup chicken broth
- ½ teaspoon salt, optional
- ½ teaspoon rubbed sage
- ½ teaspoon poultry seasoning
- ½ teaspoon pepper
- 6 cups dry bread cubes
- 1 large sweet potato, cooked, peeled and finely chopped
- ¼ cup chopped pecans

1. In a Dutch oven, heat butter over medium-high heat. Add celery and onion; cook and stir until tender. Stir in broth and seasonings. Add remaining ingredients; toss to combine.

2. Transfer to a greased 3-qt. slow cooker. Cook, covered, on low for 4 hours or until heated through.

SWEET POTATO STUFFING

Stuffing from the Slow Cooker

If you're hosting a big Thanksgiving dinner this year, add this simple slow-cooked stuffing to your menu to make the day run more smoothly. The recipe makes a good amount and comes in handy when you're out of oven space. I use it all the time!

—**DONALD SEILER** MACON, MS

PREP: 30 MIN. • **COOK:** 3 HOURS
MAKES: 10 SERVINGS

- 1 **cup chopped onion**
- 1 **cup chopped celery**
- ¼ **cup butter**
- 6 **cups cubed day-old white bread**
- 6 **cups cubed day-old whole wheat bread**
- 1 **teaspoon salt**
- 1 **teaspoon poultry seasoning**
- 1 **teaspoon rubbed sage**
- ½ **teaspoon pepper**
- 1 **can (14½ ounces) reduced-sodium chicken broth or vegetable broth**
- 2 **eggs, beaten**

1. In a small nonstick skillet over medium heat, cook onion and celery in butter until tender.

2. In a large bowl, combine the bread cubes, salt, poultry seasoning, sage and pepper. Stir in onion mixture. Combine broth and eggs; add to bread mixture and toss to coat.

3. Transfer to a 3-qt. slow cooker coated with cooking spray. Cover and cook on low for 3-4 hours or until a thermometer reads 160°.

STUFFING FROM THE SLOW COOKER

 ## Lazy-Day Cranberry Relish

My no-fuss condiment simmers away on its own while I prepare other foods on my menu. It's especially delicious with turkey.

—**JUNE FORMANEK** BELLE PLAINE, IA

PREP: 5 MIN. • **COOK:** 6 HOURS + CHILLING
MAKES: 3 CUPS

- 2 **cups sugar**
- 1 **cup orange juice**
- 1 **teaspoon grated orange peel**
- 4 **cups fresh or frozen cranberries**

1. In a 1½ qt. slow cooker, combine sugar, orange juice and peel; stir until sugar is dissolved. Add the cranberries.

2. Cover and cook on low for 6 hours. Mash the mixture. Transfer to a small bowl; cool. Refrigerate until chilled.

Mushroom Wild Rice

This is one of my favorite recipes from my mother. With only seven ingredients, it's quick to assemble in the morning. By the time I get home, mouthwatering aromas have filled the house!

—**BOB MALCHOW** MONON, IN

PREP: 5 MIN. • **COOK:** 7 HOURS
MAKES: 12-16 SERVINGS

- 2¼ **cups water**
- 1 **can (10½ ounces) condensed beef consomme, undiluted**
- 1 **can (10½ ounces) condensed French onion soup, undiluted**
- 3 **cans (4 ounces each) mushroom stems and pieces, drained**
- ½ **cup butter, melted**
- 1 **cup uncooked brown rice**
- 1 **cup uncooked wild rice**

In a 3-qt. slow cooker, combine all ingredients. Cover and cook on low for 7-8 hours or until rice is tender.

BOB MALCHOW'S
MUSHROOM WILD RICE

Saucy Scalloped Potatoes

For old-fashioned flavor, try these scalloped potatoes. They cook up tender, creamy and so comforting. Chopped ham adds a hearty touch.

—ELAINE KANE KEIZER, OR

PREP: 15 MIN. • **COOK:** 7 HOURS
MAKES: 8 SERVINGS

4 **cups thinly sliced peeled potatoes (about 2 pounds)**
1 **can (10¾ ounces) condensed cream of celery soup or mushroom soup, undiluted**
1 **can (12 ounces) evaporated milk**
1 **large onion, sliced**
2 **tablespoons butter**
½ **teaspoon salt**
¼ **teaspoon pepper**
1½ **cups chopped fully cooked ham**

In a 3-qt. slow cooker, combine the first seven ingredients. Cover and cook on high for 1 hour. Stir in ham. Reduce heat to low; cook 6-8 hours longer or until potatoes are tender.

SAUCY SCALLOPED POTATOES

POTLUCK CANDIED SWEET POTATOES

2. Using a slotted spoon, transfer potatoes to a serving dish; keep warm. Pour cooking juices into a small saucepan; bring to a boil. In a small bowl, combine cornstarch and water until smooth; stir into pan. Return to a boil, stirring constantly; cook and stir for 1-2 minutes or until thickened. Spoon over sweet potatoes.

3. Sprinkle with parsley if desired.

Butternut Squash with Whole Grain Pilaf

Fresh thyme really shines in this hearty slow-cooked side dish featuring tender butternut squash, nutritious whole grain pilaf and vitamin-packed baby spinach.
—*TASTE OF HOME* **TEST KITCHEN**

PREP: 15 MIN. • **COOK:** 4 HOURS
MAKES: 12 SERVINGS (¾ CUP EACH)

- 1 cup Kashi whole grain pilaf
- 1 medium butternut squash (about 3 pounds), cut into ½-inch cubes
- 1 can (14½ ounces) vegetable broth
- 1 medium onion, chopped
- ½ cup water
- 3 garlic cloves, minced
- 2 teaspoons minced fresh thyme or ½ teaspoon dried thyme
- ½ teaspoon salt
- ¼ teaspoon pepper
- 1 package (6 ounces) fresh baby spinach

Place pilaf in a 4-qt slow cooker. In a large bowl, combine the squash, broth, onion, water, garlic, thyme, salt and pepper; add to slow cooker. Cover and cook on low for 4-5 hours or until pilaf is tender, adding spinach during the last 30 minutes of cooking.

Potluck Candied Sweet Potatoes

To make it easier to bring this traditional Southern staple to a potluck or gathering, I updated it so that it can be cooked in a slow cooker. It's hard to go wrong with candied sweet potatoes when it comes to pleasing a crowd!
—**DEIRDRE COX** KANSAS CITY, MO

PREP: 20 MIN. • **COOK:** 5 HOURS
MAKES: 12 SERVINGS (¾ CUP EACH)

- 1 cup packed brown sugar
- 1 cup sugar
- 8 medium sweet potatoes, peeled and cut into ½-inch slices
- ¼ cup butter, melted
- 2 teaspoons vanilla extract
- ¼ teaspoon salt
- 2 tablespoons cornstarch
- 2 tablespoons cold water
    Minced fresh parsley, optional

1. In a small bowl, combine sugars. In a greased 5-qt. slow cooker, layer a third of the sweet potatoes; sprinkle with a third of the sugar mixture. Repeat layers twice. In a small bowl, combine the butter, vanilla and salt; drizzle over potatoes. Cover and cook on low for 5-6 hours or until sweet potatoes are tender.

Autumn

ENTREES

It's time to dig into flavor with these hearty autumn dinners. From satisfying roasts to sensational ethnic favorites, the main dishes shared here will lend heartwarming appeal to crisp fall days and nights.

LINDA SOUTH'S
STACK OF BONES

Stack of Bones

These lip-smacking baby back ribs always come out of the slow cooker tender and delicious. My husband devours them until there's nothing left but a stack of bones!
—**LINDA SOUTH** PINEVILLE, NC

PREP: 15 MIN. • **COOK:** 4 HOURS
MAKES: 4 SERVINGS

- 1 cup chili sauce
- 2 green onions, chopped
- 2 tablespoons brown sugar
- 2 tablespoons balsamic vinegar
- 1 tablespoon Dijon mustard
- 1 tablespoon Worcestershire sauce
- 1 tablespoon soy sauce
- 1 teaspoon ground ginger
- ¼ teaspoon crushed red pepper flakes
- ½ teaspoon liquid smoke, optional
- 4 pounds pork baby back ribs

In a large bowl, combine the first 10 ingredients. Cut the baby back ribs into individual pieces; dip each into sauce. Transfer to a 5-qt. slow cooker; top with the remaining sauce. Cover and cook on low for 4-5 hours or until meat is tender.

Family-Friendly Pizza

When it comes to kid-pleasing food, you can't go wrong with a casserole full of mozzarella cheese, seasoned sauce, pepperoni and mushrooms. Every bite is loaded with the popular flavors of pizza.
—**HOLLIE CLARK** AMES, IA

PREP: 30 MIN. • **COOK:** 3 HOURS
MAKES: 8 SERVINGS

- 6 cups uncooked egg noodles
- 1½ pounds ground beef
- 1 medium onion, chopped
- 1 medium green pepper, chopped
- 2 cans (15 ounces each) pizza sauce
- 1 can (4 ounces) mushroom stems and pieces, drained
- 2 cups (8 ounces) shredded cheddar cheese
- 2 cups (8 ounces) shredded part-skim mozzarella cheese
- 1 package (3½ ounces) sliced pepperoni

1. Cook the egg noodles according to package directions; drain. Meanwhile, in a large skillet, cook the beef, onion and green pepper over medium heat until meat is no longer pink, breaking meat into crumbles; drain. Stir in the pizza sauce and mushrooms.
2. In a greased 5-qt. slow cooker, layer half of the noodles, meat sauce, cheese and pepperoni. Repeat layers. Cover and cook on low for 3-4 hours or until heated through.

GREEN CHILI BEEF BURRITOS

Zesty Chicken Marinara

A friend of mine served this delicious chicken marinara before a church social. I think the Italian-style entree tastes like something from a restaurant.
—**LINDA BAUMANN** RICHFIELD, WI

PREP: 15 MIN. • **COOK:** 4 HOURS
MAKES: 4 SERVINGS

> 4 **bone-in chicken breast halves (12 to 14 ounces each), skin removed**
> 2 **cups marinara sauce**
> 1 **medium tomato, chopped**
> ½ **cup Italian salad dressing**
> 1½ **teaspoons Italian seasoning**
> 1 **garlic clove, minced**
> ½ **pound uncooked angel hair pasta**
> ½ **cup shredded part-skim mozzarella cheese**

1. Place chicken in a 4-qt. slow cooker. In a small bowl, combine the marinara sauce, tomato, salad dressing, Italian seasoning and garlic; pour over the chicken. Cover and cook on low for 4-5 hours or until chicken is tender.

2. Cook pasta according to package directions; drain. Serve chicken and sauce with pasta; sprinkle with cheese.

ZESTY CHICKEN MARINARA

Green Chili Beef Burritos

Here's a main course that brings in rave reviews whenever I make it. The shredded beef has that slow-simmered goodness you just can't get any other way.
—**JENNY FLAKE** NEWPORT BEACH, CA

PREP: 30 MIN. • **COOK:** 9 HOURS
MAKES: 12 SERVINGS

> 1 **boneless beef chuck roast (3 pounds)**
> 1 **can (14½ ounces) beef broth**
> 2 **cups green enchilada sauce**
> 1 **can (4 ounces) chopped green chilies**
> ½ **cup Mexican-style hot tomato sauce**
> ½ **teaspoon salt**
> ½ **teaspoon garlic powder**
> ½ **teaspoon pepper**
> 12 **flour tortillas (12 inches)**
> **Optional toppings: shredded lettuce, chopped tomatoes, shredded cheddar cheese and sour cream**

1. Cut the roast in half and place in a 3- or 4-qt. slow cooker. Add the broth. Cover and cook on low for 8-9 hours or until the meat is tender.

2. Remove beef. When cool enough to handle, shred the meat with two forks. Skim the fat from the cooking liquid; reserve ½ cup liquid. Return shredded beef and reserved liquid to the slow cooker. Stir in the enchilada sauce, green chilies, tomato sauce, salt, garlic powder and pepper.

3. Cover and cook on low for 1 hour or until heated through. Spoon the beef mixture down the center of the flour tortillas; add the toppings of your choice. Roll up.

NOTE *This recipe was tested with El Pato brand Mexican-style hot tomato sauce. If you can't find Mexican-style hot tomato sauce, you may substitute ½ cup tomato sauce, 1 teaspoon hot pepper sauce, ⅛ teaspoon onion powder and ⅛ teaspoon chili powder.*

ZESTY SAUSAGE & BEANS

Zesty Sausage & Beans

Even the biggest appetites are no match for sausage, beans and bacon served over a bed of hot rice. It's a hearty meal that leaves everyone satisfied.

—**MELISSA JUST** MINNEAPOLIS, MN

PREP: 30 MIN. • **COOK:** 5 HOURS
MAKES: 10 SERVINGS

- 2 **pounds smoked kielbasa or Polish sausage, halved and sliced**
- 2 **cans (15 ounces each) black beans, rinsed and drained**
- 1 **can (15 ounces) great northern beans, rinsed and drained**
- 1 **can (15 ounces) thick and zesty tomato sauce**
- 1 **medium green pepper, chopped**
- 1 **medium onion, chopped**
- 5 **bacon strips, cooked and crumbled**
- 3 **tablespoons brown sugar**
- 2 **tablespoons cider vinegar**
- 3 **garlic cloves, minced**
- ¼ **teaspoon dried thyme**
- ¼ **teaspoon dried marjoram**
- ¼ **teaspoon cayenne pepper**
  Hot cooked rice

In a large skillet, brown the sausage. Transfer to a 4-qt. slow cooker; add the beans, tomato sauce, green pepper, onion, bacon, brown sugar, vinegar, garlic, thyme, marjoram and cayenne. Cover and cook on low for 5-6 hours or until the vegetables are tender. Serve with rice.

Simple Sparerib & Sauerkraut Supper

I rely on this slow-cooked dinner all the time because it fits into my busy schedule, has home-style appeal and tastes great.

—**DONNA HARP** CINCINNATI, OH

PREP: 30 MIN. • **COOK:** 6 HOURS
MAKES: 4 SERVINGS

- 1 **pound fingerling potatoes**
- 1 **medium onion, chopped**
- 1 **medium Granny Smith apple, peeled and chopped**
- 3 **slices thick-sliced bacon strips, cooked and crumbled**
- 1 **jar (16 ounces) sauerkraut, undrained**
- 2 **pounds pork spareribs**
- ½ **teaspoon salt**
- ¼ **teaspoon pepper**
- 1 **tablespoon vegetable oil**
- 3 **tablespoons brown sugar**
- ¼ **teaspoon caraway seeds**
- ½ **pound smoked Polish sausage, cut into 1-inch slices**
- 1 **cup beer**

1. In a 6-qt. slow cooker, place the potatoes, onion, apple and bacon. Drain sauerkraut, reserving ⅓ cup of the liquid; add sauerkraut and reserved liquid to slow cooker.

2. Cut spareribs into serving-size portions; sprinkle with salt and pepper. In a large skillet, heat oil over medium-high heat; brown the spareribs in batches. Transfer to the slow cooker; sprinkle with brown sugar and caraway seeds.

3. Add the sausage; pour in the beer. Cover and cook on low for 6-7 hours or until ribs are tender.

SIMPLE SPARERIB & SAUERKRAUT SUPPER

TANGY TOMATO PORK CHOPS

Tangy Tomato Pork Chops

These tender chops are smothered in a delightfully rich sauce. I've also used a chuck roast instead of pork, substituted stewed tomatoes for diced and served it over rice rather than noodles.

—**LEA ANN SCHALK** GARFIELD, AR

PREP: 20 MIN. • **COOK:** 8 HOURS
MAKES: 6 SERVINGS

- 6 **bone-in pork loin chops (8 ounces each)**
- 1 **tablespoon canola oil**
- 1 **large onion, sliced**
- 1 **large sweet red pepper, sliced**
- 1 **jar (4½ ounces) sliced mushrooms, drained**
- 1 **can (28 ounces) diced tomatoes, undrained**
- 1 **tablespoon brown sugar**
- 1 **tablespoon balsamic vinegar**
- 2 **teaspoons Worcestershire sauce**
- ¼ **teaspoon salt**
- ¼ **teaspoon pepper**
  Hot cooked egg noodles, optional

1. In a large skillet, brown the pork chops in oil. Transfer to a 5-qt. slow cooker. Layer the onion, red pepper and mushrooms over pork chops.
2. In a large bowl, combine tomatoes, brown sugar, vinegar, Worcestershire sauce, salt and pepper; pour over pork and vegetables.
3. Cover and cook on low for 8-9 hours or until the pork is tender. Serve with noodles if desired.

Autumn Pot Roast

When the weather is chilly, I love coming home to a pot roast supper. Here's one of my all-time-favorite recipes.

—**MARY HANKINS** KANSAS CITY, MO

PREP: 30 MIN. • **COOK:** 6 HOURS
MAKES: 6 SERVINGS

- 1 **boneless beef chuck roast (3 pounds)**
- 1 **teaspoon salt, divided**
- ½ **teaspoon pepper, divided**
- 1 **tablespoon olive oil**
- 1½ **pounds sweet potatoes, cut into 1-inch pieces**
- 2 **medium parsnips, cut into ½ inch pieces**
- 1 **large sweet onion, cut into chunks**
- ⅓ **cup sun-dried tomatoes (not packed in oil)**
- 3 **garlic cloves, minced**
- 1 **teaspoon dried thyme**
- 2 **bay leaves**
- 1 **can (14½ ounces) reduced-sodium beef broth**
- ¾ **cup dry red wine or additional reduced-sodium beef broth**

1. Cut roast in half; sprinkle with ½ teaspoon salt and ¼ teaspoon pepper. In a large skillet, brown the meat in oil on all sides; drain.
2. Transfer to a 5-qt. slow cooker. Top with sweet potatoes, parsnips, onion, sun-dried tomatoes, garlic, thyme, bay leaves and remaining salt and pepper. Combine broth and wine; pour over vegetables.
3. Cover and cook on low for 6-8 hours or until the meat and vegetables are tender. Skim fat. Discard bay leaves. If desired, thicken cooking juices.

AUTUMN POT ROAST

CARNITAS TACOS

Carnitas Tacos

The house smells fantastic all day when I'm making the seasoned meat for these tacos. They have so much flavor, you'd never guess the recipe requires just a handful of basic ingredients.

—**MARY WOOD** MAIZE, KS

PREP: 15 MIN. • **COOK:** 6 HOURS
MAKES: 12 SERVINGS

- 1 boneless pork shoulder butt roast (3 to 4 pounds)
- 1 envelope taco seasoning
- 1 can (10 ounces) diced tomatoes and green chilies, undrained
- 12 flour tortillas (8 inches), warmed
- 2 cups (8 ounces) shredded Colby-Monterey Jack cheese
    Sour cream, optional

1. Cut roast in half; place in a 4- or 5-qt. slow cooker. Sprinkle with taco seasoning. Pour tomatoes over top. Cover and cook on low for 6-8 hours or until meat is tender.

2. Remove the meat from the slow cooker; shred with two forks. Skim fat from cooking juices. Return meat to slow cooker; heat through. Using a slotted spoon, place ½ cup on each tortilla; top with cheese. Serve with sour cream if desired.

Cranberry Pork Roast

Here's a delicious pork roast I serve to guests on cool autumn days. I love the fact that I don't have to slave away in the kitchen to prepare a main course that tastes special enough for company.

—**KIMBERLEY SCASNY** DOUGLASVILLE, GA

PREP: 5 MIN. • **COOK:** 4 HOURS + STANDING
MAKES: 6-8 SERVINGS

- 1 boneless rolled pork loin roast (2½ to 3 pounds)
- ½ teaspoon salt
- ¼ teaspoon pepper
- 1 can (14 ounces) whole-berry cranberry sauce
- ¼ cup honey
- 1 teaspoon grated orange peel
- ⅛ teaspoon ground cloves
- ⅛ teaspoon ground nutmeg

Cut roast in half and place in a 3-qt. slow cooker; sprinkle with salt and pepper. Combine the remaining ingredients; pour over roast. Cover and cook on low for 4-5 hours or until a thermometer reads 160°. Let stand 10 minutes before slicing.

CRANBERRY PORK ROAST

PORTOBELLO BEEF BURGUNDY

Portobello Beef Burgundy

Everyone will request seconds of this rich, tender beef with hearty mushrooms.

—MELISSA GALINAT LAKELAND, FL

PREP: 30 MIN. • **COOK:** 7½ HOURS
MAKES: 6 SERVINGS

- ¼ **cup all-purpose flour**
- ½ **teaspoon salt**
- ½ **teaspoon seasoned salt**
- 1½ **teaspoons minced fresh thyme or ½ teaspoon dried thyme**
- ¾ **teaspoon minced fresh marjoram or ¼ teaspoon dried thyme**
- ½ **teaspoon pepper**
- 2 **pounds beef sirloin tip steak, cubed**
- 2 **bacon strips, diced**
- 3 **tablespoons canola oil**
- 1 **garlic clove, minced**
- 1 **cup Burgundy wine or beef broth**
- 1 **teaspoon beef bouillon granules**
- 1 **pound sliced baby portobello mushrooms**
  Hot cooked noodles, optional

1. In a large resealable plastic bag, combine the first six ingredients. Add the beef, a few pieces at a time, and shake to coat.

2. In a large skillet, cook the bacon over medium heat until crisp. Remove to paper towels with a slotted spoon; drain. In the same skillet, brown the beef in oil in batches, adding the garlic to the last batch; cook 1-2 minutes longer. Drain.

3. Transfer to a 4-qt. slow cooker. Add the Burgundy wine to the skillet, stirring to loosen the browned bits from the pan. Add the beef bouillon; bring to a boil. Stir into slow cooker. Stir in the reserved bacon. Cover and cook on low for 7-9 hours or until the meat is tender.

4. Stir in the portobello mushrooms. Cover and cook on high 30-45 minutes longer or until the mushrooms are tender and the sauce is slightly thickened. Serve with hot cooked noodles if desired.

Spicy Goulash

I fired up my goulash dinner using some ground cumin, chili powder and a can of Mexican diced tomatoes.

—MELISSA POLK WEST LAFAYETTE, IN

PREP: 25 MIN. • **COOK:** 5½ HOURS
MAKES: 12 SERVINGS

- 1 **pound lean ground beef (90% lean)**
- 4 **cans (14½ ounces each) Mexican diced tomatoes, undrained**
- 2 **cans (16 ounces each) kidney beans, rinsed and drained**
- 2 **cups water**
- 1 **medium onion, chopped**
- 1 **medium green pepper, chopped**
- ¼ **cup red wine vinegar**
- 2 **tablespoons chili powder**
- 1 **tablespoon Worcestershire sauce**
- 2 **teaspoons beef bouillon granules**
- 1 **teaspoon dried basil**
- 1 **teaspoon dried parsley flakes**
- 1 **teaspoon ground cumin**
- ¼ **teaspoon pepper**
- 2 **cups uncooked elbow macaroni**

1. In a large skillet, cook beef over medium heat until no longer pink, breaking beef into crumbles; drain. Transfer to a 5-qt. slow cooker. Stir in the tomatoes, kidney beans, water, onion, green pepper, red wine vinegar, chili powder, Worcestershire sauce, beef bouillon and seasonings. Cover and cook on low for 5-6 hours or until heated through.

2. Stir in the macaroni; cover and cook 30 minutes longer or until the macaroni is tender.

SLOW-COOKED HERBED TURKEY

Slow-Cooked Herbed Turkey

As soon as the herbs are plentiful in my garden, I pull out my slow cooker and start preparing this moist turkey. When I served it to our Bible study group at a potluck, everyone wanted the recipe.

—SUE JURACK MEQUON, WI

PREP: 15 MIN. + MARINATING
COOK: 4 HOURS + STANDING
MAKES: 14-16 SERVINGS

- 2 cans (14½ ounces each) chicken broth
- 1 cup lemon juice
- ½ cup packed brown sugar
- ½ cup minced fresh sage
- ½ cup minced fresh thyme
- ½ cup lime juice
- ½ cup cider vinegar
- ½ cup olive oil
- 2 envelopes onion soup mix
- ¼ cup Dijon mustard
- 2 tablespoons minced fresh marjoram
- 3 teaspoons paprika
- 2 teaspoons garlic powder
- 2 teaspoons pepper
- 1 teaspoon salt
- 2 boneless skinless turkey breast halves (3 pounds each)

1. In a blender, combine the first 15 ingredients; cover and process until blended. Place turkey breast halves in a gallon-size resealable plastic bag; add half of the marinade. Seal the bag and turn to coat; seal and refrigerate overnight. Pour remaining marinade into a bowl; cover and refrigerate.
2. Drain and discard marinade from turkey breast halves. Transfer turkey to a 5-qt. slow cooker. Add reserved marinade; cover and cook on high for 4-5 hours or until a thermometer reads 170°. Let stand for 10 minutes before slicing.

Favorite Beef Chimichangas

Feeding a hungry crowd? You can't go wrong with golden-brown chimichangas featuring slow-roasted beef and melted cheese inside crispy tortillas.

—JUDY SANCHEZ RACINE, WI

PREP: 1 HOUR • **COOK:** 7½ HOURS
MAKES: 16 SERVINGS

- 1 boneless beef chuck roast (3½ pounds)
- 2 cups chopped peeled potatoes
- 1½ cups water
- 1 tablespoon reduced-sodium soy sauce
- 2 teaspoons garlic salt with parsley
- ¾ teaspoon pepper
- 2 cans (4 ounces each) chopped green chilies
- 2 tablespoons all-purpose flour
- 2 tablespoons taco seasoning
- 16 flour tortillas (10 inches), warmed
- 4 cups (16 ounces) shredded cheddar cheese
- ⅓ cup canola oil
  Optional toppings: guacamole, salsa or sour cream

1. Cut roast in half; place in a 4- or 5-qt. slow cooker. Arrange potatoes around the roast; pour the water over potatoes. Drizzle meat with soy sauce. Sprinkle with garlic salt and pepper. Top with green chilies. Cover and cook on low for 7-9 hours or until meat is very tender.
2. Remove roast to a platter. Shred meat with two forks and return to the slow cooker. Combine flour and taco seasoning; stir into the meat mixture. Cover and cook 30 minutes longer or until juices are thickened.
3. To assemble the chimichangas, using a slotted spoon, spoon ½ cup meat mixture off-center on each tortilla. Sprinkle with ¼ cup cheese. Fold up edge nearest filling; fold in both sides and roll up.
4. In a large skillet, fry chimichangas, folded side down, in the oil in batches for 2-3 minutes on each side or until golden brown. Drain on paper towels. Serve with toppings if desired.

Pork Chop Cacciatore

It's almost hard to believe that such a simple, easy dish could result in so much flavor. Add hot egg noodles and a tossed green salad for a complete dinner.

—**TRACY HIATT GRICE** SOMERSET, WI

PREP: 30 MIN. • **COOK:** 8 HOURS
MAKES: 6 SERVINGS

- 6 **bone-in pork loin chops (7 ounces each)**
- ¾ **teaspoon salt, divided**
- ¼ **teaspoon pepper**
- 1 **tablespoon olive oil**
- 1 **cup sliced fresh mushrooms**
- 1 **small onion, chopped**
- 1 **celery rib, chopped**
- 1 **small green pepper, chopped**
- 2 **garlic cloves, minced**
- 1 **can (14½ ounces) diced tomatoes**
- ½ **cup water, divided**
- ½ **teaspoon dried basil**
- 2 **tablespoons cornstarch**
- 4½ **cups cooked egg noodles**

1. Sprinkle the pork chops with ½ teaspoon salt and pepper. In a large skillet, brown the pork chops in oil in batches. Transfer to a 4-or 5-qt. slow cooker coated with cooking spray. Saute the mushrooms, onion, celery and green pepper in the drippings until tender. Add garlic; cook 1 minute longer. Stir in the tomatoes, ¼ cup water, basil and remaining salt; pour over pork chops.

2. Cover and cook on low for 8-10 hours or until pork chops are tender. Remove the meat to a serving platter; keep warm. Skim fat from the cooking juices if necessary; transfer to a small saucepan. Bring the liquid to a boil. Combine cornstarch and remaining water until smooth. Gradually stir into the pan. Bring to a boil; cook and stir for 2 minutes or until thickened. Serve with meat and noodles.

PORK CHOP CACCIATORE

LISA CHAMBERLAIN'S
PORK ROAST DINNER

Pork Roast Dinner

I love spending time in the kitchen and often host friends who either don't cook or work nights. They enjoy sampling new dishes, and this pork roast was a big hit. The leftover meat makes great barbecue sandwiches for dinner the next day.

—LISA CHAMBERLAIN ST. CHARLES, IL

PREP: 30 MIN. + MARINATING
COOK: 8 HOURS
MAKES: 8 SERVINGS

- 2 teaspoons minced garlic
- 2 teaspoons fennel seed, crushed
- 1½ teaspoons dried rosemary, crushed
- 1 teaspoon dried oregano
- 1 teaspoon paprika
- ¾ teaspoon salt
- ¼ teaspoon pepper
- 1 boneless whole pork loin roast (3 to 4 pounds)
- 1½ pounds medium potatoes, peeled and cut into chunks
- 1½ pounds large sweet potatoes, peeled and cut into chunks
- 2 large sweet onions, cut into eighths
- ½ cup chicken broth

1. Combine garlic, fennel, rosemary, oregano, paprika, salt and pepper; rub over the pork. Cover and refrigerate for 8 hours.

2. Place the potatoes and onions in a 5-qt. slow cooker. Top with pork. Pour chicken broth over meat. Cover and cook on low for 8-10 hours or until meat and vegetables are tender.

3. Let the meat stand 10-15 minutes before slicing.

Gingered Short Ribs with Green Rice

A fan both of Asian food and of using a slow cooker, I decided to convert one of my best Korean recipes—gingered short ribs—for my favorite appliance. I was thrilled with the resuts!

—LILY JULOW LAWRENCEVILLE, GA

PREP: 35 MIN. • **COOK:** 8 HOURS
MAKES: 6 SERVINGS

- ½ cup reduced-sodium beef broth
- ⅓ cup sherry or additional reduced-sodium beef broth
- ¼ cup reduced-sodium soy sauce
- 3 tablespoons honey
- 1 tablespoon rice vinegar
- 1 tablespoon minced fresh gingerroot
- 3 garlic cloves, minced
- 4 medium carrots, chopped
- 2 medium onions, chopped
- 3 pounds bone-in beef short ribs
- ½ teaspoon salt
- ½ teaspoon pepper
- 3 cups uncooked instant brown rice
- 3 green onions, thinly sliced
- 3 tablespoons minced fresh cilantro
- 2 tablespoons chopped pickled jalapenos
- ¾ teaspoon grated lime peel
- 1 tablespoon cornstarch
- 1 tablespoon cold water

1. In a small bowl, whisk the first seven ingredients until blended. Place carrots and onions in a 5-qt. slow cooker. Sprinkle ribs with salt and pepper; place over vegetables. Pour broth mixture over top. Cook, covered, on low 8-10 hours or until meat is tender.

2. Just before serving, prepare rice according to package directions. Stir in green onions, cilantro, jalapenos and lime peel.

3. Remove the ribs to a serving plate; keep warm. Transfer the cooking juices to a small saucepan; skim fat. Bring the juices to a boil. In a small bowl, mix the cornstarch and water until smooth; stir into juices. Return to a boil; cook and stir 2 minutes or until thickened. Serve with ribs and rice mixture.

GINGERED SHORT RIBS WITH GREEN RICE

TURKEY WITH CRANBERRY SAUCE

⑤INGREDIENTS Turkey with Cranberry Sauce

Here's an easy yet tasty way to prepare turkey breast. Ideal for holiday potlucks, the sweet-tangy cranberry sauce is a wonderful complement to the meat.

—**MARIE RAMSDEN** FAIRGROVE, MI

PREP: 15 MIN. • **COOK:** 4 HOURS
MAKES: 15 SERVINGS

- 2 **boneless skinless turkey breast halves (3 pounds each)**
- 1 **can (14 ounces) jellied cranberry sauce**
- ½ **cup plus 2 tablespoons water, divided**
- 1 **envelope onion soup mix**
- 2 **tablespoons cornstarch**

1. Place turkey in a 5-qt. slow cooker. In a large bowl, combine the cranberry sauce, ½ cup water and soup mix. Pour over turkey. Cover and cook on low for 4-6 hours or until the meat is tender. Remove turkey and keep warm.

2. Transfer cooking juices to a large saucepan. Combine the cornstarch and remaining water until smooth. Bring cranberry mixture to a boil; gradually stir in cornstarch mixture until smooth. Cook and stir for 2 minutes or until thickened. Slice turkey; serve with cranberry sauce.

Super Short Ribs

These ribs really live up to their name! They were inspired by an old oven recipe of my mom's. I added a few ingredients to her original dish to suit my taste, and now I toss everything into the slow cooker.

—**COLEEN CARTER** MALONE, NY

PREP: 20 MIN. • **COOK:** 8 HOURS
MAKES: 6 SERVINGS

- 3 **medium onions, cut into wedges**
- 3 **to 3½ pounds bone-in beef short ribs**
- 1 **bay leaf**
- 1 **bottle (12 ounces) light beer or nonalcoholic beer**
- 2 **tablespoons brown sugar**
- 2 **tablespoons Dijon mustard**
- 2 **tablespoons tomato paste**
- 2 **teaspoons dried thyme**
- 2 **teaspoons beef bouillon granules**
- 1 **teaspoon salt**
- ¼ **teaspoon pepper**
- 3 **tablespoons all-purpose flour**
- ½ **cup cold water**
  Hot cooked noodles

1. Place onions in a 5-qt. slow cooker; add ribs and bay leaf. Combine beer, brown sugar, mustard, tomato paste, thyme, bouillon, salt and pepper. Pour over meat. Cover and cook on low for 8-10 hours or until meat is tender.

2. Remove meat and vegetables to a serving platter; keep warm. Discard bay leaf. Skim fat from cooking juices; transfer juices to a small saucepan. Bring liquid to a boil.

3. Combine the flour and water until smooth. Gradually stir into pan. Bring to a boil; cook and stir for 2 minutes or until thickened.

4. Serve with meat and noodles.

SUPER SHORT RIBS

APPLE-CINNAMON PORK LOIN

Tangy Venison Stroganoff

For this change-of-pace dinner, tender chunks of venison and chopped onion are topped with a silky sour cream sauce. Meat lovers are sure to dig right in.

—**ELLEN SPES** CARO, MI

PREP: 10 MIN. • **COOK:** 3¼ HOURS
MAKES: 4 SERVINGS

- 1½ **pounds boneless venison steak, cubed**
- 1 **medium onion, sliced**
- 1 **can (10½ ounces) condensed beef broth, undiluted**
- 1 **tablespoon Worcestershire sauce**
- 1 **tablespoon ketchup**
- 1 **teaspoon curry powder**
- ½ **teaspoon ground ginger**
- ½ **teaspoon salt**
- ¼ **teaspoon pepper**
- 4½ **teaspoons cornstarch**
- ½ **cup sour cream**
- 2 **tablespoons prepared horseradish**
  Hot cooked noodles

1. Place the venison and onion in a 3-qt. slow cooker. Combine the next seven ingredients; pour over venison. Cover; cook on high for 3 to 3½ hours or until meat is tender.

2. In a small bowl, combine cornstarch, sour cream and horseradish. Gradually stir into the venison mixture. Cover and cook 15 minutes longer or until the sauce is thickened. Serve with hot cooked noodles.

DID YOU KNOW?

In general, wild game has a stronger flavor and is less tender than meat from domestic animals. For maximum tenderness, most game meat should be cooked slowly and not overdone.

Apple-Cinnamon Pork Loin

Let the comforting aroma of apples and cinnamon draw your family to the table. Mashed potatoes make the perfect side.

—**RACHEL SCHULTZ** LANSING, MI

PREP: 20 MIN. • **COOK:** 6 HOURS
MAKES: 6 SERVINGS

- 1 **boneless pork loin roast (2 to 3 pounds)**
- ½ **teaspoon salt**
- ¼ **teaspoon pepper**
- 1 **tablespoon canola oil**
- 3 **medium apples, peeled and sliced, divided**
- ¼ **cup honey**
- 1 **small red onion, halved and sliced**
- 1 **tablespoon ground cinnamon**
  Minced fresh parsley, optional

1. Sprinkle the pork roast with salt and pepper. In a large skillet, brown pork roast in the oil on all sides; cool slightly. With a paring knife, cut about sixteen 3-in.-deep slits in the sides of the roast; insert one apple slice into each slit.

2. Place half of the remaining apples in a 4-qt. slow cooker. Place roast over apples. Drizzle with honey; top with onion and remaining apples. Sprinkle with cinnamon.

3. Cover and cook on low for 6-8 hours or until meat is tender. Remove pork and apple mixture; keep warm.

4. Transfer cooking juices to a small saucepan. Bring to a boil; cook until liquid is reduced by half. Serve with pork and apple mixture. Sprinkle with parsley if desired.

CORN BREAD-TOPPED CHICKEN CHILI

Corn Bread-Topped Chicken Chili

When I discovered a recipe for a chicken potpie made in a slow cooker, I just had to give it a try. For a south-of-the-border twist, I tossed in plenty of peppers, chili powder and a golden crust that's more like a corn bread topping.

—**NICOLE FILIZETTI** JACKSONVILLE, FL

PREP: 20 MIN. • **COOK:** 4 HOURS
MAKES: 6 SERVINGS

- 1 can (16 ounces) kidney beans, rinsed and drained
- 2 cans (2¼ ounces each) sliced ripe black olives, drained
- 1 cup frozen whole kernel corn, thawed and drained
- 1 cup tomato juice
- 1 can (4 ounces) chopped green chilies, drained
- 2 tablespoons minced fresh cilantro
- 1 tablespoon chili powder
- ½ teaspoon ground chipotle pepper
- 1 small onion, finely chopped
- 1 small sweet red pepper, chopped
- 2 tablespoons canola oil, divided
- 2 garlic cloves, minced
- 1¼ pounds boneless skinless chicken breasts, cubed
- 2 tablespoons cornstarch
- ½ teaspoon salt, divided
- 1 cup cornmeal
- 2 teaspoons baking powder
- ½ teaspoon baking soda
- ½ cup 2% milk

1. In a 4-qt. slow cooker, combine the first eight ingredients. In a large skillet, saute the onion and red pepper in 1 tablespoon oil until tender. Add garlic; cook 1 minute longer. Transfer to slow cooker. In a small bowl, toss the chicken with the cornstarch and ¼ teaspoon salt; stir into the bean mixture. Cover and cook on low for 3-4 hours or until chicken is tender.

2. In a small bowl, combine the cornmeal, baking powder, baking soda and remaining salt. Stir in milk and remaining oil. Drop by tablespoonfuls over the chicken mixture. Cover and cook 1 hour longer or until a toothpick inserted in the center of the topping comes out clean.

Whether for a busy weekday or a special occasion, Cranberry-Ginger Pork Ribs are a festive choice.

—**JUDY ARMSTRONG** PRAIRIEVILLE, LA

Cranberry-Ginger Pork Ribs

PREP: 20 MIN. • **COOK:** 5 HOURS
MAKES: 8 SERVINGS

- 1 **can (14 ounces) whole-berry cranberry sauce**
- 2 **habanero peppers, seeded and minced**
- 4½ **teaspoons minced grated gingerroot**
- 3 **garlic cloves, minced**
- 2½ **pounds boneless country-style pork ribs**
- ½ **teaspoon salt**
- ½ **teaspoon cayenne pepper**
- ½ **teaspoon pepper**
- 2 **tablespoons olive oil**
  Hot cooked rice

1. In a small bowl, combine cranberry sauce, habanero peppers, ginger and garlic. Sprinkle the ribs with salt and peppers. In a large skillet, brown ribs in oil on all sides; drain.

2. Transfer meat to a 3-qt. slow cooker; pour berry mixture over ribs. Cover and cook on low for 5-6 hours or until meat is tender. Skim fat from cooking juices. Serve with pork and rice.

NOTE *Wear disposable gloves when cutting hot peppers; the oils can burn skin. Avoid touching your face.*

Slow Cooker Sauerbraten

I like to pair this easier version of German sauerbraten with spaetzle or dumplings.

—**NORMA ENGLISH** BADEN, PA

PREP: 20 MIN. • **COOK:** 6 HOURS
MAKES: 10 SERVINGS

- 1 **boneless beef chuck roast or rump roast (3 to 4 pounds)**
- 4 **cups water**
- 1 **bottle (14 ounces) ketchup**
- 1 **large onion, chopped**
- ¾ **cup packed brown sugar**
- ¾ **cup cider vinegar**
- 1 **tablespoon mixed pickling spices**
- 3 **bay leaves**
- 1½ **cups crushed gingersnap cookies (about 30 cookies)**

GRAVY
- 2 **tablespoons cornstarch**
- ¼ **cup cold water**

1. Cut the roast in half. Place in a 5-qt. slow cooker; add the water. In a large bowl, combine the ketchup, onion, brown sugar and cider vinegar; pour over the roast.

2. Place mixed pickling spices and bay leaves on a double thickness of cheesecloth; bring up the corners of the cheesecloth and tie with string to form a spice bag. Add the spice bag and gingersnap cookie crumbs to the slow cooker.

3. Cover and cook on low for 6-8 hours or until meat is tender.

4. Remove the roast and keep warm. Discard the spice bag. Strain the cooking juices; transfer 4 cups to a large saucepan. Combine cornstarch and water until smooth; stir into the cooking juices. Bring to a boil; cook and stir for 2 minutes or until thickened. Slice roast; serve with gravy.

CRANBERRY-GINGER PORK RIBS

TOP TIP

The heat level of chili peppers ranges from mild-flavored (banana) and hot (jalapeno) to fiery (habanero). The heat of the pepper is contained in the seeds and membranes.

Mandarin Turkey Tenderloin

My husband grew up in an area with a lot of turkey farms, so he learned early on to appreciate that meat in recipes. With colorful vegetables and a twist of citrus, these tenderloins make a tasty dinner without last-minute fuss.

—**LORIE MINER** KAMAS, UT

PREP: 15 MIN. • **COOK:** 4½ HOURS
MAKES: 8 SERVINGS

- 8 **turkey breast tenderloins (4 ounces each)**
- ½ **teaspoon ground ginger**
- ½ **teaspoon crushed red pepper flakes**
- 1 **can (11 ounces) mandarin oranges, drained**
- 1 **cup sesame ginger marinade**
- ½ **cup chicken broth**
- 1 **package (16 ounces) frozen stir-fry vegetable blend, thawed**
- 1 **tablespoon sesame seeds, toasted**
- 1 **green onion, sliced**
  Hot cooked rice, optional

1. Place the turkey in a 3-qt. slow cooker. Sprinkle with ginger and red pepper flakes. Top with oranges. In a small bowl, combine marinade and broth; pour over turkey. Cover and cook on low for 4-5 hours or until a thermometer reads 170°.

2. Stir the vegetables into the slow cooker. Cover and cook 30 minutes longer or until the vegetables are heated through.

3. Sprinkle with sesame seeds and green onion. Serve with rice if desired.

Bavarian Pot Roast

I ate pot roast when I was a child, but I was never a big fan until I changed it up a bit to suit my taste. Kids and adults alike enjoy the seasoned apple gravy.

—**PATRICIA GASMUND** ROCKFORD, IL

PREP: 10 MIN. • **COOK:** 7 HOURS
MAKES: 6 SERVINGS

- 1 **beef top round roast (2 pounds)**
- 1 **cup unsweetened apple juice**
- ½ **cup tomato sauce**
- 1 **small onion, chopped**
- 1 **tablespoon white vinegar**
- 1½ **teaspoons minced fresh gingerroot**
- 1 **teaspoon salt**
- 1 **teaspoon ground cinnamon**
- 2 **tablespoons cornstarch**
- ¼ **cup water**

1. In a large skillet coated with cooking spray, brown roast on all sides. Transfer to a 3-qt. slow cooker.

2. In a small bowl, combine the juice, tomato sauce, onion, vinegar, ginger, salt and cinnamon; pour over roast. Cover and cook on low for 6 hours.

3. In a small bowl, combine the cornstarch and water until smooth; stir into the cooking juices until well combined.

4. Cover and cook 1 hour longer or until the meat is tender and the gravy begins to thicken.

MANDARIN TURKEY TENDERLOIN

PATRICIA GASMUND'S
BAVARIAN POT ROAST

MOROCCAN CHICKEN

Blue Cheese and Apple Pork Chops

Tangy apple wedges combine with smoky, salty bacon to create a terrific topping for pork chops. A sprinkling of blue cheese is the perfect finishing touch.

—**NICOLE EPPERSON** SARASOTA, FL

PREP: 25 MIN. • **COOK:** 5 HOURS
MAKES: 4 SERVINGS

- 4 **bone-in pork loin chops (8 ounces each)**
- ½ **teaspoon salt**
- ¼ **teaspoon pepper**
- 1 **tablespoon olive oil**
- 2 **large tart apples, peeled and cut into wedges**
- 2 **medium onions, chopped**
- 6 **maple-flavored bacon strips, cooked and crumbled**
- 2 **tablespoons all-purpose flour**
- 1 **tablespoon sugar**
- 1 **can (14½ ounces) chicken broth**
- 1 **cup unsweetened apple juice**
- 1 **cup (4 ounces) crumbled blue cheese**

1. Sprinkle pork with salt and pepper. In a large skillet, brown pork chops in oil in batches.

2. In a 5-qt. slow cooker, combine the apples, onions and bacon. In a large bowl, combine flour, sugar, chicken broth and apple juice; pour over apple mixture. Top with pork chops. Cover and cook on low for 5-6 hours or until meat is tender.

3. Remove the pork from the slow cooker. Using a slotted spoon, remove the apples; serve with pork. Sprinkle with blue cheese.

Moroccan Chicken

With butternut squash, chickpeas and more, this dish is packed with flavor.

—**LILY JULOW**
LAWRENCEVILLE, GA

PREP: 25 MIN. • **COOK:** 6 HOURS
MAKES: 8 SERVINGS

- 1½ **pounds butternut squash, peeled, seeded and cut into 2-inch cubes**
- 1 **can (15 ounces) garbanzo beans or chickpeas, rinsed and drained**
- 1 **medium onion, chopped**
- 1 **cup chicken broth**
- ⅓ **cup raisins**
- 2 **garlic cloves, minced**
- 2 **teaspoons ground coriander**
- 2 **teaspoons ground cumin**
- ½ **teaspoon ground cinnamon**
- ½ **teaspoon salt**
- ¼ **teaspoon pepper**
- 8 **bone-in chicken thighs (about 3 pounds), skin removed**
- 2 **medium tomatoes, chopped**
- ½ **cup pitted green olives**
- 1 **tablespoon cornstarch**
- 1 **tablespoon cold water**
  Hot cooked couscous

1. In a 6-qt. slow cooker, place the squash, beans, onion, broth, raisins and garlic. Combine the coriander, cumin, cinnamon, salt and pepper; rub over chicken. Place in slow cooker.

2. Cover and cook on low for 6-8 hours or until chicken is tender, adding tomatoes and olives during the last 20 minutes of cooking.

3. Remove chicken and vegetables to a serving platter; keep warm. Skim fat from the cooking juices; transfer to a small saucepan. Bring to a boil. Combine the cornstarch and water until smooth; gradually stir into the cooking juices. Return to a boil; cook and stir for 2 minutes or until thickened. Serve with the chicken, vegetables and couscous.

CAJUN-STYLE POT ROAST

Cajun-Style Pot Roast

I often make this well-seasoned roast for guests. It's easy and goes over well with everyone—even my friend who's a chef!

—**GINGER MENZIES** OAK CREEK, CO

PREP: 15 MIN. • **COOK:** 6 HOURS
MAKES: 6 SERVINGS

- 1 **boneless beef chuck roast (2 to 3 pounds)**
- 2 **tablespoons Cajun seasoning**
- 1 **tablespoon olive oil**
- 2 **cans (10 ounces each) diced tomatoes and green chilies**
- 1 **medium sweet red pepper, chopped**
- 1½ **cups chopped celery**
- ¾ **cup chopped onion**
- ¼ **cup quick-cooking tapioca**
- 1½ **teaspoons minced garlic**
- 1 **teaspoon salt**
  Hot cooked rice

1. Cut roast in half; sprinkle with Cajun seasoning. In a large skillet, brown roast in oil on all sides. Transfer to a 5-qt. slow cooker. Combine the tomatoes, red pepper, celery, onion, tapioca, garlic and salt; pour over roast.

2. Cover and cook on low for 6-8 hours or until the meat is tender. Serve with hot cooked rice.

⑤ INGREDIENTS
Cranberry Turkey Breast with Gravy

Here's one of my favorite choices for holiday meals. The turkey breast always comes out of the slow cooker tender and moist. The fruity sauce served with the sliced meat is a delicious bonus!

—**SHIRLEY WELCH** TULSA, OK

PREP: 15 MIN. • **COOK:** 5 HOURS
MAKES: 12 SERVINGS (3 CUPS GRAVY)

- 1 **bone-in turkey breast (5 to 6 pounds)**
- 1 **can (14 ounces) whole-berry cranberry sauce**
- ¼ **cup orange juice**
- 1 **envelope onion soup mix**
- ¼ **teaspoon salt**
- ¼ **teaspoon pepper**
- 3 **to 4 teaspoons cornstarch**
- 1 **tablespoon water**

1. Place the turkey breast in a 5-qt. slow cooker. In a small bowl, combine cranberry sauce, orange juice, onion soup mix, salt and pepper; pour over turkey. Cover and cook on low for 5-6 hours or until tender.

2. Remove the turkey breast to a serving platter; keep warm. Skim the fat from the cooking juices; transfer to a small saucepan. Bring to a boil. Combine the cornstarch and water until smooth. Gradually stir into the pan. Bring to a boil; cook and stir for 2 minutes or until thickened. Serve with the turkey.

CRANBERRY TURKEY BREAST WITH GRAVY

Mushroom Pot Roast

You'll wow everyone at the table with the wine-warmed flavor of this dressed-up roast. Cooked with shiitake mushrooms, onions and other vegetables, it makes a sensational main course. Include a side of mashed potatoes so guests can savor every last drop of gravy!

—ANGIE STEWART TOPEKA, KS

PREP: 25 MIN. • **COOK:** 6 HOURS
MAKES: 10 SERVINGS

- 1 **boneless beef chuck roast (3 to 4 pounds)**
- ½ **teaspoon salt**
- ¼ **teaspoon pepper**
- 1 **tablespoon canola oil**
- 1½ **pounds sliced fresh shiitake mushrooms**
- 2½ **cups thinly sliced onions**
- 1½ **cups reduced-sodium beef broth**
- 1½ **cups dry red wine or additional reduced-sodium beef broth**
- 1 **can (8 ounces) tomato sauce**
- ¾ **cup chopped peeled parsnips**
- ¾ **cup chopped celery**
- ¾ **cup chopped carrots**
- 8 **garlic cloves, minced**
- 2 **bay leaves**
- 1½ **teaspoons dried thyme**
- 1 **teaspoon chili powder**
- ¼ **cup cornstarch**
- ¼ **cup water**
  Mashed potatoes

1. Sprinkle roast with salt and pepper. In a Dutch oven, brown roast in oil on all sides. Transfer to a 6-qt. slow cooker. Add the mushrooms, onions, broth, wine, tomato sauce, parsnips, celery, carrots, garlic, bay leaves, thyme and chili powder. Cover and cook on low for 6-8 hours or until meat is tender.

2. Remove the meat and vegetables to a platter; keep warm. Discard bay leaves. Skim fat from cooking juices; transfer to a small saucepan. Bring liquid to a boil. Combine cornstarch and water until smooth; gradually stir into pan. Bring to a boil; cook and stir for 2 minutes or until thickened. Serve with potatoes, meat and vegetables.

MUSHROOM POT ROAST

SWEET AND SAUCY CHICKEN

Creamy Celery Beef Stroganoff

Convenient canned soups lend richness to this family-favorite Stroganoff. It tastes great, and I love the fact that I can get it into the slow cooker in just 20 minutes.

—KIMBERLY WALLACE DENNISON, OH

PREP: 20 MIN. • **COOK:** 8 HOURS
MAKES: 6 SERVINGS

- 2 **pounds beef stew meat, cut into 1-inch cubes**
- 1 **can (10¾ ounces) condensed cream of celery soup, undiluted**
- 1 **can (10¾ ounces) condensed cream of mushroom soup, undiluted**
- 1 **medium onion, chopped**
- 1 **jar (6 ounces) sliced mushrooms, drained**
- 1 **envelope onion soup mix**
- ½ **teaspoon pepper**
- 1 **cup (8 ounces) sour cream**
  Hot cooked noodles

In a 3-qt. slow cooker, combine the first seven ingredients. Cover; cook on low for 8 hours or until beef is tender. Stir in sour cream. Serve with noodles.

CREAMY CELERY BEEF STROGANOFF

Sweet and Saucy Chicken

I can't remember where my saucy chicken recipe came from, but I've been enjoying it for years. The meat is so tender it falls off the bone. Just before serving, prepare rice or egg noodles for a satisfying dinner.

—PATRICIA WEIR CHILLIWACK, BC

PREP: 30 MIN. • **COOK:** 6 HOURS
MAKES: 6 SERVINGS

- 1 **broiler/fryer chicken (4 pounds), cut up and skin removed**
- ¾ **cup packed brown sugar**
- ¼ **cup all-purpose flour**
- ⅔ **cup water**
- ⅓ **cup white vinegar**
- ⅓ **cup reduced-sodium soy sauce**
- 2 **tablespoons ketchup**
- 1 **tablespoon dried minced onion**
- 1 **teaspoon prepared mustard**
- ¼ **teaspoon garlic powder**
- ¼ **teaspoon salt**
- ¼ **teaspoon pepper**
  Hot cooked rice or egg noodles, optional

1. Place the chicken in a 3-qt. slow cooker. In a small saucepan, combine the brown sugar and flour. Stir in the water, vinegar and soy sauce. Add the ketchup, minced onion, mustard, garlic powder, salt and pepper. Bring to a boil; cook and stir for 1-2 minutes or until thickened.

2. Pour over the chicken. Cover and cook on low for 6-8 hours or until the chicken juices run clear. Serve with rice or noodles if desired.

BEEF & TORTELLINI MARINARA

Pepper Steak

I freeze any leftovers of this tasty steak in individual portions for quick lunches.

—JULIE RHINE
ZELIENOPLE, PA

PREP: 30 MIN. • **COOK:** 6¼ HOURS
MAKES: 12 SERVINGS

- 1 **beef top round roast (3 pounds)**
- 1 **large onion, halved and sliced**
- 1 **large green pepper, cut into ½-inch strips**
- 1 **large sweet red pepper, cut into ½-inch strips**
- 1 **cup water**
- 4 **garlic cloves, minced**
- ⅓ **cup cornstarch**
- ½ **cup reduced-sodium soy sauce**
- 2 **teaspoons sugar**
- 2 **teaspoons ground ginger**
- 8 **cups hot cooked brown rice**

1. Place beef roast, onion and peppers in a 5-qt. slow cooker. Add water and garlic. Cook, covered, on low 6-8 hours or until meat is tender.
2. Remove the beef roast to a cutting board. Transfer the vegetables and cooking juices to a large saucepan. Bring to a boil. In a small bowl, mix the cornstarch, soy sauce, sugar and ginger until smooth; stir into the vegetable mixture. Return to a boil, stirring constantly; cook and stir 1-2 minutes or until thickened.
3. Cut the beef into slices. Stir gently into the sauce; heat through. Serve with brown rice.

Beef & Tortellini Marinara

Beef stew meat, cheese tortellini, veggies and sauce all add up to a satisfying main dish. Make it a complete meal with crusty Italian bread and a green salad.

—JOYCE FREY MACKSVILLE, KS

PREP: 30 MIN. • **COOK:** 6½ HOURS
MAKES: 11 SERVINGS

- 1 **pound beef stew meat**
- 2 **tablespoons olive oil**
- 2 **garlic cloves, minced**
- 1 **jar (26 ounces) marinara or spaghetti sauce**
- 2 **cups dry red wine or beef broth**
- 1 **pound fresh green beans, trimmed**
- 1 **can (14½ ounces) Italian diced tomatoes, undrained**
- ½ **pound small fresh mushrooms**
- 2 **envelopes thick and zesty spaghetti sauce mix**
- 2 **tablespoons minced fresh parsley**
- 1 **tablespoon dried minced onion**
- 2 **teaspoons minced fresh rosemary**
- 1 **teaspoon coarsely ground pepper**
- ¼ **teaspoon salt**
- 1 **package (9 ounces) refrigerated cheese tortellini**

1. In a large skillet, brown the beef stew meat in oil until no longer pink. Add garlic; cook 1 minute longer. Transfer to a 5- or 6-qt. slow cooker.
2. Stir in the marinara sauce, red wine, green beans, diced tomatoes, mushrooms, spaghetti sauce mix, parsley, minced onion, rosemary, pepper and salt. Cover and cook on low for 6-8 hours or until beef stew meat is tender.
3. Stir in the cheese tortellini. Cover and cook on high for 30 minutes or until tortellini are heated through.

Mushroom Chicken Florentine

Here's a simple way to prepare a classic Italian specialty. The fresh spinach, baby portobello mushrooms, white wine and herbes de Provence create an elegant backdrop for the succulent chicken.

—**NANCY SWAIN** ST. AUGUSTINE, FL

PREP: 20 MIN. • **COOK:** 4 HOURS
MAKES: 4 SERVINGS

- 1 can (10¾ ounces) condensed cream of mushroom soup, undiluted
- ½ cup white wine or chicken broth
- ½ cup sour cream
- 1 teaspoon herbes de Provence
- 1½ pounds boneless skinless chicken breasts, cut into 2-inch pieces
- 1¾ cups sliced baby portobello mushrooms
- 6 cups fresh spinach
  Hot cooked egg noodles

In a 3-qt. slow cooker, combine the soup, wine, sour cream and herbes de Provence. Stir in chicken and mushrooms. Fold in spinach. Cover and cook on low for 4-5 hours or until chicken is tender. Serve with noodles.

NOTE *Look for herbes de Provence in the spice aisle.*

Sausage-Stuffed Flank Steak

As part of a prize I won in a recipe contest, I received a slow cooker. I hadn't used one in years and started experimenting with it. My first creation was a stuffed flank steak, which became a family favorite.

—**JULIE MERRIMAN** SEATTLE, WA

PREP: 35 MIN. • **COOK:** 6 HOURS
MAKES: 4 SERVINGS

- ¼ cup dried cherries
- ¾ cup dry red wine or beef broth, divided
- 1 beef flank steak (1½ pounds)
- ¾ teaspoon salt, divided
- ½ teaspoon pepper, divided
- 1 medium onion, finely chopped
- 3 tablespoons olive oil, divided
- 4 garlic cloves, minced
- ½ cup seasoned bread crumbs
- ¼ cup pitted Greek olives, halved
- ¼ cup grated Parmesan cheese
- ¼ cup minced fresh basil
- ½ pound bulk hot Italian sausage
- 1 jar (24 ounces) marinara sauce
  Hot cooked pasta

1. In a small bowl, combine cherries and ¼ cup wine; let stand 10 minutes. Meanwhile, cut flank steak into four serving-size pieces; flatten to ¼-in. thickness. Sprinkle both sides with ½ teaspoon salt and ¼ teaspoon pepper.

2. In a large skillet, saute the onion in 1 tablespoon oil until tender. Add garlic; cook 1 minute longer. Transfer to a large bowl; stir in crumbs, olives, cheese, basil, cherry mixture and remaining salt and pepper. Crumble sausage over mixture and mix well.

3. Spread ½ cup sausage mixture over each steak piece. Roll up jelly-roll style, starting with a long side; tie with kitchen string.

4. In the same skillet, brown meat in remaining oil on all sides. Transfer to a greased 3-qt. slow cooker. Top with marinara sauce and remaining wine. Cook and cook on low for 6-8 hours or until beef is tender. Serve with pasta.

SAUSAGE-STUFFED FLANK STEAK

MATTHEW LAMAN'S
CREOLE CHICKEN THIGHS

Creole Chicken Thighs

Cajun seasoning jazzes up chicken thighs with loads of spicy flavor. After browning the meat, I toss everything—including the rice—into the slow cooker. It does the rest of the work for me, so I can take care of other things until mealtime.

—MATTHEW LAMAN HUMMELSTOWN, PA

PREP: 30 MIN. • **COOK:** 7 HOURS
MAKES: 8 SERVINGS

- 8 bone-in chicken thighs (about 3 pounds), skin removed
- 3 tablespoons Cajun seasoning, divided
- 1 tablespoon canola oil
- 3½ cups chicken broth
- 1 can (16 ounces) red beans, rinsed and drained
- 1½ cups uncooked converted rice
- 2 medium tomatoes, finely chopped
- 1 medium green pepper, chopped
- 2 tablespoons minced fresh parsley

1. Sprinkle chicken with 1 tablespoon Cajun seasoning. In a large skillet, brown chicken in oil.
2. In a 5-qt. slow cooker, combine the broth, red beans, rice, tomatoes, green pepper, parsley and remaining Cajun seasoning. Top with chicken. Cover and cook on low for 7-8 hours or until chicken is tender.

Mom's Spaghetti Sauce

My mother prepared this when we were children, and I always requested it for my birthday. Now I do the prep work in the morning and let the sauce simmer all day for a wonderful pasta dinner.

—KRISTY HAWKES SOUTH WEBER, UT

PREP: 20 MIN. • **COOK:** 4 HOURS
MAKES: 10-12 SERVINGS

- 1 pound ground beef
- 1 medium onion, chopped
- 1 medium green pepper, chopped
- 8 to 10 fresh mushrooms, sliced
- 3 celery ribs, chopped
- 1½ teaspoons minced garlic
- 2 cans (14½ ounces each) Italian stewed tomatoes
- 1 jar (26 ounces) spaghetti sauce
- ½ cup ketchup
- 2 teaspoons brown sugar
- 1 teaspoon sugar
- 1 teaspoon salt
- 1 teaspoon dried oregano
- 1 teaspoon chili powder
- 1 teaspoon prepared mustard
  Hot cooked spaghetti

1. In a large skillet, cook the ground beef, onion, green pepper, mushrooms and celery over medium heat until the meat is no longer pink, breaking the meat into crumbles. Add garlic; cook 1 minute longer. Drain.
2. In a 3-qt. slow cooker, combine the stewed tomatoes, spaghetti sauce, ketchup, brown sugar, sugar, salt, oregano, chili powder and mustard. Stir in the ground beef mixture. Cover and cook on low for 4-5 hours or until heated through.
3. Serve immediately with cooked spaghetti, or cool before placing in a freezer container. Cover and freeze for up to 3 months.

MOM'S SPAGHETTI SAUCE

OKTOBERFEST PORK ROAST

Oktoberfest Pork Roast

I adapted a recipe for pork roast that my mom used to prepare when I was a child. The tart apple wedges, tangy sauerkraut and red potatoes give it plenty of autumn appeal. Coating the slow cooker insert with cooking spray helps prevent sticking.

—**TONYA SWAIN** SEVILLE, OH

PREP: 35 MIN. • **COOK:** 8 HOURS
MAKES: 8 SERVINGS

- **16 small red potatoes**
- **1 can (14 ounces) sauerkraut, rinsed and well drained**
- **2 large tart apples, peeled and cut into wedges**
- **1 pound smoked kielbasa or Polish sausage, cut into 16 slices**
- **2 tablespoons brown sugar**
- **1 teaspoon caraway seeds**
- **1 teaspoon salt, divided**
- **1 teaspoon pepper, divided**
- **1 boneless pork loin roast (3 pounds)**
- **3 tablespoons canola oil**

1. Place the potatoes in a greased 6-qt. slow cooker. Top with the sauerkraut, apples and kielbasa. Sprinkle with the brown sugar, caraway seeds, 1/2 teaspoon salt and 1/2 teaspoon pepper.

2. Cut the roast in half; sprinkle with remaining salt and pepper. In a large skillet, brown meat in oil on all sides. Transfer to slow cooker.

3. Cover and cook on low for 8-10 hours or until the meat and vegetables are tender. Skim fat and thicken cooking liquid if desired.

Beef Stroganoff

This family-pleasing Stroganoff starts in a skillet, then cooks all day while you're away.

—**SARAH VASQUES**
MILFORD, NH

PREP: 20 MIN. • **COOK:** 6 HOURS
MAKES: 7 SERVINGS

- **2 pounds beef top sirloin steak, cut into thin strips**
- **3 tablespoons olive oil**
- **1 cup water**
- **1 envelope (1½ ounces) beef Stroganoff seasoning for the slow cooker**
- **1 pound sliced baby portobello mushrooms**
- **1 small onion, chopped**
- **3 tablespoons butter**
- **¼ cup port wine or beef broth**
- **2 teaspoons ground mustard**
- **1 teaspoon sugar**
- **1½ cups (12 ounces) sour cream**
  Hot cooked egg noodles
  Minced fresh parsley, optional

1. In a large skillet, brown meat in oil. Add water and seasoning mix, stirring to loosen browned bits from the pan. Transfer the meat and drippings to a 3-qt. slow cooker.

2. In same skillet, saute portobello mushrooms and onion in butter until tender. Combine the wine, mustard and sugar; stir into the mushroom mixture. Add to the slow cooker; stir to combine.

3. Cover and cook on low for 6-8 hours or until the meat is tender. Stir in sour cream. Serve with noodles. Sprinkle with parsley if desired.

BEEF STROGANOFF

SLOW COOKER TAMALE PIE

Slow Cooker Tamale Pie

Speed up the preparation of a zippy Southwestern dinner using supermarket convenience items—canned vegetables, enchilada sauce and corn bread mix.

—**JILL POKRIVKA** YORK, PA

PREP: 25 MIN. • **COOK:** 7 HOURS
MAKES: 8 SERVINGS

- 1 **pound ground beef**
- 1 **teaspoon ground cumin**
- ½ **teaspoon salt**
- ½ **teaspoon chili powder**
- ¼ **teaspoon pepper**
- 1 **can (15 ounces) black beans, rinsed and drained**
- 1 **can (14½ ounces) diced tomatoes with mild green chilies, undrained**
- 1 **can (11 ounces) whole kernel corn, drained**
- 1 **can (10 ounces) enchilada sauce**
- 2 **green onions, chopped**
- ¼ **cup minced fresh cilantro**
- 1 **package (8½ ounces) corn bread/ muffin mix**
- 2 **eggs**
- 1 **cup (4 ounces) shredded Mexican cheese blend**
  Sour cream and additional minced fresh cilantro, optional

1. In a large skillet, cook beef over medium heat until no longer pink, breaking beef into crumbles; drain. Stir in the cumin, salt, chili powder and pepper.
2. Transfer to a 4-qt. slow cooker; stir in the black beans, tomatoes, corn, enchilada sauce, onions and cilantro. Cover and cook on low for 6-8 hours or until heated through.
3. In a small bowl, combine muffin mix and eggs; spoon over the meat mixture. Cover and cook 1 hour longer or until a toothpick inserted near the center comes out clean.
4. Sprinkle with cheese; cover and let stand for 5 minutes. Serve with sour cream and additional cilantro if desired.

Chicken & Vegetables with Mustard-Herb Sauce

Everyone will love sitting down to this comforting meal of chicken and veggies in a delectable cream sauce.

—**MARIE RIZZIO** INTERLOCHEN, MI

PREP: 20 MIN. • **COOK:** 6 HOURS
MAKES: 4 SERVINGS

- 4 **medium red potatoes, quartered**
- 3 **medium parsnips, cut into 1-inch pieces**
- 2 **medium leeks (white portion only), thinly sliced**
- ¾ **cup fresh baby carrots**
- 4 **chicken leg quarters, skin removed**
- 1 **can (10¾ ounces) condensed cream of chicken soup with herbs, undiluted**
- 2 **tablespoons minced fresh parsley**
- 1 **tablespoon snipped fresh dill or 1 teaspoon dill weed**
- 1 **tablespoon Dijon mustard**

1. In a 5- or 6-qt. slow cooker, place the potatoes, parsnips, leeks, carrots and chicken; pour soup over the top. Cover and cook on low for 6-8 hours or until chicken is tender.
2. Remove chicken and vegetables; cover and keep warm. Stir the parsley, dill and mustard into cooking juices; serve with chicken and vegetables.

CHICKEN & VEGETABLES WITH MUSTARD-HERB SAUCE

Autumn

SOUPS, STEWS & SANDWICHES

Savory beef stews, juicy pulled-meat sandwiches and steaming soups topped with homemade dumplings...these are just a few of the fall classics shared here. Simmer up a favorite today for a meal that's sure to warm the body and the soul.

CONSTANCE SULLIVAN'S MUSHROOM BARLEY SOUP

Mushroom Barley Soup

Here's a hearty soup that's delicious and loaded with vegetables. I like to eat it with warm bread smothered in butter.
—**CONSTANCE SULLIVAN** OCEANSIDE, CA

PREP: 25 MIN. + SOAKING • **COOK:** 5 HOURS
MAKES: 12 SERVINGS (3 QUARTS)

- ½ cup dried great northern beans
- 1 pound sliced fresh mushrooms
- 2 cups chopped onions
- 1 medium leek (white portion only), sliced
- 2 tablespoons butter
- 1 to 2 garlic cloves, minced
- 2 cartons (32 ounces each) chicken broth
- 3 celery ribs, thinly sliced
- 3 large carrots, chopped
- ½ cup medium pearl barley
- 2 teaspoons dried parsley flakes
- 1½ teaspoons salt
- 1 bay leaf
- ¼ teaspoon white pepper

1. Soak beans according to package directions. In a large skillet, cook the mushrooms, onions and leek in butter over medium heat until tender. Add garlic; cook 1 minute longer.

2. Transfer to a 6-qt. slow cooker. Drain and rinse beans, discarding liquid. Add the beans, broth, celery, carrots, barley, parsley, salt, bay leaf and pepper. Cover and cook on low for 5-6 hours or until beans and vegetables are tender. Discard bay leaf.

Italian Venison Sandwiches

My slow cooker makes easy work of these hefty venison sandwiches. The meat always comes out tender and tasty.
—**ANDREW HENSON** MORRISON, IL

PREP: 10 MIN. • **COOK:** 8 HOURS
MAKES: 10-12 SERVINGS

- 2 cups water
- 1 envelope onion soup mix
- 1 tablespoon dried basil
- 1 tablespoon dried parsley flakes
- 1 teaspoon beef bouillon granules
- ½ teaspoon celery salt
- ¼ teaspoon garlic powder
- ¼ teaspoon cayenne pepper
- ¼ teaspoon pepper
- 1 boneless venison roast (3 to 4 pounds), cut into 1-inch cubes
- 10 to 12 sandwich rolls, split
  Green pepper rings, optional

In a 3-qt. slow cooker, combine the first nine ingredients. Add venison and stir. Cover and cook on low for 8 hours or until meat is tender. Using a slotted spoon, spoon into rolls. Top with pepper rings if desired.

Beef & Veggie Stew

This healthy, hearty stew is one of my husband's favorite meals. I always use fresh mushrooms, and I often rely on low-sodium beef bouillon cubes to cut the salt a bit.

—**PATRICIA KILE** ELIZABETHTOWN, PA

PREP: 25 MIN. • **COOK:** 4 HOURS
MAKES: 8 SERVINGS

- ¼ cup all-purpose flour
- 2 pounds boneless beef chuck roast, trimmed and cut into 1-inch cubes
- 2 tablespoons canola oil
- 1 can (10¾ ounces) condensed tomato soup, undiluted
- 1 cup water or red wine
- 2 reduced-sodium beef bouillon cubes
- 3 teaspoons Italian seasoning
- 1 bay leaf
- ½ teaspoon coarsely ground pepper
- 6 white onions or yellow onions, quartered
- 4 medium potatoes, cut into 1½-inch slices
- 3 medium carrots, cut into 1-inch slices
- 12 large fresh mushrooms
- ½ cup sliced celery

1. Place flour in a large resealable plastic bag. Add beef, a few pieces at a time, and shake to coat.

2. In a large skillet, brown meat in oil in batches; drain. Transfer to a 5-qt. slow cooker. Combine the tomato soup, water or wine, bouillon and seasonings; pour over beef. Add the onions, potatoes, carrots, mushrooms and celery.

3. Cover and cook on low for 4-5 hours or until meat is tender. Discard bay leaf. Serve with noodles or French bread.

Pasta e Fagioli

I've served this satisfying dish to guests and received many compliments in return. The soup is so thick and delicious that no one suspects it's actually on the lighter side.

—**PENNY NOVY** BUFFALO GROVE, IL

PREP: 30 MIN. • **COOK:** 7½ HOURS
MAKES: 8 SERVINGS (2½ QUARTS)

PASTA E FAGIOLI

- 1 pound ground beef
- 1 medium onion, chopped
- 1 carton (32 ounces) chicken broth
- 2 cans (14½ ounces each) diced tomatoes, undrained
- 1 can (15 ounces) white kidney or cannellini beans, rinsed and drained
- 2 medium carrots, chopped
- 1½ cups finely chopped cabbage
- 1 celery rib, chopped
- 2 tablespoons minced fresh basil or 2 teaspoons dried basil
- 2 garlic cloves, minced
- ½ teaspoon salt
- ½ teaspoon pepper
- 1 cup ditalini or other small pasta Grated Parmesan cheese, optional

1. In a large skillet, cook beef and onion over medium heat until beef is no longer pink and onion is tender; drain.

2. Transfer to a 4- or 5-qt. slow cooker. Stir in the broth, tomatoes, beans, carrots, cabbage, celery, basil, garlic, salt and pepper. Cover and cook on low for 7-8 hours or until vegetables are tender.

3. Stir in pasta. Cover and cook on high 30 minutes longer or until pasta is tender. Sprinkle with cheese if desired.

BEEF & VEGGIE STEW

CRANBERRY BBQ PULLED PORK

Cranberry BBQ Pulled Pork

Cranberry sauce adds a yummy twist on traditional pulled pork that my family can't get enough of! The meat cooks to tender perfection in the slow cooker, which also makes this dish conveniently portable.

—**CARRIE WIEGAND** MT. PLEASANT, IA

PREP: 20 MIN. • **COOK:** 9 HOURS
MAKES: 14 SERVINGS

- 1 **boneless pork shoulder roast (4 to 6 pounds)**
- ⅓ **cup cranberry juice**
- 1 **teaspoon salt**
SAUCE
- 1 **can (14 ounces) whole-berry cranberry sauce**
- 1 **cup ketchup**
- ⅓ **cup cranberry juice**
- 3 **tablespoons brown sugar**
- 4½ **teaspoons chili powder**
- 2 **teaspoons garlic powder**
- 1 **teaspoon onion powder**
- ½ **teaspoon salt**
- ¼ **teaspoon ground chipotle pepper**
- ½ **teaspoon liquid smoke, optional**
- 14 **hamburger buns, split**

1. Cut roast in half. Place in a 4-qt. slow cooker. Add cranberry juice and salt. Cover and cook on low for 8-10 hours or until meat is tender.
2. Remove roast and set aside. In a small saucepan, combine the cranberry sauce, ketchup, cranberry juice, brown sugar, seasonings and liquid smoke if desired. Cook and stir over medium heat for 5 minutes or until slightly thickened.
3. Skim fat from cooking juices; set aside ½ cup juices. Discard remaining juices. When cool enough to handle, shred the pork with two forks and return to slow cooker.
4. Stir in sauce mixture and reserved cooking juices. Cover and cook on low for 1 hour or until heated through. Serve on buns.

Sweet-and-Sour Beef Stew

Here's a tangy meal in one bowl that's packed with veggies!
—**FRANCES CONKLIN** GRANGEVILLE, ID

PREP: 25 MIN. • **COOK:** 8 HOURS
MAKES: 8 SERVINGS

- 2 **pounds beef top round steak, cut into 1-inch cubes**
- 2 **tablespoons olive oil**
- 1 **can (15 ounces) tomato sauce**
- 2 **large onions, chopped**
- 4 **medium carrots, thinly sliced**
- 1 **large green pepper, cut into 1-inch pieces**
- 1 **cup canned pineapple chunks, drained**
- ½ **cup cider vinegar**
- ¼ **cup packed brown sugar**
- ¼ **cup light corn syrup**
- 2 **teaspoons chili powder**
- 2 **teaspoons paprika**
- ½ **teaspoon salt**
  Hot cooked rice, optional

1. In a large skillet, brown beef in oil in batches; drain. Transfer to a 4- or 5-qt. slow cooker.
2. In a large bowl, combine the tomato sauce, onions, carrots, green pepper, pineapple, vinegar, brown sugar, corn syrup, chili powder, paprika and salt; pour over beef.
3. Cover and cook on low for 8-10 hours or until beef is tender. Serve with rice if desired.

SWEET-AND-SOUR BEEF STEW

SUNDAY STEW

Sunday Stew

We had an aunt who served this dish whenever we all got together to celebrate special occasions. It brings back so many memories. The cinnamon adds a wonderfully unique flavor.

—**JEANETTE LAZARY** ROCHESTER, NY

PREP: 25 MIN. • **COOK:** 6 HOURS
MAKES: 6 SERVINGS

- ⅓ cup all-purpose flour
- ¾ teaspoon salt
- ¾ teaspoon ground cinnamon
- ½ teaspoon pepper
- 2 pounds beef stew meat, cut into 1-inch cubes
- 2 tablespoons canola oil
- 1 package (14 ounces) frozen pearl onions
- 1 cup dry red wine or beef broth
- ¾ cup water
- 2 tablespoons red wine vinegar
- 2 tablespoons tomato paste
- 1 tablespoon honey
- 2 bay leaves
- 1 garlic clove, minced

1. In a large resealable plastic bag, combine the flour, salt, cinnamon and pepper. Add beef, a few pieces at a time, and shake to coat. In a large skillet, brown beef in oil. Transfer to a 3-qt. slow cooker. Stir in the remaining ingredients.

2. Cover and cook on low for 6-8 hours or until beef and onions are tender. Discard bay leaves.

Slow Cooker Beef Vegetable Stew

Come home to warm comfort food! This is based on my mom's fantastic recipe, though I tweaked it for the slow cooker. Add a sprinkle of Parmesan to each bowl for a tasty finishing touch.

—**MARCELLA WEST** WASHBURN, IL

PREP: 20 MIN. • **COOK:** 6½ HOURS
MAKES: 8 SERVINGS (3 QUARTS)

- 1½ pounds boneless beef chuck roast, cut into 1-inch cubes
- 3 medium potatoes, peeled and cubed
- 3 cups hot water
- 1½ cups fresh baby carrots
- 1 can (10¾ ounces) condensed tomato soup, undiluted
- 1 medium onion, chopped
- 1 celery rib, chopped
- 2 tablespoons Worcestershire sauce
- 1 tablespoon browning sauce, optional
- 2 teaspoons beef bouillon granules
- 1 garlic clove, minced
- 1 teaspoon sugar
- ¾ teaspoon salt
- ¼ teaspoon pepper
- ¼ cup cornstarch
- ¾ cup cold water
- 2 cups frozen peas, thawed

1. Set roast, potatoes, water, carrots, soup, onion, celery, Worcestershire sauce, browning sauce if desired, bouillon granules, garlic, sugar, salt and pepper in a 5- or 6-qt. slow cooker. Cover and cook on low for 6-8 hours or until meat is tender.

2. Combine cornstarch and cold water in a small bowl until smooth; gradually stir into stew. Stir in peas. Cover and cook on high for 30 minutes or until thickened.

SLOW COOKER BEEF VEGETABLE STEW

BUTTERNUT SQUASH SOUP

Butternut Squash Soup

The golden color, smooth and creamy texture, and wonderful flavor of this soup make it a welcome addition to chilly fall days. Cream cheese adds a velvety touch, and the cinnamon truly comes through nicely.

—**JACKIE CAMPBELL** STANHOPE, NJ

PREP: 30 MIN. • **COOK:** 6¼ HOURS
MAKES: 14 SERVINGS (2½ QUARTS)

- 1 **medium onion, chopped**
- 2 **tablespoons butter**
- 1 **medium butternut squash (about 4 pounds), peeled and cubed**
- 3 **cans (14½ ounces each) vegetable broth**
- 1 **tablespoon brown sugar**
- 1 **tablespoon minced fresh gingerroot**
- 1 **garlic clove, minced**
- 1 **cinnamon stick (3 inches)**
- 1 **package (8 ounces) cream cheese, softened and cubed**

1. In a small skillet, saute onion in butter until tender. Transfer to a 5-or 6-qt. slow cooker; add squash. Combine the broth, brown sugar, ginger, garlic and cinnamon; pour over squash. Cover and cook on low for 6-8 hours or until squash is tender.

2. Cool slightly. Discard cinnamon stick. In a blender, process soup in batches until smooth. Return all to slow cooker. Whisk in cream cheese; cover and cook 15 minutes longer or until cheese is melted.

Southwestern Pork and Squash Soup

Using tomatoes and Southwestern-style seasonings, I adapted a stew recipe for my husband and sons, who loved it. And leftovers are even better the next day! Try it with freshly baked corn muffins.

—**MOLLY NEWMAN** PORTLAND, OR

PREP: 20 MIN. • **COOK:** 4 HOURS
MAKES: 6 SERVINGS

- 1 **pound pork tenderloin, cut into 1-inch cubes**
- 1 **medium onion, chopped**
- 1 **tablespoon canola oil**
- 3 **cups reduced-sodium chicken broth**
- 1 **medium butternut squash, peeled and cubed**
- 2 **medium carrots, sliced**
- 1 **can (14½ ounces) diced tomatoes with mild green chilies, undrained**
- 1 **tablespoon chili powder**
- 1 **teaspoon ground cumin**
- 1 **teaspoon dried oregano**
- ½ **teaspoon pepper**
- ¼ **teaspoon salt**

In a large skillet, brown pork and onion in oil; drain. Transfer to a 4- or 5-qt. slow cooker. Stir in the remaining ingredients. Cover and cook on low for 4-5 hours or until meat is tender.

SOUTHWESTERN PORK AND SQUASH SOUP

FRENCH DIP AU JUS

French Dip au Jus

I created this sandwich because so many French Dip recipes seem bland or rely on a mix. Mine is simple, and I think it tastes better than most restaurant versions.

—LINDSAY EBERT OREM, UT

PREP: 30 MIN. • **COOK:** 8 HOURS
MAKES: 8 SERVINGS

- 1½ teaspoons beef base
- 1 teaspoon dried thyme
- 1 beef rump roast or bottom round roast (3 pounds), cut in half
- 1 medium onion, quartered
- ½ cup reduced-sodium soy sauce
- 2 garlic cloves, minced
- 1 bay leaf
- ½ teaspoon pepper
- 8 cups water
- 2 tablespoons Dijon mustard
- 2 loaves French bread (1 pound each), split and toasted
- 12 slices part-skim mozzarella cheese
- 1 jar (4½ ounces) sliced mushrooms, drained

1. Combine beef base and thyme; rub over roast and place in a 5-qt. slow cooker. Combine the onion, soy sauce, garlic, bay leaf and pepper; pour over roast. Add water.

2. Cover and cook on low for 8-9 hours or until meat is tender. Remove roast to a cutting board; cool slightly. Strain cooking juices, reserving onion; skim fat from juices. Discard bay leaf. Thinly slice meat.

3. To assemble sandwiches, spread mustard over bread. Top each bottom with three slices cheese; layer with beef, remaining cheese, mushrooms and reserved onion. Replace tops. Cut each loaf into four slices; serve with reserved juices.

NOTE *Look for beef base near the broth and bouillon at your grocery.*

Curried Turkey Soup

This colorful soup is a delight to serve the day after Thanksgiving. Best of all, it comes together in the slow cooker, allowing you some time to get a head start on your holiday shopping.

—HOLLY BAUER WEST BEND, WI

PREP: 40 MIN. • **COOK:** 8 HOURS
MAKES: 6 SERVINGS (2½ QUARTS)

- 4½ cups chicken broth
- 1 can (14½ ounces) diced tomatoes, undrained
- 2 medium carrots, chopped
- 2 celery ribs, chopped
- 1 medium onion, chopped
- 1 medium green pepper, chopped
- 1 medium tart apple, peeled and chopped
- 1 tablespoon curry powder
- ½ teaspoon salt
- ½ teaspoon pepper
- ¼ cup all-purpose flour
- ½ cup unsweetened apple juice or additional chicken broth
- 3 cups cubed cooked turkey
- 3 cups hot cooked rice

1. Combine the first 10 ingredients in a 4- or 5-qt. slow cooker. Cover and cook on low for 7-8 hours or until vegetables are tender. Mix flour and apple juice until smooth; stir into soup. Cover and cook on high for 30 minutes or until soup is thickened.

2. Stir in turkey; heat through. Serve with rice.

CURRIED TURKEY SOUP

Momma's Turkey Stew with Dumplings

My mother used to make this turkey stew every year with our Thanksgiving leftovers. It is so easy, and it really celebrates the natural flavors of simple and healthy ingredients. To this day, it's one of my favorite meals.

—STEPHANIE RABBITT-SCHAPP
CINCINNATI, OH

PREP: 20 MIN. • **COOK:** 6½ HOURS
MAKES: 6 SERVINGS

- 3 **cups shredded cooked turkey**
- 1 **large sweet onion, chopped**
- 1 **large potato, peeled and cubed**
- 2 **large carrots, chopped**
- 2 **celery ribs, chopped**
- 2 **bay leaves**
- 1 **teaspoon salt**
- ½ **teaspoon poultry seasoning**
- ½ **teaspoon dried thyme**
- ¼ **teaspoon pepper**
- 1 **carton (32 ounces) chicken broth**
- ⅓ **cup cold water**
- 3 **tablespoons cornstarch**
- ½ **cup frozen corn, thawed**
- ½ **cup frozen peas, thawed**
- 1 **cup biscuit/baking mix**
- ⅓ **cup 2% milk**

1. In a 6-qt. slow cooker, combine the first 10 ingredients; stir in broth. Cover and cook on low for 6-7 hours.
2. Remove bay leaves. In a small bowl, mix water and cornstarch until smooth; stir into turkey mixture. Add corn and peas. Cover and cook on high until mixture reaches a simmer.
3. Meanwhile, in a small bowl, mix baking mix and milk just until moistened. Drop by rounded tablespoonfuls on top of simmering liquid. Reduce heat to low; cover and cook for 20-25 minutes or until a toothpick inserted in a dumpling comes out clean.

All-Day Meatball Stew

Frozen meatballs, convenient jarred mushrooms and cans of tomato sauce and beef broth simplify this homey stew that cooks all day. It fills the house with a wonderful aroma! Each bite boasts big flavor and a comforting rich gravy. It's hard to resist second and third helpings.

—ANITA HOFFMAN HOLLAND, PA

PREP: 20 MIN. • **COOK:** 8½ HOURS
MAKES: 8 SERVINGS (3 QUARTS)

- 2 **packages (12 ounces each) frozen fully cooked Italian meatballs**
- 5 **medium potatoes, peeled and cubed**
- 1 **pound fresh baby carrots**
- 1 **medium onion, halved and sliced**
- 1 **jar (4½ ounces) sliced mushrooms, drained**
- 2 **cans (8 ounces each) tomato sauce**
- 1 **can (10½ ounces) condensed beef broth, undiluted**
- ¾ **cup water**
- ¾ **cup dry red wine or beef broth**
- ½ **teaspoon garlic powder**
- ¼ **teaspoon pepper**
- 2 **tablespoons all-purpose flour**
- ½ **cup cold water**

1. Place the meatballs, potatoes, carrots, onion and mushrooms in a 5- or 6-qt. slow cooker. In a large bowl, combine the tomato sauce, broth, water, wine, garlic powder and pepper; pour over top. Cover and cook on low for 8-10 hours or until vegetables are tender.
2. Combine flour and water until smooth; gradually stir into stew. Cover and cook on high for 30 minutes or until thickened.

MOMMA'S TURKEY STEW WITH DUMPLINGS

ANITA HOFFMAN'S
ALL-DAY MEATBALL STEW

MEXICAN BEEF & BEAN SUPPER

Mexican Beef & Bean Supper

I like that this meal is so easy to toss together and that the extras reheat well the next day. The nutritious beans and veggies taste great, and the stew warms my family up on chilly autumn days!

—**TACY FLEURY** CLINTON, SC

PREP: 20 MIN. • **COOK:** 8 HOURS
MAKES: 10 SERVINGS (2½ QUARTS)

- 1 **cup all-purpose flour**
- ¼ **teaspoon salt**
- ⅛ **teaspoon pepper**
- 1 **pound beef stew meat, cut into 1-inch cubes**
- 2 **tablespoons canola oil**
- 1 **can (16 ounces) kidney beans, rinsed and drained**
- 1 **can (15¼ ounces) whole kernel corn, drained**
- 2 **medium potatoes, cubed**
- 2 **small carrots, sliced**
- 2 **celery ribs, sliced**
- 1 **small onion, chopped**
- 2 **cans (15 ounces each) tomato sauce**
- 1 **cup water**
- 1 **envelope taco seasoning**
- ½ **teaspoon ground cumin**
   Tortilla chips and shredded cheddar cheese

1. Combine flour, salt and pepper in a large resealable plastic bag. Add beef, a few pieces at a time, and shake to coat.
2. Brown meat in batches in oil in a large skillet; drain. Transfer to a 5-qt. slow cooker. Add the beans, corn, potatoes, carrots, celery and onion.
3. Whisk the tomato sauce, water, taco seasoning and cumin; pour over top. Cover and cook on low for 8-10 hours or until meat is tender. Serve with tortilla chips and cheese.

Pulled Turkey Tenderloin

Not your ordinary turkey sandwich, this one shines—thanks to its unique yogurt sauce. We like to stack on extra slices of sweet pickles and jalapenos, or we skip the rolls entirely and serve the turkey alongside a green salad.

—**SHANA CONRADT** GREENVILLE, WI

PREP: 15 MIN. • **COOK:** 6 HOURS
MAKES: 5 SERVINGS

- 1 **package (20 ounces) turkey breast tenderloins**
- 2 **cups water**
- ½ **cup sweet pickle juice**
- 1 **envelope onion soup mix**
- 2 **tablespoons canned diced jalapeno peppers**
- ½ **cup fat-free plain Greek yogurt**
- 1 **tablespoon yellow mustard**
- ⅛ **teaspoon pepper**
- 5 **kaiser rolls, split**

1. Place turkey in a 3-qt. slow cooker. In a small bowl, combine the water, pickle juice, soup mix and jalapeno peppers; pour over turkey. Cover and cook on low for 6-8 hours or until meat is tender. Remove turkey and shred with two forks. Transfer to a small bowl.
2. Strain cooking juices, reserving ½ cup juices. In another small bowl, combine the yogurt, mustard, pepper and reserved cooking juices. Pour over turkey; toss to coat. Serve on rolls.

Spicy Shredded Beef Sandwiches

If you like your shredded beef with a little kick, then this recipe is for you! For an even zestier sandwich, add another jar of jalapenos or use hot peppers instead of the pepperoncinis.

—**KRISTEN LANGMEIER** FARIBAULT, MN

PREP: 15 MIN. • **COOK:** 8 HOURS
MAKES: 12 SERVINGS

- 1 boneless beef chuck roast (4 to 5 pounds)
- 2 medium onions, coarsely chopped
- 1 jar (16 ounces) sliced pepperoncini, undrained
- 1 jar (8 ounces) pickled jalapeno slices, drained
- 1 bottle (12 ounces) beer or nonalcoholic beer
- 1 envelope onion soup mix
- 5 garlic cloves, minced
- ½ teaspoon pepper
- 12 kaiser rolls, split
- 12 slices provolone cheese

1. Cut roast in half; place in a 4- or 5-qt. slow cooker. Add the onions, pepperoncini, jalapenos, beer, soup mix, garlic and pepper.
2. Cover and cook on low for 8-10 hours or until meat is tender.
3. Remove meat. Skim fat from cooking liquid. When cool enough to handle, shred meat with two forks and return to slow cooker; heat through. Serve ½ cup meat mixture on each roll with a slice of cheese.
NOTE *Look for pepperoncinis (pickled peppers) in the pickle and olive section of your grocery store.*

Beef Barley Soup

Here's a real stick-to-your-ribs soup. I've also used a chuck roast, rump roast and London broil that have been cut into bite-size pieces with tremendous success.

—**JANE MCMILLAN** DANIA BEACH, FL

PREP: 20 MIN. • **COOK:** 8½ HOURS
MAKES: 8 SERVINGS (2 QUARTS)

- 1½ pounds beef stew meat, cut into ½-inch cubes
- 1 tablespoon canola oil
- 1 carton (32 ounces) beef broth
- 1 bottle (12 ounces) beer or nonalcoholic beer
- 1 small onion, chopped
- ½ cup medium pearl barley
- 3 garlic cloves, minced
- 1 teaspoon dried oregano
- 1 teaspoon dried parsley flakes
- 1 teaspoon Worcestershire sauce
- ½ teaspoon crushed red pepper flakes
- ½ teaspoon pepper
- ¼ teaspoon salt
- 1 bay leaf
- 2 cups frozen mixed vegetables, thawed

1. In a large skillet, brown beef in oil; drain. Transfer to a 3-qt. slow cooker.
2. Add the broth, beer, onion, barley, garlic, oregano, parsley, Worcestershire sauce, pepper flakes, pepper, salt and bay leaf. Cover and cook on low for 8-10 hours.
3. Stir in vegetables; cover and cook 30 minutes longer or until meat is tender and vegetables are heated through. Discard bay leaf.

SPICY SHREDDED BEEF SANDWICHES

KIMBERLY NAGY'S
AUTUMN PUMPKIN CHILI

Autumn Pumpkin Chili

Everyone loves this chili...even the most finicky of my grandchildren. It also earned a thumbs up with family and friends who have tried it in other states. A satisfying dish, it's a definite keeper in my book, and I prepare it often!

—KIMBERLY NAGY PORT HADLOCK, WA

PREP: 20 MIN. • **COOK:** 7 HOURS
MAKES: 4 SERVINGS

- 1 medium onion, chopped
- 1 small green pepper, chopped
- 1 small sweet yellow pepper, chopped
- 1 tablespoon canola oil
- 1 garlic clove, minced
- 1 pound ground turkey
- 1 can (15 ounces) solid-pack pumpkin
- 1 can (14½ ounces) diced tomatoes, undrained
- 4½ teaspoons chili powder
- ¼ teaspoon pepper
- ¼ teaspoon salt
  Optional toppings: shredded cheddar cheese, sour cream and sliced green onions

1. Saute the onion and green and yellow peppers in oil in a large skillet until tender. Add garlic; cook 1 minute longer. Crumble turkey into skillet. Cook over medium heat until meat is no longer pink.
2. Transfer to a 3-qt. slow cooker. Stir in the pumpkin, tomatoes, chili powder, pepper and salt. Cover and cook on low for 7-9 hours. Serve with toppings of your choice.

Lentil and Pasta Stew

Warm up with a big bowlful of this nourishing stew that's packed with chopped smoked sausage, hearty veggies and tender lentils. It's terrific with oven-fresh baked bread.

—GERALDINE SAUCIER ALBUQUERQUE, NM

PREP: 25 MIN. • **COOK:** 8 HOURS
MAKES: 8 SERVINGS

- ½ pound smoked kielbasa or Polish sausage, chopped
- 3 tablespoons olive oil
- 3 tablespoons butter
- 1 cup cubed peeled potatoes
- ¾ cup sliced fresh carrots
- 1 celery rib, sliced
- 1 small onion, finely chopped
- 5 cups beef broth
- 1 cup dried lentils, rinsed
- 1 cup canned diced tomatoes
- 1 bay leaf
- 1 teaspoon coarsely ground pepper
- ¼ teaspoon salt
- 1 cup uncooked ditalini or other small pasta
  Shredded Romano cheese

1. Brown kielbasa in oil and butter in a large skillet. Add the potatoes, carrots, celery and onion. Cook and stir for 3 minutes over medium heat. Transfer to a 4- or 5-qt. slow cooker. Stir in the broth, lentils, tomatoes, bay leaf, pepper and salt.
2. Cover and cook on low for 8-10 hours or until lentils are tender. Cook pasta according to package directions; drain. Stir pasta into slow cooker. Discard bay leaf. Sprinkle servings with cheese.

LENTIL AND PASTA STEW

Beef Stew with Ghoulish Mashed Potatoes

Boo! Big and little ghouls alike are sure to adore the comforting flavors of this clever recipe made easy in the slow cooker. Scare up some fun this season by piping cute mashed potato ghosts over bowls of hearty beef stew.

—*TASTE OF HOME* **TEST KITCHEN**

PREP: 30 MIN. • **COOK:** 8 HOURS
MAKES: 6 SERVINGS

- 2 **pounds beef stew meat, cut into 1-inch cubes**
- 1 **pound fresh mushrooms, halved**
- 2 **cups fresh baby carrots**
- 2 **medium parsnips, peeled, halved lengthwise and sliced**
- 2 **medium onions, chopped**
- 1½ **cups beef broth**
- 3 **tablespoons tomato paste**
- 1 **tablespoon Worcestershire sauce**
- 2 **garlic cloves, minced**
- ½ **teaspoon ground cloves**
- ¼ **teaspoon pepper**
- 8 **medium potatoes (2⅓ pounds), peeled and cubed**
- ⅔ **cup sour cream**
- 6 **tablespoons butter, cubed**
- 1 **teaspoon salt, divided**
- 1 **cup frozen peas**
- 2 **tablespoons all-purpose flour**
- 2 **tablespoons water**

1. In a 5-qt. slow cooker, combine the first 11 ingredients. Cover and cook on low for 8-9 hours or until beef and vegetables are tender.

2. About 30 minutes before serving, place potatoes in a large saucepan and cover with water. Bring to a boil. Reduce heat; cover and simmer for 15-20 minutes or until tender. Drain. Return potatoes to pan; add the sour cream, butter and ½ teaspoon salt. Mash until smooth.

3. Set aside 12 peas for the ghost garnishes. Add remaining peas to the slow cooker. Increase heat to high. In a bowl, whisk the flour, water and remaining salt until smooth; stir into stew. Cover and cook for 5 minutes or until thickened.

4. Divide stew among six bowls. Place mashed potatoes in large resealable plastic bag; cut a 2-in. hole in one corner. Pipe ghost potatoes onto stew; garnish with reserved peas.

BEEF STEW WITH GHOULISH MASHED POTATOES

STEPHANIE'S SLOW COOKER STEW

Stephanie's Slow Cooker Stew

Start this heartwarming one-pot meal before you head out for the day. By the time you get home, the tender well-seasoned meat will be ready!

—STEPHANIE RABBITT-SCHAPP
CINCINNATI, OH

PREP: 20 MIN. • **COOK:** 7½ HOURS
MAKES: 5 SERVINGS

- 1 **pound beef stew meat**
- 2 **medium potatoes, peeled and cubed**
- 1 **can (14½ ounces) beef broth**
- 1 **can (11½ ounces) V8 juice**
- 2 **celery ribs, chopped**
- 2 **medium carrots, chopped**
- 1 **medium sweet onion, chopped**
- 3 **bay leaves**
- ½ **teaspoon salt**
- ½ **teaspoon dried thyme**
- ½ **teaspoon chili powder**
- ¼ **teaspoon pepper**
- 2 **tablespoons cornstarch**
- 1 **tablespoon cold water**
- ½ **cup frozen corn**
- ½ **cup frozen peas**

1. In a 3-qt. slow cooker, combine the first 12 ingredients. Cover and cook on low for 7-8 hours or until meat is tender. Discard bay leaves.

2. In a small bowl, combine cornstarch and water until smooth; stir into stew.

3. Add corn and peas. Cover and cook on high for 30 minutes or until thickened.

BUTTERNUT & PORK STEW

Butternut & Pork Stew

Cure your craving for something different with this savory stew. I like to serve it with slices of warm buttered bread and a green salad. Edamame adds an interesting protein-packed touch to this slow-cooked comfort food.

—**ERIN CHILCOAT** CENTRAL ISLIP, NY

PREP: 20 MIN. • **COOK:** 7½ HOURS
MAKES: 6 SERVINGS (2 QUARTS)

- ⅓ cup plus 1 tablespoon all-purpose flour, divided
- 1 tablespoon paprika
- 1 teaspoon salt
- 1 teaspoon ground coriander
- 1½ pounds boneless pork shoulder butt roast, cut into 1-inch cubes
- 1 tablespoon canola oil
- 2¾ cups cubed peeled butternut squash
- 1 can (14½ ounces) diced tomatoes, undrained
- 1 cup frozen corn, thawed
- 1 medium onion, chopped
- 2 tablespoons cider vinegar
- 1 bay leaf
- 2½ cups reduced-sodium chicken broth
- 1⅔ cups frozen shelled edamame, thawed

1. In a large resealable plastic bag, combine ⅓ cup flour, paprika, salt and coriander. Add pork, a few pieces at a time, and shake to coat.

2. In a large skillet, brown pork in oil in batches; drain. Transfer to a 5-qt. slow cooker. Add squash, tomatoes, corn, onion, vinegar and bay leaf. In a small bowl, combine broth and the remaining flour until smooth; stir into slow cooker.

3. Cover and cook on low for 8-10 hours or until pork and vegetables are tender. Stir in edamame; cover and cook 30 minutes longer. Discard the bay leaf.

Pumpkin Harvest Beef Stew

By the time my stew is done simmering and a batch of bread finishes baking, the house smells absolutely wonderful!

—**MARCIA O'NEIL** CEDAR CREST, NM

PREP: 25 MIN. • **COOK:** 6½ HOURS
MAKES: 6 SERVINGS

- 1 tablespoon canola oil
- 1 beef top round steak (1½ pounds), cut into 1-inch cubes
- 1½ cups cubed peeled pie pumpkin or sweet potatoes
- 3 small red potatoes, peeled and cubed
- 1 cup cubed acorn squash
- 1 medium onion, chopped
- 2 cans (14½ ounces each) reduced-sodium beef broth
- 1 can (14½ ounces) diced tomatoes, undrained
- 2 bay leaves
- 2 garlic cloves, minced
- 2 teaspoons reduced-sodium beef bouillon granules
- ½ teaspoon chili powder
- ½ teaspoon pepper
- ¼ teaspoon ground allspice
- ¼ teaspoon ground cloves
- ¼ cup water
- 3 tablespoons all-purpose flour

1. In a large skillet, heat oil over medium-high heat. Brown beef in batches; remove with a slotted spoon to a 4- or 5-qt. slow cooker. Add the pumpkin, potatoes, squash and onion. Stir in the broth, tomatoes and seasonings. Cover and cook on low for 6-8 hours or until meat is tender.

2. Remove bay leaves. In a small bowl, mix water and flour until smooth; gradually stir into stew. Cover and cook on high for 30 minutes or until liquid is thickened.

MARCIA O'NEIL'S
PUMPKIN HARVEST BEEF STEW

Autumn

DESSERTS

Fall is a great time to get cozy with warm, aromatic desserts. Bubbling with heartwarming flavor, treats such as Pumpkin Pie Pudding, Caramel-Pecan Stuffed Apples and Fudgy Peanut Butter Cake make lovely finales to autumn dinners.

ANDREA SCHAAK'S PUMPKIN PIE PUDDING

Pumpkin Pie Pudding

My husband loves anything pumpkin, and this creamy, warm dessert is one of his favorites. Although we make the super-easy pudding all year long, it's especially nice in the fall.

—**ANDREA SCHAAK** BLOOMINGTON, MN

PREP: 10 MIN. • **COOK:** 6 HOURS
MAKES: 6 SERVINGS

- 1 can (15 ounces) solid-pack pumpkin
- 1 can (12 ounces) evaporated milk
- ¾ cup sugar
- ½ cup biscuit/baking mix
- 2 eggs, beaten
- 2 tablespoons butter, melted
- 2½ teaspoons pumpkin pie spice
- 2 teaspoons vanilla extract
  Whipped topping, optional

1. In a large bowl, combine the first eight ingredients. Transfer to a 3-qt. slow cooker coated with cooking spray.

2. Cover and cook on low for 6-7 hours or until a thermometer reads 160°. Serve in bowls with whipped topping if desired.

⑤ INGREDIENTS
Old-Fashioned Tapioca

My family loves old-fashioned tapioca, but I don't always have the time to make it. That's why I developed this simple recipe that lets us enjoy the comforting treat without the fuss.

—**RUTH PETERS** BEL AIR, MD

PREP: 10 MIN. • **COOK:** 4½ HOURS
MAKES: 18 SERVINGS (½ CUP EACH)

- 8 cups 2% milk
- 1 cup pearl tapioca
- 1 cup plus 2 tablespoons sugar
- ⅛ teaspoon salt
- 4 eggs
- 1½ teaspoons vanilla extract
  Sliced fresh strawberries and
  whipped cream, optional

1. In a 4- to 5-qt. slow cooker, combine the milk, tapioca, sugar and salt. Cover and cook on low for 4-5 hours.

2. In a large bowl, beat eggs; stir in a small amount of hot tapioca mixture. Return all to slow cooker, stirring to combine. Cover and cook 30 minutes longer or until a thermometer reads 160°. Stir in vanilla.

3. Serve with strawberries and whipped cream if desired.

DID YOU KNOW?

It's easy to make pumpkin pie spice. Just combine 4 teaspoons ground cinnamon, 2 teaspoons ground ginger, 1 teaspoon ground cloves and ½ teaspoon ground nutmeg. Store in an airtight container.

Apple Betty with Almond Cream

I like making this for friends during the peak of apple-picking season. I always plan a quick, easy meal of soup and bread, so we can get right to dessert!

—**LIBBY WALP** CHICAGO, IL

PREP: 15 MIN. • **COOK:** 3 HOURS
MAKES: 8 SERVINGS

- 3 **pounds tart apples, peeled and sliced**
- 10 **slices cinnamon-raisin bread, cubed**
- ¾ **cup packed brown sugar**
- ½ **cup butter, melted**
- 1 **teaspoon almond extract**
- ½ **teaspoon ground cinnamon**
- ¼ **teaspoon ground cardamom**
- ⅛ **teaspoon salt**
- **WHIPPED CREAM**
- 1 **cup heavy whipping cream**
- 2 **tablespoons sugar**
- 1 **teaspoon grated lemon peel**
- ½ **teaspoon almond extract**

1. Place apples in an ungreased 4- or 5-qt. slow cooker. In a large bowl, combine the bread, brown sugar, butter, extract, cinnamon, cardamom and salt; spoon over apples. Cover and cook on low for 3-4 hours or until apples are tender.

2. In a small bowl, beat cream until it begins to thicken. Add the sugar, lemon peel and extract; beat until soft peaks form. Serve with apple mixture.

Fudgy Peanut Butter Cake

This recipe, which I clipped from a newspaper years ago, fills the house with a wonderful aroma as it cooks. My husband and son enjoy the warm cake with ice cream and nuts on the top.

—**BONNIE EVANS** NORCROSS, GA

PREP: 10 MIN. • **COOK:** 1½ HOURS
MAKES: 4 SERVINGS

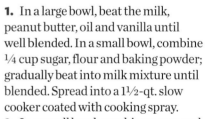

FUDGY PEANUT BUTTER CAKE

- ⅓ **cup milk**
- ¼ **cup peanut butter**
- 1 **tablespoon canola oil**
- ½ **teaspoon vanilla extract**
- ¾ **cup sugar, divided**
- ½ **cup all-purpose flour**
- ¾ **teaspoon baking powder**
- 2 **tablespoons baking cocoa**
- 1 **cup boiling water**
  Vanilla ice cream

1. In a large bowl, beat the milk, peanut butter, oil and vanilla until well blended. In a small bowl, combine ¼ cup sugar, flour and baking powder; gradually beat into milk mixture until blended. Spread into a 1½-qt. slow cooker coated with cooking spray.

2. In a small bowl, combine cocoa and remaining sugar; stir in boiling water. Pour into slow cooker (do not stir).

3. Cover and cook on high for 1½ to 2 hours or until a toothpick inserted near the center comes out clean. Serve warm with ice cream.

NOTE *Reduced-fat peanut butter is not recommended for this recipe.*

APPLE BETTY WITH ALMOND CREAM

CHOCOLATE-COVERED CHERRY PUDDING CAKE

Chocolate-Covered Cherry Pudding Cake

Growing up, I remember my grandfather cherishing the chocolate-covered cherries we'd bring him for Christmas. After he passed away, I came up with this rich recipe in his honor. It's delicious served with whipped topping.

—MEREDITH COE CHARLOTTESVILLE, VA

PREP: 20 MIN. • **COOK:** 2 HOURS + STANDING
MAKES: 8 SERVINGS

- ½ **cup reduced-fat sour cream**
- 2 **tablespoons canola oil**
- 1 **tablespoon butter, melted**
- 2 **teaspoons vanilla extract**
- 1 **cup all-purpose flour**
- ¼ **cup sugar**
- ¼ **cup packed brown sugar**
- 3 **tablespoons baking cocoa**
- 2 **teaspoon baking powder**
- ½ **teaspoon ground cinnamon**
- ⅛ **teaspoon salt**
- 1 **cup fresh or frozen pitted dark sweet cherries, thawed**
- 1 **cup fresh or frozen pitted tart cherries, thawed**
- ⅓ **cup 60% cacao bittersweet chocolate baking chips**

PUDDING
- ½ **cup packed brown sugar**
- 2 **tablespoons baking cocoa**
- 1¼ **cups hot water**

1. In a large bowl, beat the sour cream, oil, butter and vanilla until blended. Combine the flour, sugars, cocoa, baking powder, cinnamon and salt. Add to sour cream mixture just until combined. Stir in cherries and chips. Pour into a 3-qt. slow cooker coated with cooking spray.

2. In a small bowl, combine brown sugar and cocoa. Stir in hot water until blended. Pour over the batter (do not stir). Cover and cook on high for 2 to 2½ hours or until set. Let stand for 15 minutes. Serve warm.

HOT FUDGE CAKE

Hot Fudge Cake

A cake baked in a slow cooker may seem unusual, but the smiles you'll find around the dinner table prove how tasty it is! For a change of pace, I sometimes use butterscotch chips instead of chocolate.
—MARLEEN ADKINS PLACENTIA, CA

PREP: 20 MIN. • **COOK:** 4 HOURS
MAKES: 8 SERVINGS

- 1¾ cups packed brown sugar, divided
- 1 cup all-purpose flour
- 6 tablespoons baking cocoa, divided
- 2 teaspoons baking powder
- ½ teaspoon salt
- ½ cup 2% milk
- 2 tablespoons butter, melted
- ½ teaspoon vanilla extract
- 1½ cups semisweet chocolate chips
- 1¾ cups boiling water
  Vanilla ice cream

1. In a small bowl, combine 1 cup brown sugar, flour, 3 tablespoons cocoa, baking powder and salt. Combine the milk, butter and vanilla; stir into dry ingredients just until combined.
2. Spread into a 3-qt. slow cooker coated with cooking spray. Sprinkle with chocolate chips. In another bowl, combine the remaining brown sugar and cocoa; stir in boiling water. Pour over batter (do not stir).
3. Cover and cook on high for 4 to 4½ hours or until a toothpick inserted near center of cake comes out clean. Serve warm with ice cream.
NOTE *This recipe does not use eggs.*

Caramel-Pecan Stuffed Apples

This irresistible dessert is slow-cooker easy. Warm and comforting, the tender apples are filled with chewy pecans and yummy caramel topping.
—PAM KAISER MANSFIELD, MO

PREP: 20 MIN. • **COOK:** 3 HOURS
MAKES: 6 SERVINGS

- 6 large tart apples
- 2 teaspoons lemon juice
- ⅓ cup chopped pecans
- ¼ cup chopped dried apricots
- ¼ cup packed brown sugar
- 3 tablespoons butter, melted
- ¾ teaspoon ground cinnamon
- ¼ teaspoon ground nutmeg
  Granola and caramel ice cream topping, optional

1. Core apples and peel top third of each; brush peeled portions with lemon juice. Place in a 6-qt. slow cooker.
2. Combine the pecans, apricots, brown sugar, butter, cinnamon and nutmeg. Place a heaping tablespoonful of mixture in each apple. Pour 2 cups water around apples.
3. Cover and cook on low for 3-4 hours or until apples are tender. Serve with granola and caramel topping if desired.

CARAMEL-PECAN STUFFED APPLES

⑤INGREDIENTS
Crunchy Candy Clusters

Before I retired, I took these yummy peanut butter bites to work for special occasions. I still make them for holidays, because my family always looks forward to the cereal-and-marshmallow sweets. They're so simple to whip up!

—**FAYE O'BRYAN** OWENSBORO, KY

PREP: 15 MIN. • **COOK:** 1 HOUR
MAKES: 6½ DOZEN

- 2 **pounds white candy coating, coarsely chopped**
- 1½ **cups peanut butter**
- ½ **teaspoon almond extract, optional**
- 4 **cups Cap'n Crunch cereal**
- 4 **cups crisp rice cereal**
- 4 **cups miniature marshmallows**

1. Place candy coating in a 5-qt. slow cooker. Cover and cook on high for 1 hour. Add peanut butter. Stir in extract if desired.

2. In a large bowl, combine the cereals and marshmallows. Stir into the peanut butter mixture until well coated. Drop by tablespoonfuls onto waxed paper. Let stand until set. Store at room temperature.

⑤INGREDIENTS
Minister's Delight

A friend gave me this recipe years ago, saying that a minister's wife fixed it every Sunday so she named it accordingly. Best of all, you only need a few ingredients.

—**MARY ANN POTTER** BLUE SPRINGS, MO

PREP: 5 MIN. • **COOK:** 2 HOURS
MAKES: 10-12 SERVINGS

- 1 **can (21 ounces) cherry or apple pie filling**
- 1 **package yellow cake mix (regular size)**
- ½ **cup butter, melted**
- ⅓ **cup chopped walnuts, optional**

Place pie filling in a 1½-qt. slow cooker. Combine cake mix and butter (mixture will be crumbly); sprinkle over filling. Sprinkle with walnuts if desired. Cover and cook on low for 2-3 hours. Serve in bowls.

Glazed Cinnamon Apples

If you are seeking comfort food on the sweet side, this warm and tasty apple dessert, made with cinnamon and nutmeg, fits the bill.

—**MEGAN MAZE** OAK CREEK, WI

PREP: 20 MIN. • **COOK:** 3 HOURS
MAKES: 7 SERVINGS

- 6 **large tart apples**
- 2 **tablespoons lemon juice**
- ½ **cup packed brown sugar**
- ½ **cup sugar**
- 2 **tablespoons all-purpose flour**
- 1 **teaspoon ground cinnamon**
- ¼ **teaspoon ground nutmeg**
- 6 **tablespoons butter, melted**
  Vanilla ice cream

1. Peel, core and cut each apple into eight wedges; transfer to a 3-qt. slow cooker. Drizzle with lemon juice. Combine the sugars, flour, cinnamon and nutmeg; sprinkle over apples. Drizzle with butter.

2. Cover and cook on low for 3-4 hours or until the apples are tender. Top individual servings with ice cream.

CRUNCHY CANDY CLUSTERS

MEGAN MAZE'S
GLAZED CINNAMON APPLES

BUTTERSCOTCH PEARS

Butterscotch Pears

This grand finale simmers during dinner and impresses as soon as you bring it to the table. Serve as is, or with a scoop of vanilla ice cream. Leftover pear nectar is heavenly when added to sparkling wine or enjoyed over ice with breakfast.

—THERESA KREYCHE TUSTIN, CA

PREP: 20 MIN. • **COOK:** 2 HOURS
MAKES: 8 SERVINGS

- 4 **large firm pears**
- 1 **tablespoon lemon juice**
- ¼ **cup packed brown sugar**
- 3 **tablespoons butter, softened**
- 2 **tablespoons all-purpose flour**
- ½ **teaspoon ground cinnamon**
- ¼ **teaspoon salt**
- ½ **cup chopped pecans**
- ½ **cup pear nectar**
- 2 **tablespoons honey**

1. Cut pears in half lengthwise; remove cores. Brush the pears with lemon juice. In a small bowl, combine the brown sugar, butter, flour, cinnamon and salt; stir in pecans.

Spoon into pears; place in a 4-qt. slow cooker.

2. Combine pear nectar and honey; drizzle over pears. Cover and cook on low for 2-3 hours or until heated through. Serve warm.

⑤ INGREDIENTS

Easy Chocolate Clusters

You can use this simple idea to make a big batch of chocolate candy without a lot of fuss...or a lot of ingredients. I've sent these clusters to my husband's office a number of times, and I happily passed the recipe along as well.

—DORIS REYNOLDS MUNDS PARK, AZ

PREP: 10 MIN. + STANDING • **COOK:** 2 HOURS
MAKES: 3½ DOZEN

- 2 **pounds white candy coating, broken into small pieces**
- 2 **cups (12 ounces) semisweet chocolate chips**
- 4 **ounces German sweet chocolate, chopped**
- 1 **jar (24 ounces) dry roasted peanuts**

1. In a 3-qt. slow cooker, combine the candy coating, chocolate chips and German chocolate. Cover and cook on high for 1 hour. Reduce heat to low; cover and cook 1 hour longer or until melted, stirring every 15 minutes.

2. Stir in peanuts. Drop by teaspoonfuls onto waxed paper. Let stand until set. Store at room temperature.

EASY CHOCOLATE CLUSTERS

FRUIT DESSERT TOPPING

Fruit Dessert Topping

I bet you'll quickly warm up to the old-fashioned taste of my fruit topping! I like to spoon it over slices of pound cake.

—**DORIS HEATH** FRANKLIN, NC

PREP: 10 MIN. • **COOK:** 3½ HOURS
MAKES: ABOUT 6 CUPS

- 3 **medium tart apples, peeled and sliced**
- 3 **medium pears, peeled and sliced**
- 1 **tablespoon lemon juice**
- ½ **cup packed brown sugar**
- ½ **cup maple syrup**
- ¼ **cup butter, melted**
- ½ **cup chopped pecans**
- ¼ **cup raisins**
- 2 **cinnamon sticks (3 inches)**
- 1 **tablespoon cornstarch**
- 2 **tablespoons cold water**
  Pound cake or ice cream

1. In a 3-qt. slow cooker, toss apples and pears with lemon juice. Combine the brown sugar, maple syrup and butter; pour over fruit. Stir in the pecans, raisins and cinnamon sticks. Cover and cook on low for 3-4 hours.
2. Combine cornstarch and water until smooth; gradually stir into slow cooker. Cover and cook on high for 30-40 minutes or until thickened. Discard cinnamon sticks. Serve with pound cake or ice cream.

Pumpkin Cranberry Bread Pudding

Savor your favorite fall flavors with this scrumptious bread pudding, served warm with a sweet vanilla sauce. Yum!

—**JUDITH BUCCIARELLI** JOHNSON, NY

PREP: 15 MIN. • **COOK:** 3 HOURS
MAKES: 8 SERVINGS (1⅓ CUPS SAUCE)

- 8 **slices cinnamon bread, cut into 1-inch cubes**
- 4 **eggs, beaten**
- 2 **cups 2% milk**
- 1 **cup canned pumpkin**
- ¼ **cup packed brown sugar**
- ¼ **cup butter, melted**
- 1 **teaspoon vanilla extract**
- ½ **teaspoon ground cinnamon**
- ¼ **teaspoon ground nutmeg**
- ½ **cup dried cranberries**
SAUCE
- 1 **cup sugar**
- ⅔ **cup water**
- 1 **cup heavy whipping cream**
- 2 **teaspoons vanilla extract**

1. Place bread in a greased 3- or 4-qt. slow cooker. In a large bowl, combine the eggs, milk, pumpkin, brown sugar, butter, vanilla, cinnamon and nutmeg; stir in cranberries. Pour over bread cubes. Cover and cook on low for 3-4 hours or until a knife inserted near the center comes out clean.
2. For sauce, in a large saucepan, bring sugar and water to a boil over medium heat. Cook until sugar is dissolved and mixture turns a golden amber color, about 20 minutes. Gradually stir in cream until smooth. Remove from the heat; stir in vanilla. Serve warm with bread pudding.

PUMPKIN CRANBERRY BREAD PUDDING

HEIDI FLEEK'S
EASY SLOW COOKER MAC & CHEESE
page 247

APPETIZERS & BEVERAGES 236
SIDE DISHES 246
ENTREES 260
SOUPS, STEWS & SANDWICHES 286
DESSERTS 300

Winter

Ol' Jack Frost has blown into town, and that means it's time to get cozy and enjoy some piping-hot servings of your favorite comfort foods. Put a slow cooker to good use this winter season, and you'll have no trouble preparing the heartwarming delights you've craved all year.

Winter

APPETIZERS & BEVERAGES

Winter is a great time to gather with loved ones. Whether you're celebrating a holiday, cheering on your favorite football team or warming up after a day of skiing, hostessing is a snap with help from this colorful section.

LISA CASTELLI'S CRANBERRY SAUERKRAUT MEATBALLS

(5)INGREDIENTS Cranberry Sauerkraut Meatballs

I first tried these super-simple meatballs at a friend's birthday party, and now I make them all the time.
—**LISA CASTELLI** PLEASANT PRAIRIE, WI

PREP: 15 MIN. • **COOK:** 4 HOURS
MAKES: ABOUT 5 DOZEN

- 1 can (14 ounces) whole-berry cranberry sauce
- 1 can (14 ounces) sauerkraut, rinsed and well drained
- 1 bottle (12 ounces) chili sauce
- ¾ cup packed brown sugar
- 1 package (32 ounces) frozen fully cooked homestyle meatballs, thawed

In a 4-qt. slow cooker, combine the cranberry sauce, sauerkraut, chili sauce and brown sugar. Stir in the meatballs. Cover and cook on low for 4-5 hours or until heated through.

(5)INGREDIENTS Make-Ahead Eggnog

Homemade eggnog is a tradition in many families during the holiday season. Enjoy easy prep with our slow cooker version.
—*TASTE OF HOME* TEST KITCHEN

PREP: 10 MIN. • **COOK:** 2 HOURS
MAKES: 9 SERVINGS (¾ CUP EACH)

- 6 cups whole milk
- 1 cup egg substitute
- ⅔ cup sugar
- 2 teaspoons rum extract
- 1½ teaspoons pumpkin pie spice
  French vanilla whipped topping, optional

In a 3-qt. slow cooker, combine the first five ingredients. Cover and cook on low for 2-3 hours or until heated through. Serve in mugs; dollop with whipped topping if desired.

Cider House Punch

Every sip of this hot drink tastes like apple pie! For an extra-festive touch, I float clove-studded orange slices in the bowl.
—**BARBARA KAY HUMMEL** TUCSON, AZ

START TO FINISH: 20 MIN.
MAKES: 18 SERVINGS (ABOUT 3½ QUARTS)

- 2 quarts apple cider or juice
- 1 liter ginger ale
- 2⅔ cups unsweetened pineapple juice
- 1 cup cranberry juice
- ½ cup sugar
- 1 cinnamon stick (3 inches)

1. In a large kettle, combine all ingredients. Cook over medium heat until heated through, stirring occasionally.
2. Transfer to a 5-qt. slow cooker; keep warm over low heat. Discard cinnamon stick before serving.

WARM CHRISTMAS PUNCH

½ cup butter, cubed
2 cups packed brown sugar
1 can (14 ounces) sweetened
 condensed milk
1 cup light corn syrup
2 tablespoons water
1 teaspoon vanilla extract
 Apple slices

1. In a heavy 3-qt. saucepan, combine the butter, brown sugar, milk, corn syrup and water; bring to a boil over medium heat. Cook and stir until a candy thermometer reads 230° (thread stage), about 8-10 minutes. Remove from the heat; stir in vanilla.
2. Transfer to a small fondue pot or a 1½-qt. slow cooker; keep warm. Serve with apple slices.
NOTE *We recommend that you test your candy thermometer before each use by bringing water to a boil; the thermometer should read 212°. Adjust your recipe temperature up or down based on your test.*

Red Hots add a rich crimson color and spiciness to Warm Christmas Punch, while fruit juice gives it tang.

—**JULIE STERCHI** CAMPBELLSVILLE, KY

⅓ cup Red Hots
1 cinnamon stick (3½ inches)
 Additional cinnamon sticks,
 optional

1. In a 3-qt. slow cooker, combine juices, Red Hots and cinnamon stick. Cover and cook on low for 2-4 hours or until heated through and candies are dissolved.
2. Discard cinnamon stick before serving. Use additional cinnamon sticks as stirrers if desired.

(5) INGREDIENTS
Warm Christmas Punch

PREP: 5 MIN. • **COOK:** 2 HOURS
MAKES: 8 SERVINGS (2 QUARTS)

1 bottle (32 ounces) cranberry juice
5 cans (6 ounces each)
 unsweetened pineapple juice

Caramel Apple Fondue
We like to dip into this luscious treat with apple slices while watching football on TV.
—**KATIE KOZIOLEK** HARTLAND, MN

PREP/TOTAL TIME: 25 MIN.
MAKES: 3½ CUPS

CARAMEL APPLE FONDUE

Wassail Bowl Punch

The blend of spice, fruit and citrus flavors in this punch is wonderful! Stir up a batch before heading outdoors for winter fun.

—**MARGARET HARMS** JENKINS, NY

PREP: 10 MIN. • **COOK:** 1 HOUR
MAKES: 3½ QUARTS

- 4 **cups hot brewed tea**
- 4 **cups cranberry juice**
- 4 **cups unsweetened apple juice**
- 2 **cups orange juice**
- 1 **cup sugar**
- ¾ **cup lemon juice**
- 3 **cinnamon sticks (3 inches)**
- 12 **whole cloves**

1. In a 5-qt. slow cooker, combine the first six ingredients. Place cinnamon sticks and whole cloves on a double thickness of cheesecloth; bring up the corners of the cheesecloth and tie with string to form a spice bag. Add the spice bag to the slow cooker.

2. Cover and cook on high for 1 hour or until punch begins to boil. Discard spice bag. Serve warm.

---

⑤ INGREDIENTS

Hot Cocoa for a Crowd

Here's a simple but comforting hot cocoa recipe that makes plenty for guests. It has just the right amount of sweetness, too. For extra fun, add mini marshmallows or a peppermint stick to each mug.

—**DEBORAH CANADAY** MANHATTAN, KS

PREP: 10 MIN. • **COOK:** 3 HOURS
MAKES: 12 SERVINGS (1 CUP EACH)

- 5 **cups nonfat dry milk powder**
- ¾ **cup sugar**
- ¾ **cup baking cocoa**
- 1 **teaspoon vanilla extract**
- ¼ **teaspoon ground cinnamon**
- 11 **cups water**
  Miniature marshmallows and peppermint candy sticks, optional

1. In a 5- or 6-qt. slow cooker, combine the dry milk powder, sugar, baking cocoa, vanilla and cinnamon; gradually whisk in water until smooth. Cover and cook on low for 3-4 hours or until heated through.

2. Garnish with mini marshmallows and use peppermint candy sticks for stirrers if desired.

Barbecued Party Starters

These tangy homemade meatballs, mini hot dogs and pineapple chunks are sure to tide everyone over until dinner. I like to set some festive toothpicks next to the slow cooker for easy nibbling.

—**ANASTASIA WEISS** PUNXSUTAWNEY, PA

PREP: 30 MIN. • **COOK:** 2¼ HOURS
MAKES: 16 SERVINGS (⅓ CUP EACH)

- 1 **pound ground beef**
- ¼ **cup finely chopped onion**
- 1 **package (16 ounces) miniature hot dogs, drained**
- 1 **jar (12 ounces) apricot preserves**
- 1 **cup barbecue sauce**
- 1 **can (20 ounces) pineapple chunks, drained**

1. In a large bowl, combine beef and onion, mixing lightly but thoroughly. Shape into 1-in. balls. In a large skillet over medium heat, cook the meatballs in two batches until cooked through, turning occasionally.

2. Using a slotted spoon, transfer the meatballs to a 3-qt. slow cooker. Add the miniature hot dogs; stir in the apricot preserves and barbecue sauce. Cook, covered, on high 2-3 hours or until heated through.

3. Stir in the pineapple chunks; cook, covered, 15-20 minutes longer or until heated through.

WASSAIL BOWL PUNCH

ANASTASIA WEISS'
BARBECUED PARTY STARTERS

WARM BROCCOLI CHEESE DIP

Warm Broccoli Cheese Dip

Whenever my family gathers for a party or other event, this flavorful cheese dip is guaranteed to be there, too. Everyone loves the zip of the jalapeno pepper and the crunchy bits of broccoli.

—BARBARA MAIOL CONYERS, GA

PREP: 15 MIN. • **COOK:** 2½ HOURS
MAKES: 5½ CUPS

- 2 **jars (8 ounces each) process cheese sauce**
- 1 **can (10¾ ounces) condensed cream of chicken soup, undiluted**
- 3 **cups frozen chopped broccoli, thawed and drained**
- ½ **pound fresh mushrooms, chopped**
- 2 **tablespoons chopped seeded jalapeno pepper**
  Assorted fresh vegetables

1. In a 1½-qt. slow cooker, combine the process cheese sauce and cream of chicken soup. Cover and cook on low for 30 minutes or until the cheese is melted, stirring occasionally.
2. Stir in the broccoli, mushrooms and jalapeno pepper. Cover and cook on low for 2-3 hours or until the vegetables are tender. Serve with assorted fresh vegetables.
NOTE *Wear disposable gloves when cutting hot peppers; the oils can burn skin. Avoid touching your face.*

Sweet 'n' Spicy Meatballs

I usually keep a batch of these meatballs in my freezer. The slightly sweet sauce nicely complements the spicy pork sausage.

—GENIE BROWN ROANOKE, VA

PREP: 25 MIN. • **BAKE:** 15 MIN.
MAKES: ABOUT 4 DOZEN

- 2 **pounds bulk spicy pork sausage**
- 1 **egg, lightly beaten**
- 1 **cup packed brown sugar**
- 1 **cup red wine vinegar**
- 1 **cup ketchup**
- 1 **tablespoon soy sauce**
- 1 **teaspoon ground ginger**

1. In a large bowl, combine sausage and egg. Shape into 1-in. balls. Place on a greased rack in a shallow baking pan. Bake at 400° for 15-20 minutes or until a thermometer reads 160°; drain.
2. Meanwhile, in a small saucepan, combine the remaining ingredients. Bring to a boil. Reduce heat; simmer, uncovered, until sugar is dissolved.
3. Transfer the meatballs to a 3-qt. slow cooker. Add the sauce and stir gently to coat. Cover and keep warm on low until serving.

SWEET 'N' SPICY MEATBALLS

CHRISTMAS PUNCH

Chili Beef Dip

Even the biggest appetites are no match for this beefy appetizer. Set a big basket of tortilla chips next to the slow cooker and let your guests dig right in.

—**PAT HABIGER** SPEARVILLE, KS

PREP: 25 MIN. • **COOK:** 2 HOURS
MAKES: 8 CUPS

- 2 **pounds lean ground beef (90% lean)**
- 1 **large onion, chopped**
- 1 **jalapeno pepper, seeded and chopped**
- 2 **packages (8 ounces each) cream cheese, cubed**
- 2 **cans (8 ounces each) tomato sauce**
- 1 **can (4 ounces) chopped green chilies**
- ½ **cup grated Parmesan cheese**
- ½ **cup ketchup**
- 2 **garlic cloves, minced**
- 1½ **teaspoons chili powder**
- 1 **teaspoon dried oregano**
  Tortilla chips

1. In a large skillet, brown the beef, onion and jalapeno until the meat is no longer pink, breaking up the meat into crumbles; drain. Transfer to a 3- or 4-qt. slow cooker. Stir in the cream cheese, tomato sauce, chilies, Parmesan cheese, ketchup, garlic, chili powder and oregano.
2. Cover; cook on low for 2-3 hours or until heated through. Stir; serve with tortilla chips.
NOTE *Wear disposable gloves when cutting hot peppers; the oils can burn skin. Avoid touching your face.*

(5)INGREDIENTS
Christmas Punch

One year when we were having our office Christmas party, a co-worker brought her rosy red punch. It was so good, I just had to ask for the recipe. And I was delighted to discover how easy it is to prepare.

—**PATRICIA DICK** ANDERSON, IN

PREP: 15 MIN. • **COOK:** 3 HOURS
MAKES: 20 SERVINGS (¾ CUP EACH)

- 1 **quart brewed tea**
- 1 **quart apple juice**
- 1 **quart orange juice**
- 1 **quart pineapple juice**
- 1 **package (9 ounces) Red Hots**

Place all ingredients in a 6-qt. slow cooker. Cook, covered, on low 3-4 hours or until heated through and the Red Hots candies are melted, stirring occasionally.

POMEGRANATE-GLAZED TURKEY MEATBALLS

Pomegranate-Glazed Turkey Meatballs

A splash of refreshing pomegranate juice turns ordinary meatballs into something extraordinary. I love the sweet lightness of the glaze combined with the ground turkey, herbs and spices. Set these out and watch them disappear!

—DANIELLE D'AMBROSIO BRIGHTON, MA

PREP: 30 MIN. • **COOK:** 10 MIN.
MAKES: 3 DOZEN

- 1 **egg, beaten**
- ½ **cup soft bread crumbs**
- ½ **cup minced fresh parsley**
- 1 **teaspoon salt**
- 1 **teaspoon smoked paprika**
- 1 **teaspoon coarsely ground pepper**
- ¼ **teaspoon garlic salt**
- 1¼ **pounds ground turkey**
- 3 **cups plus 1 tablespoon pomegranate juice, divided**
- ½ **cup sugar**
- 1 **tablespoon cornstarch**

1. In a large bowl, combine the egg, bread crumbs, parsley, salt, paprika, pepper and garlic salt. Crumble the turkey over the mixture and mix well. Shape into 1-in. balls.

2. Divide the meatballs between two ungreased 15x10x1-in. baking pans. Bake at 375° for 10-15 minutes or until a thermometer reads 165° and the juices run clear.

3. Meanwhile, in a large skillet, combine 3 cups pomegranate juice and sugar. Bring to a boil; cook until the liquid is reduced to about 1 cup. Combine cornstarch and remaining juice; stir into skillet. Cook and stir for 1 minute or until thickened.

4. Gently stir in the meatballs and heat through. Serve in a slow cooker or chafing dish.

Hot Mulled Wine

For a holiday get-together or any occasion during those cold winter months, try this heartwarming mulled wine.

—TASTE OF HOME TEST KITCHEN

PREP: 15 MIN. • **COOK:** 4 HOURS
MAKES: 5 SERVINGS

- 2 **cinnamon sticks (3 inches)**
- 6 **whole cloves**
- 1 **fresh rosemary sprig**
- 1 **bottle (750 milliliters) cabernet sauvignon or other dry red wine**
- 1 **cup fresh or frozen cranberries**
- ⅔ **cup sugar**
- ⅓ **cup bourbon**
- ⅓ **cup orange juice**
- 4 **teaspoons grated orange peel**

1. Place the cinnamon sticks, whole cloves and rosemary sprig on a double thickness of cheesecloth; bring up the corners of the cheesecloth and tie with string to form a bag.

2. In a 1½-qt. slow cooker, combine the wine, cranberries, sugar, bourbon, orange juice and peel. Add spice bag. Cover and cook on low for 4-5 hours or until heated through. Discard spice bag. Serve warm.

HOT MULLED WINE

SLOW COOKER HOT CRAB DIP

Slow Cooker Hot Crab Dip

One batch of my hot crab dip usually isn't enough for my seafood-loving family, so I often double the recipe.

—TERRI PERRIER SIMONTON, TX

PREP: 10 MIN. • **COOK:** 2 HOURS
MAKES: 2 CUPS

- 1 **package (8 ounces) cream cheese, softened**
- ½ **cup finely chopped sweet onion**
- ¼ **cup grated Parmesan cheese**
- ¼ **cup mayonnaise**
- 2 **garlic cloves, minced**
- 2 **teaspoons sugar**
- 1 **can (6 ounces) crabmeat, drained, flaked and cartilage removed**
  Assorted crackers

In a 1½-qt. slow cooker, combine the first six ingredients; stir in crab. Cover and cook on low for 2-3 hours or until heated through. Serve with crackers.

Cheesy Pizza Fondue

I keep the ingredients for this fondue on hand for spur-of-the-moment gatherings. The taste of pizza is hard to resist!

—NEL CARVER MOSCOW, ID

PREP: 10 MIN. • **COOK:** 4 HOURS
MAKES: 4 CUPS

- 1 **jar (29 ounces) meatless spaghetti sauce**
- 2 **cups (8 ounces) shredded part-skim mozzarella cheese**
- ¼ **cup shredded Parmesan cheese**
- 2 **teaspoons dried oregano**
- 1 **teaspoon dried minced onion**
- ¼ **teaspoon garlic powder**
  Cubed Italian bread

1. In a 1½-qt. slow cooker, combine the spaghetti sauce, cheeses, oregano, onion and garlic powder.

2. Cover and cook on low for 4-6 hours or until heated through and cheese is melted. Serve with bread.

SPICED POMEGRANATE SIPPER

Spiced Pomegranate Sipper

Children and adults alike enjoy this festive hot beverage. As it simmers, it fills every room of our home with the wonderful aroma of fruit juices and spices.

—LISA RENSHAW KANSAS CITY, MO

PREP: 10 MIN. • **COOK:** 1 HOUR
MAKES: 16 SERVINGS (¾ CUP EACH)

- 1 bottle (64 ounces) cranberry-apple juice
- 2 cups unsweetened apple juice
- 1 cup pomegranate juice
- ⅔ cup honey
- ½ cup orange juice
- 3 cinnamon sticks (3 inches)
- 10 whole cloves
- 2 tablespoons grated orange peel

1. In a 5-qt. slow cooker, combine the first five ingredients. Place cinnamon sticks, whole cloves and orange peel on a double thickness of cheesecloth. Gather up the corners of cheesecloth to enclose the seasonings; tie securely with string to form a bag. Add the bag to slow cooker.

2. Cook, covered, on low 1-2 hours or until heated through. Discard the spice bag.

Cranberry Hot Wings

Chicken wings get special treatment when you add cranberries, a touch of citrus and a hint of heat. Served with blue cheese dressing and celery, this is a delicious way to warm up on a chilly winter night!

—ROBIN HAAS CRANSTON, RI

PREP: 50 MIN. • **COOK:** 2 HOURS
MAKES: ABOUT 2½ DOZEN

- 1 can (14 ounces) jellied cranberry sauce, cubed
- 2 tablespoons ground mustard
- 2 tablespoons hot pepper sauce
- 2 tablespoons reduced-sodium soy sauce
- 2 tablespoons honey
- 1 tablespoon cider vinegar
- 2 teaspoons garlic powder
- 1 teaspoon grated orange peel
- 3 pounds chicken wings
  Blue cheese salad dressing and celery ribs

1. In a 5-qt. slow cooker, combine the first eight ingredients. Cover and cook on low for 45 minutes or until the cranberry sauce is melted.

2. Meanwhile, cut the chicken wings into three sections; discard the wing tip sections. Place wings on a greased broiler pan. Broil 4-6 in. from the heat for 15-20 minutes or until lightly browned, turning occasionally.

3. Transfer the wings to slow cooker; toss to coat. Cover and cook on high for 2-3 hours or until tender. Serve wings with salad dressing and celery.
NOTE *Uncooked chicken wing sections (wingettes) may be substituted for whole chicken wings.*

TOP TIP

A cheesecloth bag makes it easy to remove spices from a slow cooker. A cloth tea sachet (available in tea shops) also makes a great spice bag.

CHEDDAR FONDUE

Cheddar Fondue

My smooth, cheesy fondue gets its spark from a little Worcestershire and ground mustard. I like to offer a platter of cubed bread, chunks of ham, small sausages or broccoli florets as dippers.

—NORENE WRIGHT MANILLA, IN

START TO FINISH: 15 MIN.
MAKES: 2½ CUPS

- ¼ **cup butter**
- ¼ **cup all-purpose flour**
- ½ **teaspoon salt, optional**
- ¼ **teaspoon ground mustard**
- ¼ **teaspoon pepper**
- ¼ **teaspoon Worcestershire sauce**
- 1½ **cups milk**
- 2 **cups (8 ounces) shredded cheddar cheese**
  Bread cubes, ham cubes, bite-size sausage and or broccoli florets

1. In a small saucepan, melt the butter; stir in the flour, salt if desired, mustard, pepper and Worcestershire sauce until smooth. Gradually add the milk. Bring to a boil; cook and stir for 2 minutes or until thickened. Reduce the heat. Add the cheese; cook and stir until cheese is melted.

2. Transfer to a fondue pot or 1½-qt. slow cooker; keep warm. Serve fondue with bread, ham, bite-size sausage and/or broccoli.

Mini Hot Dogs 'n' Meatballs

Hot appetizers just don't come any easier than this one! Feel free to vary the meats to suit your family's tastes...or give it some extra zip by using a spicy barbecue sauce or zesty spaghetti sauce.

—ANDREA CHAMBERLAIN MACEDON, NY

PREP: 5 MIN. • **COOK:** 3 HOURS
MAKES: 8 CUPS

- 1 **package (12 ounces) frozen fully cooked Italian meatballs**
- 1 **package (16 ounces) miniature hot dogs or smoked sausages**
- 1 **package (3½ ounces) sliced pepperoni**
- 1 **jar (24 ounces) meatless spaghetti sauce**
- 1 **bottle (18 ounces) barbecue sauce**
- 1 **bottle (12 ounces) chili sauce**

In a 5-qt. slow cooker, combine all ingredients. Cover and cook on low for 3-4 hours or until heated through.

MINI HOT DOGS 'N' MEATBALLS

Winter

SIDE DISHES

When it's time to complete your meal, let your slow cooker do the work! Standout sides like Vegetable-Stuffed Peppers, Jazzed-Up Green Bean Casserole and Moist Poultry Dressing are easy additions to any winter menu.

SUE LIVERMORE'S
SLOW-COOKED
BACON & BEANS

Slow-Cooked Bacon & Beans

With its smokiness and savory flavor, bacon takes a side dish of beans to the next level. No one will be able to resist!
—**SUE LIVERMORE** DETROIT LAKES, MN

PREP: 25 MIN. • **COOK:** 6 HOURS
MAKES: 12 SERVINGS (¾ CUP EACH)

- 1 **package (1 pound) sliced bacon, chopped**
- 1 **cup chopped onion**
- 2 **cans (15 ounces each) pork and beans, undrained**
- 1 **can (16 ounces) kidney beans, rinsed and drained**
- 1 **can (16 ounces) butter beans, rinsed and drained**
- 1 **can (15¼ ounces) lima beans, rinsed and drained**
- 1 **can (15 ounces) black beans, rinsed and drained**
- 1 **cup packed brown sugar**
- ½ **cup cider vinegar**
- 1 **tablespoon molasses**
- 2 **teaspoons garlic powder**
- ½ **teaspoon ground mustard**

1. In a large skillet, cook the bacon and onion over medium heat until bacon is crisp. Remove to paper towels to drain.
2. In a 4-qt. slow cooker, combine the remaining ingredients; stir in bacon mixture. Cover and cook on low for 6-8 hours or until heated through.

Maple-Almond Butternut Squash

This dressed-up butternut squash is a cinch to prepare, making it a great choice for any occasion. I sprinkle sliced almonds and Parmesan cheese on top.
—**JUDY LAWSON** DEXTER, MI

PREP: 30 MIN. • **COOK:** 5½ HOURS
MAKES: 9 SERVINGS

- 1 **medium butternut squash (about 4 pounds), peeled, seeded and cut into 2-inch cubes**
- 4 **garlic cloves, minced**
- 1 **teaspoon salt**
- ½ **teaspoon pepper**
- ½ **cup butter, melted**
- ½ **cup maple syrup**
- ½ **cup heavy whipping cream**
- ¼ **cup sliced almonds**
- ¼ **cup shredded Parmesan cheese**

1. Place the butternut squash in a 4-qt. slow cooker. Sprinkle with the garlic, salt and pepper. Add the butter and maple syrup; stir to coat. Cover and cook on low for 5-6 hours or until squash is tender.
2. Stir in the heavy whipping cream. Cover and cook 30 minutes longer or until heated through. Sprinkle with almonds and cheese.

OLD-FASHIONED DRESSING

Old-Fashioned Dressing

Remember Grandma's delicious turkey dressing? Here's a traditional recipe that's bound to take you back. You'll love both the popular combination of ingredients and the convenience of using your slow cooker—especially on hectic holidays.
—**SHERRY VINK** LACOMBE, AB

PREP: 35 MIN. • **COOK:** 3 HOURS
MAKES: 8 SERVINGS

- ½ cup butter, cubed
- 2 celery ribs, chopped
- 1 cup sliced fresh mushrooms
- 1 medium onion, chopped
- ½ cup minced fresh parsley
- 2 teaspoons rubbed sage
- 2 teaspoons dried marjoram
- 1 teaspoon dried thyme
- 1 teaspoon poultry seasoning
- ½ teaspoon pepper
- ¼ teaspoon salt
- 6 cups cubed day-old white bread
- 6 cups cubed day-old whole wheat bread
- 1 can (14½ ounces) chicken broth

1. In a large skillet, melt butter. Add the celery, mushrooms and onion; saute until tender. Stir in the seasonings. Place bread cubes in a large bowl. Stir in vegetable mixture. Add broth; toss to coat.

2. Transfer to a 3-qt. slow cooker coated with cooking spray. Cover and cook on low for 3-4 hours or until heated through.

Easy Slow Cooker Mac & Cheese

Whenever I fix this cheesy mac, my sons say, "You're the best mom in the world!"
—**HEIDI FLEEK**
HAMBURG, PA

PREP: 25 MIN. • **COOK:** 1 HOUR
MAKES: 8 SERVINGS

- 2 cups uncooked elbow macaroni
- 1 can (10¾ ounces) condensed cheddar cheese soup, undiluted
- 1 cup 2% milk
- ½ cup sour cream
- ¼ cup butter, cubed
- ½ teaspoon onion powder
- ¼ teaspoon white pepper
- ⅛ teaspoon salt
- 1 cup (4 ounces) shredded cheddar cheese
- 1 cup (4 ounces) shredded fontina cheese
- 1 cup (4 ounces) shredded provolone cheese

1. Cook macaroni according to the package directions for al dente. Meanwhile, in a large saucepan, combine the soup, milk, sour cream, butter and seasonings; cook and stir over medium-low heat until blended. Stir in the cheeses until melted.

2. Drain the macaroni; transfer to a greased 3-qt. slow cooker. Stir in the cheese mixture. Cook, covered, on low 1-2 hours or until heated through.

EASY SLOW COOKER MAC & CHEESE

SAUSAGE DRESSING

Sausage Dressing

I first used this recipe when there was no room in the oven to bake my holiday stuffing. The results were fantastic—very moist and flavorful. Even family members who don't usually eat dressing enjoyed it.

—**MARY KENDALL** APPLETON, WI

PREP: 20 MIN. • **COOK:** 4 HOURS
MAKES: 12 SERVINGS

- 1 **pound bulk pork sausage**
- 1 **large onion, chopped**
- 2 **celery ribs, chopped**
- 1 **package (14 ounces) seasoned stuffing croutons**
- 1 **can (14½ ounces) chicken broth**
- 1 **large tart apple, chopped**
- 1 **cup chopped walnuts or pecans**
- ½ **cup egg substitute**
- ¼ **cup butter, melted**
- 1½ **teaspoons rubbed sage**
- ½ **teaspoon pepper**

1. In a large skillet, cook the sausage, onion and celery over medium heat until meat is no longer pink, breaking it up into crumbles; drain. Transfer to a greased 5-qt. slow cooker. Stir in the remaining ingredients.

2. Cover and cook on low for 4-5 hours or until a thermometer reads 160°.

Jazzed-Up Green Bean Casserole

After trying many variations of traditional green bean casserole, I decided to give it a boost with crunchy water chestnuts, bacon and cheese. It was a hit!

—**SCOTT RUGH** PORTLAND, OR

PREP: 20 MIN. • **COOK:** 5½ HOURS
MAKES: 10 SERVINGS

- 2 **packages (16 ounces each) frozen cut green beans, thawed**
- 2 **cans (10¾ ounces each) condensed cream of mushroom soup, undiluted**
- 1 **can (8 ounces) sliced water chestnuts, drained**
- 1 **cup 2% milk**
- 6 **bacon strips, cooked and crumbled**
- 1 **teaspoon pepper**
- ⅛ **teaspoon paprika**
- 4 **ounces process cheese (Velveeta), cubed**
- 1 **can (2.8 ounces) French-fried onions**

In a 4-qt. slow cooker, combine the green beans, cream of mushroom soup, water chestnuts, milk, bacon, pepper and paprika. Cover and cook on low for 5-6 hours or until the beans are tender; stir in the cheese. Cover and cook for 30 minutes or until the cheese is melted. Sprinkle with the French-fried onions.

JAZZED-UP GREEN BEAN CASSEROLE

Four-Bean Medley

This tasty side featuring a variety of beans always draws compliments. Easy to put together ahead of time and then simmer, it's a convenient choice for church socials, potlucks or any bring-a-dish event.

—SUSANNE WASSON MONTGOMERY, NY

PREP: 40 MIN. • **COOK:** 6 HOURS
MAKES: 8-10 SERVINGS

- 8 **bacon strips, diced**
- 2 **medium onions, quartered and sliced**
- ¾ **cup packed brown sugar**
- ½ **cup cider vinegar**
- 1 **teaspoon salt**
- 1 **teaspoon ground mustard**
- ½ **teaspoon garlic powder**
- 1 **can (16 ounces) baked beans, undrained**
- 1 **can (16 ounces) kidney beans, rinsed and drained**
- 1 **can (16 ounces) butter beans, rinsed and drained**
- 1 **can (14½ ounces) cut green beans, drained**

1. In a large skillet, cook bacon until crisp. Drain, reserving 2 tablespoons drippings; set bacon aside. Saute the onions in drippings until tender. Stir in brown sugar, vinegar, salt, mustard and garlic powder.

2. Simmer, uncovered, for 15 minutes or until the onions are golden brown. Place the beans in a 3-qt. slow cooker. Add onion mixture and bacon; stir to combine. Cover and cook on low for 6-7 hours or until heated through. Serve with a slotted spoon.

(5) INGREDIENTS

Creamy Red Potatoes

You just can't go wrong when you serve creamy, cheesy potatoes. These require only four basic ingredients.

—**SHELIA SCHMITT** TOPEKA, KS

PREP: 5 MIN. • **COOK:** 8 HOURS
MAKES: 4-6 SERVINGS

- 2 **pounds small red potatoes, quartered**
- 1 **package (8 ounces) cream cheese, softened**
- 1 **can (10¾ ounces) condensed cream of potato soup, undiluted**
- 1 **envelope ranch salad dressing mix**

Place the red potatoes in a 3-qt. slow cooker. In a small bowl, beat the cream cheese, soup and ranch salad dressing mix until blended. Stir into potatoes. Cover and cook on low for 8 hours or until potatoes are tender.

Light Spinach Casserole

I discovered my spinach recipe in an old cookbook. The casserole went over big with our church sewing circle.

—**VIODA GEYER** UHRICHSVILLE, OH

PREP: 10 MIN. • **COOK:** 2½ HOURS
MAKES: 8 SERVINGS

- 2 **packages (10 ounces each) frozen chopped spinach, thawed and well drained**
- 2 **cups (16 ounces) 4% cottage cheese**
- 1 **cup cubed process cheese (Velveeta)**
- ¾ **cup egg substitute**
- 2 **tablespoons butter, cubed**
- ¼ **cup all-purpose flour**
- ½ **teaspoon salt**

In a 3-qt. slow cooker, combine all ingredients. Cover and cook on low for 2½ hours or until cheese is melted.

Vegetable-Stuffed Peppers

This slow-cooked side has it all—it's tasty, colorful and fun to eat. I combine kidney beans, rice, cheddar, corn and more to create a flavorful filling for green peppers. The stuffed cups are even hearty enough to make a great meatless main course.

—**SANDRA ALLEN** AUSTIN, TX

PREP: 10 MIN. • **COOK:** 8¼ HOURS
MAKES: 6 SERVINGS

- 2 **cans (14½ ounces each) diced tomatoes, undrained**
- 1 **can (16 ounces) kidney beans, rinsed and drained**
- 1½ **cups cooked rice**
- 2 **cups (8 ounces) shredded cheddar cheese, divided**
- 1 **package (10 ounces) frozen corn, thawed**
- ¼ **cup chopped onion**
- 1 **teaspoon Worcestershire sauce**
- ¾ **teaspoon chili powder**
- ½ **teaspoon pepper**
- ¼ **teaspoon salt**
- 6 **medium green peppers**

1. In a large bowl, combine the tomatoes, beans, rice, 1½ cups cheese, corn, onion, Worcestershire sauce, chili powder, pepper and salt. Remove and discard the tops and seeds of the green peppers. Fill each pepper with about 1 cup vegetable mixture. Place in a 5-qt. slow cooker. Cover and cook on low for 8 hours.

2. Sprinkle with remaining cheese. Cover and cook 15 minutes longer or until the peppers are tender and the cheese is melted.

CREAMY RED POTATOES

SANDRA ALLEN'S
VEGETABLE-STUFFED PEPPERS

MOIST POULTRY DRESSING

Moist Poultry Dressing

Mushrooms and onions blend well with the sage, thyme and other herbs in my stuffing. It also stays nice and moist.
—**RUTH ANN STELFOX** RAYMOND, AB

PREP: 20 MIN. • **COOK:** 4 HOURS
MAKES: 12-16 SERVINGS

- 2 **jars (4½ ounces each) sliced mushrooms, drained**
- 4 **celery ribs, chopped**
- 2 **medium onions, chopped**
- ¼ **cup minced fresh parsley**
- ¾ **cup butter, cubed**
- 1½ **pounds day-old bread, crusts removed and cubed (about 13 cups)**
- 1½ **teaspoons salt**
- 1½ **teaspoons rubbed sage**
- 1 **teaspoon poultry seasoning**
- 1 **teaspoon dried thyme**
- ½ **teaspoon pepper**
- 2 **eggs**
- 1 **can (14½ ounces) chicken broth or 14½ ounces vegetable broth**

1. In a large skillet, saute the mushrooms, celery, onions and parsley in butter until the vegetables are tender. In a large bowl, toss the bread cubes with salt, sage, poultry seasoning, thyme and pepper. Add the mushroom mixture. Combine eggs and chicken broth; add to the bread mixture and toss.

2. Transfer to 5-qt. slow cooker. Cover and cook on low for 4-5 hours or until a thermometer reads 160°.

Slow-Cooked Broccoli

I love making broccoli this way. Not only is it delicious, but it also frees up my oven for other items on the menu. A sprinkling of cheddar on top is the finishing touch.
—**CONNIE SLOCUM** ANTIOCH, TN

PREP: 10 MIN. • **COOK:** 2½ HOURS
MAKES: 8-10 SERVINGS

- 6 **cups frozen chopped broccoli, partially thawed**
- 1 **can (10¾ ounces) condensed cream of celery soup, undiluted**
- 1½ **cups (6 ounces) shredded sharp cheddar cheese, divided**
- ¼ **cup chopped onion**
- ½ **teaspoon Worcestershire sauce**
- ¼ **teaspoon pepper**
- 1 **cup crushed butter-flavored crackers (about 25)**
- 2 **tablespoons butter**

1. In a large bowl, combine the broccoli, cream of celery soup, 1 cup cheese, onion, Worcestershire sauce and pepper. Pour into a greased 3-qt. slow cooker. Sprinkle the crushed butter-flavored crackers on top; dot with butter.

2. Cover and cook on high for 2½ to 3 hours. Sprinkle with the remaining cheese. Cook 10 minutes longer or until the cheese is melted.

SLOW-COOKED BROCCOLI

SLOW COOKER TZIMMES

Slow Cooker Tzimmes

Tzimmes is a sweet Jewish dish that consists of a variety of fruits, veggies and sometimes meat. Like this recipe, the traditional version is tossed with honey and cinnamon, then cooked slowly over low heat to blend all of the flavors into one special treat.

—**LISA RENSHAW** KANSAS CITY, MO

PREP: 20 MIN. • **COOK:** 5 HOURS
MAKES: 12 SERVINGS (⅔ CUP EACH)

½ **medium butternut squash, peeled and cubed**
2 **medium sweet potatoes, peeled and cubed**
6 **medium carrots, sliced**
2 **medium tart apples, peeled and sliced**
1 **cup chopped sweet onion**
1 **cup chopped dried apricots**
1 **cup golden raisins**
½ **cup orange juice**
¼ **cup honey**
2 **tablespoons finely chopped crystallized ginger**
3 **teaspoons ground cinnamon**
3 **teaspoons pumpkin pie spice**
2 **teaspoons grated orange peel**
1 **teaspoon salt**
   Vanilla yogurt, optional

1. Place the first seven ingredients in a 5- or 6-qt. slow cooker. Combine the orange juice, honey, crystallized ginger, cinnamon, pumpkin pie spice, orange peel and salt; pour over the top and mix well.
2. Cover and cook on low for 5-6 hours or until the vegetables are tender. Dollop servings with vanilla yogurt if desired.

DONNA DOWNES'
CREAMY HASH BROWNS

Creamy Hash Browns

When Mom needed something to bring to social dinners, she frequently picked her comforting slow-cooked hash browns because they were always a hit. Now I get the same compliments when I fix them. Crumbled bacon, onion, cheese and sour cream dress up the potatoes.

—**DONNA DOWNES** LAS VEGAS, NV

PREP: 10 MIN. • **COOK:** 4 HOURS
MAKES: 14 SERVINGS

- 1 package (2 pounds) frozen cubed hash brown potatoes
- 2 cups (8 ounces) cubed process cheese (Velveeta)
- 2 cups (16 ounces) sour cream
- 1 can (10¾ ounces) condensed cream of celery soup, undiluted
- 1 can (10¾ ounces) condensed cream of chicken soup, undiluted
- 1 pound sliced bacon, cooked and crumbled
- 1 large onion, chopped
- ¼ cup butter, melted
- ¼ teaspoon pepper

Place the cubed hash brown potatoes in an ungreased 5-qt. slow cooker. In a large bowl, combine the remaining ingredients. Pour over potatoes and mix well. Cover and cook on low for 4-5 hours or until potatoes are tender and heated through.

DID YOU KNOW?

When a *Taste of Home* recipe calls for Italian sausage, it is referring to the sweet variety of Italian sausage. Recipes that use hot Italian sausage specifically list that type.

Everything Stuffing

Both my husband and my dad go crazy for this hearty, sausage-filled stuffing. The added bonus? It freezes really well.

—**BETTE VOTRAL** BETHLEHEM, PA

PREP: 30 MIN. • **COOK:** 3 HOURS
MAKES: 9 SERVINGS

- ½ pound bulk Italian sausage
- 4 cups seasoned stuffing cubes
- 1½ cups crushed corn bread stuffing
- ½ cup chopped toasted chestnuts or pecans
- ½ cup minced fresh parsley
- 1 tablespoon minced fresh sage or 1 teaspoon rubbed sage
- ⅛ teaspoon salt
- ⅛ teaspoon pepper
- 1¾ cups sliced baby portobello mushrooms
- 1 package (5 ounces) sliced fresh shiitake mushrooms
- 1 large onion, chopped
- 1 medium apple, peeled and chopped
- 1 celery rib, chopped
- 3 tablespoons butter
- 1 can (14½ ounces) chicken broth

1. In a large skillet, cook the sausage over medium heat until no longer pink, breaking it up into crumbles; drain. Transfer to a large bowl. Stir in the seasoned stuffing cubes, corn bread stuffing, chestnuts, parsley, sage, salt and pepper.

2. In the same skillet, saute the portobello and shiitake mushrooms, onion, apple and celery in butter until tender. Stir into the stuffing mixture. Add enough chicken broth to reach the desired moistness. Transfer to a 4-qt. slow cooker. Cover and cook on low for 3 hours, stirring once.

EVERYTHING STUFFING

Make-Ahead Mashed Potatoes

Sour cream and cream cheese bring richness to these convenient make-ahead spuds. They're a busy host's dream when time is tight because they don't require any last-minute mashing.

—**TRUDY VINCENT** VALLES MINES, MO

PREP: 20 MIN. • **COOK:** 2 HOURS
MAKES: 8-10 SERVINGS

- 1 **package (3 ounces) cream cheese, softened**
- ½ **cup sour cream**
- ¼ **cup butter, softened**
- 1 **envelope ranch salad dressing mix**
- 1 **teaspoon dried parsley flakes**
- 6 **cups warm mashed potatoes (without added milk and butter)**

In a large bowl, combine the cream cheese, sour cream, butter, dressing mix and parsley; stir in the potatoes. Transfer to a 3-qt. slow cooker. Cover and cook on low for 2-3 hours.
NOTE *This recipe was tested with fresh potatoes (not instant) in a slow cooker with heating elements surrounding the unit, not only in the base.*

⑤INGREDIENTS
Easy Sweet Potato Casserole

You need only a few ingredients to whip up a delicious side of sweet potatoes.

—*TASTE OF HOME* **TEST KITCHEN**

PREP: 20 MIN. • **COOK:** 5 HOURS
MAKES: 6 SERVINGS

- 2¼ **pounds sweet potatoes, peeled and cubed**
- ¾ **teaspoon salt**
- ⅛ **teaspoon pepper**
- 1 **cup peach pie filling**
- 2 **tablespoons butter, melted**
- ¼ **teaspoon ground cinnamon**
- ½ **cup granola without raisins, optional**

Place sweet potatoes in a 3-qt. slow cooker coated with cooking spray. Toss with salt and pepper. Top with the pie filling and drizzle with butter. Sprinkle with cinnamon. Cover and cook on low for 5-7 hours or until potatoes are tender. Sprinkle with granola if desired.

⑤INGREDIENTS ## Slow-Cooked Applesauce

Enjoy this sweet, chunky treat as a snack or as an accompaniment for a main dish. Let the applesauce cook while you head out with your family for some winter fun.

—**SUSANNE WASSON** MONTGOMERY, NY

PREP: 20 MIN. • **COOK:** 6 HOURS
MAKES: 12 CUPS

- 6 **pounds apples (about 18 medium), peeled and sliced**
- 1 **cup sugar**
- 1 **cup water**
- 1 **teaspoon salt**
- 1 **teaspoon ground cinnamon**
- ¼ **cup butter, cubed**
- 2 **teaspoons vanilla extract**

1. In a 5-qt. slow cooker, combine the apples, sugar, water, salt and cinnamon. Cover and cook on low for 6-8 hours or until tender.
2. Turn off the heat; stir in the butter and vanilla. Mash if desired. Serve warm or cold.

MAKE-AHEAD MASHED POTATOES

⑤ INGREDIENTS Italian Spaghetti Squash

Here's a simple way to serve wholesome spaghetti squash. Be sure the squash is on the small or medium side so that it fits in the slow cooker after being cut in half.

—MELISSA BROOKS SPARTA, WI

PREP: 15 MIN. • **COOK:** 6¼ HOURS
MAKES: 4 SERVINGS

- 1 **medium spaghetti squash**
- 1 **cup sliced fresh mushrooms**
- 1 **can (14½ ounces) diced tomatoes, undrained**
- 1 **teaspoon dried oregano**
- 1 **teaspoon salt**
- ¼ **teaspoon pepper**
- ¾ **cup shredded part-skim mozzarella cheese**

1. Cut squash in half lengthwise; discard seeds. Place squash, cut side up, in a 6- or 7-qt. slow cooker. Layer with mushrooms, tomatoes, oregano, salt and pepper. Cover; cook on low for 6-8 hours or until squash is tender.
2. Sprinkle with cheese. Cover and cook for 15 minutes or until cheese is melted. When squash is cool enough to handle, use a fork to separate spaghetti squash strands.

Winter Fruit Compote

You can prepare this colorful fruit relish up to a week in advance. I like to pair the compote with turkey, pork or chicken.

—ESTHER CHESNEY CARTHAGE, MO

PREP: 10 MIN. • **COOK:** 1¼ HOURS + COOLING
MAKES: 2½ CUPS

- 1 **package (12 ounces) fresh or frozen cranberries, thawed**
- ⅔ **cup packed brown sugar**
- ¼ **cup orange juice concentrate**
- 2 **tablespoons raspberry vinegar**

RANCH BEANS

- ½ **cup chopped dried apricots**
- ½ **cup golden raisins**
- ½ **cup chopped walnuts, toasted**

1. In a 1½-qt. slow cooker, combine the cranberries, brown sugar, orange juice concentrate and vinegar. Cover and cook on low for 1¼ to 1¾ hours or until cranberries pop and mixture is thickened.
2. Turn off the heat; stir in the dried apricots, golden raisins and walnuts. Cool to room temperature. Refrigerate any leftovers.

Ranch Beans

Canned goods make these tangy beans a snap to throw together. A friend passed along the fuss-free recipe to me, and I've been making it ever since.

—BARBARA GORDON ROSWELL, GA

PREP: 10 MIN. • **COOK:** 3 HOURS
MAKES: 8-10 SERVINGS

- 1 **can (16 ounces) kidney beans, rinsed and drained**
- 1 **can (15¾ ounces) pork and beans, undrained**
- 1 **can (15 ounces) lima beans, rinsed and drained**
- 1 **can (14½ ounces) cut green beans, drained**
- 1 **bottle (12 ounces) chili sauce**
- ¾ **cup packed brown sugar**
- 1 **small onion, chopped**

In a 3-qt. slow cooker, combine all the ingredients. Cover and cook on high for 3-4 hours or until heated through. **NOTE** *This dish can be cooked in the oven instead. Cover and bake in a 350° oven for 40 minutes. Remove cover and cook 10 minutes longer.*

CREAMY CORN

1. In a large bowl, combine sweet potatoes, sugar, eggs, milk, butter, salt and vanilla. Transfer to a greased 1½-qt. slow cooker. Cover and cook on low for 3 hours.
2. In a small bowl, combine brown sugar, pecans and flour; cut in butter until crumbly. Sprinkle over potatoes. Cover and cook 1-2 hours longer or until a thermometer reads 160°.

Cheesy Spinach
My daughter frequently contributes this cheese-and-spinach favorite for church suppers. Even people who say they don't care for vegetables ask for seconds of this flavorful dish—and there's never any left!
—**FRANCES MOORE** DECATUR, IL

PREP: 10 MIN. • **COOK:** 5 HOURS
MAKES: 6-8 SERVINGS

- 2 packages (10 ounces each) frozen chopped spinach, thawed and well drained
- 2 cups (16 ounces) 4% cottage cheese
- 1½ cups cubed process cheese (Velveeta)
- 3 eggs, lightly beaten
- ¼ cup butter, cubed
- ¼ cup all-purpose flour
- 1 teaspoon salt

In a large bowl, combine all ingredients. Pour into a greased 3-qt. slow cooker. Cover; cook on high for 1 hour. Reduce heat to low; cook 4-5 hours longer or until a knife inserted near the center comes out clean.

(5)INGREDIENTS Creamy Corn
This rich side requires just a handful of ingredients. I sampled it at a potluck and didn't want to leave without the recipe.
—**JUDY MCCARTHY** DERBY, KS

PREP: 5 MIN. • **COOK:** 4 HOURS
MAKES: 8 SERVINGS

- 2 packages (16 ounces each) frozen corn
- 1 package (8 ounces) cream cheese, cubed
- ⅓ cup butter, cubed
- ½ teaspoon garlic powder
- ½ teaspoon salt
- ¼ teaspoon pepper

In a 3-qt. slow cooker, combine all ingredients. Cover and cook on low for 4 hours or until heated through and the cheese is melted. Stir well before serving.

Praline Sweet Potatoes
When I had a house full of relatives and was short on cooking space, I used the basic idea of traditional sweet potato casserole and adapted it for the slow cooker. We loved the results!
—**JOANNA STANFORTH** SCOTT AFB, IL

PREP: 15 MIN. • **COOK:** 4 HOURS
MAKES: 6 SERVINGS

- 3 cups mashed sweet potatoes
- 1 cup sugar
- 3 eggs
- ½ cup 2% milk
- ¼ cup butter, melted
- 1 teaspoon salt
- 1 teaspoon vanilla extract
TOPPING
- ½ cup packed brown sugar
- ½ cup chopped pecans
- ¼ cup all-purpose flour
- 2 tablespoons cold butter

SIDE DISHES
Winter

FRANCES MOORE'S
CHEESY SPINACH

Winter

ENTREES

There's no doubt about it...winter truly is slow cooker season. From savory roasts that are ideal for entertaining to home-style spaghetti sauces perfect for frosty weeknights, these main courses offer heartwarming goodness when Old Man Winter comes calling.

JUDY CLARK'S SAVORY MUSHROOM & HERB PORK DINNER

Savory Mushroom & Herb Pork Dinner

After a long day, sit down to a traditional supper of pork roast with vegetables and gravy. I like to sprinkle French-fried onions on each serving. If you have extra time, crisp them in a dry skillet first.

—**JUDY CLARK** ADDISON, MI

PREP: 25 MIN. • **COOK:** 5 HOURS
MAKES: 8 SERVINGS

- 2 medium onions, chopped
- 16 fresh baby carrots
- 1 boneless pork shoulder butt roast (3 to 4 pounds)
- 1 can (10¾ ounces) condensed cream of mushroom soup, undiluted
- ¾ cup chicken broth
- 1 can (4 ounces) mushroom stems and pieces, drained
- ½ teaspoon dried thyme
- ½ teaspoon Worcestershire sauce
- ¼ teaspoon dried rosemary, crushed
- ¼ teaspoon dried marjoram
- ¼ teaspoon pepper
- 1 tablespoon cornstarch
- 2 tablespoons cold water
  French-fried onions, optional

1. Place chopped onions and carrots in a 5-qt. slow cooker. Cut the pork roast in half; add to slow cooker. In a small bowl, combine the soup, broth, mushrooms, thyme, Worcestershire sauce, rosemary, marjoram and pepper; pour over pork. Cover and cook on low for 5-6 hours or until meat is tender.

2. Remove the pork to a serving platter; keep warm. Skim the fat from the cooking juices; transfer to a large saucepan. Bring the liquid to a boil. Combine the cornstarch and water until smooth; gradually stir into the pan. Bring to a boil; cook and stir for 2 minutes or until thickened.

3. Serve pork with gravy. Sprinkle servings with French-fried onions if desired.

TOP TIP

Store spices in tightly closed glass or heavy-duty plastic containers in a cool, dry place. Avoid storing them in direct sunlight, over your stove or near other heat sources. For best flavor, keep ground spices for up to six months. They can be used if they are older, but the flavors may not be as intense. Whole spices can be stored for one to two years.

MEXICAN POT ROAST FILLING

Mexican Pot Roast Filling

Popular with my family, this filling is great for tacos, burritos and enchiladas.

—CONNIE DICAVOLI SHAWNEE, KS

PREP: 25 MIN. • **COOK:** 8 HOURS
MAKES: 9 SERVINGS

- 1½ teaspoons chili powder
- 1 teaspoon ground cumin
- ½ teaspoon smoked paprika
- ½ teaspoon crushed red pepper flakes
- ¼ teaspoon salt
- 1 boneless beef chuck roast (3 pounds)
- 1 can (4 ounces) chopped green chilies
- ½ cup chopped sweet onion
- 2 garlic cloves, minced
- ¾ cup beef broth
  Taco shells or flour tortillas (8 inches)
  Chopped tomatoes, shredded lettuce and shredded Mexican cheese blend

1. In a small bowl, combine the first five ingredients. Cut roast in half; rub spice mixture over meat. Transfer to a 3-qt. slow cooker. Top with chilies, onion and garlic. Pour the beef broth over meat. Cover and cook on low for 8-10 hours or until meat is tender.

2. Remove meat from slow cooker; shred with two forks. Skim fat from cooking juices. Return meat to slow cooker; heat through. Using a slotted spoon, place ½ cup meat mixture on each taco shell. Top with tomatoes, lettuce and cheese.

Slow-Simmering Beef Bourguignon

Chase away the chill of a winter evening with tender chunks of beef simmered in a rich sauce and ladled over noodles.

—ADELE ZUERNER ARDEN, NC

PREP: 30 MIN. • **COOK:** 8 HOURS
MAKES: 6 SERVINGS

- 3 pounds beef stew meat
- ¾ teaspoon salt
- ¾ teaspoon pepper
- 3 tablespoons all-purpose flour
- 1½ cups beef broth
- 1½ cups dry red wine or additional beef broth, divided
- ¾ pound medium fresh mushrooms, quartered
- 1 large sweet onion, chopped
- 2 medium carrots, sliced
- 1 thick-sliced bacon strip, chopped
- 2 garlic cloves, minced
- 2 tablespoons Italian tomato paste
  Hot cooked egg noodles

1. Sprinkle beef with salt and pepper. In a large nonstick skillet coated with cooking spray, brown beef in batches. Remove with a slotted spoon to a 4- or 5-qt. slow cooker. Add the flour; toss to coat. Add broth and 1 cup wine.

2. In same skillet, add mushrooms, onion, carrots and bacon; cook and stir over medium heat until carrots are tender. Add garlic; cook 1 minute longer. Add remaining wine, stirring to loosen browned bits from the pan; stir in the tomato paste. Transfer to slow cooker.

3. Cover; cook on low for 8-10 hours or until the beef is tender. Serve with egg noodles.

SLOW-SIMMERING BEEF BOURGUIGNON

SLOW-COOKED ASIAN CHICKEN

Slow-Cooked Asian Chicken

Ginger, soy sauce and slivered almonds give chicken a hint of the Far East. I fix this dish often for both family and guests.

—**RUTH SEITZ** COLUMBUS JUNCTION, IA

PREP: 20 MIN. • **COOK:** 5 HOURS
MAKES: 4-6 SERVINGS

- 1 broiler/fryer chicken (3 to 4 pounds), cut up
- 2 tablespoons canola oil
- ⅓ cup soy sauce
- 2 tablespoons brown sugar
- 2 tablespoons water
- 1 garlic clove, minced
- 1 teaspoon ground ginger
- ¼ cup slivered almonds

1. In a large skillet over medium heat, brown the chicken in oil on all sides. Transfer chicken to a 5-qt. slow cooker. Combine soy sauce, brown sugar, water, garlic and ginger; pour over chicken.

2. Cover and cook on low for 5-6 hours or until the chicken juices run clear. Remove chicken to a serving platter; sprinkle with almonds.

Parmesan Pork Roast

Here's proof that just a few everyday ingredients can make a special entree. The gravy is simply delectable!

—**KAREN WARNER** LOUISVILLE, OH

PREP: 15 MIN. • **COOK:** 5½ HOURS
MAKES: 10 SERVINGS

- 1 boneless whole pork loin roast (4 pounds)
- ⅔ cup grated Parmesan cheese
- ½ cup honey
- 3 tablespoons soy sauce
- 2 tablespoons dried basil
- 2 tablespoons minced garlic
- 2 tablespoons olive oil
- ½ teaspoon salt
- 2 tablespoons cornstarch
- ¼ cup cold water

1. Cut the roast in half. Transfer to a 3-qt. slow cooker. In a small bowl, combine Parmesan cheese, honey, soy sauce, basil, garlic, oil and salt; pour over pork. Cover and cook on low for 5½ to 6 hours or until a thermometer reads 160°.

2. Remove the roast to a serving platter; keep warm. Skim the fat from the cooking juices; transfer to a small saucepan. Bring the liquid to a boil. Combine cornstarch and cold water until smooth. Gradually stir into the pan. Bring to a boil; cook and stir for 2 minutes or until thickened. Slice roast; serve with gravy.

PARMESAN PORK ROAST

ITALIAN CHICKEN CHARDONNAY

Italian Chicken Chardonnay

On one especially busy day, I knew I would need to have dinner ready as soon as we walked in the door after work and school. So I thought fast and adapted one of our favorite skillet recipes for the slow cooker. When we got home, everyone enjoyed a delicious, satisfying supper.

—JUDY ARMSTRONG PRAIRIEVILLE, LA

PREP: 20 MIN. • **COOK:** 5 HOURS
MAKES: 6 SERVINGS

- 2 teaspoons paprika
- 1 teaspoon salt
- 1 teaspoon pepper
- ¼ teaspoon cayenne pepper
- 3 pounds bone-in chicken breast halves, skin removed
- ½ pound baby portobello mushrooms, quartered
- 1 medium sweet red pepper, chopped
- 1 medium onion, chopped
- 1 can (14 ounces) water-packed artichoke hearts, rinsed and drained
- 1½ cups chardonnay
- 1 can (6 ounces) tomato paste
- 3 garlic cloves, minced
- 2 tablespoons minced fresh thyme or 2 teaspoons dried thyme
- ¼ cup minced fresh parsley
  Hot cooked pasta
  Shredded Romano cheese

1. Combine the paprika, salt, pepper and cayenne pepper; sprinkle over the chicken. Place the chicken, portobello mushrooms, red pepper, onion and artichokes in a 5-qt. slow cooker. In a small bowl, combine the chardonnay, tomato paste, garlic and thyme; pour over vegetables.

2. Cover and cook on low for 5-6 hours or until the chicken is tender. Stir in the parsley. Serve with pasta; sprinkle with Romano cheese.

Spinach & Feta Stuffed Flank Steak

Want an entree that comes from your slow cooker but looks and tastes like something from an upscale restaurant? This is it! The flank steak wraps around a rich filling of sun-dried tomatoes, feta cheese, onion and spinach.

—**STEVEN SCHEND** GRAND RAPIDS, MI

PREP: 30 MIN. • **COOK:** 6 HOURS
MAKES: 6 SERVINGS

- 1 **beef flank steak (1½ pounds)**
- 2 **cups (8 ounces) crumbled feta cheese**
- 3 **cups fresh baby spinach**
- ½ **cup oil-packed sun-dried tomatoes, drained and chopped**
- ½ **cup finely chopped onion**
- 5 **tablespoons all-purpose flour, divided**
- ½ **teaspoon salt**
- ½ **teaspoon pepper**
- 2 **tablespoons canola oil**
- 1 **cup beef broth**
- 1 **tablespoon Worcestershire sauce**
- 2 **teaspoons tomato paste**
- ⅓ **cup dry red wine or additional beef broth**
  Hot cooked egg noodles, optional

1. Starting at one long side, cut the steak horizontally in half to within ½ in. of the opposite side. Open steak flat; cover with plastic wrap. Pound with a meat mallet to ½-in. thickness. Remove plastic.

2. Sprinkle 1 cup feta cheese over steak to within 1 in. of edges. Layer with spinach, tomatoes, onion and remaining cheese. Roll up jelly-roll style, starting with a long side; tie at 1½ in. intervals with kitchen string. Sprinkle with 2 tablespoons flour, salt and pepper.

3. In a large skillet, heat the oil over medium heat. Brown the beef on all sides; drain. Transfer to a 6-qt. oval slow cooker. In a small bowl, mix the beef broth, Worcestershire sauce and tomato paste; pour over the top. Cook, covered, on low 6-8 hours or until the meat is tender.

4. Remove the beef to a platter; keep warm. Transfer the cooking juices to a small saucepan; skim the fat. Bring the juices to a boil. Mix the remaining flour and wine until smooth; gradually stir into the pan. Return to a boil; cook and stir 1-2 minutes or until thickened. Serve beef with gravy and, if desired, egg noodles.

TOP TIP

To cook pasta more evenly, prevent it from sticking together and avoid boil-overs, always cook pasta in a large kettle or Dutch oven. Unless you have a very large kettle, don't cook more than 2 pounds at a time.

SPINACH & FETA STUFFED FLANK STEAK

COFFEE-BRAISED SHORT RIBS

Coffee-Braised Short Ribs

When autumn turns to winter, I start to crave hearty foods such as short ribs. Here's one of my favorite recipes, which perks up the meat with coffee.

—MELISSA TURKINGTON

CAMANO ISLAND, WA

PREP: 25 MIN. • **COOK:** 6 HOURS
MAKES: 8 SERVINGS

- **4 pounds bone-in beef short ribs**
- **1½ teaspoons salt, divided**
- **1 teaspoon ground coriander**
- **½ teaspoon pepper**
- **2 tablespoons olive oil**
- **1½ pounds small red potatoes, cut in half**
- **1 medium onion, chopped**
- **1 cup reduced-sodium beef broth**
- **1 whole garlic bulb, cloves separated, peeled and slightly crushed**
- **4 cups strong brewed coffee**
- **2 teaspoons red wine vinegar**
- **3 tablespoons butter**

1. Sprinkle the ribs with 1 teaspoon salt, coriander and pepper. In a large skillet, brown ribs in oil in batches. Using tongs, transfer ribs to a 6-qt. slow cooker. Add potatoes and onion.
2. Add the beef broth to the skillet, stirring to loosen the browned bits. Bring to a boil; cook until the liquid is reduced by half. Stir in the garlic and remaining salt; add to slow cooker. Pour the coffee over the top. Cover and cook on low for 6-8 hours or until the meat is tender.
3. Remove the ribs and potatoes to a serving platter; keep warm. Strain the cooking juices into a small saucepan; skim the fat. Bring to a boil; cook until the liquid is reduced by half. Stir in the red wine vinegar. Remove from the heat; whisk in the butter. Serve with ribs and potatoes.

(5)INGREDIENTS
No-Fuss Beef Roast

You'll need just a few pantry items to fix this easy roast and savory gravy.

—JEANIE BEASLEY TUPELO, MS

PREP: 10 MIN. • **COOK:** 6 HOURS
MAKES: 8 SERVINGS

- **1 boneless beef chuck roast (3 to 4 pounds)**
- **1 can (14½ ounces) stewed tomatoes, cut up**
- **1 can (10¾ ounces) condensed cream of mushroom soup, undiluted**
- **1 envelope Lipton beefy onion soup mix**
- **¼ cup cornstarch**
- **½ cup cold water**

1. Cut roast in half. Transfer to a 5-qt. slow cooker. In a small bowl, combine tomatoes, soup and soup mix; pour over meat. Cover and cook on low for 6-8 hours or until meat is tender.
2. Remove meat to a serving platter; keep warm. Skim fat from the cooking juices; transfer to a large saucepan. Bring the liquid to a boil. Combine cornstarch and water until smooth; stir into pan. Bring to a boil; cook and stir for 2 minutes or until thickened. Serve with roast.

NO-FUSS BEEF ROAST

Beef with Red Wine Gravy

Thanks to slow-cooker convenience, you can do a little prep in the morning and come home to this tasty entree.

—PRECI D'SILVA DALLAS, TX

PREP: 10 MIN. • **COOK:** 6¼ HOURS
MAKES: 6 SERVINGS

- 3 **pounds beef stew meat, cut into 1-inch cubes**
- 1 **pound medium fresh mushrooms, halved**
- 1 **medium onion, sliced**
- 1 **can (10½ ounces) condensed beef broth, undiluted**
- 1 **cup dry red wine**
- 1 **envelope brown gravy mix**
- 2 **tablespoons tomato paste**
- ¼ **teaspoon salt**
- 1 **bay leaf**
- ¼ **cup cornstarch**
- ¼ **cup cold water**
  Hot cooked egg noodles

1. Place the beef, mushrooms and onion in a 5-qt. slow cooker. In a small bowl, combine the broth, wine, gravy mix, tomato paste, salt and bay leaf. Pour over top.

2. Combine the cornstarch and cold water until smooth; stir into the meat mixture. Cover and cook on high for 15 minutes or until thickened. Serve with egg noodles.

Moist Italian Turkey Breast

Here's a recipe for some of the juiciest, most flavorful turkey I've ever tasted. It's a terrific way to eat lean!

—JESSICA KUNZ SPRINGFIELD, IL

PREP: 25 MIN. • **COOK:** 5 HOURS + STANDING
MAKES: 12 SERVINGS

- 1 **pound medium carrots, cut into 2-inch pieces**
- 2 **medium onions, cut into wedges**
- 3 **celery ribs, cut into 2-inch pieces**
- 1 **can (14½ ounces) chicken broth**
- 1 **bone-in turkey breast (6 to 7 pounds), thawed and skin removed**
- 2 **tablespoons olive oil**
- 1½ **teaspoons seasoned salt**
- 1 **teaspoon Italian seasoning**
- ½ **teaspoon pepper**

1. In a 6- or 7-qt. slow cooker, combine the carrots, onions, celery and broth. Place turkey in slow cooker. Brush with oil. Sprinkle with seasoned salt, Italian seasoning and pepper.

2. Cover and cook on low for 5-6 hours or until the meat is tender. Let stand for 15 minutes before slicing. Serve with vegetables.

Cranberry Chicken

I love collecting cookbooks and trying new recipes. With tangy cranberries, this chicken goes over especially well during the holiday season.

—EDITH HOLLIDAY FLUSHING, MI

PREP: 10 MIN. • **COOK:** 5 HOURS
MAKES: 6 SERVINGS

- 1 **broiler/fryer chicken (3 to 4 pounds), cut up**
- 1 **can (14 ounces) whole-berry cranberry sauce**
- 1 **cup barbecue sauce**
- 1 **small onion, finely chopped**
- 1 **celery rib, finely chopped**
- ½ **teaspoon salt**
- ¼ **teaspoon pepper**
  Hot cooked rice

Place chicken in a 3-qt. slow cooker. In a small bowl, combine cranberry sauce, barbecue sauce, onion, celery, salt and pepper; pour over chicken. Cover and cook on low for 5-6 hours or until chicken is tender. Serve with rice.

BEEF WITH RED WINE GRAVY

EDITH HOLLIDAY'S
CRANBERRY CHICKEN

Beef Roast Dinner

I love the fact that I can put a less expensive roast into the slow cooker and have the same mouthwatering results I would with a more costly cut. Here's a great example! If you prefer, change up the vegetables for variety or to suit your taste.

—SANDRA DUDLEY BEMIDJI, MN

PREP: 20 MIN. • **COOK:** 8 HOURS
MAKES: 10 SERVINGS

- 1 **pound red potatoes (about 4 medium), cubed**
- ¼ **pound small fresh mushrooms**
- 1½ **cups fresh baby carrots**
- 1 **medium green pepper, chopped**
- 1 **medium parsnip, chopped**
- 1 **small red onion, chopped**
- 1 **beef rump roast or bottom round roast (3 pounds)**
- 1 **can (14½ ounces) beef broth**
- ¾ **teaspoon salt**
- ¾ **teaspoon dried oregano**
- ¼ **teaspoon pepper**
- 3 **tablespoons cornstarch**
- ¼ **cup cold water**

1. Place the vegetables in a 5-qt. slow cooker. Cut the roast in half; place in slow cooker. Combine the broth, salt, oregano and pepper; pour over meat. Cover and cook on low for 8 hours or until meat is tender.
2. Remove the meat and vegetables to a serving platter; keep warm. Skim fat from cooking juices; transfer to a small saucepan. Bring liquid to a boil.
3. Combine cornstarch and water until smooth. Gradually stir into the pan. Bring to a boil; cook and stir for 2 minutes or until thickened. Serve with meat and vegetables.

BEEF ROAST DINNER

Chicken Merlot with Mushrooms

A dear friend of mine who liked cooking as much as I do shared her wonderful chicken-and-mushroom recipe with me. I think of her every time I make it, and I get requests for it all the time.

—SHELLI MCWILLIAM SALEM, OR

PREP: 10 MIN. • **COOK:** 5 HOURS
MAKES: 5 SERVINGS

- ¾ **pound sliced fresh mushrooms**
- 1 **large onion, chopped**
- 2 **garlic cloves, minced**
- 3 **pounds boneless skinless chicken thighs**
- 1 **can (6 ounces) tomato paste**
- ¾ **cup chicken broth**
- ¼ **cup merlot or additional chicken broth**
- 2 **tablespoons quick-cooking tapioca**
- 2 **teaspoons sugar**
- 1½ **teaspoons dried basil**
- ½ **teaspoon salt**
- ¼ **teaspoon pepper**
- 2 **tablespoons grated Parmesan cheese**
  Hot cooked pasta, optional

1. Place the mushrooms, onion and garlic in a 5-qt. slow cooker. Top with the chicken.
2. In a small bowl, combine tomato paste, broth, wine, tapioca, sugar, basil, salt and pepper. Pour over the chicken. Cover and cook on low for 5-6 hours or until chicken is tender.
3. Sprinkle with Parmesan cheese. Serve with pasta if desired.

MEATY SLOW-COOKED JAMBALAYA

Meaty Slow-Cooked Jambalaya

Satisfy even the biggest appetites with a Cajun classic—jazzy jambalaya cooked slowly and loaded with chicken, sausage, shrimp, veggies and spices. No one will leave the dinner table hungry!

—**DIANE SMITH** PINE MOUNTAIN, GA

PREP: 25 MIN. • **COOK:** 7 HOURS
MAKES: 12 SERVINGS (3½ QUARTS)

- 1 can (28 ounces) diced tomatoes, undrained
- 1 cup reduced-sodium chicken broth
- 1 large green pepper, chopped
- 1 medium onion, chopped
- 2 celery ribs, sliced
- ½ cup white wine or additional reduced-sodium chicken broth
- 4 garlic cloves, minced
- 2 teaspoons Cajun seasoning
- 2 teaspoons dried parsley flakes
- 1 teaspoon dried basil
- 1 teaspoon dried oregano
- ¾ teaspoon salt
- ½ to 1 teaspoon cayenne pepper
- 2 pounds boneless skinless chicken thighs, cut into 1-inch pieces
- 1 package (12 ounces) fully cooked andouille or other spicy chicken sausage links
- 2 pounds uncooked medium shrimp, peeled and deveined
- 8 cups hot cooked brown rice

1. In a large bowl, combine the first 13 ingredients. Place the chicken and sausage in a 6-qt. slow cooker. Pour tomato mixture over the top. Cook, covered, on low 7-9 hours or until chicken is tender.
2. Stir in the shrimp. Cook, covered, 15-20 minutes longer or until shrimp turn pink. Serve with rice.

French Onion Portobello Brisket

When I need something that will appeal to the crowd at a winter potluck, I rely on this brisket flavored with baby portobello mushrooms and French onion soup. A bit of fresh sage makes the perfect garnish.

—**AYSHA SCHURMAN** AMMON, ID

PREP: 20 MIN. • **COOK:** 8 HOURS
MAKES: 9 SERVINGS

- 1 fresh beef brisket (4 pounds)
- 1¾ cups sliced baby portobello mushrooms
- 1 small red onion, sliced
- 2 garlic cloves, minced
- 2 tablespoons butter
- 1 can (10½ ounces) condensed French onion soup
- ¼ cup dry white wine or beef broth
- ½ teaspoon coarsely ground pepper
  Fresh sage, optional

1. Cut the beef brisket in half; place in a 5-qt. slow cooker.
2. In a large saucepan, saute the mushrooms, onion and garlic in butter for 3-5 minutes or until the onion is crisp-tender. Add the soup, wine and pepper; mix well.
3. Pour mushroom mixture over beef. Cover and cook on low for 8-10 hours or until meat is tender. Garnish with sage if desired.
NOTE *This is a fresh beef brisket, not corned beef.*

FRENCH ONION PORTOBELLO BRISKET

TUSCAN-STYLE CHICKEN

Tuscan-Style Chicken

I discovered this Italian chicken recipe in a magazine and tweaked it to suit my family's tastes. Whenever I serve it at a potluck, dinner party or other event, no one guesses that I used a slow cooker. Crusty bread and a spinach salad with vinaigrette are my favorite sides.

—**MARY WATKINS** LITTLE ELM, TX

PREP: 25 MIN. • **COOK:** 6 HOURS
MAKES: 4 SERVINGS

- 2 cans (14½ ounces each) Italian stewed tomatoes, undrained
- 10 small red potatoes (about 1 pound), quartered
- 1 medium onion, chopped
- 1 can (6 ounces) tomato paste
- 2 fresh rosemary sprigs
- 4 garlic cloves, minced
- 1 teaspoon olive oil
- ½ teaspoon dried basil
- 1 teaspoon Italian seasoning, divided
- 1 broiler/fryer chicken (3 to 4 pounds), cut up and skin removed
- ½ teaspoon salt
- ½ teaspoon pepper
- 1 jar (5¾ ounces) pimiento-stuffed olives, drained

1. In a 5-qt. slow cooker, combine the first eight ingredients. Stir in ½ teaspoon Italian seasoning. Place the chicken on top. Sprinkle with the salt, pepper and remaining Italian seasoning. Top with olives.

2. Cover and cook on low for 6-7 hours or until the chicken is tender. Discard rosemary sprigs before serving.

Sweet and Sour Brisket

In our house, this main dish is always popular. The sweetness of the brown sugar combines with the sour splash of lemon to give the beef a tongue-tingling twist. We'd eat it every day if we could!

—**JOLIE ALBERTAZZIE** MORENO VALLEY, CA

PREP: 15 MIN. • **COOK:** 8 HOURS
MAKES: 10 SERVINGS

- 1 can (28 ounces) crushed tomatoes
- 1 medium onion, halved and thinly sliced
- ½ cup raisins
- ¼ cup packed brown sugar
- 2 tablespoons lemon juice
- 3 garlic cloves, minced
- 1 fresh beef brisket (3 pounds)
- ½ teaspoon salt
- ¼ teaspoon pepper

1. In a small bowl, combine tomatoes, onion, raisins, sugar, juice and garlic. Pour half into a 4- or 5-qt. slow cooker coated with cooking spray. Sprinkle meat with salt and pepper. Transfer to slow cooker. Top with remaining tomato mixture. Cover; cook on low for 8-10 hours or until meat is tender.

2. Remove brisket to a serving platter and keep warm. Skim fat from cooking juices. Thinly slice meat across the grain. Serve with tomato mixture.

NOTE *This is a fresh beef brisket, not corned beef.*

SWEET AND SOUR BRISKET

BAVARIAN PORK LOIN

Bavarian Pork Loin

My aunt used to make her Bavarian pork all the time, and now I do, too. With tart apples, sauerkraut, carrots and onion, it's an old-style German treat.

—EDIE DESPAIN LOGAN, UT

PREP: 25 MIN. • **COOK:** 6 HOURS + STANDING
MAKES: 10 SERVINGS

- 1 **boneless pork loin roast (3 to 4 pounds)**
- 1 **can (14 ounces) Bavarian sauerkraut, rinsed and drained**
- 1¾ **cups chopped carrots**
- 1 **large onion, finely chopped**
- ½ **cup unsweetened apple juice**
- 2 **teaspoons dried parsley flakes**
- 3 **large tart apples, peeled and quartered**

1. Cut roast in half; place in a 5-qt. slow cooker. In a small bowl, combine the sauerkraut, carrots, onion, apple juice and parsley; spoon over roast. Cover and cook on low for 4 hours.
2. Add apples to slow cooker. Cover and cook 2-3 hours longer or until meat is tender. Remove roast; let stand for 10 minutes before slicing. Serve with sauerkraut mixture.

TOP TIP

There are many varieties of tart apples to choose from, including Granny Smith, McIntosh, Cortland, Jonathan, Rome Beauty and Golden Russet. Experiment with different varieties and use your favorites.

SLOW-COOKED PORK VERDE

Slow-Cooked Pork Verde

Spice up any cold winter's night with a comforting and hearty Mexican entree. Warm French bread and a simple green salad are the perfect sides.

—*TASTE OF HOME* **TEST KITCHEN**

PREP: 15 MIN. • **COOK:** 4½ HOURS
MAKES: 8 SERVINGS

- 3 **medium carrots, sliced**
- 1 **boneless pork shoulder butt roast (3 to 4 pounds)**
- 1 **can (15 ounces) black beans, rinsed and drained**
- 1 **can (10 ounces) green enchilada sauce**
- ¼ **cup minced fresh cilantro**
- 1 **tablespoon cornstarch**
- ¼ **cup cold water**
  Hot cooked rice

1. Place the carrots in a 5-qt. slow cooker. Cut the pork roast in half; place in slow cooker. Add the beans, enchilada sauce and cilantro. Cover and cook on low for 4½ to 5 hours or until a meat thermometer reads 160°. Remove the roast to a serving platter; keep warm.

2. Skim fat from the cooking juices. Transfer the cooking liquid, carrots and beans to a small saucepan. Bring to a boil. Combine the cornstarch and water until smooth. Gradually stir into the pan. Bring to a boil; cook and stir for 2 minutes or until thickened. Serve with meat and rice.

Slow-Cooked Lasagna

This slow-cooked version of lasagna cuts really well. I also love the fact that it makes a smaller batch than many other recipes.

—**REBECCA O'BRYAN** ALVATON, KY

PREP: 45 MIN. • **COOK:** 4¼ HOURS + STANDING
MAKES: 6 SERVINGS

- 1 **pound ground beef**
- 1 **medium green pepper, chopped**
- 1 **medium onion, chopped**
- 1 **jar (24 ounces) herb and garlic pasta sauce**
- 4 **cups (16 ounces) shredded part-skim mozzarella cheese**
- 1 **carton (15 ounces) ricotta cheese**
- 1 **tablespoon Italian seasoning**
- ½ **teaspoon garlic powder**
- ½ **teaspoon salt**
- ¼ **teaspoon pepper**
- 4 **no-cook lasagna noodles**
- 2 **tablespoons shredded Parmesan cheese**

1. In a large skillet, cook the beef, green pepper and onion over medium heat until the meat is no longer pink, breaking up the meat into crumbles; drain. Stir in the pasta sauce; heat through. In a large bowl, combine the mozzarella and ricotta cheeses, Italian seasoning, garlic powder, salt and pepper.

2. Spread 1 cup meat sauce in an oval 3-qt. slow cooker. Break one lasagna noodle into three pieces. Layer 1⅓ lasagna noodles over the meat sauce, breaking the noodles to fit as necessary. Top with ⅔ cup meat sauce and 1⅓ cups cheese mixture. Repeat the layers twice. Top with the remaining sauce.

3. Cover and cook on low for 4-5 hours or until noodles are tender. Sprinkle with the Parmesan cheese. Cover and cook 15 minutes longer. Let stand for 10 minutes before cutting.

SLOW-COOKED LASAGNA

STOUT & HONEY BEEF ROAST

Stout & Honey Beef Roast

A splash of stout and honey make this beef a little different but delicious.

—*TASTE OF HOME* TEST KITCHEN

PREP: 15 MIN. • **COOK:** 8 HOURS
MAKES: 4 SERVINGS PLUS LEFTOVERS

- 8 **small red potatoes**
- 4 **medium carrots, cut into 1-inch pieces**
- 2 **medium onions, quartered**
- 1 **boneless beef chuck roast (4 pounds), trimmed**
- 1 **can (14½ ounces) beef broth**
- 1 **cup stout beer or additional beef broth**
- ½ **cup honey**
- 3 **garlic cloves, minced**
- 1 **teaspoon dried marjoram**
- 1 **teaspoon dried thyme**
- ½ **teaspoon salt**
- ½ **teaspoon pepper**
- ¼ **teaspoon ground cinnamon**
- 2 **tablespoons cornstarch**
- ¼ **cup cold water**

1. Place the potatoes, carrots and onions in a 5-qt. slow cooker. Cut the beef roast in half; transfer to the slow cooker. In a small bowl, combine the broth, beer, honey, garlic, marjoram, thyme, salt, pepper and cinnamon; pour over top. Cover and cook on low for 8-10 hours or until the meat and vegetables are tender.

2. Remove roast and cut a portion of the meat into cubes, measuring 2 cups; cover and save for another use. Slice the remaining beef and keep warm. Strain the cooking juices, reserving vegetables and 1 cup juices; skim fat from reserved juices.

3. Transfer to a small saucepan. Bring to a boil. Combine the cornstarch and water until smooth; gradually stir into the pan. Bring to a boil; cook and stir for 2 minutes or until thickened. Serve with beef and vegetables.

Cider-Glazed Ham

Apple cider, Dijon mustard and brown sugar combine for a glazed ham that's so good, you'll want to serve it for all of your winter holiday feasts.

—**JENNIFER FOOS-FURER** MARYSVILLE, OH

PREP: 15 MIN. • **COOK:** 4 HOURS
MAKES: 8 SERVINGS

- 1 **boneless fully cooked ham (3 pounds)**
- 1¾ **cups apple cider or juice**
- ¼ **cup packed brown sugar**
- ¼ **cup Dijon mustard**
- ¼ **cup honey**
- 2 **tablespoons cornstarch**
- 2 **tablespoons cold water**

1. Place the ham in a 5-qt. slow cooker. In a small bowl, combine the apple cider, brown sugar, Dijon mustard and honey; pour over the ham. Cover; cook on low for 4-5 hours or until heated through. Remove the ham and keep warm.

2. Pour cooking juices into a small saucepan. Combine the cornstarch and cold water until smooth; stir into cooking juices. Bring to a boil; cook and stir for 2 minutes or until thickened. Serve with ham.

Cornish Game Hens with Couscous

When I serve this to guests, they think I spent all day in the kitchen. I don't reveal that my slow cooker did most of the work!
—**BARBARA LENTO** HOUSTON, PA

PREP: 40 MIN. • **COOK:** 3 HOURS
MAKES: 4 SERVINGS

- 2 tablespoons all-purpose flour
- ½ teaspoon salt
- ½ teaspoon pepper
- ¼ teaspoon chili powder
- 2 Cornish game hens (20 to 24 ounces each), thawed
- 1 tablespoon olive oil
- 1 can (14½ ounces) reduced-sodium chicken broth
- 2 cups cubed peeled eggplant
- 2 large tomatoes, cut into wedges and seeded
- 2 cups sliced baby portobello mushrooms
- 1 medium onion, sliced
- 1 medium green pepper, chopped
- 1 garlic clove, minced
- 1 bay leaf
- 2 cups hot cooked couscous

1. In a large resealable plastic bag, combine the flour, salt, pepper and chili powder. Add the Cornish hens, one at a time, and shake to coat. In a large skillet, brown cornish hens in oil on all sides.

2. Transfer hens to a 5- or 6-qt. slow cooker. Add the chicken broth to the skillet, stirring to loosen browned bits from pan. Bring to a boil. Reduce heat; simmer, uncovered, for 1-2 minutes. Add to slow cooker.

3. Stir in the eggplant, tomatoes, portobello mushrooms, onion, green pepper, garlic and bay leaf. Cover and cook on low for 3-4 hours or until a thermometer reads 180° and the vegetables are tender. Discard bay leaf. To serve, split hens in half. Serve with couscous and vegetables.

⑤ INGREDIENTS
Cranberry-Dijon Pork Roast

Five basic ingredients are all you'll need to prepare a sweet, tangy pork roast.
—**MARY-ELLEN STEELE** BRISTOL, CT

PREP: 15 MIN. • **COOK:** 4 HOURS + STANDING
MAKES: 6 SERVINGS

- 1 boneless pork loin roast (2 to 3 pounds)
- 2 tablespoons butter
- 1 envelope golden onion soup mix
- 1 can (14 ounces) whole-berry cranberry sauce
- 2 teaspoons Dijon mustard

1. In a large skillet, brown roast in butter on all sides. Transfer to a 5-qt. slow cooker; sprinkle with soup mix. Add cranberry sauce to skillet, stirring to loosen browned bits from pan. Pour over roast.

2. Cover and cook on low for 4-5 hours or until the meat is tender. Remove the roast to a serving platter; let stand for 10 minutes before slicing. Stir the Dijon mustard into the cooking juices. Serve with roast.

CRANBERRY-DIJON PORK ROAST

SLOPPY JOE SUPPER

1 can (14½ ounces) beef broth
⅓ cup tomato paste
2 tablespoons brown sugar
2 tablespoons orange juice
   concentrate
2 tablespoons soy sauce
2 garlic cloves, minced
½ teaspoon salt
¼ teaspoon pepper
⅛ teaspoon ground allspice
1 domestic duck (4 to 4½ pounds),
   skinned, deboned and cut into
   cubes
¼ pound sliced fresh mushrooms
½ cup green pepper strips
   (¼-in. thick)
1 tablespoon butter
3 tablespoons cornstarch
¼ teaspoon ground ginger
¼ cup 2% milk
1 can (11 ounces) mandarin
   oranges, drained
   Hot cooked rice, optional

Sloppy Joe Supper

Break away from the bun and surprise kids with a tasty new take on popular sloppy joes. The seasoned meat combines with cheese soup and hash browns.

—**KARLA WIEDERHOLT** CUBA CITY, WI

PREP: 15 MIN. • **COOK:** 4 HOURS
MAKES: 8 SERVINGS

1 package (32 ounces) frozen
   shredded hash brown potatoes,
   thawed
1 can (10¾ ounces) condensed
   cheddar cheese soup, undiluted
1 egg, lightly beaten
1 teaspoon salt
½ teaspoon pepper
2 pounds ground beef
2 tablespoons finely chopped onion
1 can (15½ ounces) sloppy joe sauce

1. In a large bowl, combine potatoes, soup, egg, salt and pepper. Spread into a lightly greased 5-qt. slow cooker. In a large skillet, cook the beef and onion over medium heat until the meat is no longer pink, breaking up the meat into crumbles; drain. Stir in the sloppy joe sauce. Spoon over potato mixture.
2. Cover and cook on low for 4 to 4½ hours or until a thermometer reads 160°.

Saucy Mandarin Duck

This sweet-savory Asian entree is a great change of pace. For extra appeal, top each serving with toasted sesame seeds.

—*TASTE OF HOME* TEST KITCHEN

PREP: 30 MIN. + MARINATING
COOK: 4¾ HOURS • **MAKES:** 3 SERVINGS

1. For marinade, in a small bowl, combine first nine ingredients. Pour ¾ cup into a large resealable plastic bag; add duck. Seal the bag and turn to coat; refrigerate for 8 hours. Cover and refrigerate the remaining marinade.
2. Drain and discard the marinade. Transfer the duck to a 1½-qt. slow cooker; add the reserved marinade. Cover and cook on low for 4-5 hours or until tender. Skim fat.
3. In a small saucepan, saute the mushrooms and green pepper in the butter. Combine the cornstarch, ginger and milk until smooth. Stir into the mushroom mixture; add to the slow cooker.
4. Cover; cook on high for 45 minutes or until sauce is thickened. Just before serving, stir in the mandarin oranges. Serve with rice if desired.

Family-Favorite Spaghetti Sauce

A friend gave me her amazing recipe for spaghetti sauce, and now it's a tradition at our annual campers' potluck.

—HELEN ROWE SPRING LAKE, MI

PREP: 30 MIN. • **COOK:** 6 HOURS
MAKES: 9 SERVINGS (2¼ QUARTS)

- 1 pound bulk Italian sausage
- ½ pound ground beef
- 1 large onion, chopped
- 1 celery rib, chopped
- 3 garlic cloves, minced
- 1 tablespoon olive oil
- 1 can (28 ounces) diced tomatoes
- 1 can (10¾ ounces) condensed tomato soup, undiluted
- 1 can (8 ounces) mushroom stems and pieces, drained
- 1 can (8 ounces) tomato sauce
- 1 can (6 ounces) tomato paste
- 1 tablespoon sugar
- ½ teaspoon pepper
- ½ teaspoon dried basil
- ¼ teaspoon dried oregano
  Hot cooked spaghetti

1. In a large skillet, cook the sausage, beef, onion, celery and garlic in the oil over medium heat until the meat is no longer pink, breaking up the meat into crumbles; drain. In a 4-qt. slow cooker, combine the diced tomatoes, soup, mushrooms, tomato sauce, tomato paste, sugar and seasonings. Stir in the sausage mixture.

2. Cover and cook on low for 6-8 hours or until the flavors are blended. Serve with spaghetti.

FAMILY-FAVORITE SPAGHETTI SAUCE

ROSEMARY MUSHROOM CHICKEN

Rosemary Mushroom Chicken

Delicate rosemary lightly seasons the rich, creamy mushroom gravy in this delicious chicken dish. Add hot egg noodles and a simple tossed green salad on the side for a winning dinner anytime.

—GENNY MONCHAMP REDDING, CA

PREP: 30 MIN. • **COOK:** 7 HOURS
MAKES: 6 SERVINGS

- 6 chicken leg quarters, skin removed
- 2 cups sliced fresh mushrooms
- 2 cans (10¾ ounces each) condensed cream of mushroom soup, undiluted
- ½ cup white wine or chicken broth
- 1 teaspoon garlic salt
- 1 teaspoon dried rosemary, crushed
- ½ teaspoon paprika
- ⅛ teaspoon pepper
  Hot cooked egg noodles

Place the chicken in a 5- or 6-qt. slow cooker coated with cooking spray; top with the mushrooms. Combine cream of mushroom soup, white wine, garlic salt, rosemary, paprika and pepper; pour over top. Cover and cook on low for 7-9 hours or until the chicken is tender. Serve with noodles.

CHICKEN WITH BEANS AND POTATOES

Gingered Short Ribs

If you're a fan of ribs, you'll want to give this recipe a try. It's rich and robust.

—**MARIE RIZZIO** INTERLOCHEN, MI

PREP: 25 MIN. • **COOK:** 7 HOURS
MAKES: 4 SERVINGS

- 4 **pounds bone-in beef short ribs**
- 2 **medium parsnips, peeled and halved widthwise**
- 2 **large carrots, halved widthwise**
- ½ **cup reduced-sodium soy sauce**
- ⅓ **cup packed brown sugar**
- ¼ **cup rice vinegar**
- 1 **tablespoon minced fresh gingerroot**
- 2 **garlic cloves, minced**
- ½ **teaspoon crushed red pepper flakes**
- 1 **small head cabbage, quartered**
- 2 **tablespoons cornstarch**
- 2 **tablespoons cold water**
- 2 **teaspoons sesame oil**
- 4 **green onions, thinly sliced**
  Hot cooked couscous, optional

1. Place the short ribs, parsnips and carrots in a 5- or 6-qt. slow cooker. In a small bowl, combine soy sauce, brown sugar, rice vinegar, ginger, garlic and pepper flakes; pour over the short ribs. Top with the cabbage. Cover and cook on low for 7-8 hours or until the meat is tender.
2. Remove meat and vegetables to a serving platter; keep warm. Skim fat from the cooking juices; transfer to a small saucepan. Bring liquid to a boil. Combine the cornstarch and water until smooth. Gradually stir into the pan. Bring to a boil; cook and stir for 2 minutes or until thickened.
3. Stir in the oil. Serve with the meat and vegetables. Sprinkle with green onions. Serve with couscous if desired.

Chicken with Beans and Potatoes

Here's an all-in-one meal to toss together when you know your afternoon is going to be busy. Veggies and onion soup mix give the broth lots of flavor.

—*TASTE OF HOME* TEST KITCHEN

PREP: 20 MIN. • **COOK:** 4 HOURS
MAKES: 10 SERVINGS

- 2 **pounds boneless skinless chicken breasts, cut into 1-inch cubes**
- ½ **teaspoon lemon-pepper seasoning**
- 1 **tablespoon canola oil**
- 1 **pound fresh green beans, trimmed**
- 1 **pound small red potatoes, quartered**
- ½ **pound medium fresh mushrooms, halved**
- ½ **cup thinly sliced sweet onion**
- 2 **cans (14½ ounces each) chicken broth**
- 2 **tablespoons onion soup mix**
- 2 **teaspoons Worcestershire sauce**
- 1 **teaspoon grated lemon peel**
- ½ **teaspoon salt**
- ½ **teaspoon pepper**
- ¼ **teaspoon garlic powder**

1. Sprinkle the chicken with the lemon-pepper. In a large skillet, cook chicken in oil over medium heat for 4-5 minutes or until lightly browned.
2. In a 5- or 6-qt. slow cooker, layer green beans, potatoes, mushrooms and onion. In a small bowl, combine the remaining ingredients; pour over vegetables. Top with chicken.
3. Cover and cook on low for 4-5 hours or until vegetables are tender. Serve with a slotted spoon.

MARIE RIZZIO'S
GINGERED SHORT RIBS

SAVORY PORK CHOPS

Slow-Cooked Goose

My husband and I own a hunting lodge and host about 16 hunters each week at our camp. This flavorful goose is a favorite with guests. The recipe makes plenty of savory gravy, which everyone enjoys on homemade mashed potatoes.

—EDNA YLIOJA LUCKY LAKE, SK

PREP: 20 MIN. + MARINATING
COOK: 4 HOURS
MAKES: 4 SERVINGS

- ½ cup soy sauce
- 4 teaspoons canola oil
- 4 teaspoons lemon juice
- 2 teaspoons Worcestershire sauce
- 1 teaspoon garlic powder
- 2 pounds cubed goose breast
- ¾ to 1 cup all-purpose flour
- ¼ cup butter, cubed
- 1 can (10¾ ounces) condensed golden mushroom soup, undiluted
- 1⅓ cups water
- 1 envelope onion soup mix
  Hot cooked mashed potatoes, noodles or rice

1. In a large resealable plastic bag, combine the soy sauce, oil, lemon juice, Worcestershire sauce and garlic powder; add the goose breast. Seal and turn to coat. Refrigerate for 4 hours or overnight.

2. Drain and discard the marinade. Place flour in another large resealable plastic bag; add goose in batches and shake to coat. In a large skillet over medium heat, brown goose in butter on all sides.

3. Transfer to a 3-qt. slow cooker. Add the golden mushroom soup, water and onion soup mix. Cover and cook on high for 4-5 hours or until the meat is tender. Serve with mashed potatoes, noodles or rice.

Savory Pork Chops

By the time these delicious chops finish cooking, they're fall-apart tender. The tomato-based sauce is great over rice.

—LEA ANN SCHALK GARFIELD, AR

PREP: 20 MIN. • **COOK:** 5 HOURS
MAKES: 6 SERVINGS

- 6 bone-in pork loin chops (8 ounces each)
- 1 tablespoon canola oil
- 1 large onion, sliced
- 1 medium sweet red pepper, cut into rings
- 1 can (4 ounces) mushroom stems and pieces, drained
- 1 can (28 ounces) diced tomatoes, undrained
- 1 tablespoon brown sugar
- 1 tablespoon balsamic vinegar
- 2 teaspoons Worcestershire sauce
- ¼ teaspoon salt
- ¼ teaspoon pepper
  Hot cooked rice

1. In a large skillet, brown the pork chops in the oil in batches; drain. Transfer to a 5-qt. slow cooker. Layer with the onion, sweet red pepper and mushrooms. Combine the tomatoes, brown sugar, vinegar, Worcestershire sauce, salt and pepper; pour over the vegetables.

2. Cover and cook on low for 5-6 hours or until the pork chops are tender. Serve with rice.

GERMAN-STYLE BEEF ROAST

German-Style Beef Roast

My grandmother frequently treated our family to her wonderful German roast, and I adapted it for the slow cooker.
—**LOIS STANLEY** MYRTLE BEACH, SC

PREP: 10 MIN. • **COOK:** 8 HOURS
MAKES: 10 SERVINGS

- 1 boneless beef chuck roast (4 pounds), trimmed
- 1 teaspoon pepper
- 1 large onion, thinly sliced
- 1 bottle (12 ounces) beer or nonalcoholic beer
- 1 cup ketchup
- ¼ cup packed brown sugar
- ¼ cup all-purpose flour
- ¼ cup cold water

1. Cut the roast in half; sprinkle with pepper. Place the onion and roast in a 5-qt. slow cooker. In a small bowl, combine beer, ketchup and brown sugar; pour over the top. Cover and cook on low for 8-10 hours or until meat is tender.

2. Remove meat to a serving platter; keep warm. Skim fat from cooking juices; transfer to a small saucepan. Bring liquid to a boil.

3. Combine the flour and cold water until smooth; gradually stir into the saucepan. Bring to a boil; cook and stir for 2 minutes or until thickened. Serve with roast.

Beef with Red Sauce

Gingersnaps and a homemade spice rub with cocoa put a new spin on beef. You also can substitute crushed graham crackers for the cookies.
—**LAURIE TIETZE** LONGVIEW, TX

PREP: 25 MIN. • **COOK:** 8 HOURS
MAKES: 8 SERVINGS

- 2 tablespoons canola oil
- 2 tablespoons baking cocoa
- 1 tablespoon chili powder
- 2 teaspoons dried oregano
- 1 teaspoon salt
- 1 teaspoon pepper
- 1 teaspoon ground cumin
- ½ teaspoon ground cloves
- ½ teaspoon ground cinnamon
- 1 beef rump roast or bottom round roast (3 pounds), cut into 1½-in. cubes
- 1 large onion, chopped
- 1 can (28 ounces) whole tomatoes, undrained
- 3 tablespoons cider vinegar
- 1½ cups crushed gingersnap cookies (about 30 cookies)
- 9 garlic cloves, peeled
- 1 tablespoon sugar
   Hot cooked noodles, rice or mashed potatoes

1. In a small bowl, combine the first nine ingredients; set aside.

2. Place the beef and onion in a 4-qt. slow cooker; rub beef with the spice mixture. Pour the tomatoes over the top; sprinkle with the cider vinegar, crushed gingersnaps and garlic. Cover and cook on low for 8-10 hours or until the meat is tender. Stir in sugar. Serve with noodles, rice or potatoes.

BEEF WITH RED SAUCE

Slow-Cooked Meat Loaf

Chopped onion, garlic, Worcestershire sauce and cayenne—it all adds up to a great meat loaf from the slow cooker!

—*TASTE OF HOME* TEST KITCHEN

PREP: 25 MIN. • **COOK:** 4 HOURS
MAKES: 8 SERVINGS

- 6 tablespoons ketchup, divided
- 2 tablespoons Worcestershire sauce
- 12 saltines, crushed
- 1 medium onion, finely chopped
- 6 garlic cloves, minced
- 1 teaspoon paprika
- ½ teaspoon salt
- ½ teaspoon pepper
- ⅛ teaspoon cayenne pepper
- 2 pounds lean ground beef (90% lean)

1. Cut three 20x3-in. strips of heavy-duty foil; crisscross the strips so they resemble spokes of a wheel. Place strips on the bottom and up the sides of a 3-qt. slow cooker. Coat strips with cooking spray.

2. In a large mixing bowl, combine 2 tablespoons ketchup, Worcestershire sauce, saltines, onion, garlic, paprika, salt, pepper and cayenne. Crumble beef over mixture and mix well.

3. Shape mixture into a round loaf. Place in the center of the foil strips. Cover and cook on low for 4-5 hours or until no pink remains and a thermometer reads 160°.

4. Using foil strips as handles, remove meat loaf to a serving platter. Spread remaining ketchup over top.

PORK SATAY WITH RICE NOODLES

Pork Satay with Rice Noodles

I love to include peanut butter in savory recipes like my pork satay. To give that dish a restaurant-quality look and taste, I sprinkle it with minced fresh cilantro and chopped peanuts.

—STEPHANIE ANDERSON HORSEHEADS, NY

PREP: 20 MIN. • **COOK:** 4 HOURS
MAKES: 6 SERVINGS

- 1½ pounds boneless pork loin chops, cut into 2-inch pieces
- ¼ teaspoon pepper
- 1 medium onion, halved and sliced
- ⅓ cup creamy peanut butter
- ¼ cup reduced-sodium soy sauce
- ½ teaspoon onion powder
- ½ teaspoon garlic powder
- ½ teaspoon hot pepper sauce
- 1 can (14½ ounces) reduced-sodium chicken broth
- 3 tablespoons cornstarch
- 3 tablespoons water
- 9 ounces uncooked thick rice noodles
  Minced fresh cilantro and chopped peanuts, optional

1. Sprinkle pork with pepper. Place in a 3-qt. slow cooker; top with onion. In a small bowl, mix peanut butter, soy sauce, onion powder, garlic powder and pepper sauce; gradually add broth. Pour over onion. Cook, covered, on low 4-6 hours or until pork is tender.

2. Remove the pork from slow cooker and keep warm. Skim fat from cooking juices; transfer the cooking juices to a large skillet. Bring to a boil. In a small bowl, mix cornstarch and water until smooth and add to pan. Return to a boil; cook and stir 2 minutes or until thickened. Add pork; heat through.

3. Meanwhile, cook the rice noodles according to the package directions; drain. Serve with the pork mixture. If desired, sprinkle with cilantro and peanuts.

NOTE *Reduced-fat peanut butter is not recommended for this recipe.*

Italian Roast with Alfredo Potatoes

Surprise! This special dinner of beef and potatoes is easy enough for any night.
—*TASTE OF HOME* TEST KITCHEN

PREP: 20 MIN. • **COOK:** 7 HOURS
MAKES: 10 SERVINGS

- 1 boneless beef chuck roast (4 pounds), trimmed
- 1 envelope brown gravy mix
- 1 envelope Italian salad dressing mix
- ½ cup water
- 1 medium sweet red pepper, cut into 1-inch pieces
- 1 cup chopped green pepper
- ⅔ cup chopped onion
- 8 medium red potatoes, quartered
- 2 tablespoons cornstarch
- ¼ cup cold water
- ¾ cup refrigerated Alfredo sauce
- 2 tablespoons butter
- ¼ teaspoon pepper
- 1 tablespoon minced chives

1. Cut the roast in half; place in a 5-qt. slow cooker. In a small bowl, combine the brown gravy mix, salad dressing mix and water; pour over the roast. Top with peppers and onion. Cover and cook on low for 7-8 hours or until meat is tender.

2. Place the red potatoes in a large saucepan; cover with water. Bring to a boil. Reduce the heat; cover and simmer for 15-20 minutes or until tender.

3. Remove the roast from the slow cooker and keep warm. Skim the fat from the cooking juices if necessary; pour into a large saucepan. Combine the cornstarch and cold water until smooth; stir into cooking juices. Bring to a boil; cook and stir for 2 minutes or until thickened.

4. Drain the potatoes; mash with the Alfredo sauce, butter and pepper. Sprinkle with chives. Serve with beef and gravy.

CREAMY MUSHROOM HAM & POTATOES

Creamy Mushroom Ham & Potatoes

Have a refrigerator full of cooked ham from a holiday feast? Put the leftovers to good use in creamy comfort food.
—**TRACI MEADOWS** MONETT, MO

PREP: 25 MIN. • **COOK:** 4 HOURS
MAKES: 4 SERVINGS

- 1 can (10¾ ounces) condensed cream of mushroom soup, undiluted
- ½ cup 2% milk
- 1 tablespoon dried parsley flakes
- 6 medium potatoes, peeled and thinly sliced
- 1 small onion, chopped
- 1½ cups cubed fully cooked ham
- 6 slices process American cheese

In a small bowl, combine the cream of mushroom soup, milk and parsley. In a greased 3-qt. slow cooker, layer half of the potatoes, onion, ham, process American cheese and soup mixture. Repeat layers. Cover and cook on low for 4-5 hours or until potatoes are tender.

ITALIAN ROAST WITH ALFREDO POTATOES

JANE MCMILLAN'S
TURKEY MEATBALLS AND SAUCE

Turkey Meatballs and Sauce

In our house, we're always watching what we eat. I came up with a lower-fat take on meatballs that uses lean ground turkey but has all the flavor we crave.

—JANE MCMILLAN DANIA BEACH, FL

PREP: 40 MIN. • **COOK:** 6 HOURS
MAKES: 8 SERVINGS

- ¼ cup egg substitute
- ½ cup seasoned bread crumbs
- ⅓ cup chopped onion
- ½ teaspoon pepper
- ¼ teaspoon salt-free seasoning blend
- 1½ pounds lean ground turkey

SAUCE

- 1 can (15 ounces) tomato sauce
- 1 can (14½ ounces) diced tomatoes, undrained
- 1 small zucchini, chopped
- 1 medium green pepper, chopped
- 1 medium onion, chopped
- 1 can (6 ounces) tomato paste
- 2 bay leaves
- 2 garlic cloves, minced
- 1 teaspoon dried oregano
- 1 teaspoon dried basil
- 1 teaspoon dried parsley flakes
- ¼ teaspoon crushed red pepper flakes
- ¼ teaspoon pepper
- 1 package (16 ounces) whole wheat spaghetti

1. In a large bowl, combine the egg substitute, seasoned bread crumbs, onion, pepper and salt-free seasoning blend. Crumble the turkey over the mixture and mix well. Shape into 1-in. meatballs; place on a rack coated with cooking spray in a shallow baking pan. Bake at 400° for 15 minutes or until no longer pink.

2. Meanwhile, in a 4- or 5-qt. slow cooker, combine the tomato sauce, tomatoes, zucchini, green pepper, onion, tomato paste, bay leaves, garlic and seasonings. Stir in meatballs. Cover and cook on low for 6 hours.

3. Cook pasta according to package directions; serve with meat and sauce.

Spiced Cran-Apple Brisket

Both children and adults like the taste of this gravy-smothered brisket. With apples and cranberries, it's perfect for winter.

—AYSHA SCHURMAN AMMON, ID

PREP: 20 MIN. • **COOK:** 8 HOURS
MAKES: 9 SERVINGS

- 1 fresh beef brisket (4 pounds)
- ½ cup apple butter
- ¼ cup ruby port wine
- 2 tablespoons cider vinegar
- 1 teaspoon coarsely ground pepper
- ½ teaspoon salt
- 1 medium tart apple, peeled and cubed
- 1 celery rib, chopped
- 1 small red onion, chopped
- ⅓ cup dried apples, diced
- ⅓ cup dried cranberries
- 2 garlic cloves, minced
- 1 tablespoon cornstarch
- 3 tablespoons cold water

1. Cut the beef brisket in half; place in a 5-qt. slow cooker.

2. In a large bowl, combine butter, wine, vinegar, pepper and salt. Stir in tart apple, celery, onion, dried apples, cranberries and garlic. Pour over the brisket. Cover and cook on low for 8-10 hours or until meat is tender.

3. Remove meat to a serving platter; keep warm. Skim fat from cooking juices; transfer to a small saucepan. Bring liquid to a boil.

4. Combine cornstarch and water until smooth. Gradually stir into the pan. Bring to a boil; cook and stir for 2 minutes or until thickened. Serve with meat.

NOTES *This is a fresh beef brisket, not corned beef. This recipe was tested with commercially prepared apple butter.*

SPICED CRAN-APPLE BRISKET

Winter

SOUPS, STEWS & SANDWICHES

Winter is the ideal season to hunker down and cozy up with a casual meal of heartwarming goodness. Come home to a simmering slow cooker of chunky soup or stew. Or, savor a warm sandwich piled high with tender pork or beef. This chapter makes it easy!

MARTHA ANNE CARPENTER'S SLOW COOKER PULLED PORK SANDWICHES

Slow Cooker Pulled Pork Sandwiches

I frequently share this pork sandwich filling at potlucks because it can be made ahead of time—something I especially appreciate during the hectic Christmas season. The sweet-and-spicy sauce is always a hit. Set out a basket of fresh rolls and let the crowd dig in!

—**MARTHA ANNE CARPENTER** MESA, AZ

PREP: 20 MIN. • **COOK:** 8½ HOURS
MAKES: 10 SERVINGS

- 1 **boneless pork loin roast (4 pounds)**
- 1 **can (14½ ounces) beef broth**
- ⅓ **cup plus ½ cup Worcestershire sauce, divided**
- ⅓ **cup plus ¼ cup Louisiana-style hot sauce, divided**
- 1 **cup ketchup**
- 1 **cup molasses**
- ½ **cup prepared mustard**
- 10 **kaiser rolls, split**

1. Cut roast in half; place in a 5-qt. slow cooker. In a small bowl, combine broth, ⅓ cup Worcestershire sauce and ⅓ cup hot sauce; pour over roast. Cook, covered, on low 8-10 hours or until tender.

2. Remove the roast; discard cooking juices. Shred the pork with two forks. Return pork to slow cooker.

3. In a small bowl, combine ketchup, molasses, mustard and remaining Worcestershire sauce and hot sauce. Pour over the pork. Cook, covered, on high 30 minutes or until heated through. Serve on rolls.

Sausage Pumpkin Soup

Pairing sausage with pumpkin may seem unusual, but try it—you'll love it! Maple syrup adds just the right bit of sweetness.

—**LEAH CREMENT** COLLEGE STATION, TX

PREP: 20 MIN. • **COOK:** 3 HOURS 10 MIN.
MAKES: 8 SERVINGS (2 QUARTS)

- 1 **pound bulk pork sausage**
- ⅓ **cup chopped onion**
- 2 **cans (14½ ounces each) chicken broth**
- 1 **can (15 ounces) solid-pack pumpkin**
- ½ **cup maple syrup**
- 1 **teaspoon pumpkin pie spice**
- ½ **teaspoon garlic powder**
- ¼ **teaspoon ground nutmeg**
- 1 **can (12 ounces) evaporated milk**

1. In a large skillet, cook the sausage and onion until sausage is no longer pink, breaking up the sausage into crumbles; drain.

2. Transfer to a 4-qt. slow cooker. Add broth, pumpkin, syrup, pie spice, garlic powder and nutmeg. Cover and cook on low for 3-4 hours or until flavors are blended. Stir in milk; heat through.

CHILLY NIGHT BEEF STEW

Chilly Night Beef Stew

This hearty stew is a family favorite. Bread and a green salad make great sides.
—**JANINE TALBOT** SANTAQUIN, UT

PREP: 30 MIN. • **COOK:** 8½ HOURS
MAKES: 10 SERVINGS

- 6 tablespoons all-purpose flour
- 1½ teaspoons salt, divided
- 1 teaspoon pepper, divided
- 2 pounds beef stew meat
- ¼ cup olive oil
- 4 medium potatoes, peeled and cubed
- 6 medium carrots, sliced
- 2 medium onions, halved and sliced
- 4 celery ribs, sliced
- 2 cans (14½ ounces each) beef broth
- 2 cans (11½ ounces each) V8 juice
- 6 garlic cloves, minced
- 2 teaspoons Worcestershire sauce
- 2 bay leaves
- 1 teaspoon dried thyme
- ½ teaspoon dried basil
- ½ teaspoon paprika
- 6 tablespoons cornstarch
- ½ cup cold water

1. Combine the flour, 1 teaspoon salt and ½ teaspoon pepper in a large resealable plastic bag. Add beef, a few pieces at a time, and shake to coat.
2. Brown the beef in oil in batches in a large skillet. Transfer the meat and drippings to a 6-qt. slow cooker. Add the potatoes, carrots, onion and celery. Combine the beef broth, juice, garlic, Worcestershire sauce, bay leaves, thyme, basil, paprika and remaining salt and pepper; pour over top.
3. Cover; cook on low for 8-10 hours or until the meat and vegetables are tender. Combine the cornstarch and cold water until smooth; stir into stew. Cover and cook 30 minutes longer or until thickened. Discard bay leaves.

Barbecued Beef Chili

After a day of sledding or other outdoor fun, head inside for a meal of beefy chili.
—**PHYLLIS SHYAN** ELGIN, IL

PREP: 10 MIN. • **COOK:** 6 HOURS
MAKES: 12 SERVINGS

- 7 teaspoons chili powder
- 1 tablespoon garlic powder
- 2 teaspoons celery seed
- 1 teaspoon coarsely ground pepper
- ¼ to ½ teaspoon cayenne pepper
- 1 fresh beef brisket (3 to 4 pounds)
- 1 medium green pepper, chopped
- 1 small onion, chopped
- 1 bottle (12 ounces) chili sauce
- 1 cup ketchup
- ½ cup barbecue sauce
- ⅓ cup packed brown sugar
- ¼ cup cider vinegar
- ¼ cup Worcestershire sauce
- 1 teaspoon ground mustard
- 1 can (16 ounces) hot chili beans, undrained
- 1 can (15½ ounces) great northern beans, rinsed and drained

1. Combine the first five ingredients; rub over brisket. Cut into eight pieces; place in a 5-qt. slow cooker. Combine the green pepper, onion, chili sauce, ketchup, barbecue sauce, brown sugar, vinegar, Worcestershire and mustard; pour over meat. Cover; cook on high for 5-6 hours or until meat is tender.
2. Remove the meat; cool slightly. Meanwhile, skim fat from cooking juices. Shred meat with two forks; return to slow cooker. Reduce heat to low. Stir in the beans. Cover and cook for 1 hour or until heated through.
NOTE *This is a fresh beef brisket, not corned beef.*

BARBECUED BEEF CHILI

MACHETE SHREDDED BEEF SANDWICHES

Machete Shredded Beef Sandwiches

The shredded beef filling in these hefty sandwiches gets fantastic flavor from Worcestershire sauce, Dijon mustard, chili powder and more.

—*TASTE OF HOME* FOOD STYLING TEAM

PREP: 10 MIN. • **COOK:** 8 HOURS
MAKES: 12 SERVINGS

- 1 beef sirloin tip roast (2½ pounds)
- ½ teaspoon salt
- ¼ teaspoon pepper
- 1 tablespoon canola oil
- 1 cup each ketchup and water
- ½ cup chopped onion
- ⅓ cup packed brown sugar
- 3 tablespoons Worcestershire sauce
- 2 tablespoons lemon juice
- 2 tablespoons cider vinegar
- 2 tablespoons Dijon mustard
- 2 teaspoons celery seed
- 2 teaspoons chili powder
- 12 kaiser rolls, split

1. Sprinkle the roast with salt and pepper. In a nonstick skillet, brown the roast in the oil on all sides over medium-high heat; drain.

2. Transfer the roast to a 5-qt. slow cooker. Combine the ketchup, water, onion, brown sugar, Worcestershire sauce, lemon juice, vinegar, mustard, celery seed and chili powder; pour over roast.

3. Cover; cook on low for 8-10 hours or until the meat is tender. Remove meat; shred with two forks and return to the slow cooker. Spoon ½ cup meat mixture onto each roll.

Northwoods Beef Stew

Winter brings lots of snow to the woods of northern Wisconsin. A hearty meal like this one warms us from head to toe!

—**JANICE CHRISTOFFERSON**

EAGLE RIVER, WI

PREP: 30 MIN. • **COOK:** 8 HOURS
MAKES: 11 SERVINGS (2¾ QUARTS)

- 3 large carrots, cut into 1-inch pieces
- 3 celery ribs, cut into 1-inch pieces
- 1 large onion, cut into wedges
- ¼ cup all-purpose flour
- ½ teaspoon salt
- ¼ teaspoon pepper
- 3½ pounds beef stew meat
- 1 can (10¾ ounces) condensed tomato soup, undiluted
- ½ cup dry red wine or beef broth
- 2 tablespoons quick-cooking tapioca
- 1 tablespoon Italian seasoning
- 1 tablespoon paprika
- 1 tablespoon brown sugar
- 1 tablespoon beef bouillon granules
- 1 tablespoon Worcestershire sauce
- ½ pound sliced baby portobello mushrooms
  Hot cooked egg noodles

1. Place carrots, celery and onion in a 5-qt. slow cooker. In a large resealable plastic bag, combine the flour, salt and pepper. Add the beef, a few pieces at a time, and shake to coat. Place the beef over vegetables.

2. In a small bowl, combine the soup, red wine, tapioca, Italian seasoning, paprika, brown sugar, bouillon and Worcestershire sauce. Pour over top.

3. Cover; cook on low for 8-10 hours or until the meat and vegetables are tender, adding mushrooms during the last hour. Serve with noodles.

NORTHWOODS BEEF STEW

Beef Stew Provencal

When I was a child, my favorite food to order in a restaurant was beef stew. My mom and I decided to create our own and experimented in the kitchen until we came up with a recipe for the slow cooker. Everyone liked our Provencal version so much, it's now a tradition whenever the whole family gets together.

—**CHELSEY LARSEN** SPARKS, NV

PREP: 25 MIN. • **COOK:** 6 HOURS
MAKES: 6 SERVINGS

- 4 **medium carrots, chopped**
- 4 **celery ribs, chopped**
- 1 **cup beef broth**
- 1 **jar (7 ounces) julienned oil-packed sun-dried tomatoes, drained**
- 1 **can (6 ounces) tomato paste**
- 1 **small onion, chopped**
- ⅓ **cup honey**
- ¼ **cup balsamic vinegar**
- 1 **garlic clove, minced**
- 1 **teaspoon dried thyme**
- ½ **teaspoon onion powder**
- ¼ **teaspoon white pepper**
- 1 **boneless beef chuck roast (2½ pounds), cut into 2-inch cubes**
- ½ **cup all-purpose flour**
- ½ **teaspoon salt**
- ½ **teaspoon pepper**
- 2 **tablespoons olive oil**
  Hot cooked mashed potatoes or egg noodles

1. In a 4-qt. slow cooker, combine the first 12 ingredients. In a large bowl, combine beef, flour, salt and pepper; toss to coat. In a large skillet, brown the beef in oil in batches. Transfer to slow cooker.

2. Cover and cook on low for 6-8 hours or until the beef is tender. Serve with mashed potatoes.

Anything Goes Sausage Soup

I say "anything goes" for this chunky soup because it's so versatile. Over the years, I've substituted, left out and tossed in a variety of ingredients, and the end result is always absolutely delicious.

—**SHEENA WELLARD** NAMPA, ID

PREP: 40 MIN. • **COOK:** 9½ HOURS
MAKES: 15 SERVINGS (ABOUT 4 QUARTS)

- 1 **pound bulk pork sausage**
- 4 **cups water**
- 1 **can (10¾ ounces) condensed cream of mushroom soup, undiluted**
- 1 **can (10¾ ounces) condensed cheddar cheese soup, undiluted**
- 5 **medium red potatoes, cubed**
- 4 **cups chopped cabbage**
- 3 **large carrots, thinly sliced**
- 4 **celery ribs, chopped**
- 1 **medium zucchini, chopped**
- 1 **large onion, chopped**
- 5 **chicken bouillon cubes**
- 1 **tablespoon dried parsley flakes**
- ¾ **teaspoon pepper**
- 1 **can (12 ounces) evaporated milk**

1. In a large skillet, cook sausage over medium heat until no longer pink, breaking it up into crumbles; drain. Transfer to a 6-qt. slow cooker. Stir in water and soups until blended. Add the vegetables, chicken bouillon, parsley and pepper.

2. Cover; cook on low for 9-10 hours or until the vegetables are tender. Stir in the evaporated milk; cover and cook 30 minutes longer.

Wintertime Meatball Soup

When I really want to heat up a chilly evening, I stir a little chopped jalapeno pepper into my meatball soup. I think it's especially good served with fresh-baked corn bread on the side.

—**EUNICE JUSTICE** CODY, WY

PREP: 20 MIN. • **COOK:** 9 HOURS
MAKES: 15 SERVINGS (3¾ QUARTS)

- 2 **cans (16 ounces each) chili beans, undrained**
- 2 **cans (14½ ounces each) beef broth**
- 1 **jar (26 ounces) spaghetti sauce**
- ¼ **cup chopped onion**
- 3 **garlic cloves, minced**
- 1 **tablespoon Worcestershire sauce**
- 1 **teaspoon Italian seasoning**
- 1 **package (32 ounces) frozen fully cooked Italian meatballs**
- 1 **package (16 ounces) frozen mixed vegetables**
- 4 **cups chopped cabbage**

In a 6-qt. slow cooker, combine the chili beans, beef broth, spaghetti sauce, onion, garlic, Worcestershire sauce and Italian seasoning. Stir in Italian meatballs, mixed vegetables and cabbage. Cover and cook on low for 8-10 hours or until the vegetables are tender.

ANYTHING GOES SAUSAGE SOUP

WHITE CHILI

Lentil & Chicken Sausage Stew

This hearty, wholesome stew packs plenty of spicy sausage and veggies for a great cold-weather meal. One bowlful is never enough—unless it's a very large bowl that's filled to the brim!

—**JAN VALDEZ** CHICAGO, IL

PREP: 15 MIN. • **COOK:** 8 HOURS
MAKES: 6 SERVINGS

- 1 carton (32 ounces) reduced-sodium chicken broth
- 1 can (28 ounces) diced tomatoes, undrained
- 3 fully cooked spicy chicken sausage links (3 ounces each), cut into ½-inch slices
- 1 cup dried lentils, rinsed
- 1 medium onion, chopped
- 1 medium carrot, chopped
- 1 celery rib, chopped
- 2 garlic cloves, minced
- ½ teaspoon dried thyme

In a 4- or 5-qt. slow cooker, combine all ingredients. Cover; cook on low for 8-10 hours or until lentils are tender.

LENTIL & CHICKEN SAUSAGE STEW

White Chili

A friend and I experimented with cooked chicken breast and came up with our own white chili recipe. The Alfredo sauce sets it apart from other versions. Reduce the amount of cayenne pepper if your family prefers a milder taste.

—**CINDI MITCHELL** ST. MARYS, KS

PREP: 30 MIN. • **COOK:** 3 HOURS
MAKES: 12 SERVINGS (1 CUP EACH)

- 3 cans (15½ ounces each) great northern beans, rinsed and drained
- 3 cups cubed cooked chicken breast
- 1 jar (15 ounces) Alfredo sauce
- 2 cups chicken broth
- 1 to 2 cans (4 ounces each) chopped green chilies
- 1½ cups frozen gold and white corn
- 1 cup (4 ounces) shredded Monterey Jack cheese
- 1 cup (4 ounces) shredded pepper jack cheese
- 1 cup sour cream
- 1 small sweet yellow pepper, chopped
- 1 small onion, chopped
- 3 garlic cloves, minced
- 1 tablespoon ground cumin
- 1½ teaspoons white pepper
- 1 to 1½ teaspoons cayenne pepper
  Salsa verde and chopped fresh cilantro, optional

In a 5- or 6-qt. slow cooker, combine the first 15 ingredients. Cover and cook on low for 3-4 hours or until heated though, stirring once. Serve with salsa verde and cilantro if desired.

Chicago-Style Beef Sandwiches

Originally from the Windy City, I'm a fan of Chicago-style beef. Now in Florida, I fix my own sandwiches loaded with authentic flavor whenever I have a craving.
—**LOIS SZYDLOWSKI** TAMPA, FL

PREP: 30 MIN. • **COOK:** 8 HOURS
MAKES: 12 SERVINGS

- 1 **boneless beef chuck roast (4 pounds)**
- 1 **teaspoon salt**
- ¾ **teaspoon pepper**
- 2 **tablespoons olive oil**
- ½ **pound fresh mushrooms**
- 2 **medium carrots, cut into chunks**
- 1 **medium onion, cut into wedges**
- 6 **garlic cloves, halved**
- 2 **teaspoons dried oregano**
- 1 **carton (32 ounces) beef broth**
- 1 **tablespoon beef base**
- 12 **Italian rolls, split**
- 1 **jar (16 ounces) giardiniera, drained**

1. Cut roast in half; sprinkle with salt and pepper. In a large skillet, brown meat in oil on all sides. Transfer to a 5-qt. slow cooker.

2. In a food processor, combine the mushrooms, carrots, onion, garlic and oregano. Cover and process until finely chopped. Transfer to the slow cooker. Combine beef broth and base; pour over the top. Cover and cook on low for 8-10 hours or until tender.

3. Remove meat and shred with two forks. Skim fat from cooking juices. Return meat to the slow cooker; heat through. Using a slotted spoon, serve beef on buns; top with giardiniera.

NOTE *Look for beef base near the broth and bouillon.*

CHICAGO-STYLE BEEF SANDWICHES

Vegetarian Stew in Bread Bowls

After our third child was born, I didn't have a lot of time to spend in the kitchen, so my husband bought a slow cooker. This was our first meal out of it, and it was great!
—**MARIA KELLER** ANTIOCH, IL

PREP: 30 MIN. • **COOK:** 8 ½ HOURS
MAKES: 10 SERVINGS

- 3 **cups cubed red potatoes (about 4 medium)**
- 2 **cups chopped celery (about 4 ribs)**
- 2 **medium leeks (white portion only), cut into ½-inch pieces**
- 1¾ **cups coarsely chopped peeled parsnips (about 2 medium)**
- 1½ **cups chopped carrots (about 3 medium)**
- 1 **can (28 ounces) Italian crushed tomatoes**
- 1 **can (14½ ounces) vegetable broth**
- 2 **teaspoons sugar**
- ½ **teaspoon salt**
- ½ **teaspoon dried thyme**
- ½ **teaspoon dried rosemary, crushed**
- 3 **tablespoons cornstarch**
- 3 **tablespoons cold water**
- 10 **round loaves sourdough bread (8 to 9 ounces each)**

1. In a 4- or 5-qt. slow cooker, combine the first 11 ingredients. Cook, covered, on low 8-9 hours or until vegetables are tender.

2. In a small bowl, mix the cornstarch and water until smooth. Stir into stew. Cook, covered, on high 30 minutes or until thickened.

3. Cut a thin slice off the top of each bread loaf. Hollow out the bottoms of the loaves, leaving ½-in.-thick shells (save removed bread for another use). Serve stew in bread bowls.

MARIA KELLER'S
VEGETARIAN STEW IN BREAD BOWLS

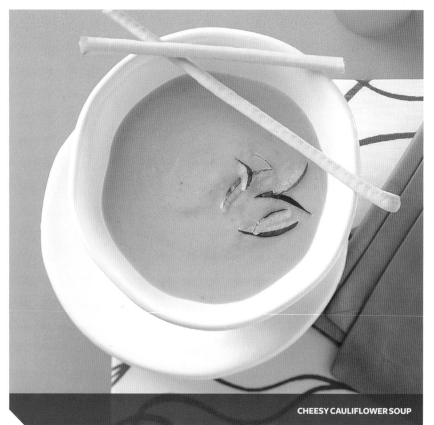

CHEESY CAULIFLOWER SOUP

Ham and Black Bean Soup

My husband likes black beans, so I tried this recipe for him. I ended up enjoying it every bit as much as he did! Even more compliments came from our neighbors, who stopped by and stayed for supper.

—**LAURA MEURER** GREEN BAY, WI

PREP: 25 MIN. • **COOK:** 4 HOURS
MAKES: 8 SERVINGS (ABOUT 2 QUARTS)

- 3 cans (15 ounces each) black beans, rinsed and drained
- 2 cans (14½ ounces each) beef broth
- 1 can (14½ ounces) diced tomatoes, undrained
- 1½ cups cubed fully cooked ham
- 1 can (4 ounces) chopped green chilies
- ¼ cup red wine vinegar
- 1 large onion, chopped
- 3 garlic cloves, minced
- 1 teaspoon dried oregano
- 1 teaspoon dried thyme
- 1 teaspoon pepper

In a 3-qt. slow cooker, combine all ingredients. Cover and cook on high for 4-5 hours or until onion is tender.

Cheesy Cauliflower Soup

Here's a true winter treat. If you'd prefer to make it chunky rather than smooth, skip using the blender—just stir in the cheese and cream, then cook everything on high heat until the cheese is melted.

—**SHERYL PUNTER** WOODSTOCK, ON

PREP: 25 MIN. • **COOK:** 5½ HOURS
MAKES: 9 SERVINGS (2¼ QUARTS)

- 1 large head cauliflower, broken into florets
- 2 celery ribs
- 2 large carrots
- 1 large green pepper
- 1 small sweet red pepper
- 1 medium red onion
- 4 cups chicken broth
- ½ teaspoon Worcestershire sauce
- ¼ teaspoon salt
- ⅛ teaspoon pepper
- 2 cups (8 ounces) shredded cheddar cheese
- 2 cups half-and-half cream

1. Place cauliflower in a 4-qt. slow cooker. Chop celery, carrots, peppers and onion; add to slow cooker. Stir in broth, Worcestershire sauce, salt and pepper. Cover and cook on low for 5-6 hours or until vegetables are tender.
2. In a blender, process the soup in batches until smooth. Return all to the slow cooker; stir in cheese and cream. Cover and cook on high for 30 minutes or until cheese is melted.

HAM AND BLACK BEAN SOUP

Slow Cooker Split Pea Soup

When I have extra ham from a holiday feast or other meal, I never wonder how I'm going to use up the leftovers. I just get busy making my favorite pea soup!

—**PAMELA CHAMBERS** WEST COLUMBIA, SC

PREP: 15 MIN. • **COOK:** 8 HOURS
MAKES: 8 SERVINGS

- 1 package (16 ounces) dried green split peas, rinsed
- 2 cups cubed fully cooked ham
- 1 large onion, chopped
- 1 cup julienned or chopped carrots
- 3 garlic cloves, minced
- ½ teaspoon dried rosemary, crushed
- ½ teaspoon dried thyme
- 1 carton (32 ounces) reduced-sodium chicken broth
- 2 cups water

In a 4- or 5-qt. slow cooker, combine all ingredients. Cover and cook on low for 8-10 hours or until peas are tender.

Easy Ropa Vieja Stew

I love the fact that I can use a slow cooker to prepare this classic Cuban stew. It has all of the bold flavors we crave without requiring a lot of hands-on time.

—**DENISE NYLAND** PANAMA CITY, FL

PREP: 25 MIN. • **COOK:** 6 HOURS
MAKES: 8 SERVINGS

- 2 pounds boneless beef chuck roast, cut in half
- 2 tablespoons olive oil
- 2 large onions, coarsely chopped
- 2 large green peppers, coarsely chopped
- 4 jalapeno peppers, seeded and minced
- 1 habanero pepper, seeded and minced
- 3 cans (14½ ounces each) diced tomatoes, undrained
- ½ cup water
- 6 garlic cloves, minced
- 2 tablespoons minced fresh cilantro
- 4 teaspoons beef bouillon granules
- 2 teaspoons pepper
- 1½ teaspoons ground cumin
- 1 teaspoon dried oregano
- ½ cup pimiento-stuffed olives, coarsely chopped
  Hot cooked rice, optional

1. In a large skillet, brown beef in oil on all sides. Transfer meat to a 5-qt. slow cooker. Add onions and peppers. Combine tomatoes, water, garlic, cilantro, beef bouillon, pepper, cumin and oregano; pour over vegetables.

2. Cover; cook on low for 6-8 hours or until meat is tender. Remove beef; cool slightly. Skim fat from cooking juices; stir in olives. Shred beef with two forks and return to slow cooker; heat through. Serve with rice if desired.

NOTE *Wear disposable gloves when cutting hot peppers; the oils can burn skin. Avoid touching your face.*

EASY ROPA VIEJA STEW

Spicy Chicken and Hominy Soup

In my native New Mexico, this is known as posole and is traditionally eaten on New Year's Day for good luck. It seems everyone has their own special version. Mine settles the age-old question—"Red or green chiles?"—by using both.

—JANET CHRISTINE MCDANIEL
ARLINGTON, TX

PREP: 15 MIN. • **COOK:** 4 HOURS
MAKES: 4 SERVINGS

- 1 pound boneless skinless chicken breasts, cubed
- 2 tablespoons olive oil
- 1 medium onion, chopped
- 3 garlic cloves, minced
- 2 chipotle peppers in adobo sauce
- 2 cans (14½ ounces each) chicken broth, divided
- 1 can (15 ounces) hominy, rinsed and drained
- 1 can (4 ounces) chopped green chilies
- 1 teaspoon dried oregano
- 1 teaspoon ground cumin
- ¼ teaspoon pepper

1. In a large skillet, brown the chicken in oil. With a slotted spoon, transfer chicken to a 3- or 4-qt. slow cooker. In the same skillet, saute onion and garlic in drippings until tender; add to chicken.
2. Place chipotle peppers and ¼ cup broth in a blender or food processor; cover and process until blended. Add to chicken mixture. Stir in the hominy, chilies, seasonings and remaining broth. Cover and cook on low for 4-5 hours or until chicken is tender.

Hungarian Goulash

Talk about heirloom recipes! As a child, my mother enjoyed many bowlfuls of my grandmother's wonderful goulash. Later, Mom fixed it for her own family, and I couldn't get enough.

—MARCIA DOYLE POMPANO, FL

PREP: 20 MIN. • **COOK:** 7 HOURS
MAKES: 12 SERVINGS

- 3 medium onions, chopped
- 2 medium carrots, chopped
- 2 medium green peppers, chopped
- 3 pounds beef stew meat, cut into 1-inch cubes
- ½ teaspoon plus ¼ teaspoon salt, divided
- ½ teaspoon plus ¼ teaspoon pepper, divided
- 2 tablespoons olive oil
- 1½ cups reduced-sodium beef broth
- ¼ cup all-purpose flour
- 3 tablespoons paprika
- 2 tablespoons tomato paste
- 1 teaspoon caraway seeds
- 1 garlic clove, minced
- Dash sugar
- 12 cups uncooked whole wheat egg noodles
- 1 cup (8 ounces) reduced-fat sour cream

1. Place the onions, carrots and green peppers in a 5-qt. slow cooker. Sprinkle the meat with ½ teaspoon salt and ½ teaspoon pepper. In a large skillet, brown meat in oil in batches. Transfer to slow cooker.
2. Add the beef broth to the skillet, stirring to loosen the browned bits from the pan. Combine the flour, paprika, tomato paste, caraway seeds, garlic, sugar and remaining salt and pepper; stir into the skillet. Bring to a boil; cook and stir for 2 minutes or until thickened. Pour over the meat. Cover and cook on low for 7-9 hours or until meat is tender.
3. Meanwhile, cook the egg noodles according to package directions. Stir sour cream into slow cooker. Drain noodles; serve with goulash.

HUNGARIAN GOULASH

Cream of Potato & Cheddar Soup

To me, this golden cream soup is total comfort—combined with the simplicity of slow cooking! My daughter contributes the Yukon Gold potatoes from her garden. Make each serving even more special with garnishes like crispy croutons, crumbled bacon or shredded cheddar cheese.

—CINDI BAUER MARSHFIELD, WI

PREP: 25 MIN. • **COOK:** 7½ HOURS
MAKES: 11 SERVINGS (2¾ QUARTS)

8 medium Yukon Gold potatoes, peeled and cubed
1 large red onion, chopped
1 celery rib, chopped
2 cans (14½ ounces each) reduced-sodium chicken broth
1 can (10¾ ounces) condensed cream of celery soup, undiluted
1 teaspoon garlic powder
½ teaspoon white pepper
1½ cups (6 ounces) shredded sharp cheddar cheese
1 cup half-and-half cream

Optional toppings: salad croutons, crumbled cooked bacon and additional shredded sharp cheddar cheese

1. Combine the first seven ingredients in a 4- or 5-qt. slow cooker. Cover and cook on low for 7-9 hours or until potatoes are tender.
2. Stir in the cheese and cream. Cover and cook 30 minutes longer or until cheese is melted. Garnish servings with toppings of your choice.

CRYSTAL KELSO'S
BROCCOLI POTATO SOUP

Broccoli Potato Soup

Even people who don't normally care for broccoli are bound to love this rich, creamy blend. Havarti cheese, chunks of red potatoes and plenty of fresh herbs give it wonderful flavor. The red pepper flakes add a bit of a kick, too!

—CRYSTAL KELSO SANDY, OR

PREP: 25 MIN. • **COOK:** 4½ HOURS
MAKES: 8 CUPS (2 QUARTS)

- 1 pound small red potatoes, cubed
- 1 large onion, chopped
- 1 large carrot, coarsely chopped
- 7 garlic cloves, minced
- 3 cups water
- 1 can (14½ ounces) condensed cream of broccoli soup, undiluted
- 1 teaspoon each minced fresh thyme, basil and parsley
- 1 teaspoon garlic powder
- ½ teaspoon salt
- ½ teaspoon crushed red pepper flakes
- ¼ teaspoon pepper
- 2 cups frozen chopped broccoli, thawed and drained
- 1 cup (4 ounces) shredded Havarti cheese

1. Place the red potatoes, onion, carrot and garlic in a 4- or 5-qt. slow cooker. Add the water, cream of broccoli soup and seasonings. Cover and cook on low for 4-5 hours or until heated through.
2. Stir in the broccoli and Havarti cheese. Cover and cook for 30 minutes or until the broccoli is tender.

Slow & Easy Minestrone

What's better on a cold day than hot soup? I often choose my minestrone because it's so simple to make—and I don't have a lot of cleanup to do after a relaxing meal.

—SALLY GOEB NEW EGYPT, NJ

PREP: 25 MIN. • **COOK:** 7 HOURS
MAKES: 6 SERVINGS (2¼ QUARTS)

- 1 can (28 ounces) diced tomatoes, undrained
- 3 celery ribs, cut into ½-inch slices
- 2 medium carrots, cut into ½-inch slices
- 2 small zucchini, halved and cut into ¾-inch slices
- 2 cups vegetable broth
- 1 cup shredded cabbage
- ¼ pound sliced fresh mushrooms
- 1 small onion, chopped
- 2 garlic cloves, minced
- 1 teaspoon dried basil
- 1 teaspoon salt
- ⅓ cup quick-cooking barley
- 1 can (15 ounces) white kidney or cannellini beans, rinsed and drained

1. In a 4- or 5-qt. slow cooker, combine the first 11 ingredients. Cover and cook on low for 7-9 hours.
2. Cook barley according to package directions; stir into soup. Add beans; heat through.

SLOW & EASY MINESTRONE

Winter

DESSERTS

From Gingerbread Pudding Cake perfect for cozy nights at home to Chocolate Peanut Drops ideal for holiday cookie trays, the comforting desserts here are sure to bring smiles and warm everyone on even the chilliest winter night.

LATONA DWYER'S
SLOW COOKER
CHOCOLATE LAVA CAKE

Slow Cooker Chocolate Lava Cake

What a great way to surprise your family on a busy winter night. Everyone who tries this dessert falls in love with it. Try using a slow cooker liner. It makes cleanup a breeze.
—**LATONA DWYER** PALM BEACH GARDENS, FL

PREP: 15 MIN. • **COOK:** 3 HOURS
MAKES: 12 SERVINGS

- 1 **package devil's food cake mix (regular size)**
- 1⅔ **cups water**
- 3 **eggs**
- ⅓ **cup canola oil**
- 2 **cups cold 2% milk**
- 1 **package (3.9 ounces) instant chocolate pudding mix**
- 2 **cups (12 ounces) semisweet chocolate chips**

1. In a large bowl, combine the cake mix, water, eggs and oil; beat on low speed for 30 seconds. Beat on medium for 2 minutes. Transfer to a greased 4-qt. slow cooker.
2. In another bowl, whisk milk and pudding mix for 2 minutes. Let stand for 2 minutes or until soft-set. Spoon over cake batter; sprinkle with the chocolate chips. Cover and cook on high for 3-4 hours or until a toothpick inserted in cake portion comes out with moist crumbs. Serve warm.

Apple Comfort

Years ago, we were without electricity for nine days during an ice storm. Luckily I was able run the slow cooker from our generator. The drastic situation called for dessert, and this has been a favorite since.
—**AWYNNE THURSTENSON**
SILOAM SPRINGS, AR

PREP: 30 MIN. • **COOK:** 4 HOURS
MAKES: 8 SERVINGS

- 8 **medium tart apples, peeled and sliced**
- 1 **cup sugar**
- ¼ **cup all-purpose flour**
- 2 **teaspoons ground cinnamon**
- 2 **eggs**
- 1 **cup heavy whipping cream**
- 1 **teaspoon vanilla extract**
- 1 **cup graham cracker crumbs**
- ½ **cup chopped pecans**
- ¼ **cup butter, melted**
  Vanilla ice cream, optional

1. In a large bowl, combine the apples, sugar, flour and cinnamon. Spoon into a greased 3-qt. slow cooker. Whisk the eggs, cream and vanilla; pour over apple mixture. Combine the cracker crumbs, pecans and butter; sprinkle over top.
2. Cover and cook on low for 4-5 hours or until apples are tender. Serve warm with ice cream if desired.

BUTTERSCOTCH-PECAN BREAD PUDDING

Hot Caramel Apples

Who ever thinks of making dessert in a slow cooker? This old-time favorite goes together quickly, and it's such a treat to come home to the comforting aroma of cinnamony baked apples.

—PAT SPARKS ST. CHARLES, MO

PREP: 15 MIN. • **COOK:** 4 HOURS
MAKES: 4 SERVINGS

- 4 **large tart apples, cored**
- ½ **cup apple juice**
- ½ **cup packed brown sugar**
- 12 **Red Hots**
- ¼ **cup butter**
- 8 **caramels**
- ¼ **teaspoon ground cinnamon**
    Whipped cream, optional

1. Peel about ¾ in. off the top of each apple; place in a 3-qt. slow cooker. Pour juice over apples. Fill the center of each apple with 2 tablespoons of sugar, three Red Hots, 1 tablespoon butter and two caramels. Sprinkle with cinnamon.
2. Cover and cook on low for 4-6 hours or until the apples are tender. Serve immediately with whipped cream if desired.

HOT CARAMEL APPLES

Butterscotch-Pecan Bread Pudding

Bread pudding fans just might hoard this yummy butterscotch dessert themselves. With whipped cream and a butterscotch drizzle, it's irresistible.

—LISA VARNER EL PASO, TX

PREP: 15 MIN. • **COOK:** 3 HOURS
MAKES: 8 SERVINGS

- 9 **cups cubed day-old white bread (about 8 slices)**
- ½ **cup chopped pecans**
- ½ **cup butterscotch chips**
- 4 **eggs**
- 2 **cups half-and-half cream**
- ½ **cup packed brown sugar**
- ½ **cup butter, melted**
- 1 **teaspoon vanilla extract**
    Whipped cream and butterscotch ice cream topping

1. Place the bread, pecans and butterscotch chips in a greased 4-qt. slow cooker. In a large bowl, whisk eggs, cream, brown sugar, melted butter and vanilla until blended. Pour over bread mixture; stir gently to combine.
2. Cook, covered, on low 3-4 hours or until a knife inserted in center comes out clean. Serve warm with whipped cream and butterscotch topping.

BURGUNDY PEARS

Burgundy Pears

These warm spiced pears elevate slow cooking to a new level of elegance, yet they're incredibly easy to make. Your friends won't believe this fancy-looking dessert came from a slow cooker.

—**ELIZABETH HANES** PERALTA, NM

PREP: 10 MIN. • **COOK:** 3 HOURS
MAKES: 6 SERVINGS

6	medium ripe pears
⅓	cup sugar
⅓	cup Burgundy wine or grape juice
3	tablespoons orange marmalade
1	tablespoon lemon juice
¼	teaspoon ground cinnamon
¼	teaspoon ground nutmeg
	Dash salt
	Whipped cream cheese

1. Peel pears, leaving stems intact. Core from the bottom. Stand pears upright in a 5-qt. slow cooker. In a small bowl, combine the sugar, wine or grape juice, marmalade, lemon juice, cinnamon, nutmeg and salt. Carefully pour over pears.

2. Cover pears and cook on low for 3-4 hours or until tender. To serve, drizzle with sauce and garnish with whipped cream cheese.

Slow Cooker Apple Pudding Cake

A comforting dessert like this is a superb treat on a chilly night. Since the pudding is made in a slow cooker, it does not require any attention from you, so it's great when entertaining. It separates into three comforting layers—apples, cake and sauce. Serve with a bit of sour cream.

—**ELLEN SCHROEDER** REEDSBURG, WI

PREP: 15 MIN. • **COOK:** 2 HOURS
MAKES: 10 SERVINGS

2	cups all-purpose flour
⅔	cup plus ¼ cup sugar, divided
3	teaspoons baking powder
1	teaspoon salt
½	cup cold butter
1	cup 2% milk
2	medium tart apples, peeled and chopped
1½	cups orange juice
½	cup honey
2	tablespoons butter, melted
1	teaspoon ground cinnamon
1⅓	cups sour cream
¼	cup confectioners' sugar

1. In a small bowl, combine the flour, ⅔ cup sugar, baking powder and salt. Cut in butter until mixture resembles coarse crumbs. Stir in milk just until moistened. Spread into the bottom of a greased 4- or 5-qt. slow cooker; sprinkle apples over batter.

2. In a small bowl, combine the orange juice, honey, melted butter, cinnamon and remaining sugar; pour over apples. Cover and cook on high for 2-3 hours or until apples are tender.

3. In a small bowl, combine sour cream and confectioners' sugar. Serve with warm pudding cake.

SLOW COOKER APPLE PUDDING CAKE

CHOCOLATE PEANUT DROPS

(5) INGREDIENTS
Chocolate Peanut Drops

This is a recipe that I got from a friend, who got it from her sister, and among the three of us we have handed it out everywhere! The chocolaty candies couldn't be easier to make in the slow cooker. Depending on the size of your spoon, you can get at least several dozen candies from this one recipe. It's so easy and great for gifts.

—ANITA BELL HERMITAGE, TN

PREP: 20 MIN. **• COOK:** 1½ HOURS + STANDING
MAKES: ABOUT 11 DOZEN

- 4 **ounces German sweet chocolate, chopped**
- 1 **package (12 ounces) semisweet chocolate chips**
- 4 **packages (10 to 12 ounces each) white baking chips**
- 2 **jars (16 ounces each) lightly salted dry roasted peanuts**

1. In a 6-qt. slow cooker, layer ingredients in order listed (do not stir). Cover and cook on low for 1½ hours. Stir to combine. (If chocolate is not melted, cover and cook 15 minutes longer; stir. Repeat in 15-minute increments until chocolate is melted.)

2. Drop mixture by rounded tablespoonfuls onto waxed paper. Let stand until set. Store in an airtight container at room temperature.

TOP TIP

Chocolate Peanut Drops are a great way to bring kids into the kitchen. Once the chocolate has melted and the ingredients are stirred together, kids can drop the mixture onto the waxed paper.

Slow Cooker Baked Apples

Coming home to this irresistible dessert on a dreary day is just wonderful; it's slow-cooker easy.

—**EVANGELINE BRADFORD** ERLANGER, KY

PREP: 25 MIN. • **COOK:** 4 HOURS
MAKES: 6 SERVINGS

- 6 **medium tart apples**
- ½ **cup raisins**
- ⅓ **cup packed brown sugar**
- 1 **tablespoon grated orange peel**
- 1 **cup water**
- 3 **tablespoons thawed orange juice concentrate**
- 2 **tablespoons butter**

1. Core apples and peel top third of each if desired. Combine the raisins, brown sugar and orange peel; spoon into apples. Place in a 5-qt. slow cooker.

2. Pour water around apples. Drizzle with orange juice concentrate. Dot with butter. Cover and cook on low for 4-5 hours or until apples are tender.

Spiced Sweet Potato Pudding

Here's one of my favorite desserts! This treat's rich flavors are well suited to the chillier months. I like to serve it over a few slices of pound cake or a scoop of vanilla ice cream.

—**AYSHA SCHURMAN** AMMON, ID

PREP: 15 MIN. • **COOK:** 3 HOURS
MAKES: 7 SERVINGS

- 2 **cans (15¾ ounces each) sweet potatoes, drained and mashed**
- 3 **eggs**
- 1 **can (12 ounces) evaporated milk**
- ⅔ **cup biscuit/baking mix**
- ½ **cup packed brown sugar**
- ½ **cup apple butter**
- 2 **tablespoons butter, softened**
- 2 **teaspoons vanilla extract**
- ⅓ **cup finely chopped pecans**
   Pound cake, optional

In a large bowl, beat the first eight ingredients until well-blended. Pour into a greased 3-qt. slow cooker. Sprinkle with pecans. Cover and cook on low for 3-4 hours or until a thermometer reads 160°. Serve with pound cake if desired.

NOTE *This recipe was tested with commercially prepared apple butter.*

Caramel Pear Pudding

This is a lovely winter dessert that uses seasonally available pears. It's easy to fix and a yummy treat after meals. I enjoy snacking on it in front of the fireplace.

—**DIANE HALFERTY** CORPUS CHRISTI, TX

PREP: 20 MIN. • **COOK:** 3 HOURS
MAKES: 10 SERVINGS

- 1 **cup all-purpose flour**
- ½ **cup sugar**
- 1½ **teaspoons baking powder**
- ½ **teaspoon ground cinnamon**
- ¼ **teaspoon salt**
- ⅛ **teaspoon ground cloves**
- ½ **cup 2% milk**
- 4 **medium pears, peeled and cubed**
- ½ **cup chopped pecans**
- ¾ **cup packed brown sugar**
- ¼ **cup butter, softened**
- ½ **cup boiling water**
   Vanilla ice cream, optional

1. In a large bowl, combine flour, sugar, baking powder, cinnamon, salt and cloves. Stir in milk until smooth. Add pears and pecans. Spread evenly into a 3-qt. slow cooker coated with cooking spray.

2. In a small bowl, combine brown sugar and butter; stir in boiling water. Pour over batter (do not stir). Cover and cook on low for 3-4 hours or until pears are tender. Serve warm with ice cream if desired.

SLOW COOKER BAKED APPLES

DIANE HALFERTY'S
CARAMEL PEAR PUDDING

SLOW-COOKED BREAD PUDDING

Slow-Cooked Bread Pudding

My warm and hearty dessert is perfect on any cold, blustery winter evening. And the slow cooker fills your kitchen with an amazing aroma. My stomach is growling just thinking about it!

—**MAIAH MILLER** EUGENE, OR

PREP: 15 MIN. • **COOK:** 3 HOURS
MAKES: 8 SERVINGS

- 4 whole wheat bagels, split and cut into ¾-inch pieces
- 1 large tart apple, peeled and chopped
- ½ cup dried cranberries
- ¼ cup golden raisins
- 2 cups fat-free milk
- 1 cup egg substitute
- ½ cup sugar
- 2 tablespoons butter, melted
- 1 teaspoon ground cinnamon
- 1 teaspoon vanilla extract

1. In a 3-qt. slow cooker coated with cooking spray, combine the bagels, apple, cranberries and raisins. In a large bowl, whisk the milk, egg substitute, sugar, butter, cinnamon and vanilla. Pour over bagel mixture and stir to combine; gently press bagels down into milk mixture.
2. Cover and cook on low for 3-4 hours or until a knife inserted near the center comes out clean.

Warm Rocky Road Cake

I didn't think a cake made in a slow cooker could be so beautiful and delicious. When it's warm it reminds me of an ooey-gooey lava cake.

—**SCARLETT ELROD** NEWNAN, GA

PREP: 20 MIN. • **COOK:** 3 HOURS
MAKES: 16 SERVINGS

- 1 package German chocolate cake mix (regular size)
- 1 package (3.9 ounces) instant chocolate pudding mix
- 1 cup (8 ounces) sour cream
- ⅓ cup butter, melted
- 3 eggs
- 1 teaspoon vanilla extract
- 3¼ cups 2% milk, divided
- 1 package (3.4 ounces) cook-and-serve chocolate pudding mix
- 1½ cups miniature marshmallows
- 1 cup (6 ounces) semisweet chocolate chips
- ½ cup chopped pecans, toasted
  Vanilla ice cream, optional

1. In a large bowl, combine the first six ingredients; add 1¼ cups milk. Beat on low speed 30 seconds. Beat on medium 2 minutes. Transfer to a greased 4- or 5-qt. slow cooker. Sprinkle cook-and-serve pudding mix over batter.
2. In a small saucepan, heat the remaining milk until bubbles form around sides of pan; gradually pour over dry pudding mix.
3. Cook, covered, on high 3-4 hours or until a toothpick inserted in cake portion comes out with moist crumbs.
4. Turn off slow cooker. Sprinkle marshmallows, chocolate chips and pecans over cake; let stand, covered, 5 minutes or until marshmallows begin to melt. Serve warm. If desired, top with ice cream.
NOTE *To toast nuts, spread in a 15x10x1-in. baking pan. Bake at 350° for 5-10 minutes or until lightly browned, stirring occasionally.*

WARM ROCKY ROAD CAKE

CRANBERRY-APPLE CRISP

Cranberry-Apple Crisp

Served with ice cream, this heartwarming dessert promises to become a favorite in your house! I love that the slow cooker simmers up the treat on its own.

—MARY JONES WILLIAMSTOWN, WV

PREP: 20 MIN. • **COOK:** 2 HOURS
MAKES: 10 SERVINGS

- 5 **large apples, peeled and sliced**
- 1 **cup fresh or frozen cranberries, thawed**
- ¾ **cup packed brown sugar, divided**
- 2 **tablespoons lemon juice**
- ½ **cup all-purpose flour**
  Dash salt
- ⅓ **cup cold butter**
  Vanilla ice cream
  Toasted chopped pecans

1. In a greased 5-qt. slow cooker, combine apples, cranberries, ¼ cup brown sugar and lemon juice. In a small bowl, mix the flour, salt and remaining brown sugar; cut in butter until crumbly. Sprinkle over fruit mixture.

2. Cook, covered, on high 2 to 2½ hours or until apples are tender. Serve with ice cream and pecans.

Gingerbread Pudding Cake

A handful of spices and half a cup of molasses give this delightful dessert a yummy old-fashioned flavor. It's pretty, too, with a dollop of whipped cream and a mint sprig on top.

—BARBARA COOK YUMA, AZ

PREP: 20 MIN. • **COOK:** 2 HOURS + STANDING
MAKES: 6-8 SERVINGS

- ¼ **cup butter, softened**
- ¼ **cup sugar**
- 1 **egg white**
- 1 **teaspoon vanilla extract**
- ½ **cup molasses**
- 1 **cup water**
- 1¼ **cups all-purpose flour**
- ¾ **teaspoon baking soda**
- ½ **teaspoon ground cinnamon**
- ½ **teaspoon ground ginger**
- ¼ **teaspoon salt**
- ¼ **teaspoon ground allspice**
- ⅛ **teaspoon ground nutmeg**
- ½ **cup chopped pecans**

TOPPING

- 6 **tablespoons brown sugar**
- ¾ **cup hot water**
- ⅔ **cup butter, melted**

1. In a large bowl, cream butter and sugar until light and fluffy. Beat in egg white and vanilla. Combine molasses and water. Combine the flour, baking soda, cinnamon, ginger, salt, allspice and nutmeg; gradually add to creamed mixture alternately with molasses mixture, beating well after each addition. Fold in pecans.

2. Pour into a greased 3-qt. slow cooker. Sprinkle with brown sugar. Combine hot water and butter; pour over batter (do not stir).

3. Cover and cook on high for 2 to 2½ hours or until a toothpick inserted near center of cake comes out clean. Turn off heat. Let stand for 15 minutes. Serve warm.

GINGERBREAD PUDDING CAKE

General Recipe Index

This handy index lists recipes by food category and major ingredient, so you can easily find recipes that suit your needs.

APPETIZERS (also see Dips, Fondue)
Barbecue Sausage Bites, 15
Barbecued Party Starters, 238
Buffet Meatballs, 163
Cranberry Hot Wings, 244
Cranberry Sauerkraut Meatballs, 236
Creamy Cranberry Meatballs, 165
Crispy Snack Mix, 15
Fruit Salsa, 16
Hawaiian Kielbasa, 96
Marinated Chicken Wings, 16
Marmalade Meatballs, 12
Mini Hot Dogs 'n' Meatballs, 245
Moist & Tender Wings, 91
Pomegranate-Glazed Turkey Meatballs, 242
Reuben Spread, 14
Slow-Cooked Salsa, 96
Slow-Cooked Smokies, 166
Slow Cooker Party Mix, 95
Southwestern Nachos, 8
Sweet & Sour Turkey Meatballs, 170
Sweet & Spicy Chicken Wings, 165
Sweet 'n' Spicy Meatballs, 240
Sweet & Spicy Peanuts, 93
Sweet 'n' Tangy Chicken Wings, 13
Tangy Barbecue Wings, 167

APPLES
Apple Betty with Almond Cream, 227
Apple-Cinnamon Pork Loin, 195
Apple Comfort, 300
Apple Granola Dessert, 152
Applesauce Sweet Potatoes, 174
Apricot-Apple Cider, 171
Banana Applesauce, 24
Blue Cheese and Apple Pork Chops, 200
Butterscotch Apple Crisp, 78
Butterscotch Mulled Cider, 170
Caramel Apple Fondue, 237
Caramel-Pecan Stuffed Apples, 229
Chunky Applesauce, 81
Cranberry-Apple Crisp, 307
Cranberry Apple Topping, 178
Easy Hot Spiced Cider, 165
Ginger Applesauce, 175
Glazed Cinnamon Apples, 230
Granola Apple Crisp, 82

Hot Caramel Apples, 301
Hot Spiced Cherry Sipper, 168
Hot Spiced Wine, 162
Pretty Orange Cider, 12
Slow-Cooked Apple Cranberry Cider, 166
Slow-Cooked Applesauce, 256
Slow Cooker Apple Pudding Cake, 302
Slow Cooker Baked Apples, 304
Spiced Cran-Apple Brisket, 285
Spicy Apple Tea, 14

APRICOTS
Apricot-Apple Cider, 171
Spiced Lamb Stew with Apricots, 63

ARTICHOKES
Cheese-Trio Artichoke & Spinach Dip, 95
Five-Cheese Spinach & Artichoke Dip, 168
Makeover Creamy Artichoke Dip, 91
Spinach Artichoke Dip, 11

BACON & CANADIAN BACON
Bacon Cheese Dip, 97
Bayou Gulf Shrimp Gumbo, 118
Beer-Braised Stew, 113
Brat Sauerkraut Supper, 132
Creamy Hash Browns, 255
Easy Beans & Potatoes with Bacon, 28
Four-Bean Medley, 249
Green Beans with Bacon and Tomatoes, 27
Hearty Split Pea Soup, 69
Jazzed-Up Green Bean Casserole, 248
Loaded Mashed Potatoes, 19
Maple Baked Beans, 99
Mint Lamb Stew, 75
Simple Sparerib & Sauerkraut Supper, 186
Slow-Cooked Bacon & Beans, 246
Slow-Cooked Ranch Potatoes, 100
Spanish Hominy, 25
Stuffed Sweet Onions, 35
Sweet & Sour Turkey Meatballs, 170
Zesty Sausage & Beans, 186

BANANAS
Banana Applesauce, 24
Bananas Foster, 79
Elvis' Pudding Cake, 80

BARLEY
Beef Barley Soup, 219
Mushroom Barley Soup, 210
Vegetable Beef Barley Soup, 150

BEANS
Black Bean Potato au Gratin, 27
Chicken with Beans and Potatoes, 278
Chuck Wagon Beans, 177
Cowboy Calico Beans, 25
Easy Beans & Potatoes with Bacon, 28
Fiesta Corn and Beans, 109
Four-Bean Medley, 249
Green Beans and New Potatoes, 105
Ham and Black Bean Soup, 294
Hawaiian Barbecue Beans, 101
Louisiana Red Beans and Rice, 117
Maple Baked Beans, 99
Mexican Beef & Bean Supper, 218
Navy Bean Dinner, 72
Ranch Beans, 257
Slow-Cooked Bacon & Beans, 246
Slow-Cooked Cannellini Turkey Soup, 64
Slow-Cooked Pork and Beans, 113
Smoky Baked Beans, 108
Southwestern Chicken & Lima Bean Soup, 138
Spinach Bean Soup, 147
Sweet & Spicy Beans, 32
Zesty Sausage & Beans, 186

BEEF (also see Ground Beef)
Appetizers
Creamy Chipped Beef Fondue, 12
Reuben Spread, 14
Main Dishes
Autumn Pot Roast, 187
Bavarian Pot Roast, 198
Beef & Tortellini Marinara, 204
Beef Braciole, 61
Beef Osso Bucco, 122
Beef Roast Dinner, 268
Beef Stroganoff, 208
Beef with Red Sauce, 281
Beef with Red Wine Gravy, 266
Best Short Ribs Vindaloo, 37
Cajun-Style Pot Roast, 201
Caramelized Onion Chuck Roast, 57

Coffee-Braised Short Ribs, 265
Creamy Celery Beef Stroganoff, 203
Favorite Beef Chimichangas, 190
Fiesta Beef Bowls, 51
French Onion Portobello Brisket, 269
German-Style Beef Roast, 281
Gingered Short Ribs, 278
Gingered Short Ribs with Green Rice, 193
Green Chili Beef Burritos, 185
Italian Roast with Alfredo Potatoes, 283
Java Roast Beef, 114
Louisiana Round Steak, 54
Lucky Corned Beef, 42
Mexican Pot Roast Filling, 261
Mushroom Pot Roast, 202
No-Fuss Beef Roast, 265
Pepper Steak, 204
Polynesian Roast Beef, 136
Portobello Beef Burgundy, 189
Sausage-Stuffed Flank Steak, 205
Slow-Cooked Caribbean Pot Roast, 62
Slow Cooker Sauerbraten, 197
Slow Cooker Two-Meat Manicotti, 43
Slow-Simmering Beef Bourguignon, 261
Special Sauerbraten, 40
Spiced Cran-Apple Brisket, 285
Spinach & Feta Stuffed Flank Steak, 264
Steak San Marino, 50
Stout & Honey Beef Roast, 274
Sunday Dinner Brisket, 130
Super Short Ribs, 194
Sweet and Sour Brisket, 270
Tender Salsa Beef, 130

Sandwiches
Chicago-Style Beef Rolls, 150
Easy Philly Cheesesteaks, 144
Machaca Beef Dip Sandwiches, 67
Sweet & Savory Slow-Cooked Beef, 70
Teriyaki Sandwiches, 140
Tex-Mex Beef Sandwiches, 146
Tex-Mex Shredded Beef Sandwiches, 65
Very Best Barbecue Beef Sandwiches, 145

Soups, Stews & Chili
Barbecued Beef Chili, 287
Beef & Potato Soup, 67
Beef & Veggie Stew, 211
Beef Barley Soup, 219
Beef Stew Provencal, 289
Beef Stew with Ghoulish Mashed Potatoes, 222
Chicago-Style Beef Sandwiches, 292

Chilly Night Beef Stew, 287
Easy Ropa Vieja Stew, 295
French Dip au Jus, 215
Hungarian Goulash, 296
Machete Shredded Beef Sandwiches, 288
Mexican Beef & Bean Supper, 218
Northwoods Beef Stew, 288
Pumpkin Harvest Beef Stew, 224
Slow Cooker Beef Vegetable Stew, 213
Spicy Shredded Beef Sandwiches, 219
Stephanie's Slow Cooker Stew, 223
Sunday Stew, 213
Sweet-and-Sour Beef Stew, 212
Vegetable Beef Barley Soup, 150

BEETS
Harvard Beets, 20

BERRIES
Black and Blue Cobbler, 155
Blueberry Cobbler, 159
Blueberry Grunt, 156
Chocolate Bread Pudding, 82
Chocolate-Raspberry Fondue, 79
Pear-Blueberry Granola, 83
Slow-Cooker Berry Cobbler, 152
Strawberry Rhubarb Sauce, 155
Warm Strawberry Fondue, 9

BEVERAGES
Apricot-Apple Cider, 171
Butterscotch Mulled Cider, 170
Chai Tea, 94
Christmas Punch, 241
Cider House Punch, 236
Easy Hot Spiced Cider, 165
Hot Cocoa for a Crowd, 238
Hot Mulled Wine, 243
Hot Spiced Cherry Sipper, 168
Hot Spiced Wine, 162
Make-Ahead Eggnog, 236
Mocha Mint Coffee, 88
Mulled Dr Pepper, 170
Pretty Orange Cider, 12
Slow-Cooked Apple Cranberry Cider, 166
Spiced Coffee, 167
Spiced Pomegranate Sipper, 244
Spicy Apple Tea, 14
Sunny Ambrosia Punch, 89
Sweet Kahlua Coffee, 93

Warm Christmas Punch, 237
Wassail Bowl Punch, 238

BREAD PUDDING
Butterscotch-Pecan Bread Pudding, 301
Caribbean Bread Pudding, 154
Chocolate Bread Pudding, 82
Pumpkin Cranberry Bread Pudding, 233
Raisin Bread Pudding, 78
Slow-Cooked Bread Pudding, 306
Slow-Cooker Bread Pudding, 159

BROCCOLI
Broccoli Potato Soup, 299
Corn and Broccoli in Cheese Sauce, 107
Creamy Chicken & Broccoli Stew, 62
Hearty Broccoli Dip, 17
Slow-Cooked Broccoli, 252
Warm Broccoli Cheese Dip, 240

CABBAGE & SAUERKRAUT
Bavarian Pork Loin, 271
Brat Sauerkraut Supper, 132
Cranberry Sauerkraut Meatballs, 236
German Potato Salad with Sausage, 55
Oktoberfest Pork Roast, 208
Reuben Spread, 14
Simple Sparerib & Sauerkraut Supper, 186
Slow-Cooked Reuben Brats, 149

CANDIES
Chocolate Peanut Drops, 303
Crunchy Candy Clusters, 230
Easy Chocolate Clusters, 232

CARROTS
Glazed Spiced Carrots, 30
Lucky Corned Beef, 42
Marmalade-Glazed Carrots, 98
Slow Cooker Rotisserie-Style Chicken, 135

CHEESE
Appetizers
Bacon Cheese Dip, 97
Buffalo Wing Dip, 11
Cheddar Fondue, 245
Cheese-Trio Artichoke & Spinach Dip, 95
Cheesy Pizza Fondue, 243
Chili Cheese Dip, 163
Creamy Onion Dip, 162

CHEESE

Appetizers (continued)
Five-Cheese Spinach & Artichoke Dip, 168
Reuben Spread, 14
Seafood Cheese Dip, 14
Slow Cooker Cheese Dip, 94
Southwestern Nachos, 8
Warm Broccoli Cheese Dip, 240

Dessert
Pink Grapefruit Cheesecake, 83

Main Dishes
Blue Cheese and Apple Pork Chops, 200
Cajun Chicken Lasagna, 119
Family-Friendly Pizza, 184
Hearty Cheese Tortellini, 41
Parmesan Pork Roast, 262
Slow-Cooked Lasagna, 273
Slow Cooker Buffalo Chicken Lasagna, 126
Slow Cooker Two-Meat Manicotti, 43
Spinach & Feta Stuffed Flank Steak, 264
Spinach and Sausage Lasagna, 63

Sandwiches
Easy Philly Cheesesteaks, 144
Italian Sausages with Provolone, 129

Side Dishes
Cheddar Spirals, 22
Cheesy Potatoes, 98
Cheesy Sausage Gravy, 172
Cheesy Spinach, 258
Corn and Broccoli in Cheese Sauce, 107
Easy Slow Cooker Mac & Cheese, 247
Potluck Macaroni and Cheese, 31
Slow-Cooked Mac 'n' Cheese, 33

Soups
Cheesy Cauliflower Soup, 294
Cream of Potato & Cheddar Soup, 297

CHERRIES
Amaretto Cherries with Dumplings, 158
Cherry & Spice Rice Pudding, 153
Cherry Cola Chocolate Cake, 84
Chocolate-Covered Cherry Pudding
    Cake, 228
Hot Spiced Cherry Sipper, 168

CHICKEN & CHICKEN SAUSAGE

Appetizers
Buffalo Wing Dip, 11
Cranberry Hot Wings, 244
Hot Wing Dip, 166

Marinated Chicken Wings, 16
Moist & Tender Wings, 91
Sweet & Spicy Chicken Wings, 165
Sweet 'n' Tangy Chicken Wings, 13
Tangy Barbecue Wings, 167

Main Dishes
Amazing Slow Cooker Orange Chicken, 58
BBQ Chicken Baked Potatoes, 47
Cajun Chicken Lasagna, 119
Casablanca Chutney Chicken, 50
Chicken & Mushroom Alfredo, 49
Chicken & Vegetables with Mustard-Herb
    Sauce, 209
Chicken Merlot with Mushrooms, 268
Chicken Mole, 36
Chicken Thighs with Ginger-Peach Sauce, 43
Chicken Thighs with Sausage, 112
Chicken with Beans and Potatoes, 278
Chili-Lime Chicken Tostadas, 123
Cranberry Chicken, 266
Creole Chicken Thighs, 207
Fiesta-Twisted Brunswick Stew, 116
Greek Orzo Chicken, 116
Indonesian Peanut Chicken, 52
Italian Chicken Chardonnay, 263
Jamaica-Me-Crazy Chicken Tropicale, 111
Lemon Chicken Breasts with Veggies, 41
Lemon Cilantro Chicken, 118
Lime Chicken Tacos, 117
Mango-Pineapple Chicken Tacos, 59
Meaty Slow-Cooked Jambalaya, 269
Mediterranean Chicken in Eggplant Sauce, 52
Moroccan Chicken, 200
Moroccan Vegetable Chicken Tagine, 124
Mushroom Chicken Florentine, 205
Pineapple Curry Chicken, 45
Red, White and Brew Slow-Cooked Chicken, 131
Rosemary Mushroom Chicken, 277
Savory Lemonade Chicken, 136
Simple Chicken Tagine, 126
Slow-Cooked Asian Chicken, 262
Slow Cooker Buffalo Chicken Lasagna, 126
Slow Cooker Rotisserie-Style Chicken, 135
Slow-Roasted Chicken with Vegetables, 121
Southwest Chicken, 114
Soy-Ginger Chicken, 61
Spicy Chicken and Rice, 129
Spring-Thyme Chicken Stew, 56
Sweet and Saucy Chicken, 203
Sweet 'n' Tangy Chicken, 131

Tangy Chicken Thighs, 38
Tasty Chicken Marsala, 124
Tempting Teriyaki Chicken Stew, 133
Tex-Mex Chicken & Rice, 132
Tuscan-Style Chicken, 270
Zesty Chicken Marinara, 185

Sandwiches
BBQ Chicken Sliders, 68

Soups, Stews & Chili
Corn Bread-Topped Chicken Chili, 196
Creamy Chicken & Broccoli Stew, 62
Fiesta-Twisted Brunswick Stew, 116
Herbed Chicken & Spinach Soup, 70
Lentil & Chicken Sausage Stew, 291
Lime Chicken Chili, 142
Mango & Coconut Chicken Soup, 141
Mulligatawny Soup, 69
Navy Bean Dinner, 72
Posole Verde, 146
Southwestern Chicken & Lima Bean Soup, 138
Southwestern Chicken Soup, 145
Spicy Chicken and Hominy Soup, 296

CHILI
Autumn Pumpkin Chili, 221
Barbecued Beef Chili, 287
Corn Bread-Topped Chicken Chili, 196
Lime Chicken Chili, 142
Navy Bean Dinner, 72
Vegetarian Chili Ole!, 74
White Chili, 291

CHOCOLATE
Cherry Cola Chocolate Cake, 84
Chocolate Bread Pudding, 82
Chocolate-Covered Cherry Pudding
    Cake, 228
Chocolate Malt Pudding Cake, 80
Chocolate Peanut Drops, 303
Chocolate Pecan Fondue, 158
Chocolate-Raspberry Fondue, 79
Easy Chocolate Clusters, 232
Fudgy Peanut Butter Cake, 227
Hot Cocoa for a Crowd, 238
Hot Fudge Cake, 229
Minty Hot Fudge Sundae Cake, 153
Mocha Mint Coffee, 88
Slow Cooker Chocolate Lava Cake, 300
Sweet Kahlua Coffee, 93
Warm Rocky Road Cake, 306

COBBLERS & CRISPS
Black and Blue Cobbler, 155
Blueberry Cobbler, 159
Butterscotch Apple Crisp, 78
Cranberry-Apple Crisp, 307
Granola Apple Crisp, 82
Slow-Cooker Berry Cobbler, 152

COCONUT
Butternut Coconut Curry, 99
Coconut-Pecan Sweet Potatoes, 175
Mango & Coconut Chicken Soup, 141
Pecan-Coconut Sweet Potatoes, 24

CORN
Corn and Broccoli in Cheese Sauce, 107
Corn Spoon Bread, 173
Creamed Corn, 109
Creamy Corn, 258
Fiesta Corn and Beans, 109
Jalapeno Creamed Corn, 100
Shoepeg Corn Side Dish, 18

CORNISH HENS
Cornish Game Hens with Couscous, 275

CRANBERRIES
Cranberry-Apple Crisp, 307
Cranberry Apple Topping, 178
Cranberry BBQ Pulled Pork, 212
Cranberry Chicken, 266
Cranberry-Dijon Pork Roast, 275
Cranberry-Ginger Pork Ribs, 197
Cranberry Hot Wings, 244
Cranberry Pork Roast, 188
Cranberry Sauerkraut Meatballs, 236
Cranberry Turkey Breast with Gravy, 201
Creamy Cranberry Meatballs, 165
Ham with Cranberry-Pineapple Sauce, 57
Lazy-Day Cranberry Relish, 180
Pumpkin Cranberry Bread Pudding, 233
Slow-Cooked Apple Cranberry Cider, 166
Spiced Cran-Apple Brisket, 285
Turkey with Cranberry Sauce, 194

DESSERTS (also see Bread Pudding, Candies, Cobblers & Crisps)
Amaretto Cherries with Dumplings, 158
Apple Betty with Almond Cream, 227
Apple Comfort, 300

Apple Granola Dessert, 152
Bananas Foster, 79
Blueberry Grunt, 156
Burgundy Pears, 302
Butterscotch Dip, 81
Butterscotch Pears, 232
Caramel Pear Pudding, 304
Caramel-Pecan Stuffed Apples, 229
Caribbean Bread Pudding, 154
Cherry & Spice Rice Pudding, 153
Cherry Cola Chocolate Cake, 84
Chocolate-Covered Cherry Pudding Cake, 228
Chocolate Malt Pudding Cake, 80
Chocolate-Raspberry Fondue, 79
Chunky Applesauce, 81
Elvis' Pudding Cake, 80
Fruit Compote Dessert, 154
Fruit Dessert Topping, 233
Fudgy Peanut Butter Cake, 227
Gingerbread Pudding Cake, 307
Glazed Cinnamon Apples, 230
Hot Caramel Apples, 301
Hot Fudge Cake, 229
Maple Creme Brulee, 156
Minister's Delight, 230
Minty Hot Fudge Sundae Cake, 153
Old-Fashioned Tapioca, 226
Pear-Blueberry Granola, 83
Pink Grapefruit Cheesecake, 83
Pumpkin Cranberry Bread Pudding, 233
Pumpkin Pie Pudding, 226
Rice Pudding, 81
Slow Cooker Apple Pudding Cake, 302
Slow Cooker Baked Apples, 304
Slow Cooker Chocolate Lava Cake, 300
Spiced Sweet Potato Pudding, 304
Strawberry Rhubarb Sauce, 155
Tropical Compote Dessert, 84
Warm Rocky Road Cake, 306

DIPS (also see Fondue)
Bacon Cheese Dip, 97
Buffalo Wing Dip, 11
Butterscotch Dip, 81
Cheese-Trio Artichoke & Spinach Dip, 95
Chili Beef Dip, 241
Chili Cheese Dip, 163
Creamy Onion Dip, 162
Five-Cheese Spinach & Artichoke Dip, 168
Green Olive Dip, 89

Hearty Broccoli Dip, 17
Hot Chili Dip, 90
Hot Crab Dip, 13
Hot Wing Dip, 166
Jalapeno Spinach Dip, 9
Loaded Veggie Dip, 90
Makeover Creamy Artichoke Dip, 91
Pepperoni Pizza Dip, 88
Pizza Dip, 17
Seafood Cheese Dip, 14
Slow-Cooked Crab Dip, 93
Slow Cooker Cheese Dip, 94
Slow Cooker Hot Crab Dip, 243
Spinach Artichoke Dip, 11
Taco Joe Dip, 171
Warm Broccoli Cheese Dip, 240

DUCK
Saucy Mandarin Duck, 276

DUMPLINGS
Amaretto Cherries with Dumplings, 158
Momma's Turkey Stew with Dumplings, 216

FISH (also see Seafood)
Cioppino, 77
Slow Cooker Salmon Loaf, 125

FONDUE (also see Dips)
Caramel Apple Fondue, 237
Cheddar Fondue, 245
Cheesy Pizza Fondue, 243
Chocolate Pecan Fondue, 158
Chocolate-Raspberry Fondue, 79
Creamy Chipped Beef Fondue, 12
Mexican Fondue, 11
Tomato Fondue, 97
Warm Strawberry Fondue, 9

FRUIT (also see specific kinds)
Fruit Compote Dessert, 154
Fruit Dessert Topping, 233
Fruit Salsa, 16
Tropical Compote Dessert, 84
Tropical Triple Pork, 133
Warm Fruit Salad, 172
Winter Fruit Compote, 257

GOOSE
Slow-Cooked Goose, 280

GROUND BEEF

Appetizers
Barbecued Party Starters, 238
Buffet Meatballs, 163
Chili Beef Dip, 241
Chili Cheese Dip, 163
Creamy Cranberry Meatballs, 165
Green Olive Dip, 89
Hearty Broccoli Dip, 17
Marmalade Meatballs, 12
Mini Hot Dogs 'n' Meatballs, 245
Slow Cooker Cheese Dip, 94

Main Dishes
Family-Favorite Spaghetti Sauce, 277
Family-Friendly Pizza, 184
Healthy Slow-Cooked Meat Loaf, 49
Hearty Cheese Tortellini, 41
Mom's Spaghetti Sauce, 207
Potato Pizza Casserole, 45
Sloppy Joe Supper, 276
Slow-Cooked Lasagna, 273
Slow-Cooked Meat Loaf, 282
Slow Cooker Tamale Pie, 209
Spicy Goulash, 189
Zippy Spaghetti Sauce, 59

Sandwiches
Chili Coney Dogs, 111

Side Dish
Cowboy Calico Beans, 25

Soups & Stew
All-Day Meatball Stew, 216
Pasta e Fagioli, 211
Wintertime Meatball Soup, 290
Zippy Spanish Rice Soup, 139

HAM & PROSCIUTTO

Beef Braciole, 61
Black-Eyed Peas & Ham, 23
Cider-Glazed Ham, 274
Creamy Mushroom Ham & Potatoes, 283
Easy Citrus Ham, 46
Ham and Black Bean Soup, 294
Ham with Cranberry-Pineapple Sauce, 57
Hash Browns with Ham, 104
Light Ham Tetrazzini, 58
Mom's Scalloped Potatoes and Ham, 40
Saucy Scalloped Potatoes, 182
Scalloped Potatoes & Ham, 29
Slow Cooker Split Pea Soup, 295
Tropical Triple Pork, 133

LAMB

Glazed Lamb Shanks, 123
Gyro Soup, 74
Mint Lamb Stew, 75
Spiced Lamb Stew with Apricots, 63
Tangy Lamb Tagine, 42

LEMONS

Lemon Chicken Breasts with Veggies, 41
Lemon Cilantro Chicken, 118
Lemon Red Potatoes, 20
Savory Lemonade Chicken, 136

LENTILS

Lentil & Chicken Sausage Stew, 291
Lentil and Pasta Stew, 221
Lentil Stew, 73

LIMES

Chili-Lime Chicken Tostadas, 123
Conga Lime Pork, 48
Lime Chicken Chili, 142
Lime Chicken Tacos, 117

MANGOES

Mango & Coconut Chicken Soup, 141
Mango-Pineapple Chicken Tacos, 59
Tropical Triple Pork, 133

MEATBALLS

All-Day Meatball Stew, 216
Barbecued Party Starters, 238
Buffet Meatballs, 163
Cranberry Sauerkraut Meatballs, 236
Creamy Cranberry Meatballs, 165
Marmalade Meatballs, 12
Mini Hot Dogs 'n' Meatballs, 245
Pomegranate-Glazed Turkey
    Meatballs, 242
Sweet & Sour Turkey Meatballs, 170
Sweet 'n' Spicy Meatballs, 240
Turkey Meatballs and Sauce, 285
Wintertime Meatball Soup, 290

MEATLESS MAIN DISHES

Enchilada Pie, 110
Lentil Stew, 73
Vegetarian Chili Ole!, 74
Vegetarian Stew in Bread Bowls, 292
Vegetarian Stuffed Peppers, 51

MUSHROOMS

Beef Stroganoff, 208
Chicken & Mushroom Alfredo, 49
Chicken Merlot with Mushrooms, 268
Creamy Celery Beef Stroganoff, 203
Creamy Mushroom Ham & Potatoes, 283
French Onion Portobello Brisket, 269
Italian Mushrooms, 34
Mushroom Barley Soup, 210
Mushroom Chicken Florentine, 205
Mushroom Pot Roast, 202
Mushroom Wild Rice, 180
Rosemary Mushroom Chicken, 277
Savory Mushroom & Herb Pork Dinner, 260
Slow Cooker Mushroom Rice Pilaf, 102

NUTS & PEANUT BUTTER

Apple Betty with Almond Cream, 227
Butterscotch Pears, 232
Butterscotch-Pecan Bread Pudding, 301
Caramel Pear Pudding, 304
Caramel-Pecan Stuffed Apples, 229
Chocolate Peanut Drops, 303
Chocolate Pecan Fondue, 158
Coconut-Pecan Sweet Potatoes, 175
Crispy Snack Mix, 15
Crunchy Candy Clusters, 230
Easy Chocolate Clusters, 232
Elvis' Pudding Cake, 80
Fudgy Peanut Butter Cake, 227
Indonesian Peanut Chicken, 52
Maple-Almond Butternut Squash, 246
Pecan-Coconut Sweet Potatoes, 24
Praline Sweet Potatoes, 258
Slow-Cooked Asian Chicken, 262
Slow Cooker Party Mix, 95
Sweet & Spicy Peanuts, 93
Warm Rocky Road Cake, 306

ONIONS

Caramelized Onion Chuck Roast, 57
Creamy Onion Dip, 162
French Onion Portobello Brisket, 269
Onion-Garlic Hash Browns, 33
Stuffed Sweet Onions, 35
Sunday Stew, 213

ORANGES

Amazing Slow Cooker Orange Chicken, 58
Mandarin Turkey Tenderloin, 198

Marmalade-Glazed Carrots, 98
Marmalade Meatballs, 12
Pretty Orange Cider, 12
Saucy Mandarin Duck, 276

PASTA & COUSCOUS
Main Dishes
Beef & Tortellini Marinara, 204
Beef Stroganoff, 208
Beef with Red Wine Gravy, 266
Beer-Braised Stew, 113
Cajun Chicken Lasagna, 119
Chicken & Mushroom Alfredo, 49
Cornish Game Hens with Couscous, 275
Creamy Celery Beef Stroganoff, 203
Family-Favorite Spaghetti Sauce, 277
Family-Friendly Pizza, 184
Greek Orzo Chicken, 116
Greek Shrimp Orzo, 54
Hearty Cheese Tortellini, 41
Italian Chicken Chardonnay, 263
Light Ham Tetrazzini, 58
Mom's Spaghetti Sauce, 207
Moroccan Chicken, 200
Mushroom Chicken Florentine, 205
Pork Chop Cacciatore, 191
Pork Satay with Rice Noodles, 282
Portobello Beef Burgundy, 189
Ratatouille with a Twist, 36
Red, White and Brew Slow-Cooked Chicken, 131
Rosemary Mushroom Chicken, 277
Sausage-Stuffed Flank Steak, 205
Simple Chicken Tagine, 126
Slow-Cooked Lasagna, 273
Slow Cooker Buffalo Chicken Lasagna, 126
Slow Cooker Two-Meat Manicotti, 43
Slow-Simmering Beef Bourguignon, 261
Spiced Lamb Stew with Apricots, 63
Spicy Goulash, 189
Spinach and Sausage Lasagna, 63
Super Short Ribs, 194
Tangy Venison Stroganoff, 195
Turkey Meatballs and Sauce, 285
Zesty Chicken Marinara, 185
Zippy Spaghetti Sauce, 60
Side Dishes
Cheddar Spirals, 22
Easy Slow Cooker Mac & Cheese, 247
Potluck Macaroni and Cheese, 31
Slow-Cooked Mac 'n' Cheese, 33

Soups & Stews
Hungarian Goulash, 296
Lentil and Pasta Stew, 221
Northwoods Beef Stew, 288
Pasta e Fagioli, 211
Pepperoni Pizza Soup, 141
Vegetable Minestrone, 149
Zesty Italian Soup, 144

PEACHES
Chicken Thighs with Ginger-Peach Sauce, 43
Pork with Peach Sauce, 121

PEARS
Burgundy Pears, 302
Butterscotch Pears, 232
Caramel Pear Pudding, 304
Pear-Blueberry Granola, 83

PEAS & BLACK-EYED PEAS
Best Short Ribs Vindaloo, 37
Black-Eyed Peas & Ham, 23
Hearty Split Pea Soup, 69
Slow Cooker Split Pea Soup, 295

PEPPERONI
Family-Friendly Pizza, 184
Mini Hot Dogs 'n' Meatballs, 245
Pepperoni Pizza Dip, 88
Pepperoni Pizza Soup, 141
Pizza Dip, 17
Potato Pizza Casserole, 45

PEPPERS
Chili-Lime Chicken Tostadas, 123
Jalapeno Creamed Corn, 100
Jalapeno Spinach Dip, 9
Pork and Green Chili Stew, 112
Spicy Shredded Beef Sandwiches, 219
Vegetable-Stuffed Peppers, 250
Vegetarian Stuffed Peppers, 51

PINEAPPLE
Barbecue Sausage Bites, 15
Barbecued Party Starters, 238
Cantonese Sweet and Sour Pork, 46
Caribbean Bread Pudding, 154
Ham with Cranberry-Pineapple Sauce, 57
Hawaiian Barbecue Beans, 101
Hawaiian Kielbasa, 96

Hawaiian Sausage Subs, 138
Island Pork Roast, 56
Mango-Pineapple Chicken Tacos, 59
Pineapple Curry Chicken, 45
Polynesian Roast Beef, 136

POMEGRANATE
Pomegranate-Glazed Turkey Meatballs, 242
Spiced Pomegranate Sipper, 244

PORK (also see Bacon & Canadian Bacon, Ham & Prosciutto, Pepperoni, Sausage)
Appetizers
Slow Cooker Cheese Dip, 94
Southwestern Nachos, 8
Main Dishes
Apple-Cinnamon Pork Loin, 195
Asian Ribs, 55
Bavarian Pork Loin, 271
Blue Cheese and Apple Pork Chops, 200
Cantonese Sweet and Sour Pork, 46
Carnitas Tacos, 188
Cola Barbecue Ribs, 122
Conga Lime Pork, 48
Cranberry-Dijon Pork Roast, 275
Cranberry-Ginger Pork Ribs, 197
Cranberry Pork Roast, 188
Island Pork Roast, 56
Lip Smackin' Ribs, 128
Mexican Pork Roast, 119
No-Fuss Pork Roast Dinner, 135
Oktoberfest Pork Roast, 208
Parmesan Pork Roast, 262
Pork Chop Cacciatore, 191
Pork Roast Cubano, 137
Pork Roast Dinner, 193
Pork Satay with Rice Noodles, 282
Pork with Peach Sauce, 121
Savory Mushroom & Herb Pork Dinner, 260
Savory Pork Chops, 280
Simple Sparerib & Sauerkraut Supper, 186
Slow-Cooked Pork and Beans, 113
Slow-Cooked Pork Verde, 273
Slow-Cooked Pulled Pork with Mojito Sauce, 125
Stack of Bones, 184
Sweet and Spicy Jerk Ribs, 114
Tangy Tomato Pork Chops, 187
Thai Pork, 38
Tropical Triple Pork, 133

PORK (continued)
Sandwiches
Coffee-Braised Pulled Pork Sandwiches, 77
Country Rib Sandwiches, 147
Cranberry BBQ Pulled Pork, 212
Cuban-Style Pork Sandwiches, 151
Italian Pulled Pork Sandwiches, 73
Mojito Pulled Pork, 75
Slow Cooked Barbecued Pork Sandwiches, 139
Slow-Cooked Spicy Portuguese Cacoila, 142
Slow Cooker Pulled Pork Sandwiches, 286
Southwest Pulled Pork, 140
Side Dishes
Cheesy Sausage Gravy, 172
Slow-Cooked Sausage Dressing, 177
Soups & Stews
Butternut & Pork Stew, 224
Pork and Green Chili Stew, 112
Posole Verde, 146
Satay-Style Pork Stew, 65
Southwestern Pork and Squash Soup, 214
Vegetable Pork Soup, 72

POTATOES (also see Sweet Potatoes)
Au Gratin Garlic Potatoes, 19
BBQ Chicken Baked Potatoes, 47
Beef & Potato Soup, 67
Beef Stew with Ghoulish Mashed
    Potatoes, 222
Black Bean Potato au Gratin, 27
Broccoli Potato Soup, 299
Cheesy Potatoes, 98
Chicken with Beans and Potatoes, 278
Cream of Potato & Cheddar Soup, 297
Creamy Hash Brown Potatoes, 23
Creamy Hash Browns, 255
Creamy Mushroom Ham & Potatoes, 283
Creamy Red Potatoes, 250
Easy Beans & Potatoes with Bacon, 28
Garlic & Herb Mashed Potatoes, 18
German Potato Salad with Sausage, 55
Glazed Lamb Shanks, 123
Green Beans and New Potatoes, 105
Hash Browns with Ham, 104
Italian Roast with Alfredo Potatoes, 283
Lemon Red Potatoes, 20
Loaded Mashed Potatoes, 19
Lucky Corned Beef, 42
Make-Ahead Mashed Potatoes, 256
Mom's Scalloped Potatoes and Ham, 40

Mushroom Pot Roast, 202
Nacho Hash Brown Casserole, 34
Onion-Garlic Hash Browns, 33
Potato Pizza Casserole, 45
Rich & Creamy Mashed Potatoes, 178
Saucy Scalloped Potatoes, 182
Scalloped Potatoes & Ham, 29
Scalloped Taters, 108
Sloppy Joe Supper, 276
Slow-Cooked Ranch Potatoes, 100
Summer Side Dish, 101
Tuscan-Style Chicken, 270

PUMPKIN
Autumn Pumpkin Chili, 221
Pumpkin Cranberry Bread Pudding, 233
Pumpkin Harvest Beef Stew, 224
Pumpkin Pie Pudding, 226
Sausage Pumpkin Soup, 286

RICE
Amazing Slow Cooker Orange Chicken, 58
Bayou Gulf Shrimp Gumbo, 118
Best Short Ribs Vindaloo, 37
Brown Rice and Vegetables, 107
Cajun-Style Pot Roast, 201
Cantonese Sweet and Sour Pork, 46
Cherry & Spice Rice Pudding, 153
Chicken Thighs with Ginger-Peach Sauce, 43
Cranberry Chicken, 266
Cranberry-Ginger Pork Ribs, 197
Creole Chicken Thighs, 207
Curried Turkey Soup, 215
Fiesta Beef Bowls, 51
Gingered Short Ribs with Green Rice, 193
Indonesian Peanut Chicken, 52
Jamaica-Me-Crazy Chicken Tropicale, 111
Lentil Stew, 73
Louisiana Red Beans and Rice, 117
Meaty Slow-Cooked Jambalaya, 269
Mushroom Wild Rice, 180
Pepper Steak, 204
Pineapple Curry Chicken, 45
Rice Pudding, 81
Saucy Mandarin Duck, 276
Savory Pork Chops, 280
Slow-Cooked Pork Verde, 273
Slow Cooker Mushroom Rice Pilaf, 102
Soy-Ginger Chicken, 61
Spicy Chicken and Rice, 129

Steak San Marino, 50
Tender Salsa Beef, 130
Tex-Mex Chicken & Rice, 132
Thai Pork, 38
Zesty Sausage & Beans, 186
Zippy Spanish Rice Soup, 139

SALAD
Warm Fruit Salad, 172

SANDWICHES
BBQ Chicken Sliders, 68
Chicago-Style Beef Rolls, 150
Chicago-Style Beef Sandwiches, 292
Coffee-Braised Pulled Pork Sandwiches, 77
Country Rib Sandwiches, 147
Cranberry BBQ Pulled Pork, 212
Cuban-Style Pork Sandwiches, 151
Easy Philly Cheesesteaks, 144
French Dip au Jus, 215
Hawaiian Sausage Subs, 138
Italian Pulled Pork Sandwiches, 73
Italian Venison Sandwiches, 210
Machaca Beef Dip Sandwiches, 67
Machete Shredded Beef Sandwiches, 288
Mojito Pulled Pork, 75
Pulled Turkey Tenderloin, 218
Slow Cooked Barbecued Pork Sandwiches, 139
Slow-Cooked Reuben Brats, 149
Slow-Cooked Spicy Portuguese Cacoila, 142
Slow Cooker Pulled Pork Sandwiches, 286
Southwest Pulled Pork, 140
Spicy Shredded Beef Sandwiches, 219
Sweet & Savory Slow-Cooked Beef, 70
Teriyaki Sandwiches, 140
Tex-Mex Beef Sandwiches, 146
Tex-Mex Shredded Beef Sandwiches, 65
Turkey Sloppy Joes, 64
Very Best Barbecue Beef Sandwiches, 145

SAUSAGE (also see Chicken & Chicken Sausage, Pepperoni, Turkey & Turkey Sausage)
Appetizers
Barbecue Sausage Bites, 15
Barbecued Party Starters, 238
Hawaiian Kielbasa, 96
Mini Hot Dogs 'n' Meatballs, 245
Slow-Cooked Smokies, 166
Sweet 'n' Spicy Meatballs, 240

Main Dishes

Brat Sauerkraut Supper, 132
Family-Favorite Spaghetti Sauce, 277
German Potato Salad with Sausage, 55
Glazed Kielbasa, 37
Hearty Cheese Tortellini, 41
Italian Sausages with Provolone, 129
Oktoberfest Pork Roast, 208
Ratatouille with a Twist, 36
Sausage-Stuffed Flank Steak, 205
Simple Sparerib & Sauerkraut Supper, 186
Slow Cooker Two-Meat Manicotti, 43
Spinach and Sausage Lasagna, 63
Tropical Triple Pork, 133
Zesty Sausage & Beans, 186

Sandwiches

Chili Coney Dogs, 111
Hawaiian Sausage Subs, 138
Slow-Cooked Reuben Brats, 149

Side Dishes

Chuck Wagon Beans, 177
Everything Stuffing, 255
Sausage Dressing, 248
Slow Cooker Goetta, 30
Smoky Baked Beans, 108

Soups & Stews

Anything Goes Sausage Soup, 290
Fiesta-Twisted Brunswick Stew, 116
Lentil and Pasta Stew, 221
Sausage Pumpkin Soup, 286
Zesty Italian Soup, 144

SEAFOOD (also see Fish)

Bayou Gulf Shrimp Gumbo, 118
Cioppino, 77
Greek Shrimp Orzo, 54
Hot Crab Dip, 13
Meaty Slow-Cooked Jambalaya, 269
Seafood Cheese Dip, 14
Slow-Cooked Crab Dip, 93
Slow Cooker Hot Crab Dip, 243

SIDE DISHES & CONDIMENTS

Beans

Black Bean Potato au Gratin, 27
Chuck Wagon Beans, 177
Cowboy Calico Beans, 25
Easy Beans & Potatoes with Bacon, 28
Fiesta Corn and Beans, 109
Four-Bean Medley, 249
Green Beans with Bacon and Tomatoes, 27
Hawaiian Barbecue Beans, 101
Jazzed-Up Green Bean Casserole, 248
Maple Baked Beans, 99
Ranch Beans, 257
Slow-Cooked Bacon & Beans, 246
Smoky Baked Beans, 108
Sweet & Spicy Beans, 32

Fruit

Banana Applesauce, 24
Cranberry Apple Topping, 178
Ginger Applesauce, 175
Lazy-Day Cranberry Relish, 180
Slow-Cooked Applesauce, 256
Warm Fruit Salad, 172
Winter Fruit Compote, 257

Miscellaneous

Cheesy Sausage Gravy, 172
Everything Stuffing, 255
Moist Poultry Dressing, 252
Old-Fashioned Dressing, 247
Sausage Dressing, 248
Slow-Cooked Sausage Dressing, 177
Slow Cooker Goetta, 30
Spanish Hominy, 25
Stuffing from the Slow Cooker, 180

Pasta

Cheddar Spirals, 22
Easy Slow Cooker Mac & Cheese, 247
Potluck Macaroni and Cheese, 31
Slow-Cooked Mac 'n' Cheese, 33

Potatoes & Sweet Potatoes

Applesauce Sweet Potatoes, 174
Au Gratin Garlic Potatoes, 19
Black Bean Potato au Gratin, 27
Cheesy Potatoes, 98
Coconut-Pecan Sweet Potatoes, 175
Creamy Hash Brown Potatoes, 23
Creamy Hash Browns, 255
Creamy Red Potatoes, 250
Easy Beans & Potatoes with Bacon, 28
Easy Sweet Potato Casserole, 256
Garlic & Herb Mashed Potatoes, 18
Hash Browns with Ham, 104
Lemon Red Potatoes, 20
Make-Ahead Mashed Potatoes, 256
Nacho Hash Brown Casserole, 34
Onion-Garlic Hash Browns, 33
Pecan-Coconut Sweet Potatoes, 24
Potluck Candied Sweet Potatoes, 183
Praline Sweet Potatoes, 258
Rich & Creamy Mashed Potatoes, 178
Saucy Scalloped Potatoes, 182
Scalloped Potatoes & Ham, 29
Scalloped Taters, 108
Slow-Cooked Ranch Potatoes, 100
Summer Side Dish, 101
Sweet Potato Stuffing, 179

Rice

Brown Rice and Vegetables, 107
Mushroom Wild Rice, 180
Slow Cooker Mushroom Rice Pilaf, 102

Vegetables

Black-Eyed Peas & Ham, 23
Brown Rice and Vegetables, 107
Butternut Coconut Curry, 99
Butternut Squash with Whole Grain Pilaf, 183
Cheesy Spinach, 258
Corn and Broccoli in Cheese Sauce, 107
Corn Spoon Bread, 173
Creamed Corn, 109
Creamy Corn, 258
Easy Squash Stuffing, 174
Fall Garden Medley, 175
Fiesta Corn and Beans, 109
Glazed Spiced Carrots, 30
Green Beans and New Potatoes, 105
Harvard Beets, 20
Italian Mushrooms, 34
Italian Spaghetti Squash, 257
Jalapeno Creamed Corn, 100
Light Spinach Casserole, 250
Maple-Almond Butternut Squash, 246
Marmalade-Glazed Carrots, 98
Shoepeg Corn Side Dish, 18
Slow-Cooked Broccoli, 252
Slow-Cooked Vegetables, 29
Slow Cooker Ratatouille, 102
Slow Cooker Tzimmes, 253
Spiced Acorn Squash, 173
Stewed Zucchini and Tomatoes, 101
Stuffed Sweet Onions, 35
Vegetable Medley, 105
Vegetable-Stuffed Peppers, 250

SOUPS (also see Chili, Stews)

Anything Goes Sausage Soup, 290
Beef & Potato Soup, 67
Beef Barley Soup, 219
Broccoli Potato Soup, 299

SOUPS (continued)

Butternut Squash Soup, 214
Cheesy Cauliflower Soup, 294
Cream of Potato & Cheddar Soup, 297
Curried Turkey Soup, 215
Gyro Soup, 74
Ham and Black Bean Soup, 294
Hearty Split Pea Soup, 69
Herbed Chicken & Spinach Soup, 70
Mango & Coconut Chicken Soup, 141
Mulligatawny Soup, 69
Mushroom Barley Soup, 210
Pasta e Fagioli, 211
Pepperoni Pizza Soup, 141
Posole Verde, 146
Sausage Pumpkin Soup, 286
Slow & Easy Minestrone, 299
Slow-Cooked Cannellini Turkey Soup, 64
Slow Cooker Split Pea Soup, 295
Southwestern Chicken & Lima Bean Soup, 138
Southwestern Chicken Soup, 145
Southwestern Pork and Squash Soup, 214
Spicy Chicken and Hominy Soup, 296
Spinach Bean Soup, 147
Vegetable Beef Barley Soup, 150
Vegetable Minestrone, 149
Vegetable Pork Soup, 72
Wintertime Meatball Soup, 290
Zesty Italian Soup, 144
Zippy Spanish Rice Soup, 139

SPINACH

Cheese-Trio Artichoke & Spinach Dip, 95
Cheesy Spinach, 258
Five-Cheese Spinach & Artichoke Dip, 168
Herbed Chicken & Spinach Soup, 70
Jalapeno Spinach Dip, 9
Light Spinach Casserole, 250
Mushroom Chicken Florentine, 205
Spinach & Feta Stuffed Flank Steak, 264
Spinach and Sausage Lasagna, 63
Spinach Artichoke Dip, 11
Spinach Bean Soup, 147

SQUASH

Butternut & Pork Stew, 224
Butternut Coconut Curry, 99
Butternut Squash Soup, 214
Butternut Squash with Whole Grain Pilaf, 183
Easy Squash Stuffing, 174
Italian Spaghetti Squash, 257
Maple-Almond Butternut Squash, 246
Moroccan Vegetable Chicken Tagine, 124
Southwestern Pork and Squash Soup, 214
Spiced Acorn Squash, 173
Stewed Zucchini and Tomatoes, 101

STEWS

All-Day Meatball Stew, 216
Beef & Veggie Stew, 211
Beef Stew Provencal, 289
Beef Stew with Ghoulish Mashed Potatoes, 222
Beer-Braised Stew, 113
Butternut & Pork Stew, 224
Chilly Night Beef Stew, 287
Cioppino, 77
Creamy Chicken & Broccoli Stew, 62
Easy Ropa Vieja Stew, 295
Fiesta-Twisted Brunswick Stew, 116
Hungarian Goulash, 296
Lentil & Chicken Sausage Stew, 291
Lentil and Pasta Stew, 221
Lentil Stew, 73
Mexican Beef & Bean Supper, 218
Mint Lamb Stew, 75
Momma's Turkey Stew with Dumplings, 216
Northwoods Beef Stew, 288
Pork and Green Chili Stew, 112
Pumpkin Harvest Beef Stew, 224
Satay-Style Pork Stew, 65
Slow Cooker Beef Vegetable Stew, 213
Spiced Lamb Stew with Apricots, 63
Spring-Thyme Chicken Stew, 56
Stephanie's Slow Cooker Stew, 223
Sunday Stew, 213
Sweet-and-Sour Beef Stew, 212
Tangy Lamb Tagine, 42
Tempting Teriyaki Chicken Stew, 133
Vegetarian Stew in Bread Bowls, 292

STUFFING & DRESSING

Easy Squash Stuffing, 174
Everything Stuffing, 255
Moist Poultry Dressing, 252
Old-Fashioned Dressing, 247
Sausage Dressing, 248
Slow-Cooked Sausage Dressing, 177
Stuffing from the Slow Cooker, 180
Sweet Potato Stuffing, 179

SWEET POTATOES

Applesauce Sweet Potatoes, 174
Coconut-Pecan Sweet Potatoes, 175
Easy Sweet Potato Casserole, 256
Pecan-Coconut Sweet Potatoes, 24
Potluck Candied Sweet Potatoes, 183
Praline Sweet Potatoes, 258
Spiced Sweet Potato Pudding, 304
Sweet Potato Stuffing, 179

TOMATOES

Family-Favorite Spaghetti Sauce, 277
Green Beans with Bacon and Tomatoes, 27
Mom's Spaghetti Sauce, 207
Stewed Zucchini and Tomatoes, 101
Tangy Tomato Pork Chops, 187
Tomato Fondue, 97
Zippy Spaghetti Sauce, 59

TORTILLAS

Carnitas Tacos, 188
Enchilada Pie, 110
Favorite Beef Chimichangas, 190
Green Chili Beef Burritos, 185
Lime Chicken Tacos, 117

TURKEY & TURKEY SAUSAGE

Appetizers
Pomegranate-Glazed Turkey Meatballs, 242
Sweet & Sour Turkey Meatballs, 170
Main Dishes
Butter & Herb Turkey, 47
Chicken Thighs with Sausage, 112
Cranberry Turkey Breast with Gravy, 201
Italian Sausage and Vegetables, 137
Louisiana Red Beans and Rice, 117
Mandarin Turkey Tenderloin, 198
Moist Italian Turkey Breast, 266
Moist Turkey Breast with White Wine Gravy, 128
Slow-Cooked Herbed Turkey, 190
Turkey Meatballs and Sauce, 285
Turkey with Cranberry Sauce, 194
Sandwiches
Pulled Turkey Tenderloin, 218
Turkey Sloppy Joes, 64
Soups, Stew & Chili
Autumn Pumpkin Chili, 221
Curried Turkey Soup, 215
Momma's Turkey Stew with Dumplings, 216
Slow-Cooked Cannellini Turkey Soup, 64

VEGETABLES (also see specific kinds)
Autumn Pot Roast, 187
Bavarian Pot Roast, 198
Beef & Veggie Stew, 211
Beef Roast Dinner, 268
Brown Rice and Vegetables, 107
Cheesy Cauliflower Soup, 294
Chicken & Vegetables with Mustard-Herb
   Sauce, 209
Fall Garden Medley, 175
Gingered Short Ribs, 278
Green Beans with Bacon and Tomatoes, 27
Italian Sausage and Vegetables, 137
Lemon Chicken Breasts with Veggies, 41

Loaded Veggie Dip, 90
Louisiana Round Steak, 54
Mandarin Turkey Tenderloin, 198
Mediterranean Chicken in Eggplant Sauce, 52
Moroccan Chicken, 200
Moroccan Vegetable Chicken Tagine, 124
No-Fuss Beef Roast, 265
Pork Roast Dinner, 193
Ratatouille with a Twist, 36
Savory Mushroom & Herb Pork Dinner, 260
Slow & Easy Minestrone, 299
Slow-Cooked Vegetables, 29
Slow Cooker Beef Vegetable Stew, 213
Slow Cooker Ratatouille, 102

Slow Cooker Tzimmes, 253
Slow-Roasted Chicken with Vegetables, 121
Stewed Zucchini and Tomatoes, 101
Vegetable Beef Barley Soup, 150
Vegetable Medley, 105
Vegetable Minestrone, 149
Vegetable Pork Soup, 72
Vegetable-Stuffed Peppers, 250
Vegetarian Chili Ole!, 74
Vegetarian Stew in Bread Bowls, 292

VENISON
Italian Venison Sandwiches, 210
Tangy Venison Stroganoff, 195

Alphabetical Recipe Index

This handy index lists every recipe in alphabetical order, so you can easily find your favorite dishes.

A
All-Day Meatball Stew, 216
Amaretto Cherries with Dumplings, 158
Amazing Slow Cooker Orange Chicken, 58
Anything Goes Sausage Soup, 290
Apple Betty with Almond Cream, 227
Apple-Cinnamon Pork Loin, 195
Apple Comfort, 300
Apple Granola Dessert, 152
Applesauce Sweet Potatoes, 174
Apricot-Apple Cider, 171
Asian Ribs, 55
Au Gratin Garlic Potatoes, 19
Autumn Pot Roast, 187
Autumn Pumpkin Chili, 221

B
Bacon Cheese Dip, 97
Banana Applesauce, 24
Bananas Foster, 79
Barbecue Sausage Bites, 15
Barbecued Beef Chili, 287
Barbecued Party Starters, 238
Bavarian Pork Loin, 271
Bavarian Pot Roast, 198
Bayou Gulf Shrimp Gumbo, 118
BBQ Chicken Baked Potatoes, 47
BBQ Chicken Sliders, 68
Beef & Potato Soup, 67
Beef & Tortellini Marinara, 204

Beef & Veggie Stew, 211
Beef Barley Soup, 219
Beef Braciole, 61
Beef Osso Bucco, 122
Beef Roast Dinner, 268
Beef Stew Provencal, 289
Beef Stew with Ghoulish Mashed Potatoes, 222
Beef Stroganoff, 208
Beef with Red Sauce, 281
Beef with Red Wine Gravy, 266
Beer-Braised Stew, 113
Best Short Ribs Vindaloo, 37
Black and Blue Cobbler, 155
Black Bean Potato au Gratin, 27
Black-Eyed Peas & Ham, 23
Blue Cheese and Apple Pork Chops, 200
Blueberry Cobbler, 159
Blueberry Grunt, 156
Brat Sauerkraut Supper, 132
Broccoli Potato Soup, 299
Brown Rice and Vegetables, 107
Buffalo Wing Dip, 11
Buffet Meatballs, 163
Burgundy Pears, 302
Butter & Herb Turkey, 47
Butternut & Pork Stew, 224
Butternut Coconut Curry, 99
Butternut Squash Soup, 214
Butternut Squash with Whole Grain Pilaf, 183
Butterscotch Apple Crisp, 78

Butterscotch Dip, 81
Butterscotch Mulled Cider, 170
Butterscotch Pears, 232
Butterscotch-Pecan Bread Pudding, 301

C
Cajun Chicken Lasagna, 119
Cantonese Sweet and Sour Pork, 46
Caramel Apple Fondue, 237
Caramel Pear Pudding, 304
Caramel-Pecan Stuffed Apples, 229
Cajun-Style Pot Roast, 201
Caramelized Onion Chuck Roast, 57
Caribbean Bread Pudding, 154
Carnitas Tacos, 188
Casablanca Chutney Chicken, 50
Chai Tea, 94
Cheddar Fondue, 245
Cheddar Spirals, 22
Cheese-Trio Artichoke & Spinach Dip, 95
Cheesy Cauliflower Soup, 294
Cheesy Pizza Fondue, 243
Cheesy Potatoes, 98
Cheesy Sausage Gravy, 172
Cheesy Spinach, 258
Cherry & Spice Rice Pudding, 153
Cherry Cola Chocolate Cake, 84
Chicago-Style Beef Rolls, 150
Chicago-Style Beef Sandwiches, 292
Chicken & Mushroom Alfredo, 49

Chicken & Vegetables with Mustard-Herb Sauce, 209
Chicken Merlot with Mushrooms, 268
Chicken Mole, 36
Chicken Thighs with Ginger-Peach Sauce, 43
Chicken Thighs with Sausage, 112
Chicken with Beans and Potatoes, 278
Chili Beef Dip, 241
Chili Cheese Dip, 163
Chili Coney Dogs, 111
Chili-Lime Chicken Tostadas, 123
Chilly Night Beef Stew, 287
Chocolate Bread Pudding, 82
Chocolate-Covered Cherry Pudding Cake, 228
Chocolate Malt Pudding Cake, 80
Chocolate Peanut Drops, 303
Chocolate Pecan Fondue, 158
Chocolate-Raspberry Fondue, 79
Christmas Punch, 241
Chuck Wagon Beans, 177
Chunky Applesauce, 81
Cider-Glazed Ham, 274
Cider House Punch, 236
Cioppino, 77
Coconut-Pecan Sweet Potatoes, 175
Coffee-Braised Pulled Pork Sandwiches, 77
Coffee-Braised Short Ribs, 265
Cola Barbecue Ribs, 122
Conga Lime Pork, 48
Corn and Broccoli in Cheese Sauce, 107
Corn Bread-Topped Chicken Chili, 196
Corn Spoon Bread, 173
Cornish Game Hens with Couscous, 275
Country Rib Sandwiches, 147
Cowboy Calico Beans, 25
Cranberry-Apple Crisp, 307
Cranberry Apple Topping, 178
Cranberry BBQ Pulled Pork, 212
Cranberry Chicken, 266
Cranberry-Dijon Pork Roast, 275
Cranberry-Ginger Pork Ribs, 197
Cranberry Hot Wings, 244
Cranberry Pork Roast, 188
Cranberry Sauerkraut Meatballs, 236
Cranberry Turkey Breast with Gravy, 201
Cream of Potato & Cheddar Soup, 297
Creamed Corn, 109
Creamy Celery Beef Stroganoff, 203
Creamy Chicken & Broccoli Stew, 62
Creamy Chipped Beef Fondue, 12

Creamy Corn, 258
Creamy Cranberry Meatballs, 165
Creamy Hash Brown Potatoes, 23
Creamy Hash Browns, 255
Creamy Mushroom Ham & Potatoes, 283
Creamy Onion Dip, 162
Creamy Red Potatoes, 250
Creole Chicken Thighs, 207
Crispy Snack Mix, 15
Crunchy Candy Clusters, 230
Cuban-Style Pork Sandwiches, 151
Curried Turkey Soup, 215

E
Easy Beans & Potatoes with Bacon, 28
Easy Chocolate Clusters, 232
Easy Citrus Ham, 46
Easy Hot Spiced Cider, 165
Easy Philly Cheesesteaks, 144
Easy Ropa Vieja Stew, 295
Easy Slow Cooker Mac & Cheese, 247
Easy Squash Stuffing, 174
Easy Sweet Potato Casserole, 256
Elvis' Pudding Cake, 80
Enchilada Pie, 110
Everything Stuffing, 255

F
Fall Garden Medley, 175
Family-Favorite Spaghetti Sauce, 277
Family-Friendly Pizza, 184
Favorite Beef Chimichangas, 190
Fiesta Beef Bowls, 51
Fiesta Corn and Beans, 109
Fiesta-Twisted Brunswick Stew, 116
Five-Cheese Spinach & Artichoke Dip, 168
Four-Bean Medley, 249
French Dip au Jus, 215
French Onion Portobello Brisket, 269
Fruit Compote Dessert, 154
Fruit Dessert Topping, 233
Fruit Salsa, 16
Fudgy Peanut Butter Cake, 227

G
Garlic & Herb Mashed Potatoes, 18
German Potato Salad with Sausage, 55
German-Style Beef Roast, 281
Ginger Applesauce, 175
Gingerbread Pudding Cake, 307

Gingered Short Ribs, 278
Gingered Short Ribs with Green Rice, 193
Glazed Cinnamon Apples, 230
Glazed Kielbasa, 37
Glazed Lamb Shanks, 123
Glazed Spiced Carrots, 30
Granola Apple Crisp, 82
Greek Orzo Chicken, 116
Greek Shrimp Orzo, 54
Green Beans and New Potatoes, 105
Green Beans with Bacon and Tomatoes, 27
Green Chili Beef Burritos, 185
Green Olive Dip, 89
Gyro Soup, 74

H
Ham and Black Bean Soup, 294
Ham with Cranberry-Pineapple Sauce, 57
Harvard Beets, 20
Hash Browns with Ham, 104
Hawaiian Barbecue Beans, 101
Hawaiian Kielbasa, 96
Hawaiian Sausage Subs, 138
Healthy Slow-Cooked Meat Loaf, 49
Hearty Broccoli Dip, 17
Hearty Cheese Tortellini, 41
Hearty Split Pea Soup, 69
Herbed Chicken & Spinach Soup, 70
Hot Caramel Apples, 301
Hot Chili Dip, 90
Hot Cocoa for a Crowd, 238
Hot Crab Dip, 13
Hot Fudge Cake, 229
Hot Mulled Wine, 243
Hot Spiced Cherry Sipper, 168
Hot Spiced Wine, 162
Hot Wing Dip, 166
Hungarian Goulash, 296

I
Indonesian Peanut Chicken, 52
Island Pork Roast, 56
Italian Chicken Chardonnay, 263
Italian Mushrooms, 34
Italian Pulled Pork Sandwiches, 73
Italian Roast with Alfredo Potatoes, 283
Italian Sausage and Vegetables, 137
Italian Sausages with Provolone, 129
Italian Spaghetti Squash, 257
Italian Venison Sandwiches, 210

J

Jalapeno Creamed Corn, 100
Jalapeno Spinach Dip, 9
Jamaica-Me-Crazy Chicken Tropicale, 111
Java Roast Beef, 114
Jazzed-Up Green Bean Casserole, 248

L

Lazy-Day Cranberry Relish, 180
Lemon Chicken Breasts with Veggies, 41
Lemon Cilantro Chicken, 118
Lemon Red Potatoes, 20
Lentil & Chicken Sausage Stew, 291
Lentil and Pasta Stew, 221
Lentil Stew, 73
Light Ham Tetrazzini, 58
Light Spinach Casserole, 250
Lime Chicken Chili, 142
Lime Chicken Tacos, 117
Lip Smackin' Ribs, 128
Loaded Mashed Potatoes, 19
Loaded Veggie Dip, 90
Louisiana Red Beans and Rice, 117
Louisiana Round Steak, 54
Lucky Corned Beef, 42

M

Machaca Beef Dip Sandwiches, 67
Machete Shredded Beef Sandwiches, 288
Make-Ahead Eggnog, 236
Make-Ahead Mashed Potatoes, 256
Makeover Creamy Artichoke Dip, 91
Mandarin Turkey Tenderloin, 198
Mango & Coconut Chicken Soup, 141
Mango-Pineapple Chicken Tacos, 59
Maple-Almond Butternut Squash, 246
Maple Baked Beans, 99
Maple Creme Brulee, 156
Marinated Chicken Wings, 16
Marmalade-Glazed Carrots, 98
Marmalade Meatballs, 12
Meaty Slow-Cooked Jambalaya, 269
Mediterranean Chicken in Eggplant Sauce, 52
Mexican Beef & Bean Supper, 218
Mexican Fondue, 11
Mexican Pork Roast, 119
Mexican Pot Roast Filling, 261
Mini Hot Dogs 'n' Meatballs, 245
Minister's Delight, 230
Mint Lamb Stew, 75

Minty Hot Fudge Sundae Cake, 153
Mocha Mint Coffee, 88
Moist & Tender Wings, 91
Moist Italian Turkey Breast, 266
Moist Poultry Dressing, 252
Moist Turkey Breast with White Wine Gravy, 128
Mojito Pulled Pork, 75
Momma's Turkey Stew with Dumplings, 216
Mom's Scalloped Potatoes and Ham, 40
Mom's Spaghetti Sauce, 207
Moroccan Chicken, 200
Moroccan Vegetable Chicken Tagine, 124
Mulled Dr Pepper, 170
Mulligatawny Soup, 69
Mushroom Barley Soup, 210
Mushroom Chicken Florentine, 205
Mushroom Pot Roast, 202
Mushroom Wild Rice, 180

N

Nacho Hash Brown Casserole, 34
Navy Bean Dinner, 72
No-Fuss Beef Roast, 265
No-Fuss Pork Roast Dinner, 135
Northwoods Beef Stew, 288

O

Oktoberfest Pork Roast, 208
Old-Fashioned Dressing, 247
Old-Fashioned Tapioca, 226
Onion-Garlic Hash Browns, 33

P

Parmesan Pork Roast, 262
Pasta e Fagioli, 211
Pear-Blueberry Granola, 83
Pecan-Coconut Sweet Potatoes, 24
Pepper Steak, 204
Pepperoni Pizza Dip, 88
Pepperoni Pizza Soup, 141
Pineapple Curry Chicken, 45
Pink Grapefruit Cheesecake, 83
Pizza Dip, 17
Polynesian Roast Beef, 136
Pomegranate-Glazed Turkey Meatballs, 242
Pork and Green Chili Stew, 112
Pork Chop Cacciatore, 191
Pork Roast Cubano, 137
Pork Roast Dinner, 193
Pork Satay with Rice Noodles, 282

Pork with Peach Sauce, 121
Portobello Beef Burgundy, 189
Posole Verde, 146
Potato Pizza Casserole, 45
Potluck Candied Sweet Potatoes, 183
Potluck Macaroni and Cheese, 31
Praline Sweet Potatoes, 258
Pretty Orange Cider, 12
Pulled Turkey Tenderloin, 218
Pumpkin Cranberry Bread Pudding, 233
Pumpkin Harvest Beef Stew, 224
Pumpkin Pie Pudding, 226

R

Raisin Bread Pudding, 78
Ranch Beans, 257
Ratatouille with a Twist, 36
Red, White and Brew Slow-Cooked Chicken, 131
Reuben Spread, 14
Rice Pudding, 81
Rich & Creamy Mashed Potatoes, 178
Rosemary Mushroom Chicken, 277

S

Satay-Style Pork Stew, 65
Saucy Mandarin Duck, 276
Saucy Scalloped Potatoes, 182
Sausage Dressing, 248
Sausage Pumpkin Soup, 286
Sausage-Stuffed Flank Steak, 205
Savory Lemonade Chicken, 136
Savory Mushroom & Herb Pork Dinner, 260
Savory Pork Chops, 280
Scalloped Potatoes & Ham, 29
Scalloped Taters, 108
Seafood Cheese Dip, 14
Shoepeg Corn Side Dish, 18
Simple Chicken Tagine, 126
Simple Sparerib & Sauerkraut Supper, 186
Sloppy Joe Supper, 276
Slow & Easy Minestrone, 299
Slow-Cooked Apple Cranberry Cider, 166
Slow-Cooked Applesauce, 256
Slow-Cooked Asian Chicken, 262
Slow-Cooked Bacon & Beans, 246
Slow Cooked Barbecued Pork Sandwiches, 139
Slow-Cooked Bread Pudding, 306
Slow-Cooked Broccoli, 252
Slow-Cooked Cannellini Turkey Soup, 64
Slow-Cooked Caribbean Pot Roast, 62

Slow-Cooked Crab Dip, 93
Slow-Cooked Goose, 280
Slow-Cooked Herbed Turkey, 190
Slow-Cooked Lasagna, 273
Slow-Cooked Mac 'n' Cheese, 33
Slow-Cooked Meat Loaf, 282
Slow-Cooked Pork and Beans, 113
Slow-Cooked Pork Verde, 273
Slow-Cooked Pulled Pork with Mojito Sauce, 125
Slow-Cooked Ranch Potatoes, 100
Slow-Cooked Reuben Brats, 149
Slow-Cooked Salsa, 96
Slow-Cooked Sausage Dressing, 177
Slow-Cooked Smokies, 166
Slow-Cooked Spicy Portuguese Cacoila, 142
Slow-Cooked Vegetables, 29
Slow Cooker Apple Pudding Cake, 302
Slow Cooker Baked Apples, 304
Slow Cooker Beef Vegetable Stew, 213
Slow-Cooker Berry Cobbler, 152
Slow Cooker Bread Pudding, 159
Slow Cooker Buffalo Chicken Lasagna, 126
Slow Cooker Cheese Dip, 94
Slow Cooker Chocolate Lava Cake, 300
Slow Cooker Goetta, 30
Slow Cooker Hot Crab Dip, 243
Slow Cooker Mushroom Rice Pilaf, 102
Slow Cooker Party Mix, 95
Slow Cooker Pulled Pork Sandwiches, 286
Slow Cooker Ratatouille, 102
Slow Cooker Rotisserie-Style Chicken, 135
Slow Cooker Salmon Loaf, 125
Slow Cooker Sauerbraten, 197
Slow Cooker Split Pea Soup, 295
Slow Cooker Tamale Pie, 209
Slow Cooker Two-Meat Manicotti, 43
Slow Cooker Tzimmes, 253
Slow-Roasted Chicken with Vegetables, 121
Slow-Simmering Beef Bourguignon, 261
Smoky Baked Beans, 108
Southwest Chicken, 114
Southwest Pulled Pork, 140
Southwestern Chicken & Lima Bean Soup, 138
Southwestern Chicken Soup, 145
Southwestern Nachos, 8
Southwestern Pork and Squash Soup, 214
Soy-Ginger Chicken, 61
Spanish Hominy, 25
Special Sauerbraten, 40
Spiced Acorn Squash, 173

Spiced Coffee, 167
Spiced Cran-Apple Brisket, 285
Spiced Lamb Stew with Apricots, 63
Spiced Pomegranate Sipper, 244
Spiced Sweet Potato Pudding, 304
Spicy Apple Tea, 14
Spicy Chicken and Hominy Soup, 296
Spicy Chicken and Rice, 129
Spicy Goulash, 189
Spicy Shredded Beef Sandwiches, 219
Spinach & Feta Stuffed Flank Steak, 264
Spinach and Sausage Lasagna, 63
Spinach Artichoke Dip, 11
Spinach Bean Soup, 147
Spring-Thyme Chicken Stew, 56
Stack of Bones, 184
Steak San Marino, 50
Stephanie's Slow Cooker Stew, 223
Stewed Zucchini and Tomatoes, 101
Stout & Honey Beef Roast, 274
Strawberry Rhubarb Sauce, 155
Stuffed Sweet Onions, 35
Stuffing from the Slow Cooker, 180
Summer Side Dish, 101
Sunday Dinner Brisket, 130
Sunday Stew, 213
Sunny Ambrosia Punch, 89
Super Short Ribs, 194
Sweet and Saucy Chicken, 203
Sweet & Savory Slow-Cooked Beef, 70
Sweet-and-Sour Beef Stew, 212
Sweet and Sour Brisket, 270
Sweet & Sour Turkey Meatballs, 170
Sweet & Spicy Beans, 32
Sweet & Spicy Chicken Wings, 165
Sweet and Spicy Jerk Ribs, 114
Sweet 'n' Spicy Meatballs, 240
Sweet & Spicy Peanuts, 93
Sweet 'n' Tangy Chicken, 131
Sweet 'n' Tangy Chicken Wings, 13
Sweet Kahlua Coffee, 93
Sweet Potato Stuffing, 179

T
Taco Joe Dip, 171
Tangy Barbecue Wings, 167
Tangy Chicken Thighs, 38
Tangy Lamb Tagine, 42
Tangy Tomato Pork Chops, 187
Tangy Venison Stroganoff, 195

Tasty Chicken Marsala, 124
Tempting Teriyaki Chicken Stew, 133
Tender Salsa Beef, 130
Teriyaki Sandwiches, 140
Tex-Mex Beef Sandwiches, 146
Tex-Mex Chicken & Rice, 132
Tex-Mex Shredded Beef Sandwiches, 65
Thai Pork, 38
Tomato Fondue, 97
Tropical Compote Dessert, 84
Tropical Triple Pork, 133
Turkey Meatballs and Sauce, 285
Turkey Sloppy Joes, 64
Turkey with Cranberry Sauce, 194
Tuscan-Style Chicken, 270

V
Vegetable Beef Barley Soup, 150
Vegetable Medley, 105
Vegetable Minestrone, 149
Vegetable Pork Soup, 72
Vegetable-Stuffed Peppers, 250
Vegetarian Chili Ole!, 74
Vegetarian Stew in Bread Bowls, 292
Vegetarian Stuffed Peppers, 51
Very Best Barbecue Beef Sandwiches, 145

W
Warm Broccoli Cheese Dip, 240
Warm Christmas Punch, 237
Warm Fruit Salad, 172
Warm Rocky Road Cake, 306
Warm Strawberry Fondue, 9
Wassail Bowl Punch, 238
White Chili, 291
Winter Fruit Compote, 257
Wintertime Meatball Soup, 290

Z
Zesty Chicken Marinara, 185
Zesty Italian Soup, 144
Zesty Sausage & Beans, 186
Zippy Spaghetti Sauce, 60
Zippy Spanish Rice Soup, 139